AF498398

Elizabeth, the Wife of Oliver Cromwell.

Drawn and Engraved by W. Bond, from a
half length Portrait in the Possession of Oliver Cromwell Esq.ʳ

Published by Longman, Hurst, Rees, Orme & Brown, London, Jan.ʸ 2.ᵈ 1820.

MEMOIRS

OF THE

PROTECTOR, OLIVER CROMWELL,

AND OF HIS SONS,

RICHARD AND HENRY.

ILLUSTRATED BY

ORIGINAL LETTERS, AND OTHER FAMILY PAPERS.

By OLIVER CROMWELL, Esq.

A DESCENDANT OF THE FAMILY.

WITH PORTRAITS FROM ORIGINAL PICTURES.

Second Edition.

IN TWO VOLUMES.

VOL. II.

LONDON:

PRINTED FOR LONGMAN, HURST, REES, ORME, AND BROWN,

PATERNOSTER-ROW.

1821.

CONTENTS

OF

THE SECOND VOLUME.

CHAPTER XI.

Charge against Cromwell considered, of the removal of the
King from Holmby House. — Formidable power of the Agitators, the authors of this measure, and Cornet Joyce, wholly
their agent. — Reality and sincerity of Cromwell's negotiations for the King's restoration; and Major Huntington's
charge against Cromwell respecting those negotiations, and
his motives for making it, considered. — Sir John Berkley's
narrative of those negotiations, and of the King's escape from
Hampton Court, and of his going to the Isle of Wight. —
Sufficient evidence of the fact of those negotiations, and of
Cromwell's sincerity; and of Cromwell's privity to the King's
escape, and that he had no concern in his going to the Isle
of Wight. — Supposed cause of Cromwell's alleged desertion
of the King's interest. — Moderate terms of the Independents' propositions to the King. — Probable cause of the
King's rejection of them. — Lord Clarendon's observations
upon the removal of the King from the Isle of Wight to
Hurst Castle by the Army. — Observations upon Colonel
Pride's exclusion of the members, to show it to be the act of
the Republicans to bring forward the trial of the King, and
Cromwell not concerned in it. — The improbability of Cromwell's supposed influence over Fairfax, from Whitelock's and
others' account of his temper and disposition. — Ludlow's

CHAPTER XIV.

CHAPTER XV.

MEMOIRS

OF

OLIVER CROMWELL,

AND OF

HIS SONS RICHARD AND HENRY.

CHAPTER XI.

CHARGE AGAINST CROMWELL CONSIDERED, OF THE REMOVAL
OF THE KING FROM HOLMBY HOUSE. — FORMIDABLE
POWER OF THE AGITATORS, THE AUTHORS OF THIS MEA-
SURE, AND CORNET JOYCE WHOLLY THEIR AGENT. —
REALITY AND SINCERITY OF CROMWELL'S NEGOTIATIONS
FOR THE KING'S RESTORATION; AND MAJOR HUNTING-
DON'S CHARGE AGAINST CROMWELL RESPECTING THOSE
NEGOTIATIONS, AND HIS MOTIVES FOR MAKING IT CON-
SIDERED. — SIR JOHN BERKLEY'S NARRATIVE OF THOSE
NEGOTIATIONS AND OF THE KING'S ESCAPE FROM HAMP-
TON-COURT, AND OF HIS GOING TO THE ISLE OF WIGHT.
— SUFFICIENT EVIDENCE OF THE FACT OF THOSE NEGO-
TIATIONS, AND OF CROMWELL'S SINCERITY; AND OF
CROMWELL'S PRIVITY TO THE KING'S ESCAPE, AND THAT
HE HAD NO CONCERN IN HIS GOING TO THE ISLE OF
WIGHT. — SUPPOSED CAUSE OF CROMWELL'S ALLEGED
DESERTION OF THE KING'S INTEREST. — MODERATE
TERMS OF THE INDEPENDENTS' PROPOSITIONS TO THE

THE next charge against Cromwell is, his supposed
concern in the removal of the King from Holmby
House, by Cornet Joyce.

Rushworth gives a paper published by the army,
entitled " A true impartial Narrative concerning
the Army's Preservation of the King, to show that
the Army did thereby intend the Good, Life, Property, and Liberty, of all the Commons of England." It states the grounds of this their undertaking to remove the King, to be chiefly an intimation to them of a design of some to surprise
and carry him off; and which design they were
able to prove, and was justly suspected to be intended by some that were with His Majesty; the
execution whereof was to be followed by the
raising another army to suppress them, the present
army. — It proceeds to state that Cornet Joyce,
an appointed agent by the army, observing some

circumstances in the conduct of the King and of those about him, affording ground of suspicion of the determined immediate execution of such intention, proceeded to remove the King in the manner related in this narrative.

Mr. Denzil Holles, referring to the same transaction, says, at first it must seem only an act of Mr. Joyce, Cromwell protesting he knew nothing of it, though, adds Mr. Holles, he was the man who appointed it to be done, as appears, he says, by some passages taken out of some of their own authors, as one that calls him Sirrah Niho, and others. He (Mr. Holles) proceeds, — that Sir Thomas Fairfax also, in a letter to the House, professes the same for himself as in the presence of God, with a large undertaking for the rest of his officers and the body of the army. And perhaps, says he, he said true ; I would fain be so charitable as to believe it ; nor indeed do I think the good man is privy to all their plots ; he must have no more than what they are pleased to carve and chew for him, but must swallow all, and own them when they come abroad. Here then, says he, they have the King ; Joyce drives away the guards ; forces Colonel Greaves to fly, whom else they threatened to kill, for no man's life must stand in their way (murder being no crime in the visible saints) ; carries away His Majesty and the commissioners that attend him prisoners, and immediately sends up a letter to certify what he had done, with directions it should be delivered to Cromwell, and, he absent, to Sir Arthur Haslerig or Colonel Fleetwood, which was given to Colonel Fleetwood as one Lieutenant Markham informed the House, saying, the messenger that brought it told him so; nor did Sir Arthur Haslerig make a clear answer when he was asked concerning it in the House, Colonel Fleetwood being at that time gone to the army, so as he could not be examined. Whitelock, mentioning this transaction, says, that a party of horse, sent from the committee of troopers of the army, came to Holmby, where, after they had secured the guards, they demanded His Majesty; the commissioners, amazed at it, demanded of them what warrant they had for what they did; but they would give no other account but that it was the pleasure of the army. He then proceeds to give a similar account of the rest of that affair to that before given. He says, that the General sent to the Parliament the grounds of the soldiers' undertaking of themselves the business of Holmby; which were, that they had intimation of a design which they were able to make good, of some to surprise the King. Also, that he refused to return to Holmby, when offered to be conducted back by the General.

Lord Clarendon, after describing the manner of the King's removal from Holmby, says, that the committee with the King quickly gave notice to the Parliament of what had passed, with all the circumstances; and that it was received with all imaginable consternation, nor could any body imagine what the purpose and resolution was. Nor were they, proceeds His Lordship, at the more ease, nor in any degree pleased with the account they received from the General himself; who, by his letter, informed them that the soldiers at Holmby had brought the King from thence, and that His Majesty lay the next night at Colonel Montague's house, and would be the next day at Newmarket: that the ground thereof was, from an apprehension of some strength gathered to force the King from thence; whereupon he had sent Colonel Whalley's regiment to meet the King: that he (the General) protested that his remove was without his consent, or of the officers about him, and without their desire or privity: that he would take care for the security of His Majesty's person from danger; and assured the Parliament that the whole army endeavoured peace; and were far from opposing presbytery, or affecting independency, or from any purpose to obtain a licentious freedom in religion, or the interest of any particular party; but were resolved to leave the absolute determination of all to the Parliament.

Mrs. Hutchinson, mentioning this removal of the King from Holmby, only says, the soldiers, led on by one Cornet Joyce, took the King from

Holmby, out of the Parliament commissioners'
hands.

Much has been endeavoured to be made to the
prejudice of those who have been supposed to have
been the contrivers of this removal of the King,
particularly by the enemies of Cromwell, upon
whom they wish to throw all the supposed odium
of the measure. Real odium there could be none,
in the perilous situation in which the army and its
principal officers felt themselves, under the apprehension of the power and inveteracy of the presbyterian party in the Parliament. The army having,
it appears, certain information of an intention to
take the King out of the hands in which he had
been placed, for purposes hostile to, and destructive of them, they deemed it necessary to frustrate
that intention by bringing him amongst them:
and, as the King did not suffer by the exchange,
— on the contrary, from Lord Clarendon's own
account of these proceedings, he appears to have
been much more liberally and respectfully treated,
than when with the Parliament's commissioners, —
no harm was done. The act itself was solely one
of self-defence and preservation, which fully justified the proceeding.

This granted, no criminalty attached to the
General or Cromwell, or to any others of the army,
who should be proved to have contrived it; and
they might, without any discredit to themselves,
have openly avowed it. But if Cromwell or the

General really formed or knew of this determination to remove the King, and authorised or connived at the employment of Joyce in the enterprise, and should be found to have positively denied their previous knowledge thereof, no justification can be offered for so deliberate a falsehood, nor can their veracity be depended upon in any other transaction in which they had been, or were thereafter engaged; and Cromwell, as particularly aimed at, must be taken for that deliberate liar and hypocrite his enemies seem so anxious to show him to be. Now what is the proof of either the General's or Cromwell's contrivance or knowledge of this intended removal? Lord Clarendon describes the agitators as known to be wholly Cromwell's creatures, and under his direction; and that the presbyterian party had no suspicion of the General, whom they knew to be perfect presbyterian in his judgment; but that Cromwell had obtained the ascendancy over him by his dissimulation and pretences of sincerity.

Cornet Joyce's alleged letter to Cromwell, supposing it true, is no proof of Cromwell's previous knowledge of the design; for had Cromwell been really privy to it, it is not probable that a letter that must have referred to such privity would have been directed to be delivered to any other than Cromwell's own hand, and not left to be delivered indiscriminately to any other. The whole of this story appears to be a weak attempt tò fix upon Cromwell the supposed odium of the removal of the King. All the evidence respecting the letter is, the testimony of a Lieutenant Markham, as he is called, whose informer was the messenger that brought the letter, and Sir Arthur Heselrigge's supposed hesitation in answering the enquiries of the House concerning it. This is all conjecture upon which to found His Lordship's favourite hypothesis, — the hypocrisy of Cromwell. Ludlow, speaking of the agitators, says that they (the agitators) sent a party of horse under the command of Cornet Joyce with an order in writing to take the King from Holmby. He also says, that they (the agitators) were jealous of Cromwell. He gives the following account of the purposed rendezvous, which was held in a field called Cockbush Field, between Hertford and Ware : that the time for the general rendezvous being come, the commonwealth party amongst them declared to stand to their engagement, not to be dispersed till the things they had demanded were effected, and the government of the nation established ; to make good which resolution several regiments appeared in the field with distinguishing marks in their hats ; but that Cromwell, not contenting himself with his part in an equal government, puffed up by his successes to an expectation of greater things, and having driven a bargain with the grandees in the House, either to comply with the King, or to settle things in a factious way without him, procured a party to stand by him in the seizing some of those who appeared at the rendezvous in opposition to his designs: that to this end, being accompanied with divers officers whom he had preferred and thereby made his creatures, he rode up to one of the regiments which had the distinguishing marks, requiring them to take them out, which they not doing, he caused several of them to be seized; and then, their hearts failing, they yielded obedience to his commands. He ordered one of them to be shot dead upon the place, delivering the rest of those whom he had seized, being eleven in number, to the marshal; and having dispersed the army to their quarters, went to give an account of his proceedings to the Parliament.

This (Ludlow's) account of the proceedings of the agitators must be deemed a complete refutation of His Lordship's assertion of Cromwell's influence over them; instead of acting under his influence, they were evidently suspicious of his desire to restore the King: they were republicans (called by Ludlow the commonwealth party), and so was Ludlow; they were determined upon a republican form of government, and would not listen to the return of monarchy, which they had declared to be inconsistent with the prosperity of the nation. This strong language of the agitators alarmed Cromwell and Ireton, and determined them if possible to get rid of them: and they appear to have subdued them, for the time at least, at this rendezvous.

Lord Clarendon founds his assertion of Cromwell's privity to the King's removal from Holmby also upon his (Cromwell's) leaving London the morning of Cornet Joyce's arrival at Holmby; of the truth of which he produces no evidence of dates, or otherwise, nor does this circumstance appear in any other account of the transaction; and if it were true, it would amount to no more than a suspicious circumstance in the minds of those who are disposed to indulge any the most trifling surmise to Cromwell's prejudice.

In further proof of Cromwell's ignorance of Cornet Joyce's undertaking, it appears from Rushworth, that the General (Fairfax), in the conversation between the King and him, and Cromwell, Ireton, and Hammond, and divers other officers, at Lady Cutts's house at Childersley, upon the King charging them all with their privity to this proceeding, Joyce having, he said, told him that he had the commission of the whole army for what he did, and consequently that he must have had the General's, as being the principal part of it; Joyce declared he had not the General's commission; and that the General declared for himself, and was confident for the other officers about him, and the body of the army, that the King's removal was without their desire or privity: and Whitelock says, that the party of horse that removed the King was from the committee of troopers of the army, by which he must mean the council of agitators. Ludlow expressly says that the agitators sent a party of horse under the command of Cornet Joyce, on the 4th of June (1647), with an order in writing to take the King out of the hands of the commisioners of Parliament. The truth appears clearly to be, that this design of removing the King was conceived and directed by the council of agitators, without the authority or privity of their officers; of the dispositions of the principal of whom, to treat with the King, they were evidently become very jealous: and Ludlow, it is observable, says, that the principal officers of the army made it so much their business to get the good opinion of the King, that Whalley, being sent from them, with orders to use all means but constraint to cause him to return to Holmby, and the King refusing, was contented to bring him to the army. The General (Fairfax), Rushworth states, offered to take back the King to Holmby. Sir Philip Warwick does not mention the interview of the King and the principal officers of the army at Childersley; but he says, that at Royston Fairfax and Cromwell waited on the King together: that he asked them, whether they commissioned Joyce to remove him, and that they denied it: " I'll not believe you," says the King, " unless you hang him." Lord Fairfax, in his short memorials, says, that being at Saffron Walden, in Essex, he had

notice, that Cornet Joyce, an arch-agitator, who
quartered about Oxford, had seized on the King's
person, removed his guards, and given such a
check to the commissioners of Parliament attending the King, that they refused to act any farther
on their commission, being so unwarrantably interrupted. " That it might appear what a real
trouble this act was to me, though the army was
almost wholly infected with this humour of agita-
tion, I called for a council of war, to proceed
against Joyce for this high offence, and breach of
the articles of war ; but the officers, whether for
fear of the distempered soldiers, or rather, as he
suspected, secret allowance of what was done,
made all my endeavours in this ineffectual." Mr.
Denzil Holles, a most inveterate enemy to Cromwell, in his forementioned memoirs, charges Cromwell with being the abettor of this enterprise,
(allowing at the same time Cromwell's absolute
denial of the charge,) which he founds upon passages taken out of some books of those times, and
upon a letter, which he says was sent by Joyce to
Cromwell, containing an account of this proceeding ; referring probably to the forementioned
letter mentioned by Lord Clarendon. Mr. Holles,
in whatever he says respecting Cromwell, is not to
be relied on : his memoirs are the performance of
an enraged and disappointed man of the presbyterian party, frustrated by the superior abilities of
Cromwell and others of the independent party, in

their views of establishing the presbyterian form of church-government, in exclusion of all other modes of religious worship, and of disbanding the army, and thereby getting into their hands Cromwell and all others who did not fall in with their views of absolute power.

Cromwell is, on the one hand, accused of insincerity in his negotiations with the King for his restoration, and, on the other hand, the reality of his negotiations are brought forward in the shape of accusation.

Dr. Harris, in his Life of Cromwell, in proof of his supposed arts and ambition, gives, in a note, a paper to be found in the first volume of Thurloe's State Papers; nothing so fully as which paper, he says, set forth those arts and ambition: and it is written, he adds, with such a spirit and air of truth as strongly inclines one to believe it. How this paper found its way into these state papers does not appear, but it is marked at the conclusion " *Copia vera.*" It is also to be found amongst Mr. Baron Masere's tracts, taken from the same state papers: it is entitled " Sundry Reasons inducing Major Huntington to lay down his Commission; humbly presented to the Honourable Houses of Parliament." He describes himself as having, at the modelling of the army, been appointed by the Parliament a major in Cromwell's regiment; and having lately quitted that situation, he held it incumbent on him to assign his reasons for so doing : which were, because the principles, designs, and actions of those officers who had a great influence upon the army, were, as he conceived, very repugnant and destructive to the honour and safety of the Parliament and kingdom, from whom they derived their authority. He then gives what he conceives to be the particular instances.

Dr. Harris, in his eager desire to establish his favourite position (Cromwell's supposed arts and ambition), attaches much consequence to this paper, considering it sufficient evidence of the truth of his position. The truth, however, appears to be, that this Huntington thinks proper to desert his friends in the army, and join himself to the presbyterian party in the Parliament : and, in proof of the sincerity of his conversion, betrays the confidence he alleges to have been reposed in him, under the pretence of assigning his reasons for such desertion. The first great crime he imputes to Cromwell and Ireton is their impeding the disbanding the army : their so doing they do not deny ; and the reasons that have been already assigned must surely be deemed sufficient; namely, their well-founded apprehensions of the vengeance of the presbyterian party, so soon as the army should be broken and dispersed, and the obnoxious leaders at their mercy. Another charge is their advising, for the effecting of their further purposes, the removal of the King from Holmby, to

secure him from the influence of those appointed
to be about him by the Parliament, which, he says,
was done by the private soldiery, and promoted by
the agitators, by Cromwell's and Ireton's advice.
But it is conceived to be evident, from what has
been heretofore stated, that neither Cromwell nor
Ireton had any concern in that removal, nor were
in any degree privy to it. Huntington's relation
of the answer of Joyce to the General, that Cromwell gave him orders for this removal, is mere assertion ; he (Huntington) not saying that he heard
him so declare ; and it is quite improbable. The
agitators appear to have given Joyce the directions for so doing, unknown to Cromwell, and
under suspicion of his being in private treaty with
the King. Joyce does not mention Cromwell as
in any way engaged in this business, and Cromwell positively denies to the King himself all
knowledge of it, nor does the General hint it in
his memorial. This narrative proves no more than
every one knew, that the army were aware of the ill
disposition of the Parliament towards them, and of
their endeavours to get possession of the King for
the purpose of separately treating with him, or of
raising a separate army: and of the means used
by the army to counteract them by themselves
treating with the King. All the remainder of this
paper is, in like manner, mere unproved invective
against Cromwell and Ireton, particularly Cromwell, retailing every word supposed to have escaped

them, upon which he (Huntington) could put any construction to their prejudice. The undenied endeavours of Cromwell to come to an agreement with the King is surely no proof of the ambitious views imputed to him, of aiming at supreme power.

This paper, Whitelock says, was presented to the House of Lords: and, in a subsequent article, that he (Huntington) made oath in the Lords' House that the narrative given in by him was true and would be attested.

Rushworth says of this paper: — A paper was delivered to and read in the House of Lords from Major Huntington, of reasons why he left the army — that they were very large, being a narrative of pretended carriages of Lieutenant-general Cromwell and Commissary-general Ireton, since the Parliament's going to disband the army, in relation to overtures with His Majesty, and the proceedings against the Lords, Commons, and aldermen that were impeached: and, proceeds Rushworth, on Tuesday, August 8th, Major Huntington appeared before the Lords, and took his oath, that what he had affirmed in his narrative given in, of his own knowledge, was true, and that what upon hearsay, he believed would be attested; the Lords required his attendance, and ordered him protection.

The time of the delivery of this paper appears, from its date, to have been about the time of the commencement of the treaty of the Isle of Wight.

Lord Clarendon pompously introduces this Major Huntingtoh, to prove Cromwell's insincerity in his treaty with the King. He describes him as one of Cromwell's best officers; that he was in his own regiment of horse, and upon whom he entirely relied; and that he had been employed by him to the King to say those things from him which had given the King the most confidence, and was much more than he had ever said to Ashburnham. And, adds His Lordship, the Major did believe that he had meant all he said, and that the King had a good opinion of the Major's integrity: that he, the Major, when he observed Cromwell to grow colder in his expressions for the King than he had formerly been, expostulated with him in very sharp terms, for abusing him and making him the instrument to cozen the King: and that the other endeavoured to persuade him that all should be well; but that he, the Major, informed the King that Cromwell was a villain, and would destroy him if he were not prevented: and that, in a short time after, he gave up his commission, and would serve no longer in the army.

All this amounts but to a weak endeavour of Huntington to recommend himself to his new friends, and to convince them of the sincerity of his apostacy, by betraying the confidence of those who had entrusted him. It may be true that he might be authorised by Cromwell and Ireton to give to the King a favourable representation of their dispositions towards him; and there is every reason to believe that they were sincere in these their professions; but their discovery of the King's private negotiations with the Parliament and the Scots, acknowledged by Lord Clarendon himself, would necessarily terminate their treaty with the King, and occasion Cromwell's subsequent coolness, and to which Huntington could not be a stranger if he really was so much in their confidence as he professes; but the ill-construction he here chooses to put thereon was likely best to please his new employers. His narrative delivered to the House of Lords does not mention his supposed sharp expostulation with Cromwell, nor is it very likely he would venture it with him.

Rushworth shows his opinion of the charges exhibited against Cromwell and Ireton in this paper, by calling them pretended carriages.

Ludlow, in reference to this charge of Huntington, says, — These affairs (an apparent disposition in Scotland in favour of the King) necessitated the Parliament to raise the militia, in order to oppose this malevolent spirit which threatened them from the north, and also prevailed with them to discountenance a charge of high treason framed by Major Huntington, an officer of the army, with the advice of some members of both Houses, against Lieutenant-general Cromwell, for endeavouring, by betraying the King, Parliament, and army, to advance himself; it being, he (Ludlow) adds, manifest that the preferring this accusation at that time, was principally designed to take him off from his command, and thereby to weaken the army, that their enemies might be the better enabled to prevail against them.

Hence it is plain that Ludlow (no friend to Cromwell) considered this charge a contrivance of the enemies of Cromwell in both Houses, to remove him from his command, and probably destroy him and ruin the army: and that Huntington was only their tool in this business, not improbably seduced by his employers from his former friends for that purpose. And there is in Milton's prose works the following passage:— " Whilst he (Cromwell) staves off the enemy at the peril of his life, these (the Presbyterians) accuse him, fighting bravely for them, and amidst the very encounter itself, of feigned crimes, and suborn one Major Huntington against his head. And that accuser, Huntington, unpunished, and left to his own liberty, at length struck with remorse, came of himself and besought Cromwell's pardon, and freely confessed by whom he had been suborned."

There can be no reason to dispute Milton's veracity in this account, and Ludlow evidently considers this business as a contrivance to take off Cromwell. But Dr. Harris, anxious to establish the credibility of Huntington's testimony against Cromwell, concludes his note upon this passage with observing, that Mr. Wood, in his Athenæ

Oxonienses, informs that Major Huntington hated Oliver for his diabolical proceedings, and was hated by him again, so much that he imprisoned him several times. This looks, adds Dr. Harris, not as if he had asked pardon and confessed his fault. That Cromwell should hate Huntington for his baseness is not surprising; and his frequent imprisonment of him has not the appearance of any apprehension on the part of Cromwell of any disclosure he might be thought capable of making to his (Cromwell's) prejudice.

Major Huntington (in this his memorial) affects to have been very much in the confidence of the King, and all the other parties to this negotiation; but it is worthy of remark, and proves his unworthiness of credit, that Sir John Berkley, in his after-given narrative of this negotiation, mentions his name only twice: the first time he mentions him, he says, that upon a conference with the King, he found that His Majesty discovered, not only to him, but to every one he was pleased to converse with, a total diffidence of all the army, except Huntington (as he calls him), grounding such diffidence chiefly upon the other officers' backwardness to treat of receiving any favour or advantage from His Majesty. Huntington therefore appears to have been little more than a messenger from the King in this negotiation, and to have been singled out by him (not for his, Huntington's, credit) as the only officer upon whom the

King could prevail to accept any compensation (or, perhaps more properly, bribe) for these his services. Enough, it is conceived, has been already said in proof of the invalidity of his narrative. But thereto may be added a letter of a Mr. Chidley, in Milton's State Papers, to Cromwell, speaking of Divine Providence having ordered his (Cromwell's) conclusion of the insurrection in Wales, to be upon the very entrance of the Scots, — " Though contrary (he says) to the malicious expectation of all wicked men, whereof Major Huntington, none of the least, as appeared by his railing book in print against you and your son-in-law, whereof Your Honour may remember that I once gave you an answer, also in print, at that inch of time."

But the following narrative of Sir John Berkley appears to be a faithful and impartial account of the negotiations between the King, himself, and Cromwell and Ireton, and other principal officers of the Parliament army, for the restoration of the King — of the King's escape from Hampton-court — and of subsequent proceedings during the treaty of Newport.

They commence with stating, that in the year 1647, the Queen and the Prince of Wales sent him (Sir John Berkley) into Holland, to condole the death of the Prince of Orange; and that, having performed that office, he returned with Mr. John and Mr. William Ashburnham to France, by the way of Calais, where they met with the news of

His Majesty being seized by one Cornet Joyce, in
Holmby House; from whence he had been carried
with a guard of four hundred horse towards the
army; the Cornet producing no authority whereby
to warrant this proceeding. That the next post
informed them that His Majesty was well received
by the officers and soldiers of the army, and that
there were great hopes conceived, that they would
both concur to establish His Majesty in his just
right.

That Sir John was sent into England by the
Queen, to assist the King in this negotiation, accompanied by Mr. William Legge, of the King's
bed-chamber.

That two miles on this side Tunbridge, they
met with Sir Allen Apsley, who had been his (Sir
John's) Lieutenant-governor of Exeter, and afterwards Governor of Barnstaple, who told him, that
he was going to him (Sir John) from Cromwell,
and some other officers of the army, with letters,
and a cypher and instructions, which were to this
effect: — That he (Sir Allen Apsley) should desire him (Sir John Berkley) to remember that, in
some conferences with Colonel Lambert and other
officers of the army, upon the rendering of Exeter,
he (Sir John) had taken notice of the army's bitter
inveighing against the King's person, as if he had
been the worst of men, and their excessive extol-
ling the Parliament; both which being without
any colour of ground, he (Sir John) had concluded

that those discourses were not out of any persuasion of mind, but affected to prepare men to receive the alteration of government, which they intended that the Parliament should effect, by the
assistance of the army; which he (Sir John) had
said was not only a most wicked, but a very difficult, if not an impossible design, for a few men,
not of the greatest quality, to introduce a popular
government, against the King and his party,
against the Presbyterians, against the nobility and
gentry, against the laws established, both ecclesiastical and civil, and against the whole genius of
the nation, that had been accustomed for so many
ages to a monarchical government : that, on the
other side, if they would but consider, that those
of their party had no particular obligations to the
crown, (as many of the Presbyterians had,) and
therefore ought less to despair of His Majesty's
grace and favour : that the presbyter began this
war upon specious pretences of making the King
a glorious king : that, under that pretext, they
had deceived many well-meaning men, and had
brought great things to pass; but that now, the
mask was taken off, and they were discovered to
have sought their own advantages, and, at the
same time, that the power to do themselves much
good, or much hurt to others, was now almost
wrested out of their hands; and that this had been
done by the independent party, who could establish themselves no way under Heaven, so justly

and prudently, as by making good what the Presbyterians had only pretended to do, — that is, the restoring the King and people to their just and ancient rights, which would so ingratiate them with both, that they would voluntarily invest them with as much trust and power as subjects were capable of; whereas, if they grasped at more, it would be with the general hatred, and with their own destruction: that to this discourse of him (Sir John) they now informed him, that at that time they had only given a hearing, but no consent, as proceeding from an interest much divided from theirs; but that they had since found, by experience, all, or the most part of it to be so reasonable, that they were resolved to put it in practice, as he (Sir John) might perceive by what had already passed : that they desired, for the present, nothing of him, but that he would present them humbly to the Queen and Prince, and be suitor to them in their names, not to condemn them absolutely; but to suspend their opinions of them, and their pretensions towards His Majesty, and judge them rather by their future behaviour; of the innocence whereof they had already given some testimonies to the world, and would do more and more daily: that when he (Sir John) should have done this office, they desired he would come over into England, and become an eye-witness of their proceedings. Sir John says, that he thought this rencounter no ill omen to his future proceedings :

that Sir Allen Apsley told him he would have to
do with subtle men, that governed themselves by
other maxims than the rest of the world : that he
(Sir John) remembered to have answered, that the
caution was good, and that he would arm himself
the best he could ; but that it was hard to secure
ourselves from malicious men, when we were absolutely in their power : that he took the best information he could from Sir Allen Apsley, and
resolved with him to go into London, before he
went to the King, or to the army, that he might
be enlightened by the most able men of the King's
party ; which he did : that from London he went
to the head-quarters at Reading, with intention,
after he had delivered his message, to desire leave
to wait on His Majesty at Causum : that upon his
arrival at Reading, he spoke with Sir Edward
Ford, (who was brother-in-law to Ireton,) and
Mr. John Denham, who had been sent before upon
the same mission, both of whom were much of the
same advice with those he had discoursed with at
London, concerning the present power of the adjutators, by whom the most important affairs of the
kingdom and army were transacted : that, in sum,
they doubted that His Majesty hearkened to some
secret propositions of the Presbyterians, and had
bent all his thoughts to make an absolute breach
between the army and Parliament, which Ireton
had discerned, and told His Majesty plainly,
" Sir, you have an intention to be the arbitrator

between the Parliament and us, and we mean to
be it between Your Majesty and the Parliament :"
that two or three hours after his (Sir John's) arrival, Cromwell sent an officer to excuse him (Cromwell), that he could not wait on him till ten at
night, by reason he was sitting with the committee
of Parliament, and should not rise till then : that
he came then, accompanied with Rainsborough
and Sir Hardress Waller: that after general discourse, he (Sir John) told Cromwell the sum of
his instructions from the Queen and Prince;
which were to assure them, that Her Majesty and
His Highness were not partial to the Presbyterians,
nor any way averse to them : that he (Sir John)
would endeavour to incline His Majesty to comply with them, as far as would stand with his
honour and conscience, and to dispose them to
press His Majesty no farther: that his (Cromwell's) answer was in these words, — That whatever the world might judge of them, they would
be found no seekers of themselves, farther than to
have leave to live as subjects ought to do, and to
preserve their consciences; and that they thought
no men could enjoy their lives and estates quietly,
without the King had his rights; which they had
declared in general terms already to the world,
and would more particularly very speedily, wherein
they would comprise the several interests of the
royal presbyterian and independent parties, as far
as they were consisting with each other; which

he (Sir John) says, he understood afterwards to be meant of the proposals of the army : that he went the next day to the General (Fairfax) by Cromwell's direction, to ask his leave to see the King, which he was pleased to grant : that he delivered his letters and instructions to His Majesty : that he found that His Majesty discovered, not only to him, but to every one he was pleased to converse with, a total diffidence of all the army, except Huntington, and grounded it chiefly upon the officers' backwardness to treat of receiving any favour or advantage from His Majesty : that he (Sir John) was of His Majesty's sense, that men, whose hands were yet hot with the blood of his most faithful subjects, ought not entirely to be trusted, but thought they ought absolutely to be well dissembled with, whilst His Majesty was in their hands ; at least, that he might the better get out of them ; and that, to this end, he offered several expedients ; — as to suffer Hugh Peters to preach before His Majesty, of which he was very ambitious, and to converse with him and others of the army with freedom, and by all means to endeavour to gain the good opinion of the most active adjutators and the like : but that His Majesty concurred in none of them ; which made him (Sir John) doubt that His Majesty valued his reasons something the worse on account of the author of them ; and, therefore, that he (Sir John) meditated nothing so much as to procure a pass for

Mr. John Ashburnham, with whom he hoped he might prevail, and he with His Majesty; and which, within a few days after, he did obtain, and caused it to be delivered to his servant: that, however it was, upon some surmises of him (Sir John) being an engaged presbyterian, Cromwell came to expostulate the matter plainly with him; to which he (Sir John) replied, " That he was as much presbyterian as independent; that he (Sir John), as well as others, were inclined to think the better of them (the Independents), because they pretended to mind the King's restoration; but bid them be assured, that as soon as he should discover they were not real, he, and he thought all the King's party, would join with any that would but dissemble better than they; and concluded, that he thought nothing would separate the crown and the King's party:" that Cromwell seemed not unsatisfied with this plain dealing, and so left him: that the next day Huntington, who was sent to me by the King, made him acquainted with two general officers, whom he durst not name, because they were obnoxious to the then present power: that with these he had often and free communication; and, enquiring what opinion they had of the army in general, as to a conjunction with the King, they replied, " That they did believe, that it was universally desired, both by the officers and adjutators:" that if Cromwell was not real in it, he was a great dissembler, and so was Ireton: that, for the present, the whole army was so bent upon it, that they durst not be otherwise;—that, if they should ever happen to change, they should easily discover it; and, because they had been, in great part, the cause that Sir Allen Apsley was sent to him (Sir John), they thought themselves obliged to give him all the light they could of things and persons; which to the best they performed, in· his (Sir John's) opinion, most sincerely: that he (Sir John) informed them at their first meeting, that he doubted there would be three great difficulties which would obstruct the agreement;—first, that they would expect that the King should not only give them liberty of conscience, but alter the established ecclesiastical government, which His Majesty was persuaded he could not in conscience do; the second, that they would not be contented to separate some few men from the court, and from bearing great offices, unless they and their posterity were ruined, and that by the King's act, which His Majesty could not in honour permit; and, thirdly, that they would not be contented with a security of the militia, during His Majesty's life; and His Majesty could not grant it further, but infinitely to the prejudice of his posterity: that they assured him, that His Majesty would be pressed in none of these particulars, and that there was a draught of proposals, which Ireton had drawn, and which would certainly be voted by the whole army,

wherein there was nothing tending to any such
purpose; and, that if His Majesty would consent
to them, there would be an end of all difficulties;
and they thought that the sooner His Majesty did
it the better it would be; because there was no
certainty in the temper of the army, which they
had observed to have altered more than once already: that he (Sir John) asked whether he might
not have a sight of these proposals; they answered, when he pleased: that they went with them to
Ireton for that purpose, and remained with him
almost till morning: that he (Ireton) permitted
him (Sir John) to alter two of the articles, and
that, in most material points, and that he would
have done a third, which was, the excluding seven
persons (that were not named) from pardon, and
the admitting of the King's party to sit in the next
Parliament; — to the first he answered, that being
they had prevailed in the war, if they should not
in the sight of the world make some distinction
between themselves and those that were worsted,
(who always bear the blame of public quarrels,) they
had so many malicious enemies, both in the Parliament and army, that they should be censured of
betraying their party, and to have sought their own
ends by private and indirect means; to the second,
he confessed that he should himself be afraid of a
Parliament, wherein the King's party should have
the major vote; but that after the agreement, if
the King's party and they could piece kindly and

cordially together, there would be nothing easier
than to procure His Majesty satisfaction in those
two particulars: he concluded, by conjuring him
(Sir John), as he tendered His Majesty's good and
welfare, that he would endeavour to prevail with
him to grant the proposals, that they might with
the more confidence propound them to the Parliament, and make an end of all differences : that
Sir John, out of his discourses and enquiries, collected these observations ;—that the army was
governed partly by a council of war, and partly by
a council of the army, or adjutators, wherein the
General had but a single voice ;—that Fairfax (the
General) had little power in either ;—that Cromwell and his son Ireton, with their friends and partizans, governed the council of war absolutely,
but not that of the army, which was the most
powerful, though they had a strong party there
also ; but that the major part of the adjutators
carried it ;—that amongst these adjutators, there
were many ill-wishers of Cromwell, looking on
him as one who would always make his advantages out of the army. Sir John proceeds,—that
when he came to Reading, he found many of the
adjutators jealous that Cromwell was not sincere
for the King; and they desired him, if he found
him false to their engagement, that he would let
them know it, and they did not doubt to set him
right, either with, or against, his will. But he
adds, that in all his conferences with him (Crom-

well), he found no man, in appearance, so zealous
for a speedy blow as he: sometimes wishing that
the King was more frank, and would not tie himself so strictly to narrow maxims; sometimes complaining of his son Ireton's slowness in perfecting
the proposals, and his not accommodating more to
His Majesty's sense; always doubting, that the
army would not preserve their good inclinations
for the King: that he (Sir John) met with him
(Cromwell) about three days after he came to
Reading, as he was coming from the King, then at
Causum: that he told him that he had lately seen
the tenderest sight that ever his eyes beheld, which
was the interview between the King and his children, and wept plentifully at the remembrance of
it; saying that never man was so abused as he, in
his sinister opinions of the King, who, he thought,
was the uprightest and most conscientious man of
his three kingdoms: that they, of the independent
party, (as they were called,) had infinite obligations to him, for not consenting to the Scots propositions at Newcastle, which would have totally
ruined them, and which His Majesty's interest
seemed to invite him to: and concluded, with
wishing that God would be pleased to look upon
him according to the sincerity of his heart towards
His Majesty: that he (Sir John) immediately acquainted His Majesty with this passage; who
seemed not well edified with it, and did believe
that all proceeded out of the use Cromwell and

the army had of His Majesty, without whom he thought they could do nothing : and this he (Sir John) conceived was inculcated daily by Bampfield and Loe, at first, and afterwards by the Lord Lauderdale, who had frequent accesses to His Majesty from the Scots, the Presbyterians, and the city of London, who knew there was nothing so fatal to them as a conjunction between the King and the army : that out of all his observations, he (Sir John) drew these conclusions, which he prosecuted to the best of his power; — that His Majesty was concerned to come to a speedy issue with the army; that he might either agree with them or discover that they intended not to agree with him ; and in that case, that His Majesty should secure his escape ; and that, in the mean time, His Majesty should not give them the least colour of exception to his actions ; that seeing the officers were more easily fixed to His Majesty by a visible prospect of their interest, in case of a conjunction, he took the least pains with them, and applied himself to Hugh Peters and the adjutators, who swayed their officers more than their officers commanded them ; and that it was more hard to satisfy them (being many) in point of interest than their officers, who were few :—that about ten days after his (Sir John's) arrival at the army the contentions grew high and hot between them and the presbyterian party in the House, (which was the major part by much,) and the city of London ; the one

contending to have the Parliament purged of corrupt members, and the other to have the army
removed farther from the city: that this caused
the army's march from Reading to Bedford, and
consequently His Majesty's remove, with his wonted guard, from Causum to Woburn, (a house of
the Earl of Bedford,) where he (Sir John) procured His Majesty a sight of the army's proposals,
six or eight days before they were offered to him
in public: that His Majesty was much displeased
with them in general, saying, that if they had a
mind to close with him, they would never impose
so hard terms upon him, to which he (Sir John)
replied, that if they had demanded less than they
had done, he should have suspected them, more
than he now did, of intending not really to serve
His Majesty, but only to abuse him; since it was
not likely that men who had, through so great
dangers and difficulties, acquired so great advantages, should ever sit down with less than was
contained in the proposals; and, on the other side,
never was a crown, that had been so near lost, so
cheaply recovered, as His Majesty's would be, if
they agreed upon such terms: that His Majesty
was of another advice, and returned, that they
could not subsist without him, and therefore he
did not doubt but that he should see them very
shortly be glad to condescend farther; and then
objected to three particular points of the proposals;—the first was, the exception of seven not

named from pardon; the second, the excluding his párty from being eligible in the next ensuing Parliament; and the third, that though there was nothing against the church-government established, yet there was nothing done to assert it: that to these he (Sir John) replied, that after His Majesty and the army were accorded, it would be no impossible work to make them remit in the first point; and, if he could not, when His Majesty was re-instated in his throne, he might easily supply seven persons beyond the seas, in such sort, as to make their banishment supportable to them; to the second, that the next Parliament would be necessitated to lay great bur-dens upon the kingdom, and it would be a happi-ness to the King's party to have no voice in them; to the third, that the law was security enough for the church, and it was happy that men, who had fought against the church, should be reduced (when they were superiors) not to speak against it; that His Majesty broke from him (Sir John) with this expression, — " Well, I shall see them glad ere long to accept more equal terms." I now began to long impatiently for Mr. Ashburnham, as hoping he had some better topics for His Majesty; and within a few days after he arrived, to His Majesty's great contentment, as well as mine: that his instructions referred to his (Sir John's), which they were to prosecute jointly: that he (Sir John) gave him (Mr. Ashburnham) presently all the light he had, which he seemed to embrace at first;

but that after he had discoursed more amply with His Majesty, he (Sir John) found him, so far from crossing him (His Majesty) that he abounded in His Majesty's sense, and held afterwards this discourse with Sir John ; — That, for his part, he was always bred in the best company, and, therefore, could not converse with such senseless fellows as the adjutators were ; that if we would gain the officers sure to the King, there was no doubt but they would be able to command their own army ; and therefore he was resolved to apply himself totally to them ; — and so he did : and there grew immediately great familiarities between him and Whalley, captain of the guard that waited on the King, and then with Cromwell and Ireton ; and daily messages between His Majesty and the head-quarters, which Mr. Ashburnham carried, and sometimes him (Sir John) with him, though he seldom knew the message ; at least, he (Mr. Ashburnham) would have him believe he did not, for he chose to speak apart with Cromwell and Ireton, when he (Sir John) was present, alleging that they would not speak freely to two at once : that, what with the pleasure of having so concurring a second as Mr. Ashburnham, and what with the encouraging messages which His Majesty had by Lord Lauderdale and others from the presbyterian party and the city of London, who pretended to despise the army, and to oppose them to death, His Majesty seemed very much erected ; insomuch, that,

when the proposals were solemnly sent to him, and
his concurrence most humbly and earnestly desired,.
His Majesty (not only to the astonishment of Ireton and the rest, but even of him, Sir John,) entertained them with very tart and bitter discourses,
saying, sometimes, that he would have no man to
suffer for his sake, and that he repented of nothing
so much as the bill against the Lord Strafford,
which, though most true, was unpleasant for them
to hear; that he would have the church established
according to law, by the proposals. They replied,
it was none of their work to do it; that it was
enough for them to wave the point, and, they
hoped, enough for His Majesty, since he had waved
the government itself in Scotland. His Majesty
said, that he hoped God had forgiven him that sin,
and repeated often, " You cannot be without me;
you will fall to ruin if I do not sustain you." That
many of the army who were present, and wished
well (at least as they pretended) to the agreement,
looked wishfully and with wonder, upon him (Sir
John) and Mr. Ashburnham; and he (Sir John), as
much as he durst, upon His Majesty, who would
take no notice of it, until he (Sir John) was forced
to step to him, and whisper in his ear — "Sir,
Your Majesty speaks as if you had some secret
strength and power that I do not know of; and
since Your Majesty hath concealed it from me, I
wish you had concealed it from these men too."
That His Majesty soon recollected himself, and

began to sweeten his former discourse with great
power of language and behaviour; but it was now
of the latest; for that Colonel Rainsborough, (who
of all the army seemed the least to wish the accord,)
in the middle of the conference, stole away, and
posted to the army, which he inflamed against the
King with all the artificial malice he had: that as
soon as the conference ended, he (Sir John) followed him to Bedford, where the army then lay:
that he met with some of the adjutators, who asked
him what His Majesty meant, to entertain their
commissioners so harshly? He told them that
Rainsborough had delivered it amiss to them, as
indeed he had, by adding to the truth, and then
desired a meeting with Ireton, and the rest of the
superior officers, and obtained it; and there asked
them, if the King should grant the proposals, what
would ensue? they replied, they would offer them
to the Parliament: but if they refused them, what
would they do then? They replied, they would
not tell him: that he (Sir John) then returned in
answer, that he would tell them that he would lose
no more time with them; for that if there came of
the propsals nothing but the propounding, he could
then propound as well as they: that they all replied,
that it was not for them to say, directly, what they
would do against the Parliament; but intimated,
that they did not doubt of being able to prevail
with the Parliament: that when he (Sir John)
appeared not fully satisfied with this reply, Rains-

borough spoke out in these words, "If they will not agree, we will make them;" to which the whole company assented. But, proceeds Sir John, we had harder work with His Majesty, who was so far from granting, that he sent for Sir Thomas Gardiner, Mr. Jeffry Palmer, and Sir Orlando Bridgman (his learned counsel), men indeed of great abilities and integrity; to these were added, Mr. Philip Warwick, Mr. Ashburnham, Mr. Denham, Sir Richard Ford, Dr. Gough, (who came over with Mr. Ashburnham from France,) Dr. Sheldon, Dr. Hammond, and himself (Sir John); that these easily answered the proposals, both in point of law and reason; but they had to do with what was stronger. All this while, continues Sir John, there wanted not those that meditated a better understanding between the Parliament and the army; but that not taking effect, the army advanced nearer London, and lodged at Windsor, and His Majesty at Stoke: that at this time, those that were supposed best inclined to His Majesty, in the army, seemed much afflicted with His Majesty's backwardness to concur with the army in the proposals; and the rather, because they conceived great hopes that, within a few days, they should be masters of London, which they doubted might alter the temper of the army towards the King: that Cromwell and Ireton, and the rest of the superior officers of the army, knew that London would certainly be theirs two days before they

communicated it to the army; and therefore sent
an express to Mr. Ashburnham and to him (Sir
John), to inform them, that although His Majesty
would not yield to the proposals, yet he should at
least send a kind letter to the army, before it were
commonly known that London would submit: that
they (Sir John and Mr. Ashburnham) caused a
meeting of the above-named persons at Windsor,
where the letter was immediately drawn, but His
Majesty would not sign it till after three or four
several debates, which lost at least one whole day's
time: that they (Mr. Ashburnham and Sir John)
went with it at last; and upon the way met with
messages to hasten it; but before they came to
Sion, the commissioners from London were arrived,
and the letter was out of season; for, that though
His Majesty was ignorant of the success when he
signed the letter, yet coming after it was known,
it lost both its grace and its efficacy: that all that
the officers could do, they did; which was, whilst
the army was in the act of thanksgiving to God for
their success, to propose that they should not be
elevated with it, but keep still to their former engagement to His Majesty; and, once more, solemnly vote the proposals, which was accordingly
done: that the next day the army marched into
London; and some few of the Presbyterian party,
that had been most active against the army, dis-
appeared: that from London the head-quarters
came to Putney, and His Majesty was lodged at

Hampton-court: Mr. Ashburnham had, daily, some message or another from the King to Cromwell and Ireton, who had enough to do, both in the Parliament and council of the army; the one abounding with Presbyterians, and the other with Levellers; and both really jealous that Cromwell and Ireton had made a private compact and bargain with the King; Lilburn printing books weekly to that effect: and that Sir Lewis Dives, afterwards, acknowledged to him (Sir John), that being his fellow-prisoner, he had daily endeavoured to possess him with that opinion, of which, although he were not persuaded himself, yet that he judged it for the King's service to divide Cromwell and the army: that on the other side, the Presbyterians were no less confident of their surmises; and that Cromwell told him (Sir John) that Lady Carlisle affirmed, that he (Sir John) had told her that he (Cromwell) was to be Earl of Essex, and captain of the King's guards: that these and the like discourses made great impression on the army, to which Mr. Ashburnham's secret and long conferences contributed not a little; insomuch, that the adjutators, who were wont to complain that Cromwell went too slow towards the King, began now to suspect that he had gone too fast, and left them behind him; from whence there were frequent complaints in the council of the army, of the intimacy Mr. Ashburnham and he (Sir John) had in the army: that Cromwell's and Ireton's doors

were open to them when it was shut to the army;
that they knew not why malignants should have
so much countenance in the army, and liberty
with the King: that with these discourses, both in
public and private, Cromwell seemed highly offended; and when he could carry any thing to
His Majesty's advantage amongst the adjutators,
could not rest until he had made them (Sir John
and Mr. Ashburnham) privately partakers of it;
but telling them, that if he were an honest man,
he had said enough of the sincerity of his intentions;
if he were not, nothing was enough; and therefore
conjured them, as they tendered His Majesty's
service, not to come so frequently to his quarters,
but send privately to him; the suspicions of him
being grown to that height, that he was afraid to
lie in his own quarters. But, continues Sir John,
this had no operation upon Mr. Ashburnham, who
alleged that we must show them the necessity of
agreeing with the King, from their own disorders:
that about three weeks after the army had entered
London, the Scots had prevailed with the Parliament for another solemn address to His Majesty;
which was performed in the old propositions of
Newcastle, some particulars in respect to the Scots
only excepted: that the army was very unwilling
that the King should grant these propositions, of
which the King advised with all the persons above
mentioned, who were all of opinion that it was unsafe for His Majesty to close with the enemies of

the army, whilst he was in it. And therefore he
followed the advice of all the leading part of the
independent party, both in the Parliament and
army, by refusing the articles, and desiring a personal treaty; whereof His Majesty thought the
proposals of the army a better ground than the
articles, though there were something in them to
which His Majesty could not consent: that they
(Sir John and Mr. Ashburnham) gave their friends
in the army a sight of this answer the day before
it was sent, with which they seemed infinitely satisfied, and promised to use their utmost endeavours
to procure a personal treaty; and (adds Sir John),
to his understanding, performed it: for that both
Cromwell and Ireton, with Vane and all their
friends, seconded, with great resolution, this desire
of His Majesty. But that, contrary to their and
all men's expectations, they found a most general
opposition, and that this message of His Majesty
had confirmed the jealousy of their private agreement with the King; so that the more it was urged
by Cromwell and his friends, the more it was rejected by the rest, who looked on them as their be-
trayers: that the suspicions were so strong in the
House, that they lost almost all their friends there;
and the army, that lay then about Putney, were no
less ill satisfied; for there came down shoals every
day from London of the presbyterian and levelling
parties that fomented those jealousies: insomuch
that Cromwell thought himself, or pretended it,

not secure in his own quarters: that the adjutators now began to change their discourses, and complained openly in their councils both of the King and the malignants about His Majesty: that one of the first they voted from him was himself (Sir John); they said, that since His Majesty had not accepted of their proposals, they were not obliged any farther to them; that they were obliged to consult their own safety, and the good of the kingdom, and to use such means towards both as they should find rational: and, adds Sir John, because they met with strong opposition from Cromwell and Ireton, and most of the superior officers, and some even of the adjutators, they had many private solemn meetings in London, where they humbled themselves before the Lord, and sought his good pleasure, and desired that he would be pleased to reveal it to his saints, which they interpreted those to be who were most violent or zealous, as they called it, in the work of the Lord: that these found it apparent, that God had, on the one side, hardened the King's heart, and blinded his eyes, in not passing the proposals, whereby they were absolved from offering him any more; and that, on the other side, the Lord had led captivity captive, and put all things under their feet; and that, therefore, they were bound to finish the work of the Lord, which was, to alter the government, according to their first design: and that to this end they resolved to seize the King's person, and take him out of Cromwell's hands. That these

proceedings struck so great a terror into Cromwell
and Ireton, with others of the officers, whom they
(Sir John and Mr. Ashburnham) supposed best affected to the King, that they were of opinion the
army, should be drawn to a rendezvous, and their
endeavours used to engage them once more to adhere to the proposals : that, as soon as the tumultuous part of the army had notice of it, they resolved, before the day of rendezvous, to seize the
King's person : that he (Sir John) had been then
about three weeks removed from the King, and
about a fortnight after him, Mr. Ashburnham :
that Mr. Leg still continued with His Majesty,
and waited in his bed-chamber : that about eight
or ten days before the time appointed for the drawing together of the army, Mr. Ashburnham invited
him (Sir John) from London, and Mr. Leg, from
Hampton-court, to dine with him on a Sunday at
Ditton, being on the other side of the water : that
they were both there long before him, and he a
good while before dinner; but that just as dinner
was ready to come in, they took him (Sir John)
aside in the room, and told him that His Majesty
was really afraid of his life by the tumultuous part
of the army, and was resolved to make his escape,
and that they had order from His Majesty to command him (Sir John), in his name, to wait on him
in his intended escape : that he (Sir John) replied,
" That it was a great honour, and accompanied
with not a little danger;" but that it being new to

him, nothing then occurred to him but two things ; — the first was, that he thought it absolutely necessary that Mr. Ashburnham, who kept the King's money, should immediately employ his servant, Dutton, who was well acquainted with the coast, to provide three or four ships in several ports, to be ready in all events; the second, that he (Sir John) also might receive His Majesty's commands immediately from himself: that to the first they seemed to concur, but nothing was ever done in it, which to that day amazed him (Sir John): that the other was effected; and he (Sir John) went the Tuesday night after to Hampton-court privately, being introduced a back way by Mr. Leg: that the King told him he was afraid of his life, and that he would have him assist in person in his escape: that he (Sir John) asked which way His Majesty would go? His Majesty replied, "That both Mr. Ashburnham (who was present) and he should know that by Will. Leg:" that the Monday before, Mr. Ashburnham and he (Sir John) went to the head-quarters, to desire passes to return beyond the seas; and, by the way back, he (Mr. Ashburnam) told him, that the Scots had much tampering with the King, but could come to no agreement: that they would fain have His Majesty out of the army, and to that end had much augmented his just fears; and, therefore, asked him (Sir John) what he thought of His Majesty's coming privately to London, and appearing in the

House of Lords? that he replied, "Very ill! because the army were absolutely masters both of the city and Parliament, and would undoubtedly seize His Majesty; and, if there should be but two swords drawn in the scuffle, they would accuse His Majesty of beginning a new war, and proceed with him accordingly." He then asked him what he thought of the Isle of Wight? he replied, Better than of London; though he knew nothing of it, nor who was governor: that he (Ashburnham) replied, that he had some communication with the governor of late, and conceived good hopes of him, but had no assurance from him: that he (Sir John) then asked him, why His Majesty could not make his retreat secure by quitting the kingdom? he replied, that he would not for two reasons; the first was, that the rendezvous would be a week after, and His Majesty was not willing to quit the army before that were passed; because, if the superior officers prevailed, they would be able to make good their public engagement; and, if they were overtopped, they must apply themselves to him for their own security: the second was, that the Scots were in treaty with the King, and very near to a conclusion of it; which they would never come to, but out of their desire to separate the King and the army; that, if the King went to them before the conclusion of it, they would hold him to impossible conditions; and, therefore, His Majesty was resolved to con-

clude with them first: in which advice Mr.
Ashburnham was most positive, and told him (Sir
John) often, that the world would laugh at us, if
we quitted the army before we had agreed with
the Scots : — " And let them do so," replied Sir
John, " provided His Majesty be secure." · That
on or about the Wednesday, they had orders to
send spare horses to Sutton, in Hampshire, a place
where he (Sir John) never had been; and the
Thursday after, His Majesty, with Will. Leg, came
out at the closing of the evening, and immediately
went towards Oatlands, and so through the forest,
where His Majesty was their guide ; but they lost
their way, through the excessive darkness and
storminess of the night: that when His Majesty
first set out, he discoursed long with Mr. Ashburnham, and at last called him (Sir John) to him, and
complained very much of the Scots commissioners,
who were the first that presented his dangers to
him, and offered him expedients for his escape ;
but that, when he proposed to make use of those
they had offered, they were full of objections to
them, saying, that his coming into London was
desperate, his hiding in England chimerical, and
his escape to Jersey prevented, because his (Sir
John's) ship was discovered ; which particular the
King said the Lord Lanerick had affirmed : that
the King thereupon asked him (Sir John) if he
had ever a ship ready ; to which he answered, that
he neither had nor could have any, having not

one penny of money: that he had desired Mr.
Ashburnham earnestly to make provision, but
knew not what he had done in it: that the King
then asked him, what he thought might be the
reason they should say that he had, and that it
had been discovered, if he had none? That he replied, it was hard for him to affirm what was their
meaning in that particular, or in general, in their
manner of proceeding with His Majesty; but that
he did conjecture, that they were very desirous to
have His Majesty out of the army, which made
them present his dangers to him so frequently as
they had done; and that, in the next place, they
desired that His Majesty should put himself again
into their hands, but wanted confidence, or believed
it would be ineffectual to move it directly to His
Majesty, because they had given so ill an account
of him, when he was last with them; and that,
therefore, they objected against their own expedient of either coming openly into London, or of
obscuring himself in England: and that, because
they could find no other reason against his going
to Jersey, they pretended that he (Sir John) had
a ship, which had been discovered; believing,
perhaps, that he was totally separated from His
Majesty, and so should not have had any opportunity of contradicting it; and that, by these
means, His Majesty being excluded from all other
means of escaping, should have been necessitated
to make use of Scotland: that His Majesty then

laid his hand upon his (Sir John's) shoulder, and said, "I think thou art in the right;" and believed it afterward more confidently than I did : that he (Sir John) then asked His Majesty which way he would go ? to which His Majesty replied, that he hoped to be at Sutton three hours before day, and that while their horses were making ready, they would consider what course to take ; but that, by the length and badness of the road, the darkness of the night, and going at least ten miles out of the way, it was daybreak when they came to their inn at Sutton ; where their servant came out to them, and told them there was a committee of the county then sitting about the Parliament business : that His Majesty thereupon sent for their horses out, and they continued their way towards South-ampton ; and His Majesty resolved that they should walk down the next hill, with their horses in their hands, and as they walked, consult what they were to do : that then he (Sir John) enquired if Mr. Ashburnham had gotten a ship, and finding he had not, proposed going farther west; where he (Sir John) was sure he had some friends, who would favour their escape. And here again, says Sir John, he found the two reasons prevail, of not leaving the army before the rendezvous was passed, and the treaty with the Scots finished : that His Majesty then resolved (and that for the first time, for aught he (Sir John) could then discover) to go to the Isle of Wight, whither he ordered Mr.

Ashburnham and him to go with their instructions,
by word of mouth, to the governor, Hammond,
and return to His Majesty, who went with Will.
Leg, to a house of Lord Southampton, at Titchfield : that they should carry him a copy of the
letter His Majesty left at Hampton-court, and
copies of two letters sent to him, one from Cromwell, the other without a name : that Cromwell's,
and the other letter, contained great apprehensions
and fears of the ill intentions of the levelling party
in the army and city against His Majesty; and
that from Cromwell added, that, in prosecution
thereof, a new guard was the next day to be put
upon His Majesty of that party : His Majesty's
letter contained his distrust of the disorderly part
of the army, and his necessity thereupon of providing for his own safety, which he would so do,
as not to desert the interest of the army : that in
order thereunto, we should let the governor know,
that of all the army His Majesty had made choice
of him, to put himself upon, as being a person of
good extraction, and one that, though he had been
engaged against him in the war, yet it had been
prosecuted by him without any animosity to his
person; to which he had been informed he had no
aversion : only His Majesty, that he might not
surprise him, thought fit to send them (Sir John
and Mr. Ashburnham) before, to advertise him,
and to obtain his promise to protect His Majesty
and his servants to the best of his power ; and that

if it should happen that he might not be able to do it, then the governor should oblige himself to leave them (the King and his attendants) in as good a condition as he found them, that is, suffer them to make their escape: that with these instructions they quitted the King; but that before he (Sir John) had gone ten yards, he returned to His Majesty, and said, " I have no knowledge of the governor, and therefore cannot tell whether he may not detain us in the island;" he therefore advised His Majesty, if they came not to him the next day, that he (His Majesty) should think no more of them, but secure his own escape: that His Majesty thanked him (Sir John) for the caution, and pursued his way, and Mr. Ashburnham and him theirs: that the first thing they resolved was, that since His Majesty went towards the east side of the island, we would go on to the west, to a place called Lymington, where Mr. Ashburnham told him there was a short passage over: by the way, Sir John asked Mr. Ashburnham if he had any acquaintance with Hammond the governor; he replied, " Not very much;" but that he had lately had some discourse with him upon the highways near Kingston, and found him not very averse to His Majesty; but that which made him conceive the best hopes of him was, the character Mr. Durham, and the commendations Lady Isabella Thynne gave of him: that they came to Lymingtom that night, but could not pass by reason of a violent storm.; but the next morning they got over, and had then eight miles to the castle of Carisbrooke, where the governor dwelt : that they came thither after ten in the morning, and found that the governor was newly gone out, towards Newport : that when they overtook him, Mr. Ashburnham desired him (Sir John) to open the matter to him, which he would afterwards second : that after he had saluted him, he took him aside and delivered their message to him, word by word; but he grew so pale, and fell into such a trembling, that he (Sir John) did really believe he would have fallen off his horse; which trembling continued with him at least an hour after, in which he broke out into passionate and distracted expressions, sometimes saying, " O, gentlemen! you have undone me, by bringing the King into the island; if, at least, you have brought him : and, if you have not, pray let him not come; for, what between my duty to His Majesty, and my gratitude for this fresh obligation of confidence, on the one hand; and my observing my trust to the army, on the other, I shall be confounded :" that, other-while he would talk to a quite contrary purpose : he (Sir John) remembered, that to settle him the better, he said, that " God be thanked, there was no harm done; that His Majesty intended a favour to him and his posterity, in giving him an occasion to lay a great obligation upon him, and such as was very consisting with his relation to the army, who had

so solemnly engaged themselves to His Majesty;
but that if he thought otherwise, His Majesty
would be far from-imposing his person upon him:"
that he replied, that then, if His Majesty should
come to any mischance, what would the army and
kingdom say to him, that had refused to receive him?
to this he (Sir John) replied, that he did not refuse
him, who was not come to him: that he (the governor) returned, that he must needs know where
His Majesty was, because he knew where we were;
Sir John told him, he was never the nearer for his
(Sir John's) part: that he then began a little to
sweeten, and to wish that His Majesty would have
reposed himself absolutely upon him; because it
would have been much the better for both: that
he (Sir John) then went to Mr. Ashburnham, and
told him, that this governor was not a man for
their purpose; and that, for his part, he would
never give his consent that His Majesty should
trust him: that Mr. Ashburnham acknowledged
that he did not like him; yet, on the other side,
he much feared what would become of His Majesty,
if he should be discovered before he had made his
point, and made appear what his intention was;
for then he would be accused of what his enemies
pleased to lay upon him: that he (Sir John) replied, that if they returned not that night, His
Majesty would be gone to sea: that he perceived
that Mr. Ashburnham liked not that so well, and
therefore took the governor to task apart; and,
after some conference, they both came to him (Sir

John), and the governor said, that since they desired it, he would say, that because His Majesty,
he believed, had made choice of him as a person
of honour and honesty, to lay this great trust
upon, therefore he would not deceive His Majesty's
expectation: that he (Sir John) replied, that expression was too general, and did not come home
to their instructions. He then made many discourses, not much to the purpose; during which
time he kept himself between Mr. Ashburnham
and him (Sir John), and when he found him (Sir
John) still unsatisfied, he added, that he was
harder to content than Mr. Ashburnham, and
that he did believe, that His Majesty would be
much easier pleased than either; and thereupon
concluded, that he (Sir John) should go into the
castle, and that Mr. Ashburnham should take his
horse and go to the King, and tell His Majesty
what he said: that he (Sir John) embraced the
motion most readily, and immediately went over
the bridge into the castle, though he had the
image of the gallows very perfectly before him:
that Mr. Ashburnham went, he believed, with a
better heart to horse; but before he had gone
half-a-flight-shot, the governor (being before the
castle-gate) called to him, and had a conference of
at least a quarter of an hour with him; to what
purpose he (Sir John) never knew until he came
into Holland; where a gentleman of good worth
and quality told him, that the governor affirmed

afterwards in London, and in many places, that
he then offered to Mr. Ashburnham, that he (Sir
John) should go, and he (Ashburnham) should
stay; as believing His Majesty to be less willing
to expose him (Ashburnham) than him (Sir John);
but that Mr. Ashburnham absolutely refused: that
whatever passed between them, he (Sir John) was
sure they came both back to him; and the governor
putting himself between them, said, that he would
say that which he was sure ought to content any
reasonable man, which was, that he did believe
His Majesty relied on him, as a person of honour
and honesty, and therefore he did engage himself
to them, to perform whatever could be expected
from a person of honour and honesty: that before
he could make any answer, Mr. Ashburnham replied, " I will ask no more:" that the governor
then added, " Let us then all go to the King, and
acquaint him with it:" that Mr. Ashburnham
answered, " With all my heart:" that he (Sir
John) then broke from the governor, who held him
in his hand, and went to Mr. Ashburnham, and
said, " What! do you mean to carry this man to
the King before you know whether he will approve
of this undertaking or no? undoubtedly you will
surprise him:" Mr. Ashburnham said nothing but
" I'll warrant you:" — " And so you shall," said he
(Sir John), " for you know the King much better
than I do; and, therefore, when we shall come
where the King is, I assure you I will not see him

before you have satisfied His Majesty concerning
your proceeding:" — well, he would take that
upon him: that he (Sir John) then desired
he would not let the governor take any other
person with him, that in all events they might
the more easily secure him; which he consented
to : that, nevertheless, when they came to Cowes
castle, where they were to take boat, Hammond
took Basket, the governer of that castle, along
with him; and when Sir John complained of it
to Mr. Ashburnham, he answered, " It was no
matter, for that we should be able to do well
enough with them two :" that when they came to
Titchfield, the Lord of Southampton's house, Mr.
Ashburnham, according to his promise, went up to
the King, and left him (Sir John) below, with
Hammond and Basket, who (Sir John) afterwards
understood, that when Mr. Ashburnham had given
an account of their message, and the governor's
answer, and came to say that he was come along
with them to make good what he had promised,
His Majesty struck himself upon his breast, and
said, " What! have you brought Hammond with
you? O, you have undone me; for I am by this
means made fast from stirring." Mr. Ashburnham
replied, that, if he mistrusted Hammond, he would
undertake to secure him. His Majesty said, " I
understand you well enough; but the world would
not excuse me; for if I should follow that council,
it would be said, and believed, that he (Hammond)

had ventured his life for me, and that I had unworthily taken it from him : no ; it is too late now to think of any thing, but going through the way you have forced upon me, and to leave the issue to God." But when His Majesty began anew to wonder that he could make so great an oversight, Mr. Ashburnham, having no more to reply, wept bitterly : that, in the mean time, Hammond and Basket were so impatient at this long stay below in the court, that he (Sir John) was forced to send a gentleman of Lord Southampton, to desire that His Majesty and Mr. Ashburnham would remember that they were below : that about half an hour after, they were sent for up ; but before Hammond and Basket kissed his hand, His Majesty took him (Sir John) aside, and said, " Sir John Berkley, I hope you are not so passionate as Jack Ashburnham ; do you think you have followed my directions ?" to which Sir John answered, " No, indeed, Sir ; but it is none of my fault, as Mr. Ashburnham can tell you, if he please : I have exposed my life to prevent it :" and then told His Majesty the sum of what had passed, and particularly of his being a prisoner in the castle, and of Mr. Ashburnham's coming away without him ; which Mr. Ashburnham had omitted : that His Majesty judged it was then to late to boggle, and therefore received Hammond cheerfully, who promised more to His Majesty than he had done to them ; and they all went over that night to the

Cowes: that, in the morning, His Majesty went
with the governor to Carisbrooke, and was met in
the way by divers gentlemen of the island, from
whom he learned, that he was more fortunate than
he was aware of; for that the whole island was
unanimously for the King, except the governors
of the castles and Hammond's captains: that
there were but twelve old men in the castle, and
they had served under the Earl of Portland, and
were all well affected: that Hammond might
easily be gained, if not more easily forced, the
castle being day and night full of loyal subjects
and servants of His Majesty; and that His Majesty,
having daily liberty to ride abroad, might choose
his own time of quitting the island. Indeed, adds
Sir John, not only His Majesty and all that were
about him, but those that were at a further distance,
approved by their letters this resolution of His
Majesty: that both His Majesty and Mr. Ashburnham attacked the governor very prosperously;
for that both he and his captains seemed to desire
nothing of His Majesty, but that he would send a
civil message to the Houses, signifying his pro-
pension to peace: which was done to their satisfaction: that, three days after their coming to
the island, a messenger was sent by the Parliament for Mr. Ashburnham, himself (Sir John),
and Mr. Leg; but the governor refused to let
them go: that, the fifth day after their arrival,
they heard that in the rendezvous of the army,

the superior officers had carried it, and that one or
two soldiers had been shot, and eleven more of
the mutinying levellers made prisoners; that
this made them bless God for the resolution of
coming into the island: and now Mr. Ashburnham and the governor were frequent and fervent
in private conferences, and as he (Sir John)
had heard, came to particulars of accommodation for him, in case of the King's recovery of
his kingdom, insomuch, that now the governor
seemed solicitous of nothing so much as that
the army should resume its wonted discipline,
and clear themselves of their importunate and impertinent adjutators; of whose authority in the
army he had never approved, and therefore he
sent his chaplain immediately to the army, to con-
jure the superior officers to make use of their
success upon the adjutators: that, two or three
days after, he moved earnestly, that His Majesty
would send one of the three, Sir John, Mr. Ashburnham, or Mr. Leg, to the army, with colour-
able letters to the General; but that he should
write with confidence to Cromwell and Ireton, to
whom he (the governor) would also write; and he
did accordingly write to them, conjuring them by
their engagement, by their interest, by their honour, and their consciences, to come to a speedy
close with the King, and not to expose themselves
still to the fantastic giddiness of the adjutators.
Sir John proceeds:—his two comrades were very

well contented that he should go this voyage; which he did, not without some apprehension of the event as to his own particular: that His Majesty charged him to require Will. Ashburnham to provide a ship for him upon the coast of Sussex; but Mr. Ashburnham thought not fit that he should be furnished with money for that, or for his journey: that he (Sir John) desired that, in case the army should not intend well, he might have a commission to the Scots; but Mr. Ashburnham did not think it fit: that he (Sir John) took a cousin-german of his with him, a Mr. Henry Berkley, son to Sir Henry Berkley, and procured a pass from the governor of the Cowes, for his return within four or five days, which had otherwise been forgotten: that between Bagshot and Windsor (then the head-quarters) he met Traughton, the governor's chaplain, who told him he could carry no good news back, the army being as yet come to no resolution as to the King: that, as he (Sir John) was half-way between Bagshot and Windsor, Cornet Joyce (a great adjutator, and he that had taken the King from Holmby) overtook him; he seemed much to wonder, that he durst adventure to come to the army: that, upon his discourses with him, he found that it had been discoursed among the adjutators, " whether, for their justification, the King ought not to be brought to a trial?" which he held in the affirmative; not, he said, that he would have one hair of his head to suffer, but that they might not bear the blame of the war : that he (Sir John) was quickly weary of his discourse, but perceived he (Joyce) would not leave him until he saw him in Windsor, and knew where he lodged : that, about an hour after, he (Sir John) went to the General's quarters, and found a general meeting of the officers there : that after an hour's waiting he was admitted, and after he had delivered his compliments and letters to the General, he was desired to withdraw; and having attended half an hour, he was called in : that the General looked very severely upon him, and, after his manner, said, that they were the Parliament's army, and therefore could not say any thing to His Majesty's motion of peace, but must refer those matters to them, to whom they would send His Majesty's letters : that he then looked about upon Cromwell and Ireton, and the rest of his acquaintance, who saluted him very coldly, and had their countenances quite changed towards him, and showed him Hammond's letter, which he had delivered to them, and smiled with much disdain upon it. Sir John says, he saw that that was no place for him, and therefore went to his lodgings, where he staid from four until six, and none of his acquaintance came to him, which appeared sad enough : that at last he sent his servant out, and wished him to see if he could light upon any of his (Sir John's) acquaintance ; who met with one that was a general officer, who whispered in his

ear, and bade him tell his master that he would
meet him at twelve at night, in a close behind the
Garter Inn : that he (Sir John) came at the hour,
and the officer not long after. Sir John asked
what news? he replied, " None good ;" and then
continued this discourse,—" You know that I and
my friend engaged ourselves to you ; that we were
zealous for an agreement ; and, if the rest were
not so, we were abused : that, if there was an intention to cozen us, it would not be long hid from
us ; that, whatever we should discover, should not
be secret to you ; that, ever since the tumult of
the army, I did mistrust Cromwell, and not long
after Ireton, whereof I informed you ; I come now
to tell you, that we mistrust neither, but know
them, and all of us, to be the archest villains in
the world : for, we are resolved, notwithstanding
our engagements, to destroy the King and his posterity ; to which end Ireton made two propositions
this afternoon, one that you should be sent prisoner to London; the other, that none should
speak with you upon pain of death, and I do
hazard my life now by doing of it ; the way that
is intended to ruin the King is, to send 800 of the
most disaffected of the army to secure his person,
(as believing him not so now,) and then bring him
to a trial ; and I dare think no farther : this will
be done in ten days, and therefore if the King can
escape, let him do it, as he loves his life." That
he (Sir John) then enquired what was the reason

of this horrid change,—what had the King done to deserve it? He said, " Nothing; and that to our grief, for we would leap for joy, if we could have any advantage against him. I have pleaded hard against this resolution this day, but have been laughed at for my pains." He (Sir John) then said, " Well, but still why is this horrid perfidiousness resolved on, since there appears no occasion for it, the officers being superior at the rendezvous?" He answered, that he could not tell certainly, but he conceived this to be the ground of it, — that though one of the mutineers was shot at the late rendezvous, and eleven made prisoners, and the rest in appearance overquelled, yet that they were so far from being so indeed, that there have been with Cromwell and Ireton, one after another, two third parts of the army, to tell them, that though they were certainly to perish in the attempt, they would leave nothing unessayed, to bring the army to their sense; and, if all failed, they would make a division in the army, and join with any that would assist in the destruction of their opposers: that Cromwell and Ireton therefore argued thus; — if the army divide, the greatest part will join with the Presbyterians, and will, in all likelihood, prevail to our ruin, and we shall be forced to make applications to the King, wherein we shall rather crave than offer any assistance; and when His Majesty shall give it us, and afterwards have the good fortune to prevail, if he shall then pardon us,

it is all we can pretend to, and more than we
can promise ourselves; and thereupon concluded,
That if we cannot bring the army to our sense,
we must go to theirs; a schism being evidently
destructive: and that therefore Cromwell bent all
his thoughts to make his peace with the party that
was most opposite to the King, in which Peters was
instrumental: that he (Sir John) then asked this
gentleman, whether he (Sir John) should not endeavour to deliver his letters from the King to
Cromwell and Ireton: he replied, by all means,
lest they should mistrust that he (Sir John) had
discovered them: that as soon as Sir John came
to his lodging, he dispatched his cousin, Harry
Berkley, to the Isle of Wight, with two letters;
the one containing a general relation, and doubtful
judgment of things in the army, which he intended
should be shown to the governor; the other was
in cypher, wherein he gave a particular account of
this conference, naming the person, and concluding
with a most passionate supplication to His Majesty,
to meditate nothing but his immediate escape: that
the next morning he sent Colonel Cook to Cromwell, to let him know that he had letters and
instructions to him from the King; that he (Cromwell) sent him word by the same messenger, that
he durst not see him, it being very dangerous to
them both; and bid me be assured, that he would
serve His Majesty as long as he could do it without
his own ruin; but desired that he (Sir John) would

not expect that he should perish for his (the King's) sake: that as soon as he had this answer he took horse for London, with this resolution,—not to acquaint any man with the intentions of the army, nor of His Majesty's intended escape; which he (Sir John) presumed would be within a few days, the wind serving, and the Queen having sent a ship to that purpose, and pressed it earnestly by her letters: that Sir John, the next day after his arrival at London, had a letter from Lord Lanerick and Lord Lauderdale, desiring a meeting with him, as presuming he had a commission to treat with them from His Majesty: that at this meeting they wondered to find the contrary. In his (Sir John's) discourse with them, he happened to say, " The last words His Majesty said to me, at parting, were, that whatever he (Sir John) should undertake to any person in his name, His Majesty would make it good, on the word of a King." That Lord Lanerick thereupon replied, that he would ask no more commission; believing it to be true, both because he (Sir John) affirmed it, and because he had received the like from His Majesty upon the like occasion: that their first conference was interrupted through Lord Lauderdale's vehement indignation against the letter of Mr. Ashburnham to the Speaker, wherein he had this passage, " That he would not expose his honour to the discretion of either Scot or adjutator:" that this letter was written by Mr. Ash-

burnham before he (Sir John) had left the island,
upon the occasion of Whalley's complaint to the
House of Commons: that Mr. Ashburnham had
broken his engagement with him, at his first coming to Woburn; wherein he said, he (Ashburnham)
undertook that the King should not leave the
army without his knowledge and consent: that
Dr. Sheldon, Dr. Hammond, Mr. Leg, and himself,
objected hard against this expression; but that
Mr. Ashburnham liked it so well, that he could
not be prevailed on to depart from it.   Sir John
proceeds, — on Friday after, they (the two Scots
Lords and himself) had another meeting, wherein
they discoursed themselves well towards an agreement, and resolved, on the Monday following, to
conclude one way or other: that the next day, being Saturday, he (Sir John) had a letter from Mr.
Ashburnham, requiring him, in His Majesty's
name, to lay by all other business whatsoever, and
to return instantly to His Majesty; he sent therefore his excuse to these Lords, and went that night
out of town: which they took very ill, though
they had no reason for it; for that he would as
willingly have excused his journey as they; as believing it was only to assist in His Majesty's escape;
for that he had more than once observed, that
though Mr. Ashburnham was willing enough to
appropriate employments of honour and profit, yet
that he was contented to communicate those of
danger with his friends: that the next morning he

(Sir John) was with His Majesty, who received him more graciously than ordinary, and told him that he had always a good opinion of his honesty and discretion, but was never so much confirmed in it, as by his dispatch from Windsor ; for which His Majesty thanked him : that after he had returned his acknowledgements for His Majesty's favour, he asked, if His Majesty approved the advice so well, why did he not follow it? why was he still in the island, where he could not long promise himself the liberty he now had, since there were forces designed, both by sea and land, to secure his person : that His Majesty replied, that he would have a care of that time enough, and that he was to conclude with the Scots before he left the kingdom ; because, from their desire to have him out of the army's hands, they would listen to reason ; whereas, if he went away before, they would never treat with him but upon their own terms : and in this opinion Mr. Ashburnham fully concurred with His Majesty : that against this he (Sir John) argued the best he could ; and when he saw it was in vain, he desired His Majesty would dispatch this treaty, for that his condition would admit no delays : that His Majesty then ordered him to withdraw with Mr. Ashburnham, Dr. Sheldon, Dr. Hammond, and Mr. Leg, to see how far His Majesty had gone in a treaty with the Scots. This treaty, observes Sir John, had been managed in London by Dr. Gough, who,

in the Queen's name, conjured His Majesty to
make his speedy escape: and in all his letters, and
in his own name, had beseeched His Majesty not
to insist upon nice terms in this present exigence
of his affairs; but that Mr. Ashburnham refined
much upon several expressions of the articles, that
concerned the covenant and Church of England,
of which he was a great professor, and made many
replies and alterations, and moved that messenger
should be sent after messenger about it, and, at
last, insisted, that the King should send for the
Scots commissioners to come to him : that the next
day he (Sir John) fell sick, but the day following
he went to His Majesty, and, as soon as he could
be admitted, spoke to him in these words;—" Sir,
if you make no more haste than you do, I doubt
you will not be able to secure your escape; and,
therefore, I humbly beseech you to make two
papers or draughts, the one containing the utmost
extent of what you will give the Scots, and sign
it; and, at the same time, send another, containing
the least you will receive of them, and let the
Scots sign, and deliver that to Dr. Gough, at the
same time that he shall deliver Your Majesty's
concessions to them, and provide instantly for your
safety :" that about the middle of this discourse
with the King, Mr. Ashburnham came in; and
when he (Sir John) had ended, very graciously
smiling, said, that this proposition would be good,
if it were practicable, which it was not; for that.

though the Scots should agree to the substance of
all the articles, yet they and all men else would
have their several senses concerning the expressions ; which must be satisfied, or no agreement
could be made, and, therefore, he concluded, that
the Scots were to be sent for : that to this he (Sir
John) replied, that Mr. Ashburnham had reason,
ordinarily speaking, for what he objected ; but that
His Majesty's danger made this a very extraordinary case : that his reasons however carried it clear,
and Sir William Fleming, or Mr. Mungo Murray,
(for they both went and came by turns,) was sent
to invite the Scots commissioners to come to His
Majesty : that the next day, after his departure, in
the evening, the King called him (Sir John) to
him, and told him, " I think you are a prophet,
for the Scots commissioners at London have sent
an express, desiring me to do the same thing, in
effect, as you had moved ; but that it was now too
late, for they would be come away, before another
express could be gone out of the island towards
them :" that he (Sir John) replied that their concurrence was accidental ; for that he had not the
least intelligence with the Scots commissioners ;
but, that when he saw there was no remedy, he
applied himself to what was the next best he could :
and, proceeds Sir John, God knows, there was
work enough for abler men than any of them were ;
for that at the same time that they, the Scots, were
coming to the King, there were also commissioners

sent by the Parliament to His Majesty, with offers
of a treaty, upon condition that His Majesty, as a
pledge of his future sincerity, would grant four
preliminary bills, meaning the bills heretofore described, which they had brought with them: Sir
John proceeds, — many well-wishing persons were
induced to believe, that, by all means, His Majesty
ought to pass those bills, for many reasons; but
especially, because his enemies would deliver him
to the world, as obstinate to his own and the kingdom's ruin, if he should not accept this offer : that
to avoid both the inconveniences of granting or
refusing, he (Sir John) drew an answer of the
treaty before it began : that if they would needs
think it expedient to require so great hostages from
His Majesty they would not be backward to give
some token to him of their reality; and then desired, that at the same time that His Majesty
should pass these four bills, the Houses would pass
four of His Majesty's drawing, which were all most
popular, and such as they durst not pass, nor would
deny; at least, if they did, they could, with no
colour of justice, accuse His Majesty for not granting what was most unjust and most unpopular : the
first was a bill for payment of the army, which
contained their disbanding, as soon as they were
paid; the second, a period to the present Parliament; the third, for restoring the King, Queen,
and royal family, to their revenues; the fourth,
the settling of the church-government, without

any coercive power; and, in the mean time, till such a government were agreed on, the old one to stand, without coercive authority: that he (Sir John) showed this answer, first to Mr. Leg, then to Dr. Hammond, and Dr. Sheldon; who seemed to approve of the expedient, and desired Mr. Ashburnham would acquaint the King with it; but he (Sir John) never heard any thing from His Majesty; and was resolved never to have it obtruded, lest he should appear fond of his own conceptions; that by His Majesty's directions an answer was drawn, that gave a full denial; which was, in his (Sir John's) judgment, very well penned: but, adds he, I thought good penning did not signify much at that time, and therefore made this objection, that it was very possible, that upon His Majesty's giving an absolute negative, the commissioners might have orders to enjoin the governor to look more strictly to his person, and so his intended escape would be prevented. His Majesty replied immediately, that he had thought of a remedy, which was, to deliver his answer, sealed, to the commissioners; and so left us: that he (Sir John) could not hold from letting Mr. Ashburnham find his sense of this sorry 'expedient, by saying, that the commissioners would either open the answer, or conclude that, in effect, it was a denial, and proceed accordingly; but all was in vain: that some few days after, the English commissioners arrived,

and delivered their message, and desired an answer
within three or four days: that, the next day, the
Lords Loudon, Lanerick, Lauderdale, Chiesly, and
others, commissioners for the kingdom of Scotland,
delivered a protestation to the King, subscribed by
them, against this message, as not according with
their covenant: that, from that time, they began
to treat seriously with His Majesty, but would not
permit that either Mr. Ashburnham or him (Sir
John) should assist at the treaty; for which, he
says, he forgave them with all his heart; for that
it would have been very insecure for them to have
had any communication with them at that time:
that, at last, they came to such a conclusion as
they could get; not such an one as they desired,
from the King, but much short of it; which gave
an advantage to the Lord Argyle, and the clergy
party in Scotland, to oppose it as not satisfactory;
and thereby retarded the proceeding of Duke Hamilton, and that army, four months; which was consequently the ruin of Langharn in Wales, and of
the forces in Kent and Essex, and of the Scots
army also, which consisted of twenty-four thousand
men: all which forces were the result of the treaty,
which appeared to him (Sir John), if it had been
sooner dispatched, to have been one of the most
prudent acts of His Majesty's reign, however un-
prosperous: that when the time was come that the
King was to deliver his answer to the English
commissioners, His Majesty sent for them, and

before he delivered it, asked the Lord Denbigh
(who was the chief commissioner) whether they
had power to alter any substantial or circumstantial
part of their message; and they replying they had
not, His Majesty delivered his answer to the Lord
Denbigh, sealed: that after they had withdrawn
awhile, the Lord Denbigh returned with the rest,
and seemed offended with His Majesty for delivering the message sealed, and expressed his indignation in harsher terms than one gentleman ought
to use to another: that after long expostulations
His Majesty was persuaded to open his answer;
which was so far from allaying the storm, that it
increased it, both in the commissioners and the
governor, who, all together, retired from the castle
of Carisbrooke to Newport, an English mile from
the castle: that as soon as they were gone, he (Sir
John) went to Mr. Ashburnham, who told him, he
had newly dispatched away a footman over the
water, to order four or five horses to be removed
from the place where they then stood, lest they
should be found and seized by the soldiers that
were coming into the island: that he (Sir John)
conjured him by no means to do it, lest the winds
or the Parliament's frigates might frustrate their
escape, and they should want horses: that he
(Ashburnham) thereupon sent a groom after him,
and brought him back; but within a few hours
after, sent him again with the first order, but upon
what ground he (Sir John) knew not, unless that

of good husbandry: that, that night or the next
morning, His Majesty resolved to endeavour his
escape, but he met with two great obstacles, the
wind in the very instant became cross, and the
governor returned from Newport full of fury, and
locked up the gates, and doubled his guards, and
went not to bed that night: that in the morning
he commanded all His Majesty's servants from
him; but before they took their leaves, they acquainted him that they had left the captain of the
frigate and two honest and trusty gentlemen of the
island to assist his escape, and that all things would
be in readiness on the other side of the water:
that His Majesty commanded them to draw a declaration in his name that night, and send it to him
in the morning, when they came to Newport:—
that Will. Leg and he (Sir John) left Mr. Ashburnham and the rest in the inn, and went to an
acquaintance's house of theirs in the town; where,
after they had staid an hour, they heard a drum
beat confusedly, and, not long after that, one
Captain Burley, with divers others, were risen to
rescue the King; whereupon Mr. Leg and he (Sir
John) went to the inn, where they found Mr. Ashburnham making speeches to those poor well-
affected people, advising them to desist from their
vain enterprise. Sir John says, " I must confess I
thought any communication of ours with them
dangerous; and therefore advised Mr. Ashburnham
not to say any thing to them; for that when his

words were out of his mouth, others would interpret them, and say he said what they pleased :"
and, he adds, it was well for him and us that we
did so ; for the prisoners were not only examined
concerning us, · but even promised liberty and
pardon in case they would accuse us : and the governor of the Cowes had orders from Hammond to
put us on ship-board and to carry us to London,
upon suspicion that we were accessary to this rising ;
which was a design so impossible for those that
undertook it to effect, (they consisting chiefly of
women and children, without any arms save one
musket,) that no sober man could possibly have
been engaged in it. Sir John says, he was desired,
that night, to draw the declaration for His Majesty,
which he did, and it was approved of by all but
Mr. Ashburnham, and at last published in His
Majesty's name : that, after they had staid on the
other side the water about three weeks, expecting
His Majesty's coming over to them ; and beginning
at last to despair of it, he (Sir John) moved to
Mr. Ashburnham, Mr. Leg, and Mr. Denham, (who
was then come to them from London,) that some
one might be sent to the Queen from them all,
which was consented to, and he (Sir John) was
made choice of by the rest to go on that business.

This memorial or narrative is to be found in Mr.
Baron Masere's publication of tracts. It is given
at length, as containing sufficient evidence of the
fact of the negotiation with the King, of Cromwell,

and of Ireton, and of other the superior officers of the army, which was also well known in various other ways, as before shown, and affords no reason to suspect the sincerity of these officers.

It is thence evident, that Cromwell, and some others of the principal officers of the army, made the first advances towards the negotiation with the King for his restoration: that Ireton drew the proposals to be offered to the King, which were first shown to Sir John, who, in a long conference with Ireton, was permitted to alter some of the articles in some material points. . Sir John supposes himself to have discovered, in his discourses and enquiries, that the army was governed, partly by a council of war, and partly by a council of the army or adjutators; that the General (Fairfax) had little power in either; that Cromwell and Ireton, with their friends and partizans, governed the council of war absolutely, but not that of the army, which was the most powerful, though they had a strong party there also; but that the major part of the adjutators carried it; and that, amongst these adjutators, there were many ill-wishers of Cromwell: that Sir John, in all his conferences with Cromwell, found no man apparently so jealous for a speedy blow as he, doubting, nevertheless, of the continuance of the army's favourable disposition towards the King: that Sir John recommended to the King to agree to the army's proposals, of which he had the perusal before they were offered to him in public; but that he rejected them with tart and bitter expressions in the presence of the officers that presented them: that after the King's removal to Hampton-court, Mr. Ashburnham had daily messages from the King to Cromwell and Ireton, who, Sir John says, had enough to do, both in the Parliament and in the council of the army; the one abounding with Presbyterians, the other with Levellers, and both jealous of Cromwell and Ireton, having made a private bargain with the King: and that Cromwell becoming alarmed, desired them (Sir John and Mr. Ashburnham) not to come so frequently to his quarters, but send privately to him; the suspicions of him being grown to that height, that he was afraid to lie in his own quarters.

It further appears from the above memorial or narrative, that the King rejected the Parliament's propositions, and desired a personal treaty, for which he deemed the army's proposals a better ground than those propositions. And that the King's party's friends in the army, much satisfied with this rejection, promised their utmost endeavours to procure such personal treaty, and to Sir John's understanding performed it; both Cromwell and Ireton, with all their friends, seconding with great resolution this desire of His Majesty.

The cause of Cromwell's alleged desertion of the King's interest is said to be, that, notwithstanding the officers' superiority at the rendezvous,

the mutineers not quelled had at different times,
to the amount of two-thirds of the army, been with
Cromwell and Ireton, to tell them that they would
leave nothing untried to bring the army to their
(the mutineers') sense; and that, if all failed, they
would make a division in the army, and join with
any that would assist in the destruction of their
opposers; and that Cromwell and Ireton thereupon
became apprehensive, that in the division of the
army, the greatest part would join the Presbyterians, and would prevail to their ruin, and they
should be compelled to apply to the King, rather
craving than offering any assistance. And so it
is supposed they (Cromwell and Ireton) concluded,
that if they could not bring the army to their own
sense, they must go to theirs, a schism being evidently destructive; and that therefore Cromwell
thenceforth bent all his thoughts to make his
peace with the party that was most opposite to the
King.

It is conceived, that a doubt cannot remain in
the minds of unprejudiced readers of this memorial,
of Cromwell's sincerity, and honest and anxious
exertions, to bring to a successful termination this
negotiation for the restoration of the King, and
that upon much more moderate terms than those
offered by the presbyterian party, particularly in
respect of the church, which he appears to have
left untouched. This forbearance was agreeable
to their moderate and tolerant principles as inde-

pendents. The other propositions are not stated;
but the King appears to have objected to only two,
besides the above respecting the church, and they
all probably might have been got over, or reasonably
settled by temperate management. But the King
appears to have ruined all by his violent and indiscreet conduct towards the presenters of these propositions, and by his tampering with the different
parties, and confiding in none of them. These
circumstances and the threats of the agitators
were evidently the causes of Cromwell's and the
other principal officers' desertion of the King, and
joining the army in their subsequent proceeding
to his trial.

The King was unfortunate in his advisers: Mr.
Ashburnham appears to have been his principal
counsellor in these negotiations, who does not
seem equal to the situation; particularly in the
very imprudent and unjustifiable disposal of the
King's person to Hammond. Sir John Berkley's
memorial shows him (Sir John) to have been an
able and honourable man, nevertheless he advises
the King to dissimulation, notwithstanding the
repeated charges of dissimulation and duplicitty
by the royal party against the very men upon whom
it was to be exercised. He advises their being
well dissembled with, whilst the King should be
in their hands, that he might the better get out of
them: and to this end he offered several expedients.

This was bad advice; and the King does not, in this instance, appear to have followed it.

Ludlow follows Sir John Berkley, in his account of these transactions; which he adopts from his above memorial, having, he says, seen the manuscript, written by Sir John himself, and left in the hands of a merchant at Geneva.

Mrs. Hutchinson, referring to the same subject, the above treaty with the King, and discontinuance of their intercourse with him, says, the King, by reason of his daily converse with the officers, began to be trinkling with them, not only then, but before; and had drawn in some of them to engage to corrupt others to fall in with him. But, says she, to speak the truth of all, Cromwell was at that so uncorruptibly faithful to his trust, and to the people's interest, that he could not be drawn in to practise his own usual and natural dissimulations, in this occasion: that his son-in-law Ireton, that was as faithful as he, was not so fully of the opinion, (till he·had tried it and found to the contrary,) but that the King might have been managed to comply with the public good of his people, after he could no longer uphold his own violent will: but that upon some discourses with him, the King uttering these words to him — " I shall play my game as well as I can;" Ireton replied, " If Your Majesty have a game to play, you must give us also the liberty to play ours:" that Colonel Hutchinson (her husband), privately, discoursing with his cousin (Ireton) about the communications he had with the King, Ireton's expressions were these: "He gave us words; and we paid him in his own coin, when we found he had no real intention to the people's good, but to prevail by our factions, to regain by art what he had lost in fight."

Mr. Baron Maseres, in a note in his publication of this memoir, (with other tracts,) referring to Cromwell's abandonment of the treaty with the King, which he observes he had been carrying on for more than five months, (from the beginning of June to the middle of November, 1647,) for restoring him to the exercise of his royal authority, observes that Sir John Berkley's account is so clear and circumstantial, and supported by the testimony of so many respectable persons who were concerned in the management of it, that it seems highly deserving of credit, without seeking any other motive for this change of his (Cromwell's) conduct towards the King, besides the fear of losing his influence over the army, if he should persist in his endeavours to restore him to his authority, after a great part of the army had resolved to act against him. But, continues the Baron, it has been supposed by some writers, that Cromwell had another reason for abandoning the King's interest, and concurring with the party of the army that was adverse to him, arising from a discovery which he had made, (by means of a letter from the King to his Queen, who

was then in France, which he had intercepted,)
that the King was resolved, when he should be
restored to his authority, to break all the promises
of favour, which he had made to Cromwell and
other officers of the army in the course of the
negotiation then on foot, and to punish them as
rebels. The Baron then gives the copy of the
supposed letter, (said to have been the cause of
the death of the King,) of which the writer he
mentions gives the following account:— That
Lord Bolingbroke told them (Mr. Pope and
Lord Marchmont), June 12. 1742, that Lord Oxford (the second Earl of Oxford) had often told
him that he had seen, and had in his hands, an
original letter that the King wrote to the Queen,
in answer to one of hers that had been intercepted,
and then forwarded to him; wherein she had re-
proached him for having made those villains too
great concessions, viz. that Cromwell should be
Lord-lieutenant for life without account; that that
kingdom should be in the hands of the party with
an army there kept, which should have no head
but the Lieutenant; and that Cromwell should
have a Garter, &c.: that in this letter of the King's,
it was said that she should leave him to manage,
who was better informed of all circumstances than
she could be; but that she might be entirely easy
as to whatever concessions he should make them;
for that he should know in due time how to deal
with the rogues, who, instead of a silken garter,

should be fitted with a hempen cord: that so the letter ended; which answer, as they waited for, so they intercepted accordingly; and that it determined his fate: and for which letter Lord Oxford said he had offered five hundred pounds.

This letter seems to be the same as is referred to in the following passage from the Memoirs of Lord Broghill, afterwards Earl of Orrery, written by his chaplain: it is related to be the subject of a conversation between His Lordship and Cromwell and Ireton, respecting and after the King's death; in which Cromwell is stated to have said, that if the King had followed his own mind, and had had trusty servants about him, he had fooled them all; and added that once they had a mind to have closed with him; but upon something that happened, they fell off from that design: that in answer to a question of His Lordship, why they once would have closed with the King, and why they did not; Cromwell is stated to have said, that they would have closed with the King, because they found that the Scots and the Presbyterians began to be more powerful than themselves, and that if they made up matters with the King, they (Cromwell and his party) would have been left in the lurch: that therefore they thought it best to prevent them, by offering, first, to come in upon any reasonable condition; but that while they were busied in these thoughts, there came a letter from one of their spies, acquainting them that on that

day their final doom was decreed, referring to a
letter sent from the King to the Queen, which the
spy described as sewed up in the skirt of a saddle,
to be taken that night to the Blue Boar inn, in
Holborn, to be taken from thence to Dover.
Then follows the particulars of finding the letter
in the saddle by Cromwell and Ireton, who attended there for that purpose, in the habits of
troopers: that by this letter they found that the
King had acquainted the Queen that he was then
courted by both the factions, the Scotch Presbyterians and the army; and that which bid fairest
for him should have him; but that he thought he
should close with the Scotch sooner than the other:
that upon this, added Cromwell, we took horse and
went to Windsor, and finding we were not likely
to have any tolerable terms from the King, we
immediately from that time forward resolved his
ruin. Neal, in his History of the Puritans, states
the substance of this letter, given by different
writers in different terms; but adds, that Doctor
Lane, of the Commons, had frequently declared,
that he had seen this original letter; that he knew
it to be the King's own hand, and that the contents
were as above.

The preceding account of Cromwell's conversation with Lord Broghill may be correct or incorrect; much, however, depends upon the very words
of a conversation, which it is difficult, if not almost
impossible, after the shortest time, accurately to

remember; but, as it appears to have been related long afterwards by His Lordship to Mr. Morrice, his chaplain, and by him given from memory, many years after His Lordship's death, and he, Mr. Morrice, is described in the preface to these memoirs as regarding neither dates nor order of time, but jumbling circumstances together as they occurred to his remembrance, this account cannot be wholly relied on. The substance however may be true; and does not affect the fact of Cromwell's negotiation with the King for his restoration. The contents of the supposed intercepted letter, so far as concerns the promised promotion of Cromwell and others, are not consistent with Lord Fairfax's assertion in one of his letters to the Parliament, (hereafter mentioned by Whitelock,) referring to this negotiation with the King, that they had not done, nor should do any thing which they should desire to hide from the Parliament and the world, and should not avow to the faces of their adversaries : that several officers had been sent to the King about his removes and for other purposes, but that they had not bargained nor asked any thing of the King, as to any private interest of their own. Nor is this promised promotion of Cromwell and others agreeable to Sir John Berkley's account of the officers' backwardness to treat of receiving any favour or advantage from His Majesty.

Mr. Holles, referring to the King's escape from

Hampton-court, and finally going to the Isle of Wight, asserts, in his forementioned memorial, in his usual violent style, without producing any evidence in support of his assertion, that the King's going to the Isle of Wight was Cromwell's contrivance; where, he says, he had provided a jailer in Colonel Hammond the governor. This will appear, like the remainder of Mr. Holles's memorial, to be mere unfounded, ill-natured assertion, in addition to the obloquy with which he has already endeavoured to load Cromwell, and deserves no more credit than the rest of his work. The forenamed Dr. Bates only says, he privately made his escape from the army, and, as fate would have it, fled to the Isle of Wight, the government of which, as it seems probable, was just before put into the hands of Colonel Hammond, a dear friend to Cromwell, that there he might play his part in the business. To this man, adds Bates, the King commits himself, running of his own accord into the snare which the rebels had long laid for him.

Lord Clarendon, who is as ill-disposed towards Cromwell as Mr. Holles, or Dr. Bates, does not venture so far as to make this assertion. He says, that there was at this time a new faction grown up in the army, which were either by their own denomination, or with their own consent, called Levellers, who spoke insolently and confidently against the King and Parliament, and the great officers of the army, and professed as great malice against all the Lords, as against the King; and declared that all degrees should be levelled, and that an equality should be established, both in titles and estates through the kingdom. Whether, continues His Lordship, the raising this spirit was a piece of Cromwell's ordinary witchcraft, in order to some of his designs, or whether it grew amongst those tares which had been sowed in that confusion, certain it is, it gave him real trouble at last; but that the present use he made of it was, that upon the licentious discourse of that kind, which some soldiers upon the guard usually made, the guard upon the King's person was doubled, a restraint put upon the great resort of people, who came to see the King; and all pretended to. be for his security, and to prevent any violence that might be attempted upon his life, which they seemed to apprehend and detest: that in the mean time they neither hindered His Majesty from riding abroad to take the air,˙ nor from doing any thing he had a mind to, nor restrained those who waited upon him in his bed-chamber, nor his chaplains from performing their functions; though towards all these there was less civility exercised than had been; and the guards which waited nearest were more rude, and made more noise at unseasonable hours, than they had been accustomed to do; that the King every day received little billets or letters secretly conveyed to him without any name, which advertised him of wicked designs upon his life, and some of them advised him to make an escape, and repair secretly into the city, where he should be safe; some letters directing him to such an alderman's house; all which His Majesty looked upon as artifice to lead him into some straits, from whence he should not easily extricate himself; and yet many who repaired to him brought the same advice from men of unquestionable sincerity, by what reason soever they were swayed.

That the King found himself in great perplexity from what he discerned and observed himself, as well as what he heard from others; but what use to make of the one or the other was very hard to resolve: he did really believe that their malice was at the height, and that they did design his murder; but knew not which was a probable way to prevent it: that the making an escape, if it were not contrived with wonderful sagacity, would expose him to be assassinated by pretending ignorance, and would be charged upon himself; and if he could avoid their guards and get beyond them undiscovered, whither should he go, and what place would receive and defend him? That there was reason to believe that he did resolve to transport himself beyond the seas, which had been no hard matter to have brought to pass; but with whom he consulted for the way of doing it, is not to this day discovered; they who were instrumental in his remove, pretending to know nothing of the resolution or counsel. Then follows the account of the King's escape on the 11th of November, from Hampton-court, and his going finally to the Isle of Wight, with Lord Clarendon's various conjectures upon that transaction. He adds, that amidst the alarm this had occasioned, and the uncertainty where the King was, Cromwell informed the House that he had received letters from Colonel Hammond of all the manner of the King's coming to the Isle of Wight, and the company that came with him, that he remained there, in the castle of Carisbrooke, till the pleasure of the Parliament should be known. He assured them that Colonel Hammond was so honest a man, and so much devoted to their service, that they need have no jealousy that he might be corrupted by any body; and, adds His Lordship, that all this relation he made with so unusual a gaiety, that all men concluded that the King was where he wished he should be.

Amongst all His Lordship's conjectures upon the King's escape, he does not venture to charge Cromwell as the cause of his going to the Isle of Wight. He only describes him as pleased with the information, he (His Lordship) says, he re-received from Colonel Hammond. Sir John Berkley does not say to whom Colonel Hammond wrote, to inform the Parliament of the King's arrival in the Isle of Wight; but it must be to the Parliament, and not to Cromwell as an individual. This passage from Lord Clarendon is highly improbable, and not supported by Sir John's narrative. Indeed, all His Lordship says upon this subject, of the · first information to the House of the King's arrival in the Isle of Wight by Cromwell, may · be considered as positively contradicted by the Journals of the House of Commons. In them is the following entry:— " Saturday, 13th November, 1647. Colonel Whalley called in, and made a particular relation of all the circumstances concerning the King's going away from Hampton-court. He likewise delivered in a letter directed to him (Whalley) from Lieutenant-general Cromwell, concerning some rumours and reports of some design of danger to the person and life of the King; which was read, and a copy given to the House."

15th same November. " Letter from Captain Baskett, of Cowes castle, of 13th same month, and one from Colonel Robert Hammond, of same day, signifying that the King was come into the Isle of Wight; both read, and directed to be communicated to the Lords. Ten pounds ordered to the messenger that brought the letter from Captain Baskett, and twenty pounds to Captain Rolfe that brought the letter from the governor of the Isle of Wight, directed to Mr. Speaker."

The above renders it perfectly certain, that the letters read were addressed to the House and not to Cromwell, and consequently not read by him; the House would not have given rewards for private letters; and the letter from Colonel Hammond is expressly said .to be directed to the Speaker. His Lordship considers the King's going to the Isle of Wight as unpremeditated and accidental; and that when he quitted Hampton-court, he had not formed any plan of future proceeding, and had not resolved whither to go.

Mr. Hume, observing that Lord Clarendon was positive that the King, when he fled from Hampton-court, had no intention of going to the Isle of Wight, adds, that there remained a letter of Charles's to the Earl of Lanerick, secretary of Scotland, in which he plainly insinuates that that measure was voluntarily embraced; and that if he had thought proper, he might have been at Jersey, or any other place of safety.

Rushworth, in his account of the King's quitting Hampton-court, and his arrival in the Isle of Wight, and the circumstances, only says, that information had been given to the House: that many that had relation and access to His Majesty were privy to the design.

Ludlow says, — at last the King resolved to go to the Isle of Wight, being, as is most probable, recommended thither by Cromwell, who, as well as the King, had a good opinion of Colonel Hammond, the governor there. This is merely conjectural, but does not imply any ill intention in Cromwell towards the King.

But Sir Philip Warwick, who was attendant upon the King's person, and no friend to Cromwell, says, that it came not within his knowledge who gave the counsel for the King's flight, or what was resolved about it; but that, by one that did know it, he (Sir Philip) had it at that time communicated to him, before he (the King) went away, and perhaps with too much imprudence. "I," continues Sir Philip, "could not concur for his making a mean (since it was likely to be a dangerous) flight; but that, being carried off by Sir John Ashburnham, Sir John Berkley, and Mr. William Legg only, the next we heard of him was, that he was in Carisbrooke castle, where his terms certainly were not beforehand made." Sir Philip adds, that he had occasion but once, at the Isle of Wight, to speak with the King about this affair; and that it was by an accident, or the King's letting himself into that discourse, that he did but touch upon it, nor durst I seem more inquisitive. "But," says he, "when I mentioned that the world had an ill opinion of my friend Mr. Ashburnham's guiding him thither, I remember he freely replied, ' I do no way believe he was unfaithful to me; but I think he wanted courage at that time, (which, says Sir Philip, I interpreted His Majesty meant his not staying with the governor,) whom I never knew wanted it before.' If," adds Sir Philip, "it be lawful to conjecture at an affair of this nature, the choosing this place did not arise from a belief either of the King or Mr. Ashburnham in the governor, but from the failing of some ship there expected. But," adds Sir Philip, " it might be admitted, that they might think the officers of the army would be true to him, when his person was out of the power of being apprehended by the agitators : and that, too probably, His Majesty, wearied with the thoughts of the French having cast him into the hands of the Scots who had used him no better, and of the unconcernedness of other princes in his case, and of the Scotch and English presbyterians' remorselessness towards him, like a sick man, he was willing to change his bed, and see whether it would better his condition; and I am induced to credit this, because the King had given his word to Cromwell and his jailer, Colonel Whalley, at Hampton-court; and the King, by Ashburnham, very few days before his flight, discharged himself of this engagement; which (if Whalley had not been directed otherwise) he would have lain hold of him, and have put it out of his power to have escaped." Here, Sir Philip supposes the King to have withdrawn his promise to Cromwell, not to endeavour his escape, which must amount to a notice of his intention to attempt it, and supposes Whalley to have received instructions probably from Cromwell not to prevent it.

All these circumstances, from these several writers, confirm the accuracy and truth of Sir

John Berkley's narrative of the King's escape, had it wanted confirmation ; and, together, leave no ground for doubt, that Cromwell, finding himself no longer able to serve the King in his restoration, apprised him of his (the King's) personal danger from the agitators, and advised, and probably assisted in his escape. The state of perfect liberty to go where he pleased, in which the King found himself upon his arrival upon the coast of Hampshire, and the letter from Cromwell to the King, a copy whereof he sent by Sir John Berkley and Mr. Ashburnham, the substance whereof Sir John gives in his memoirs, prove Cromwell's anxiety for the personal safety of the King, and that nothing was wanting on his part to enable him to quit the kingdom.

In a publication by Dr. Birch, of letters between the forenamed Colonel Hammond and the committee of Lords and Commons at Derby House, General Fairfax, Lieutenant-general Cromwell, Commissary-general Ireton, and others relating to the King during his confinement in Carisbrooke castle, is a letter from the above Mr. Ashburnham to a friend concerning his deportment towards the King, in his attendance on him at Hampton-court, and in the Isle of Wight. This letter is therein mentioned to have been first printed in 1648. He describes himself as charged with the scandal of having betrayed His Majesty into the Isle of Wight, by compact with the Parliament and army, before his departure from Hampton-court, by affrighting him from thence, to afford them a better opportunity, being at a greater distance from London, to destroy him; for which service he was to have a great sum of money. He commences his justification with stating that the King's alarms for his personal safety, from the information he had received, of a resolution of a violent party in the army to take away his life, and his resolution in consequence to quit Hampton-court, and his positive determination not to desert·the kingdom, either by crossing the seas or going to Scotland, determined the King's choice of the Isle of Wight to avoid the present danger, and where he might give least offence to the Parliament and army, and have frequent intercourse with both for settling a peace, of which he then despaired not; and where he might expect the abatement of the ruinous power of the levellers and their faction to be the fruits of the general rendezvous, which was immediately to follow. He then describes Sir John Berkley's and his interview and engagement with the governor (Hammond), suppressing this part of Sir John's narrative and his censures of his conduct therein. He positively denies that any member of the Parliament or army had any knowledge from him of the King's quitting Hampton-court. In this statement, not the most distant hint is given of any·part Cromwell had in this transaction. Ireton, in a letter to Hammond, in contradiction of the pretence of the King's keeping himself within the protection of the army, by coming into his hands, (to be found in the above publication,) observes, that the King's own declaration, left behind upon his table, plainly discovered that he, in his going away, had other intentions; and that his surrendering himself to him (Hammond) was besides his first purpose. This is a further proof that Cromwell had no concern in the King's going to the Isle of Wight.

Lord Clarendon, referring to the King's situation at Newmarket with the army, after his quitting Holmby, says, that the King found himself at Newmarket attended by greater troops and superior officers, so that he was presently freed from any subjection to Mr. Joyce, which was no small satisfaction to him; and they who were about him appeared men of better breeding than the former, and paid His Majesty all the respect imaginable, and seemed to desire to please him in all things: that all restraint was taken off from persons resorting to him, and he saw every day the faces of many who were grateful to him; and he no sooner desired that some of his chaplains might have leave to attend upon him for his devotion, but it was yielded to; and they who were named by him (who were Dr. Sheldon, Dr. Morley, Dr. Saunderson, and Dr. Hammond,) were presently sent for, and gave their attendance, and performed their functions at the ordinary hours,

in their accustomed formalities, all persons who
had a mind to it being suffered to be present, to
His Majesty's infinite satisfaction, who began to
believe that the army was not so much his enemy
as it was reported to be : and the army had sent
an address to him full of protestation of duty,
and besought him that he would be content for
some time to reside among them, until the affairs
of the kingdom were put into such a posture as he
might find all things to his own content and security, which they infinitely desired to see as soon as
might be ; and to that purpose made daily instances
to the Parliament: that, in the mean time, His
Majesty sat still or removed to such places as were
most convenient for the march of the army, being
in all places as well provided for and accommodated
as he had used to be in any progress; the best
gentlemen of the several counties through which
he passed daily resorted to him, without distinction : he was attended by some of his old trusty
servants in the places nearest his person ; and that
which gave him most encouragement to believe
that they meant well was, that, in the army's address to the Parliament, they desired that care
might be taken for settling the King's rights according to the several professions they had made
in their declarations, and that the royal party
might be treated with more candour and less
rigour ; and many good officers, who had served
His Majesty faithfully, were civilly received by

the officers of the army, and lived quietly in their
quarters, which they could not do any where else;
which raised a great reputation to the army throughout the kingdom, and as much reproach upon the
Parliament.

That the Parliament at this time had recovered
its spirit, when they saw the army did not march
nearer towards them, and not only stopped at St.
Albans, but was drawn back to a further distance;
which persuaded them that their General was displeased with their former advance; and so they
proceeded with all passion and vigour against
those principal officers, who they knew contrived
all these proceeedings. They published declarations to the kingdom, that they desired to bring
the King in honour to his Parliament, which was
their business from the beginning, and that he
was detained prisoner, against his will, in the
army; and that they had great reason to apprehend the safety of his person: that the army, on
the other hand, declared that His Majesty was
neither prisoner, nor detained against his will;
and appealed to His Majesty himself, and to all his
friends, who had liberty to repair to him, whether
he had not more liberty, and was not treated with
more respect since he came into the army than he
had been at Holmby, or during the time he remained in those places and with that retinue that
the Parliament had appointed; that there was
nothing they (the Parliament) did really fear so

much, as that the army would make a firm conjunction with the King and unite with his party,
of which there was so much show; and many
unskilful men, who wished it, bragged too much:
and that therefore the Parliament sent a committee
to His Majesty with an address of another style
than they had lately used, with many professions
of duty, and declaring that if he was not, in all
respects, treated as he ought to be, and as he desired, it was not their fault, who desired he might
be at full liberty, and do what he would; hoping
that the King would have been induced to desire to
come to London, and to make complaint of the army's
having taken him from Holmby; by which they
believed the King's party would be disabused and
withdraw their hopes of any good from the army;
and then they thought they should be hard enough
for them.

That the King was in great doubt how to carry
himself: he thought himself so barbarously used
by the Presbyterians, and had so ill an opinion of
all the principal persons who governed them, that
he had no mind to put himself into their hands.
On the other side, he was far from being satisfied
with the army's good intention towards him; and
though many of his friends were suffered to resort
to him, they found that their being long about him
would not be acceptable; and though the officers
and soldiers appeared for the most part civil to
him, they were all at least as vigilant as the former

guards had been; so that he could not, without great difficulty, have got from them if he had desired it: that Fairfax had been with him and kissed his hand, and made such professions as he could well utter, which was with no advantage in the delivery; his authority was of no use because he resigned himself entirely to Cromwell, who had been, and Ireton likewise, with the King, without either of them offering to kiss his hand, otherwise they behaved themselves with good manners towards him: that His Majesty used all the address he could towards them, to draw some promise from them; but they were so reserved, and stood so much upon their guard, and used so few words, that nothing could be concluded from what they said. They excused themselves for not seeing His Majesty often, upon the great jealousies the Parliament had of them, towards whom they professed all fidelity: that the persons who resorted to His Majesty, and brought advices from others, who durst not yet offer to come themselves, brought several opinions to him, some thinking the army would deal sincerely with him; others expecting no better from them, than they afterwards performed; so that the King well concluded that he would neither reject the Parliament addresses by any neglect, nor disoblige the army by appearing to have jealousy of them, or desire to be out of their hands; which he could hardly have effected if he had known a better place to have resorted to. So he desired both parties to hasten their consultations, that the kingdom might enjoy peace and happiness, in which he should not be without a share; and he would pray to God to bring this to pass as soon as possible.

That the very high contests between the Parliament and the army, in which neither side could be persuaded to yield to the other or abate any of their asperity, made many prudent men believe that both sides would in the end be willing to make the King the umpire, which neither of them ever intended to do.

That in the House of Commons, which was now the scene of all the actions that displeased and incensed the army, (for the House of Peers was shrunk into so inconsiderable a number, and their persons not considerable after the death of the Earl of Essex, except those who were affected or might be disposed by the army,) they were wholly guided by Holles, and Stapleton, Lewis, and Glyn, who had been very popular and notorious from the beginning, and by Waller, and Massey, and Brown, who had served in commands in the army, and performed at sometimes very signal service, and were exceedingly beloved in the city; and two or three others, who followed their dictates and were subservient to their directions. These were all men of parts, interest, and signal courage, and did not only heartily abhor the intentions which they discerned the army to have, and that it was wholly to be disposed according to the designs of Cromwell, but had likewise declared animosities against the persons of the most active and powerful officers; but that Cromwell had that power in the House, and that reputation abroad, that when he could not absolutely control their designs, he did so obstruct them, that they could not advance to any conclusion.

That they (the army) resorted therefore to an expedient, which they had observed, by the conduct of those very men against whom they meant to apply it, had brought to pass all that they desired; and in the council of officers prepared an impeachment of high treason in general terms against Mr. Holles and other the forementioned persons, and others, to the number of eleven members of the House of Commons. Then, in Lord Clarendon's history, follows the statement of that transaction, and their finally, in consequence, withdrawing from the House.

His Lordship, relating the removal of the King to Hampton-court, says, it was prepared and put into as good order for his reception as could have been done in the best time.

Referring to the rendezvous upon Hounslow Heath, and the presence there, of the Speakers of both Houses (who had, according to His Lordship's statement, privately before met with the chief officers of the army) with their maces, and such other members as accompanied them, complaining to the General, that they had not freedom at Westminster, but were in danger of their lives by the tumults; and appealed to the army for their protection. His Lordship observes, that this looked like a new act of Providence to vindicate the army from all reproaches, and to justify them in all they had done, as absolutely done for the preservation of the Parliament and kingdom : that if this had been a retreat of Sir Harry Vane and some other discontented men, who were known to be independents and fanatics in their opinions in religion, and of the army faction, who being no longer able to oppose the wisdom of the Parliament had fled to their friends for protection from justice, they would have got no reputation, nor the army been thought the better of for their company; but neither of the Speakers were ever looked upon as inclined to the army; Lenthall was generally believed to have no malice towards the King, and not to be without good inclination to the church; and the Earl of Manchester, who was Speaker of the House of Peers, was known to have all prejudice imaginable against Cromwell, and had formerly accused him of want of duty to the Parliament; and the other hated him above all men, and desired to have taken away his life : that the Earl of Manchester and the Earl of Warwick were the two pillars of the presbyterian party; and that they two, with the Earl of Northumberland, and some other of the Lords and some of the Com-

mons, who had appeared to disapprove all the proceedings of the army, should now join with Sir
Harry Vane, and appeal to the army for protection, with that formality as if they had brought
the whole Parliament with them, and had been entirely driven and forced away by the city, appeared,
to every stander-by, so stupendous a thing, that it
is not, says His Lordship, to this day understood
otherwise, than that they were resolved to have
their particular shares in the treaty, which they
believed the chief officers of the army to have near
concluded with the King : for that they never intended to put the whole power into the hands of
the army, nor had any kindness to, or confidence
in the officers thereof, was very apparent by their
carriage and behaviour after, as well as before ;
and if they had continued together, considering
how much the city was devoted to them, it is probable that the army would not have used any force,
which might have received a fatal repulse ; but
that some good compromise might have been made
by the interposition of the King. But this schism,
adds His Lordship, carried all the reputation and
authority to the army, and left none in the Parliament ; for though it presently appeared that the
number of those who left the Houses was small in
comparison of those who remained behind, and
who proceeded with the same vigour in declaring
against the army : and the city seemed as resolute
in putting themselves into a posture and preparing

for their defence, all their works and fortifications
being still entire; so that they might have put the
army to great trouble, if they had steadily pursued
their resolutions (which they did not seem in any
degree to decline); yet this rent made all the
accused members, who were the men of parts and
reputation to conduct their counsels, to withdraw
themselves upon the astonishment; some concealing themselves till they had opportunity to make
their peace, and others withdrawing and transport-
ing themselves beyond the seas.

Then follows the account of the army's becoming masters of the city, and conducting the
Speaker and members who had come to them to
their respective Houses of Parliament.

Whilst, proceeds His Lordship, these things
were thus agitated between the army and the Parliament and city, the King enjoyed himself at
Hampton-court much more to his content than he
had of late; the respects of the chief officers of
the army seeming much greater than they had
been; Cromwell himself came oftener to him, and
had long conferences with him; talked with more
openness to Mr. Ashburnham than he had done,
and appeared more cheerful: that persons of all
conditions repaired to His Majesty of those who
had served him; with whom he conferred without
reservation; and the citizens flocked thither as
they had used to do at the end of a progress, when
the King had been some months absent from Lon-

don : but that which pleased him most was, that his children were permitted to come to him, in whom he took great delight. They were all at the Earl of Northumberland's house, at Sion, from the time the King came to Hampton-court, and had liberty to attend His Majesty when he pleased ; so that sometimes he sent for them to come to Hampton-court, and sometimes he went to them to Sion, which gave him great satisfaction.

That in this manner the King made use of the liberty he enjoyed, and considered as well what remedies to apply to the worst that could fall out, as to caress the officers of the army in order to the improvement of his condition, of which he was not yet in despair, the chief officers and all the heads of that party looking upon it as their wisest policy to cherish the King's hopes by the liberty they gave him, and by a very flowing courtesy towards all who had been of his party, whose reputation, and good word and testimony, they found did them much good both in the city and in the country : that, to the Lord Capel who had come to visit him, the King imparted all his hopes and what great overtures the Scots had again made to him, and that he did really believe that it could not be long before there would be a war between the two nations, in which the Scots promised themselves an universal concurrence from all the Presbyterians in England ; and that, in such a conjuncture, he wished that his own party would put themselves in arms, without which he could not expect great benefit by the success of the other; and therefore desired Lord Capel to watch such a conjuncture, and draw his friends together, which he promised to do effectually, and did very punctually afterwards to the loss of his own life: and many things, adds Lord Clarendon, were then adjusted upon the foresight of future contingencies, which were afterwards though fit to be executed. But that none were more full of professions of duty and a resolution to run all hazards than the Scots commissioners, who, from the time they had delivered up the King, resided at London with their usual confidence, and loudly complained of the presumption of the army in seizing upon the person of the King; insinuated themselves to all those who were thought to be most constant and inseparable from the interest of the crown, with passionate undertaking that their whole nation would be united, to a man, in any enterprise for his service: and now, adds His Lordship, they came to him (the King) with as much presumption as if they had carried him to Edinburgh. Here, adds His Lordship, the foundation of that engagement was laid, which was endeavoured to be performed in the ensuing year, and which the Scots themselves then communicated to the Marquis of Ormond, the Lord Capel, and other trusty persons, as if there was nothing else intended in it than a full vindication of all His Majesty's rights and interest.

That when the army had thus subdued all opposition, and the Parliament and they seemed all of a piece, and the refractory humours of the city seemed to be suppressed and totally tamed, the army seemed less regardful to the King than they had been; the chief officers came rarely to Hampton-court, nor had the same countenance towards Ashburnham and Berkley as they used to have; they were not at leisure to speak with them, and when they did, asked captious questions, and gave answers themselves of no signification: that the adjutators and council of officers sent some propositions to the King, as ruinous to the church and destructive to the regal power as had been yet made by the Parliament, and in some respects much worse, and more dishonourable; and said, if His Majesty would consent thereto, they would apply themselves to the Parliament, and do the best they could to persuade them to be of the same opinion; but His Majesty rejected them with more than usual indignation, not without some reproaches upon the officers for having deluded him, and having prevailed in all their own designs, by making the world believe that they intended His Majesty's restoration and settlement upon better conditions than the Parliament was willing to admit: that, by this manner of resentment, the

army took itself to be disobliged, and used another
language in their discourse of the King, than they
had for some months done ; and such officers who
had formerly served the King and had been civilly
treated and sheltered in the quarters of the army,
were now driven from thence.   They who had
been kind to them withdrew themselves from their
acquaintance; and the sequestrations of all the
estates of the cavaliers which had been intermitted
were revived with as much rigour as ever had been
before practised, and the declared delinquents
racked to as high compositions, which if they refused to make, their whole estates were taken from
them, and their persons exposed to affronts and
insecurity ; but this was imputed to the prevalence
of the presbyterian humour in the Parliament
against the judgment of the army ; and that it was
very true, that though the Parliament was so far
subdued, it no more found fault with what the
army did, nor complained that it meddled in determining what settlement should be made in the
government, yet, that in all their own acts and
proceedings, they prosecuted a presbyterian settlement as earnestly as they could : that the covenant was pressed in all places, and the Anabaptists
and other sects, which began to abound, were
punished, restrained, and discountenanced, which
the army liked not, as a violation of the liberty of
tender consciences, which they pretended was as
much the original of the quarrel as any other

grievance whatsoever. This statement of proceedings (by His Lordship), from the arrival of the
King at Newmarket, does not differ substantially
from the before-given accounts of those transactions, making all due allowance for His Lordship's
usual glosses in favour of his own side of the
question.

Referring to the King's removal from the Isle
of Wight to Hurst Castle, after the unsuccessful
termination of the treaty of Newport, and the vote
of the House of Commons, that it was without
their consent, which His Lordship says had little
contradiction, because no one would own the
advice; also relating the General's (Fairfax) march
to London, and the resolution of the House, notwithstanding, after a very long debate, that the
answer of the King to the propositions was a ground
for the Houses to proceed upon, for the settlement
of the peace of the kingdom ; also the resumption
of the above question, which, after a long debate,
notwithstanding the late exclusion of so many members ; and the termination in the negative of the
above resolution, consequently that the above
answer was not satisfactory, — says, that no one
owned the above act of exclusion ; that Fairfax
knew nothing of it ; and that the guards themselves, being asked what authority they had, only
answered that they had orders. Respecting the
removal of the King, Rushworth gives a letter, dated
the 1st of December, 1648, from Carisbrooke

Castle to the House, signed by Major Rolph and others, who had the care of the King, informing of the arrival of Lieutenant-colonel Cobbett and Captain Merriman, with instructions from the General (Fairfax) and council of war, forthwith to secure the King's person in Carisbrooke Castle, as before the treaty, till they should receive the resolution of the Houses upon their late remonstrance; and that, whilst Rolph and the other officers were in debate thereon, whether they ought or ought not to obey these instructions, a messenger arrived from the General (Fairfax), with an order under his hand and seal, directed to the same persons, commanding them immediately to take the person of the King into their charge, and to remove him to Hurst Castle, which was done. Rushworth, it should be remembered, was at that time the General's secretary, and would not have given this letter, had he not known it to be authentic, or would certainly have commented upon it, had he had reason to doubt its authenticity. Whitelock says that the King was removed by order of the General and council of the army. Sir Philip Warwick speaks of this removal of the King as done by directions from the army; but admits the General's (Fairfax) giving the warrant for it, only saying that he had been wrought on to give it.

In further confutation of Lord Clarendon's statement, that General Fairfax knew nothing of the intended exclusion of the members, Rushworth says that they were seized and kept in custody by special order from the General and council of the army; and that on the same day, (December 6. 1648,) a committee of the Commons was sent to the General (Fairfax), to enquire the reason thereof, who, not disavowing the proceeding, referred the committee to his council of war for his answer, meaning their and his reasons for their procedure. Whitelock gives a similar account. He (Rushworth) further states the committee's report, that at another attendance of the committee, the General had answered, that the matter was of great concernment, and supposed they did not expect a present answer from him, but that he would prepare one speedily, and desired the House would not trouble itself to send any more concerning that business : that this answer did not appear satisfactory to the House, who directed the application to be received. Rushworth adds, that sixteen of these members were liberated on that day with permission to resume their seats.

Dr. Harris, in his Life of Cromwell, takes upon himself to determine that he was the author and abettor of this measure of purging the House of Commons, by Colonel Pride seizing and surprising many of its members, thence commonly called Pride's purge. He allows that his name does not appear therein ; but, he says, that some say, that it was done by his (Cromwell's) command : and he (Dr. Harris) adds, that there need be no doubt that

Ireton and the other chief officers concerned, were fully satisfied they had Cromwell's approbation, they would not have taken such a step without it: for though, he adds, Fairfax was easy and manageable, Cromwell was very different, nor would he have failed showing his resentment against those who should have presumed to have acted opposite to his will. This is mere conjecture, for the purpose of introducing Cromwell into this transaction, without regard to the, it may be safely said, decisive evidence to the contrary. But Ludlow says, that Lieutenant-general Cromwell, the night after the interruption of the House, arrived from Scotland, and lay at Whitehall, (having been absent from London with the army, as before mentioned, from the month of May, 1648, preceding,) where, and at other places, he declared, that he had not been acquainted with this design. Rushworth confirms this account of the army under General Fairfax's command entering London on the 2d of December, 1648; this interruption by seizure of the members to have happened on the 6th, and Cromwell not to have taken his seat until the 7th, being the day following. In the before-mentioned publication of letters by Dr. Birch, Cromwell's last letter to Hammond is dated 25th November, 1648, by which he appears to be then in the north.

Notwithstanding Cromwell's above declaration, given by Ludlow, that he did not know of the design of seizing the members, which Dr. Harris has extracted in a note, he (Dr. Harris) chooses to have no opinion of his (Cromwell's) veracity; he says, " His declarations on this head are not, I think, much to be regarded;" and he seems to make a sort of sarcastic apology for charging Cromwell with uttering an absolute falsehood, by ranking him with other politicians as bad as he supposes Cromwell to be, who, he says, have a language of their own: they, he says, abound with quirks, subtleties, and distinctions; they explain away and interpret as they imagine will best suit their circumstances and conveniences. To all this, if, continues he, we add Cromwell's known dissimulation, we shall see little cause to rely on them. This is not liberal, either towards Cromwell or towards politicians universally: it is easier to find an opprobrious epithet than to establish a proof: Cromwell, it is conceived, has not yet been proved a liar or a dissembler.

The truth appears to be, that the agitators, who were the republican party in the army, had become too powerful for their General and the other principal officers; and, being determined upon a republican form of government, had intimidated Cromwell, and the other officers who were friendly to the King's return upon proper terms, from further treaty with him: this appears from the preceding extracts from the several forementioned writers. This republican party were in like manner determined to prevent all renewal of treaty with

the King; they were also determined upon bringing the King to a trial.   To accomplish these, their
designs, they adopt the measure of what they term
purging the House of Commons, meaning the exclusion of those members from sitting therein
whom they knew to be favourable to a continuance
or renewal of the treaty of Newport, and unfavourable to the purposed measure of bringing the
King to a trial.   With these views, they probably
hastened the coming of the part of the army with
Fairfax, and, with its assistance, this exclusion of
the obnoxious members, during the absence of
Cromwell, lest he should, by his presence, prevent
or impede their designs; and overawed the General
(Fairfax) and his council of officers, into the sanction of their proceedings.   Thus the whole was
accomplished before Cromwell's arrival, and resum-
ing his seat in the House: and this accords with
and confirms the truth of his (Cromwell's) declaration of his ignorance of these designs, and acquits
him of the foul charge of the deliberate falsehood
with which his enemies wish to fix him.   And
Ludlow takes to himself, and a few others, the
whole merit, as he deems it, of this transaction of
the exclusion, (not referring to Cromwell,) where
he relates, that being come to the resolution, three
of the members of the House, and three of the
officers of the army, withdrew into a private room,
to consider of the best means to attain the ends of
such resolution; when we (Ludlow being therefore

one of them) agreed, that the army should be
drawn up the next morning, and guards placed in
Westminster-hall, the Court of Requests, and the
lobby, that none might be permitted to pass into
the House but such as had continued faithful to
the public interest : and, to this end, says he, we
went over the names of all the members, one by
one.   He adds, that General Ireton went to Sir
Thomas Fairfax, and acquainted him with the necessity of this extraordinary way of proceeding;
having taken care to have the army drawn up the
next morning by seven of the clock.

It can hardly be doubted that Ludlow, and his
republican party, availed themselves of Cromwell's
absence to accomplish this and their other measures, preparatory to their great object of bringing
the King to trial, and establishing a commonwealth.

· But it is indispensably necessary to these writers, that the perfidy and hypocrisy of Cromwell
should be established, and that at the expense even
of General Fairfax's understanding, whom, for the
purpose of making Cromwell the principal actor,
they reduce almost to idiocy.   It is admitted by
all these writers, that Cromwell was absent at the
time of the General's entry with his army into
London, and of the army's seizure of the members,
40 or more in number.   Rushworth states the
large remonstrance of the army, presented to the
House of Commons, to have been dated 18th, and

presented on Monday the 20th of November (1648), consequently during the treaty, and Cromwell's absence; and that it was accompanied by a letter from the General to the Speaker, desiring, on behalf of the officers and himself, that it might have a present reading and consideration. This remonstrance, signed by John Rushworth, secretary by the appointment of the General (Fairfax) and his general council of officers, recommends to the Parliament to lay aside the treaty, and to return to their votes of no more addresses to the King, and that he should return no more to government; and that they should proceed against the King in a way of justice, for evils done by him, and as the capital cause of all: and, that in order thereto, to have him kept in safe custody; and that no king should be thereafter admitted but by election. He (Rushworth) also states the letter from the General and council of the army, referring to the remonstrance, for their reasons for moving towards London.

The declaration of the army, subsequent to the remonstrance, puts the General's (Fairfax) privity to the expulsion beyond all doubt, had any doubt remained; they would rejoice, say they, if the majority of the House of Commons would become sensible of the destructiveness of their late way, and would exclude from communication in their councils all such corrupt and apostatized members as had obstructed justice, safety, and public interest: they desire that so many of them, as God had kept upright, would withdraw from such as per-sisted in their guilt; and declare, that for these ends they were approaching London.

No further evidence can be necessary to prove the General's (Fairfax) privity, both to the removal of the King to Hurst Castle, and to the exclusion of the members, and that they were done by the direction of himself and his council of officers; and it is not credible that he could be prevailed on to concur in these important acts against his own judgment: he must have been weak indeed, and very unfit for the important command in which he was placed, to be thus influenced.

Lord Clarendon says, that Fairfax never sat in the High Court of Justice, though, he says, he was overwitted by Cromwell, and made a property to bring that to pass which could have hardly been otherwise effected. This is wholly assertion; it is a serious impeachment of the General's understanding, to suppose him thus wholly a tool of Cromwell: but his understanding must have been defective indeed, not to see, in the presentment of the remonstrance, and his accompanying letter, that he joined the remonstrants in their several objects of — no more addresses to the King; his return no more to government; the trial of the King; and, necessarily, the sentence that might be passed upon him; and an elective monarchy.

Rushworth also says, that the General (Fairfax) was present at the sitting, on the 6th of January, of the commissioners for preparing the proceedings for the trial of the King, he being one of them; but sat not at the table, and went away immediately. He therefore went, in effect, the whole length of those who brought on the trial and sat in judgment upon the King, except only the not taking his seat in the High Court of Justice: and it appears from Whitelock, that, immediately after the King's death, he agreed to join the Parliament, and faithfully serve them, — most of them the very men who had been chiefly instrumental to the bringing the King to trial and to death. Nor does it appear that he, at the time when he must have seen that things were approaching to extremities, ever expressed his disapprobation of the proceedings, or used any means to prevent them. Ludlow says, that in the debate, in the Convention Parliament, preparatory to the Restoration, upon the subject of the purposed bill of indemnity, and the exceptions therein of particular persons, the Lord Fairfax plainly said, that if any person must be excepted, he knew no man that deserved it more than himself, who being General of the army at that time, and having power sufficient to prevent the proceedings against the King, had not thought fit to make use of it to that end.

His Lordship introduces with some pomp a circumstance that he considers fit to be remembered; — that on the calling over the names of the Court of Justice, the name of the General being called next

to the President, Lady Fairfax, his wife, said aloud,
" He has more wit than to be here :" and that presently, upon the reading the impeachment, and the
expression used of "all the good people of England," the same voice, in a louder tone answered,
" No, nor the hundredth part of them." This
appears to introduce her and her husband to His
Lordship's favour, and induces him to give a high
account of Her Ladyship's family; and he seems
to think the General merely absenting himself
from the High Court of Justice a sufficient excuse
for his concurrence in all the proceedings that
brought the King there, without the least exertion
on his part to prevent it. If this lady, of so high
a spirit, and having so great influence over her
husband, as she is by different writers represented
to have had, and he, the weak, undetermined
character he is described to be, had exerted her
influence with him, she might perhaps have prevented this melancholy catastrophe of the trial and
death of the King. But Whitelock does not represent the General as of this very ductile spirit :
he says of him, that he was a person of as meek
and humble carriage as ever he saw in great employment, and but of few words in discourse, or
council; yet, that when his reason and judgment
were satisfied, he was unalterable, except it were
by letter, whereof (as was fit) he was the only
judge. But, adds Whitelock, " I have observed
him at councils of war, that he has said little, but

hath ordered things expressly contrary to the judgment of all his council; and in action in the field, I have seen him so highly transported, that scarce any one durst speak a word to him; and he would seem more like a man distracted and furious, than of his ordinary mildness and so far different temper." Yet, for the purpose of rendering Cromwell odious, by making him the author of all the mischief with which they (the royalist writers) think proper to charge him, and exonerating the General, they reduced him (the General) to a mere cipher, a tool in the hands of Cromwell, to carry into execution such of his designs as he did not think fit himself to appear in. The editor of His Lordship's (Fairfax) forementioned memorial says, that he governed the army not as a cipher, but with great prudence and conduct, in councils of war as well as animated by his personal courage in the field. Nevertheless, upon the ground of the General's supposed incapacity, Cromwell is made responsible for all the General's actions, as well as his own: on the contrary, Fairfax, by concurring in the above proceedings, appears to have determined upon bringing the King to trial, whilst Cromwell was, according to Bishop Burnet, hesitating upon it. He says, Ireton was the person that drove it on, for that Cromwell was all the while in some suspense about it.

Ludlow states the army's sending Major-general

Harrison with a party of horse, to bring the King from the Isle of Wight to Windsor.

In a preceding part of these memoirs of Ludlow, he says, being fully persuaded that an accommodation with the King was unsafe to the people of England, and unjust and wicked in the nature of it; of the former, as it was obvious to all men that the King himself had proved, by the duplicity of his dealings with the Parliament, which manifestly appeared in his own papers taken at the battle of Naseby and elsewhere : of the latter, he (Ludlow) was convinced by the express words of God's law, that blood defileth the land, and the land cannot be cleansed of the blood that is shed therein, but by the blood of him that shed it. And therefore, says he, "I could not consent to the counsels of those who were contented to leave the guilt of so much blood upon the nation; and thereby to draw down the just vengeance of God upon us all, when it was most evident that the war had been occasioned by the invasion of our rights, and open breach of our laws and constitution on the King's part." He (Ludlow) says, the army were for bringing the King to trial for levying war against the Parliament and people of England; and that the common council of the city of London presented a petition to Parliament to that effect; but that some of the commonwealth's men desired, that before they consented to that method, it might be resolving what government to establish, fearing a design in the army to set up some one of themselves in his room : that others endeavoured to persuade them that the execution of justice ought to be their first work, in respect to their duty to God and the people : that the failure therein had been already the occasion of a second war, which was justly to be charged on the Parliament for neglecting that duty : that those who were truly commonwealth's men, ought to be of that opinion, as the most probable means to attain their desires, in the establishment of an equal and just government : and that the officers of the army, who were chiefly to be suspected, could not be guilty of so much imprudence and folly, to erect an arbitrary power in any one of themselves, after they had in so public a manner declared their detestation of it in another.

Mr. Hume and other royalist writers attribute the proceedings against the King to the Independents ; but the preceding history does not justify this charge upon them, or upon the Presbyterians exclusively ; the agitators or republican party, headed by Ludlow and others, composed probably of persons of all religious denominations, and of many of none, brought about the trial and death of the King. This party had become, as is before observed, formidable to Cromwell himself : Ludlow, who was one of them, so describes them, and that to be one of the causes of him (Cromwell) and his party's discontinuance of their negotiation with the King.

Ludlow, in the preceding passages, avows and justifies this part of the army taking the subsequent proceedings into their own hands; by first seizing the obnoxious members and excluding them from the House, and then rescinding the vote allowing of a renewal of the treaty with the King, and voting no further addresses or applications to him.

Lord Clarendon says, that it had been acknowledged since, by some officers and others, who were present at the consultations, that from the time of the King's being at Hampton-court, and after the army had mastered both the Parliament and the city, and were weary of having the King with them, and knew not well how to be rid of him, there were many secret consults what to do with him: and that it was generally concluded that they should never be able to settle their new form of government whilst he lived; and that after he was a prisoner in the Isle of Wight, they were more solicitous for a resolution and determination in that particular: and that after the vote of no more addresses, the most violent party thought they could do nothing in order to their own ends, till he should be first dead; and that therefore, one way or other, that was to be compassed in the first place: that some of them were for deposing him; others for depriving him of his life by poison, as making the least noise, or by assassination: and a third sort for his being brought to a public trial as a malefactor; which, they said, would be most for

the honour of the Parliament, and would teach all
kings to know that they were accountable and
punishable for the wickedness of their lives : that
many of the officers were for the first (his de-
position), for which they had precedents, and that
they could in that case better settle the government than if he were dead ; for that his son could
pretend no right during his life ; but that when he
should be dead, his son would presently call himself king, and others would call him so too, and
other kings and princes might own him for such.
And that if he were kept alive in a close prison,
he might afterwards be made use of, or removed
upon any appearance of a revolution : that there
were as many officers of the second judgment,
that he should be presently dispatched (poisoned
or assassinated) ; for that, whilst living, there
would be always plots and designs to set him at
liberty, and he would have parties throughout the
kingdom, and in a short time a faction in their
most secret councils, and perhaps in the army itself ;
and that where his liberty would yield so great a
price, it would be too great a trust to repose in
any man that he would long resist the temptation ;
whereas, if he were dead, all those fears would be
over, especially if they proceeded with that circumspection and severity towards all his party as in
prudence they ought to do. This party, adds
His Lordship, would probably have carried it, if
Colonel Hammond could have been wrought upon

to have concurred; but that he had too much
conscience to have exposed himself to that infamy;
and without his privity or connivance it could not
have been done: that the third party, which were
all the levellers and agitators of the army, in the
head of which were Ireton and Harrison, would
not endure either of the other ways; for that they
could as easily bring him to justice in the sight of
the sun as depose him, since the authority of the
Parliament could do one as well as the other: that
their precedent of deposing had no reputation with
the people, but was looked upon as the effect of
some potent faction, which always oppressed the
people more after than they had been before; that
besides, those deposings had always been attended
with assassinations and murders, which were the
more odious and detested, because nobody owned
and avowed the bloody actions they had done;
but that if he were brought to a public trial for
the notorious ill things he had done, and for his
misgovernment, upon the complaint and prosecution of the people, the superiority of the people
would be thereby vindicated and made manifest,
and they should receive the benefit and be for
ever free from those oppressions which he had
imposed upon them, and for which he ought to
pay so dear; and that such an exemplary proceeding and execution as this, where every circumstance should be clear and notorious, would
be the best foundation and security of the govern-

ment they intended to establish; and no man would be ambitious to succeed him and be a king in his place, when he saw in what manner he must be accountable to the people : that this argument- ation, or the strength and obstinacy of that party, carried it; and thereupon all that formality of proceeding, which afterwards was exercised, was resolved upon and consented to.

The preceding narrative, as given by His Lordship, must be received with great caution, as coming from persons acknowledging themselves to have been personally engaged in consultations that went the length of dethroning the King, only by different means: and it must be observed, that these acknowledgments were made by these officers after the Restoration, for the purpose of extenuating their own conduct, and of obtaining from the then prevailing party the most favourable construction of the part they had taken in these transactions; their testimony must therefore have been very suspicious. His Lordship's account, however, of the third party's determination to bring the King to trial, agrees in substance with Ludlow's account, in proving the levellers and agitators, (the republican party of the army,) headed by Ireton and Harrison, to have brought on this trial, and not separately the Presbyterians or Independents as such. And in justice to Crom- well it ought to be particularly noticed, that he is not here named as having had any concern in these deliberations, nor in this final resolution of bringing the King to trial: he would not have escaped His Lordship's vigilance and de-tection, had he been even hinted at in these transactions.

Mrs. Hutchinson, referring to these proceedings, and to the part her husband, the Colonel, took therein, says, that when he was sufficiently recovered from his then late illness to attend the House, he found the presbyterian party so prevalent there, that the victories obtained by the army displeased them, and so hot they grew in the zeal of their faction, that they from thenceforth resolved and endeavoured to close with the common enemy, that they might thereby compass the destruction of their independent brethren : that to this end, and to strengthen their faction, they got in again the late suspended members ; whereof it was said, and by the consequence appeared true, that Mr. Holles, during his secession, had been in France, and there meeting with the Queen, had pieced up an ungodly accommodation with her ; although he were the man, that when, at the beginning, some of the sober men who foresaw the sad issues of war and victory on either side, were labouring an accommodation, openly in the House said, " He abhorr'd that word accommodation :" that after these were gotten in again, and encouraged by the presbyterian ministers, and the people in the

city, they procured a revocation of the votes formerly made of no more addresses to the King; and
that then nothing was agitated with more violence
than a new personal treaty with honour and freedom; and even his (the King's) coming to the
city before any security given, was laboured for,
but that prevailed not: that such were the heats of
the two parties, that Mr. Holles challenged Ireton
even in the House; out of which they both went
to have fought; but that one, who sat near them,
overheard the wicked whisper, and prevented the
execution of it: that amidst these things, at last a
treaty was sent to the King by commissioners,
and although, continues Mrs. Hutchinson, there
were some honourable persons in this commission,
yet that it could not be denied but that they were
carried away by the other, and concluded, upon
most dangerous terms, an agreement with the
King; and that such were the terms upon which
the King was to be restored, that the whole cause
was evidently given up to him: that the commissioners that treated with him had been cajoled
and biassed with the promises of great honours and
offices to every one of them; and so they brought
back their treaty to be confirmed by the Houses;
where there was a very high dispute about them,
and they sat up most part of the night, when at
length it was voted to accept his concessions, the
dissenting party being fewer than the other that

were carried on in the faction : that Colonel Hutchinson was that night among them, and being convinced in his conscience that both the cause and all those who with an upright honest heart asserted and maintained it were betrayed and sold for nothing, he addressed himself to these commissioners he had most honourable thoughts of, and urged his reasons and apprehensions to them, that the King, after having been exasperated, vanquished, and captured, would be restored to that power which was inconsistent with the liberty of the people; who, for all their blood, treasure, and misery, would reap no fruit, but a confirmation of bondage; and that it had been a thousand times better never to have struck one stroke in the quarrel, than, after victory, to yield up a righteous cause; whereby they should not only betray the interest of their country, and the trust reposed in them and those zealous friends who had engaged to the death for them, but be false to the covenant of their God, which was to extirpate prelacy, not to lease it. This refers to the King's refusal to give up bishops, and his proposal to lease out their revenues. Mrs. Hutchinson proceeds, — that they acknowledged that the conditions were not so secure as they ought to be; but in regard of the growing insolence of the army, it was best to accept them. They further said, that they, enjoying those trusts and places which they had secured for themselves and other honest men, should be able to curb the King's exorbitances : and such other things they said, wherewith the Colonel, dissatisfied, opposed their proceedings as much as he could : that by this violent proceeding of the Presbyterians, they finished the destruction of him in whose restitution they were then so fiercely engaged; for this gave heart to the vanquished cavaliers, and such courage to the captive King, that it hardened him and them to their ruin: that on the other side, it so frightened all the honest people, that it made them as violent in their zeal to pull down as the others were in their madness to restore this kingly idol; and the army, who were principally levelled and marked out for the sacrifice and peace-offering of this ungodly reconciliation, had some colour to pursue their late arrogant usurpations upon that authority which it was their duty rather to have obeyed than interrupted; but that the debates of that night, which produced such destructive votes to them and all their friends, being reported to them, they, the next morning, seized the members.

The above extract from Mrs. Hutchinson most satisfactorily proves the clandestine and interested proceedings of the presbyterian party in their transactions with the King at Newport; and of Mr. Holles in particular, in spite of his affectedly disinterested declaration at the conclusion of his angry and malignant work, of his having no thought of personal revenge towards any particular in case

his party had prevailed.   This account is from her
husband, Colonel Hutchinson, who appears to have
been an honest, moderate man, not of any particu-
cular party, but acting according to the best of his
own judgment.   He here describes the presbyterian
party as prevalent in the House, and their object
in endeavouring to close with the King, to be the
destruction of the independent party.   He describes Mr. Holles as having when abroad, come
to an accommodation with the Queen, notwithstanding his forementioned declarations,   He relates the influence the King had obtained over the
leading commissioners by his promise of honours
and offices, to induce them to consent to a disad-
vantageous and insecure treaty; all which they
acknowledged and justified to him, Colonel Hutchinson.   And he is disposed to allow these proceedings to be a degree of justification of the army's
subsequent apparently violent conduct, who were
principally marked out as the victims of this, as he
calls it, ungodly reconciliation.   And Lord Clarendon observes, that some of the commissioners found
means to advertise the King in private, that they
were of His Majesty's judgment about church-
government, which they hoped might yet be preserved, but not by the method His Majesty pursued : that all the reasonable hope of preserving
the crown was in dividing the Parliament from
the army, which could be only done by his giving

satisfaction in what was demanded with reference to the church : that this might probably unite the Parliament and the city of London, where the Presbyterians were most powerful, and enable them, the Parliament, to reform their army, and to disband those who should be refractory, and then to bring His Majesty to London with honour, where he might have an opportunity of gaining more abatements than he could ever expect by refusing to sign the preliminaries: that many advertisements came from His Majesty's friends in London, and other places, that it was high time the treaty was at an end before the army drew nearer London, which it would shortly do, as soon as those in the north had finished their works.

And this account from Lord Clarendon fully establishes the truth of Colonel Hutchinson's above narrative of the presbyterian party's secret negotiations with the King; the discovery whereof by the army well accounts for their subsequent conduct, and which theywould deem no more than an act of self-preservation against their inveterate enemies, who were plotting their destruction. The principal officers were accused, as has been observed, in their negotiations with the King, of obtaining from him promises of preferments and other rewards, which the General (Fairfax) has positively denied; declaring that they bargained not, nor

asked any thing of the King for any private interest of their own.

Lord Clarendon, with his usual asperity towards
every one connected with Cromwell, describes Mr.
Holles as having, one day, upon a very hot debate
in the House, and some rude expressions which
fell from Ireton, persuaded him (Ireton) to walk
out of the House with him, and then telling him
that he should presently go over the water and
fight with him: that Ireton replying that his conscience would not suffer him to fight a duel, Holles,
in choler, pulled him by the nose, telling him, that
if his conscience would keep him from giving men
satisfaction, it should keep him from provoking
them: and to this affront, given to a man whom
he describes of the most virulent, malicious, and
revengeful nature of all the pack, he attributes
the impeachment of Mr. Holles and the other ten
members. Ireton's established courage in various
actions in which he had been engaged, renders this
account utterly improbable, and is entitled to no
more credit than is due to Mr. Holles's impeachment of Cromwell's courage; both proceeding from
the same ill disposition towards these extraordinary
characters. Mrs. Hutchinson, however, in her
preceding account of this quarrel, expressly says,
that Holles challenged Ireton in the House, from
whence they went to have fought, but were prevented by the interposition of one of the members,

who had overheard them. Ludlow, in confirmation of this account, says, that Mr. Holles, thinking some expressions used by Ireton, respecting
himself and others of the secluded members, to be
injurious to them, passing by him in the House,
whispered him in the ear, telling him it was false,
and that he would justify it to be so, if he would
follow him; and thereupon immediately went out
of the House, with the other following him : that
some members who had observed their passionate
carriage to each other, and seen them hastily leaving the House, acquainted the House with their
apprehensions; whereupon they sent their sergeant-
at-arms to command their attendance, which letting
them understand as they were taking boat to go
to the other side of the water, they returned, and
the House enjoined them to forbear all words or
actions of enmity towards each other, which they
promised to do. These two relations must be
deemed of themselves a sufficient contradiction of
Lord Clarendon's narrative of this transaction ;
nor is it probable that Mr. Holles would have
omitted to mention this affair with the circumstances related by His Lordship, so creditable to
his own courage and disgraceful to Ireton, had
His Lordship's account been correct.

This misunderstanding of Holles and Ireton
would not have been here noticed, but for the purpose of showing the small degree of credit to which

these narratives are entitled, where they are manifestly introduced for the sole purpose of vilifying and destroying those characters that wese most obnoxious to the writers, and of building upon the ruins of them their own fabricated histories, to serve a party purpose.

CHAPTER XII.

LUDLOW, referring to the Scots preparations for
raising an army, in pursuance of their treaty with
the King, wherein he says the Presbyterians and
cavaliers joined, though with different designs,
says, that in the mean time Lieutenant-general
Cromwell, not forgetting himself, procured a
meeting of divers leading men amongst the Presbyterians and Independents, both members of Parliament and ministers, at a dinner in Westminster,
under a pretence of endeavouring a reconciliation
between the two parties; but that he found it a

work too difficult for him to compose the differences between these two ecclesiastical interests;
one of which would endure no superior, the other
no equal; so that this meeting produced no effect:
that he contrived another conference to be held
in King-street, (he does not say when, seldom
giving dates,) between those called the grandees
of the House and army, and the commonwealth's
men; in which the grandees, of whom Lieutenant-
general Cromwell was the head, kept themselves
in the clouds, and would not declare their judgments either for a monarchical, aristocratical, or
democratical government; maintaining that any
of them might be good in themselves, or for them,
according as Providence should direct them: that
the commonwealth's men declared that monarchy
was neither good in itself nor for us: that it was
not desirable in itself, they urged from the 8th
chapter and 8th verse of the first book of Samuel,
where the rejection of the judges and the choice
of a king was charged upon the Israelites by God
himself as a rejection of him; and from another
passage in the same book, where Samuel declares
it to be a great wickedness; with divers more texts
of Scripture to the same effect: and that it was no
way conducing to the interest of this nation, was
endeavoured to be proved by the infinite mischiefs
and oppressions we had suffered under it and by
it: that, indeed, our ancestors had consented to be
governed by a single person, but with this proviso,

— that he should govern according to the direction of the law, which he always bound himself by oath to perform: that the King had broken this oath, and thereby dissolved our allegiance, protection and obedience being reciprocal: that having appealed to the sword for the decision of the things in dispute, and thereby caused the effusion of a deluge of the people's blood, it seemed to be a duty incumbent upon the representatives of the people to call him to an account for the same; more especially, since the controversy was determined by the same means which he had chosen; and then to proceed to the establishment of an equal commonwealth, founded upon the consent of the people, and providing for the rights and liberties of all men, that we might have the hearts and hands of the nation to support it, as being most just, and in all respects most conducing to the happiness and prosperity thereof: that, notwithstanding what was said, Lieutenant-general Cromwell, not for want of conviction, but in hopes to make a better bargain with another party, professed himself unresolved; and having learned what he could of the principles and inclinations of those present at the conference, took up a cushion and flung it at his (Ludlow's) head, and then ran down the stairs; but he overtook him with another, which made him hasten down faster than he desired: that the next day, passing by him (Ludlow) in the House, he told

him he was convinced of the desirableness of
what was proposed, but not of the feasibleness of
it ; thereby, as he (Ludlow) supposed, designing to
encourage him to hope that he was inclined to join
with them, though unwilling to publish his opinion,
lest the grandees should be informed of it, to whom
he (Ludlow) presumed he professed himself to be
of another judgment. Ludlow thus takes upon
himself to attribute Cromwell's irresolution to
base motives ; but it is generally allowed that he
always hesitated about bringing the King to trial ;
nor is it probable he should communicate this
supposed alteration in his sentiments in so loose a
way ; nor was Ludlow likely to be his confidant in
a disclosure of so much importance, of whom he
does not appear upon other occasions to have had a
very high opinion, though Ludlow seems anxious
to have it otherwise supposed. Nothing in these
passages from Ludlow criminate Cromwell, who
at the first meeting was very properly endeavouring
to reconcile the presbyterian and independent
parties, who were destroying the common cause
by their animosities ; but which he found impracticable. His object at the second meeting appears
to have been to hear the sentiments of the different
parties, to enable him and those acting with him
to determine the best measures to be taken upon
consideration of all their reasonings in the then
very momentous crisis. Cromwell appears to
have long continued in doubt, (Ludlow says he

was unresolved,) and therefore carefully avoided giving any opinion at these meetings; and probably purposely terminated this last meeting in the odd way mentioned by Ludlow, to avoid further and more serious discussion.

And now, says Whitelock, (about the 23d of December,) was a sharp debate in the Parliament about bringing the great delinquents of the kingdom to speedy punishment; and now, adds he, was set on foot and begun their great design of taking away the King, whom divers in the debate did not stick to name for the greatest delinquent, and to be proceeded against in justice : that others insisted upon it that he was not capable of being brought to justice by his subjects, but by God alone ; and that having subdued him and his party, there was no need of any thing further, but to secure the Parliament from their enemies' rising against them any more; and that might be done without bringing the King to any judicial trial,—a thing not read of in any history. He does not even hint at Lord Clarendon's suggestion of assassination ; nor is it credible that any one should dare to avow, or have the wickedness to entertain, such a thought; it is probably thrown out for the chance of increasing the odium so desirable to be fixed upon the parties engaged in these transactions. But, says he, those of the fierce party prosecuted their design with all eagerness, and those of a contrary opinion either durst

not oppose, knowing they should be presently
secluded the House if they did, or seeing that no
opposition would be to any effect or purpose ; that
it was endeavoured wholly to have put the business
upon the army, that if they would have the thing
done, they should do it themselves, as most proper
for such an irregular and unheard-of business, to
be done in an irregular way, and by such irregular
men ; but they were subtle enough to see and
avoid that, and to make those whom they left
sitting in the Parliament to be their stales and to
do their most dirty work for them : many of whom
they found, and persuaded to be strangely forward
to engage in it : insomuch, that it was carried by
vote in the House of Commons to name a committee of thirty-eight persons, to consider of drawing up a charge; and for that purpose to receive
all informations, and examinations of all witnesses
for the matters of fact against the King, and all
other delinquents that might be thought fit to be
brought to condign punishment.

That Sir Thomas Widdrington and he (Whitelock), being together on the 26th of the same
December, received a message from the committee, requiring them to come to them to advise
them ; but they resolving not to meddle in the
business of the trial of the King, it being contrary to their judgment, went out of town to
Whitelock's house.   He gives an account of the
proceedings preparatory to the trial : and adds,

that on the morning of the 9th of January, Sir
Thomas Widdrington and himself, by agreement,
went into the House, the trial of the King being
begun; that some looked very shy upon them, others
bid them welcome, and seemed glad to see them.
He then gives a particular account of the trial, of
the sentence, and of the execution; the same in
substance with the accounts given by Lord Clarendon, Rushworth, and others.

It appears, however, certain, that subsequent to
the termination of the treaty of Newport, there
were many meetings of the principals of the different parties, to consider of the then critical state
of the affairs of the nation. Whitelock mentions
one of these meetings to have been on the 18th of
December (1648). He says, that when the chancery business was over, Sir Thomas Widdrington
and he went to the Rolls by appointment, where
Lieutenant-general Cromwell and Colonel Dean
met them; and with the Speaker, they had a long
discourse together about the present affairs: and
that then, another time was appointed by the
Lieutenant-general for them to meet again and to
consider and confer how the settlement of the
kingdom might be best effected, and to join counsels for the public good: and that in the afternoon
of the 21st of the same month there was another
meeting of the Speaker, Cromwell, Sir Thomas
Widdrington, and himself, when they discoursed
freely about the present affairs, and actions of the

army and the settlement of the kingdom : and that
in the conclusion, Sir Thomas Widdrington and
himself were desired to draw up some heads
upon the discourse, to be considered by the same
company : and that on the 22d Sir Thomas Widdrington and himself met, staid all the day together to draw some heads upon the preceding
day's discourse, and to endeavour to bring the
army into some fitter temper : that they were
likewise desired to frame somewhat in order to
the restitution of the secluded members, — for
an answer for the army to the messages of the
House to the army, touching their members under
restraint, and heads for a declaration what the
Parliament intended for the settlement of the
kingdom, to be considered of and offered to the
Parliament and council of the army. — This, proceeds Whitelock, was a work of no small difficulty
and danger, yet at this time not to be declined by
them ; both the members of the House and chief
officers of the army, having engaged and trusted
them only therein : they prayed to God to direct
them in it, and that neither of them might receive
any prejudice, but that the kingdom might receive
good by this their employment, and the courses of
the army be moderated, (as it was in some measure
at this time,) though it broke out again into violence afterwards.

It is here observable, that these two meetings
appear to have been private meetings, at which

only Cromwell and a very few more were present,
for the express purpose of consulting upon the
then state of the affairs of the nation, and upon
the best settlement of the kingdom : and, Whitelock adds, that they discoursed freely thereof, and
of the actions of the army ; and that Sir Thomas
Widdrington and he (they were then two of the
commissioners of the great seal) were employed to
form a plan thereon, and for the purpose of bringing the army into a better temper, and for the
restoration of the secluded members, and of a declaration of the Parliament's intention for the
settlement of the kingdom ; to be offered to the
Parliament and council of the army.

Also, that neither Ireton, nor Ludlow, nor Harrison, nor any others of the republican party, were
present ; and that the Speaker, and Whitelock,
and Widdrington, were adverse to the bringing the
King to trial: and that this subject, therefore,
could not form any part of Cromwell's consultations with them ; that, on the contrary, it appears,
that the actions of the army in excluding the
members, and the means of preventing their carrying into effect their design of bringing the King
to a trial ; and a settlement of the kingdom in
peace and security, were the real and only objects
of this meeting : whether this settlement was to be
with or without the King, does not appear ; and
hence it is to be fairly inferred that Cromwell did
all he could to prevent this measure of bringing

the King to trial, and to accomplish a settlement of the kingdom in some other way, not then having a view to his own advancement.

The same writer (Whitelock) mentions a meeting of the general council of the army on the same day (the 22d December), on which Sir Thomas Widdrington and himself met for the before-mentioned purposes; at which the council, he says, had much debate concerning the matters of religion, — relating to their new representation, and of the power of the representatives. — He adds, (under the date of the 23d of the same December,) that he and Sir Thomas Widdrington went together, according to appointment, to the Speaker's house: that there met them divers gentlemen of the House, and they consulted about settling the kingdom by the Parliament, and not to leave all to the sword; and that Sir Thomas and he spake their minds freely to them; that some of them were wholly against any king at all, others were against having the present King, or his eldest, or second son to be king; others were for the third son, the Duke of Gloucester, (who was among them, and might be educated as they should appoint,) to be made king: that they came, after a long debate, to no resolution, but appointed to meet again on the next Monday: that the Commons sat on the 25th, though it was Christmas-day:—that the committee named to consider how to proceed in a way of justice against the King were enjoined to meet

on that afternoon; and a debate whether the se‑
cluded members should be admitted.—And to
proceed to the consideration of the measure of
bringing the King to a trial.

From the foregoing extracts from Rushworth,
and from the Journals of the House of Commons,
it appears, that the Commons, after the exclusion
of the members, having rescinded the resolution
of the House, " That the King's concessions to
the Parliament's propositions were a sufficient
ground for the House to proceed upon for settling
the peace of the kingdom ;" and having voted his
concessions at the Isle of Wight not satisfactory,
and that no more addresses should be made to
him, they proceeded to prepare a charge against
him, and passed an ordinance for attainting him of
high treason, and for trying him by commissioners :
that they sent up this charge to the Lords for
their concurrence, who, after much debate, post‑
poned its further consideration, and adjourned;
but that the Commons, upon searching the Lords'
journal-book, finding that they had rejected it, re‑
solved to proceed without them : and then came
to the following resolutions:—They declared it to
be treason, by the fundamental laws of the king‑
dom, in the king for the time being to levy war
against the Parliament and kingdom of England;
—the people, under God, to be the original of all
just power : that the Commons of England in Par‑
liament, being chosen by, and representing the

people, had the supreme power of the nation; and that all things declared by them to be law had the force of law, and all the people of the nation concluded thereby, without the concurrence of the King and House of Peers. And then the ordinance of the Commons for the trial of the King was passed.

The King denying the authority of the court, they proceeded to pronounce the sentence.

The King's speech at the execution of the sentence does not appear to possess any particular merit: he insists upon his innocence, alleging that he did not begin the war, nor did ever intend to encroach on their privileges: that the Parliament began upon the militia (army), after acknowledging it to be his, taking it from him: and that they began the troubles.

The King, in his declaration of his reasons for refusing to acknowledge the jurisdiction of the court, intended to have been delivered by him in court, but forbidden, proceeds to show the grounds of his confidence that they could not judge him, or the meanest man in England: that no proceeding could be just that was not warranted either by the laws of God, or by the municipal laws of the country: that this was not warranted by God's laws; for that, on the contrary, obedience unto kings was clearly and strictly warranted and commanded both in the Old and New Testament: that there it is said, Where the word of a king is, there

is power, and who may say unto him, What doest
thou?   Then, for the law of the land, — that no
impeachment can lie against a king, they all going
in his name; and one of the legal maxims is, that
a king can do no wrong: that the law upon which
these proceedings were grounded must be either
old or new; if old, show it; if new, tell what authority, warranted by the fundamental laws of the
land, hath made it, and when? that the House of
Commons could not erect a court of justice, which
was not one itself: that admitting, but not granting, that the people's commission could grant this
power, the question was never asked of the tenth
man in the kingdom; and, in this way, the poorest
ploughman was manifestly wronged, if his free
consent not demanded; nor could any colour be
pretended for this commission without the consent,
at least, of the major part of every man in England of whatsoever quality or condition; which
was never sought.

Rapin, in his History of England, confining himself, he says, wholly to the kingdom of England,
and supposing the constitution of the government
such as it was, from the Conquest to Charles I., he
should briefly set forth what had been said for and
against so extraordinary a trial.   In the first place,
says he, it has been demanded — on what law, natural or positive, was founded the right assumed
by the Parliament of England to try the King?
He proceeds, — the most plausible answer in vin-

dication of the Parliament's proceedings is as follows: that, according to the constitution of the
English government, the King is no less bound
than the subject to observe the laws to which
himself or predecessors assented, which is the
principal clause of the coronation-oath: that if
this obligation be equal on both sides, there must
be, therefore, equally means to cause them to
discharge it, in case they neglect it: that as for
the subject, there is no manner of difficulty; the
penalties against offenders are universally known,
and the courts of justice are appointed to inflict
them: that it is true the laws had ordained no
penalty upon kings who discharge not their duty;
as well out of respect to the regal dignity, as because it cannot be supposed that the king, to
whom the execution of the laws is committed,
should be the first to break them, and betray the
trust lodged in him by the people: that he is,
nevertheless, bound to observe them himself, and
cause them to be observed by the subject: that this
is a principle generally acknowledged; but what is
this obligation, if the observance of the laws depends solely on his will, and there be no just means
to compel him to observe them, or punish him,
when he breaks them? will it not be an empty
sound without any meaning? and will not the English government be as arbitrary as that of any
other country in the world? That since, therefore, the laws have not decreed any penalty against

a king that should neglect his duty, or the manner to constrain him to discharge it; and as, nevertheless, he is bound by the same laws to procure
the observance thereof, and to observe them himself, the nation's representative in Parliament is,
of course, to call him to an account, since it is not
possible to imagine any other way : that, supposing
the King to have violated the most fundamental
laws of the realm, shall foreigners be applied to, to
bring him to justice ?   Can it be supposed, contrary to experience, that the King is under an impossibility of breaking the fundamental laws of the
kingdom, of endeavouring to subvert them, and of
establishing an arbitrary government ? will it be
maintained that he may do it with impunity ? —
but, if he is assured of impunity, what difference
is there between the English government and the
most despotic ; since its preservation will solely
depend on the King's probity and will ?   If he
runs no hazard in trying to alter the constitution,
after ten attempts, he will try again, even until he
succeeds : that as to the objection, that less violent
means than war may be used to oblige the King to
the observance of the laws, and less unjust and extraordinary than the taking away his life, to punish
him for the breach of them, it is answered, — this
is true ; and the Parliament had accordingly tried
to secure the government by other methods, as by
demanding of the King, that the power of the
militia might be lodged in both Houses : that if the

King had agreed to it, the realm would have been
in peace, and the people's jealousies have ceased :
but that he had taken up arms to prevent the Parliament's using these means ; a clear evidence that
his design was to maintain himself in a condition
to alter the government when he should have opportunity : that this unjust war had been the occasion of infinite mischiefs, of the death of thou-
sands of his subjects, and the ruin of the rest ; and
that, if he was brought to a trial, it was not so
much to punish him for violating the laws, as for
preferring the unjust and violent way of arms before the expedients offered him to prevent his
breaking them for the future.

Rapin proceeds, — That the advocates for the
King say, that though the kings of England have
not so much authority in their realm as some other
kings, it does not follow that they may be put upon
a level with subjects, and made equally accountable for their actions : that the principle laid down
for foundation, that there is an equal obligation
upon the King and the subjects to observe the
law, is false, and consequently the whole reasoning
founded thereon of no force ; for that private persons being entrusted only with their own conduct,
nothing can exempt them from the observance of the
laws : but that the King being entrusted with the
government of the state, and the execution of the
laws, he has consequently power to qualify them
on certain occasions, otherwise this trust would be

to no purpose : that the laws could not foresee
every thing, and that there are occasions where it
is absolutely necessary for the public good to act
contrary to them, or at least to suspend the observance of them, and that therefore the obligation
of the King and the subject is not equal : that
supposing the King had violated some of the fundamental laws of the kingdom, and levied war
against the Parliament after the most unjust manner, it did not follow that he might be punished
with death, by reason he has neither superior nor
equal in the kingdom, and he could have none but
subjects for his judges; besides, that he was the
fountain of justice, and it was absurd to make him
liable to justice, from whom it flows and derives its
whole authority : that supposing the chance of war
had put him in the power of his enemies, he might
have been detained in prison, and prevented from
doing mischief till he was prevailed with to grant
all the securities required : but that there was a
wide difference between imprisonment and death ;
as the first could be considered as a reasonable and
necessary precaution, and the other as a punishment subjects were not empowered to inflict on
their sovereign ; as indeed the like had never been
heard of.

The forementioned arguments seem to comprise all that can be said on both sides of this very
momentous question, and they certainly, either
way, present great difficulties. One thing is clear,

and worthy of observation, — that the King, to his last moment, adhered to the principle he brought with him to the throne, that of passive obedience and non-resistance : this he distinctly avows in his above declaration ; and upon this principle he must, as hath been before observed, have considered all the opposition of his subjects from the beginning of his reign to have been nothing short of absolute rebellion ; nor can there be a doubt, from the various circumstances disclosed in the histories of these times, that he always, in his several treaties with them, so considered them ; consequently, that he would feel himself under no obligation to adhere to his engagements with them longer than might suit his convenience. — The Parliament was well aware of his adherence to this principle, and never thought they could obtain from him sufficient security against the breach of any treaties he might make with them.

There seems, however, much weight in the objections of the King to the right claimed by the Commons to erect the High Court of Justice. — It doth not seem that both Houses, perfectly complete, could do it : the Commons were chosen to represent the people in Parliament, the King being then one of the constituent parts. The King being absent, and the House of Lords in effect dissolved, and the Commons, by force and otherwise, much reduced from their original and proper number, it should seem that, for this particular purpose of forming a competent court for the trial of the King, resort should have been then again had to the people for their special authority for the formation of such court, supposing the people at large to have been competent to give such authority. The then Commons' resolutions in favour of the people's, or of their own power, could not make that to be law which was not already so. By the laws of this country, every one has a right to be tried by his equals; the King could not be tried by his equals; and his judges were his subjects, supposed to be aggrieved, consequently not impartial or unprejudiced; this was placing the King in a worse condition than the meanest of his people. The King's case has been compared to a trustee, his people the objects of his trust. Upon a breach of his trust, the people, it has been said, had a right to resume the trust and punish the trustee, as in the case of other trustees; but this does not apply to the King's case, because in the common case of unfaithful trustees, they are not amenable to the persons by whom they are entrusted, but to a court of judicature; and their default will be triable by an impartial judge, or by a jury of their equals. If this reasoning be just, it does not appear that, according to the laws or constitution of this country, a court of judicature could be instituted for the trial of the King, and consequently that the High Court of Justice was not legally competent thereto; therefore that the King was correct in denying its jurisdiction.

But this is a deep and solemn subject, not lightly or unnecessarily to be discussed. Judge Blackstone, in his Commentaries, treating of the revolution, and the declaration of the vacancy of the throne by the Lords and Commons, in consequence of the King's abdication, says, — "Whenever a question arises between the society at large and any magistrate vested with powers originally delegated by that society, it must be decided by the voice of the society itself: there is not upon earth any other tribunal to resort to. And that these consequences were fairly deduced from those facts, (the abdication of the throne, &c.) our ancestors have solemnly determined in a full parliamentary convention representing the whole society: that the reasons upon which they decided may be found at large in the parliamentary proceedings of the times; and may be matter of instructive amusement for us to contemplate as a speculative point of history." But, adds he, "care must be taken not to carry this enquiry farther, than merely for instruction or amusement: that the idea, that the consciences of posterity were concerned in the rectitude of their ancestors' decisions, gave birth to those dangerous political heresies which so long distracted the state, but at length are all happily extinguished. I therefore rather choose to consider this great political measure upon the solid footing of authority, rather

than to reason in its favour from its justice, moderation, and expedience: because that might imply a right of dissenting or revolting from it, in
case we should think it to have been unjust, oppressive, or inexpedient.   Whereas our ancestors
having most indisputably a competent jurisdiction
to decide this great and important question, and
having in fact decided it, it is now become our
duty at this distance of time to acquiesce in their
determination; being born under that establishment which was built upon this foundation, and
obliged by every tie, religious as well as civil, to
maintain it."   He adds, "While we rest this fundamental transaction, in point of authority, upon
grounds the least liable to cavil, we are bound both
in justice and gratitude to add, that it was conducted with a temper and moderation which naturally arose from its equity; that, however it
might in some respects go beyond the letter of
our ancient laws, it was agreeable to the spirit of
our constitution and the rights of human nature."
The same writer observes, " That the supposition
of law is, that neither the King nor either House
of Parliament (collectively taken) is capable of
doing any wrong; since in such cases the law feels
itself incapable of furnishing any adequate remedy.
For which reason all oppression, which may happen
to spring from any branch of the sovereign power,
must necessarily be out of the reach of any stated
rule or express legal provision: but that if ever

they unfortunately happen, the prudence of the times must provide new remedies upon new emergencies : that it is found by experience, that whenever the unconstitutional oppressions, even of the sovereign power, advance with gigantic strides, and threaten desolation to a state, mankind will not be reasoned out of the feelings of humanity ; nor will sacrifice their liberty by a scrupulous adherence to those political maxims which were originally established to preserve it."

Had King James the Second stood his ground, not vacating, as he did, the throne by his own act, and been made prisoner, the two cases of himself and King Charles the First would have closely approached each other ; and the difficulties of proceedings would have been probably very similar.

Upon these transactions, the best and wisest men have held different opinions ; which should mitigate the severity with which the writers on the King's part have chosen to express themselves respecting those who were concerned in bringing forward the great and dreadful catastrophe. These writers seem delighted with the terms regicides and murderers, and similar opprobrious epithets, not doing them the justice to allow that they acted upon principles they thought legal and right, however erroneous those principles might be ; nor allowing for the confusion and terror by which the whole nation was then agitated. Most of those of the King's judges who were brought to trial ap-

pear to have been religious professors, and the
irreproachableness of their moral characters and
conduct in private life afford strong grounds for
believing that they were really religious persons.
They must have been legally advised they were
right, and their defence, made twelve years afterwards, affording ample time for consideration and
repentance, shows them to have continued in the
same mind; and even in the moment of expiring
life, under the most cruel sentence, inflicted with
the most unrelenting and strict severity, and which
they underwent with the most patient and religious
fortitude, they expressed no contrition; on the
contrary, they justified the part they had taken to
their last moments. These circumstances certainly
do not prove them to have acted legally right, but
they do prove their continued, unabated conviction of the rectitude of their own conduct and
motives. They appear to have entered seriously
and solemnly upon the measure. Rushworth says,
that the officers at the head-quarters at Windsor
had serious councils, and days spent wholly in
prayer for direction of their proceedings. Lord
Clarendon (though sarcastically) observes, that the
preliminaries to these conferences were always
fastings and prayers, made by Cromwell or Ireton,
or some other inspired person, as most of the officers were. Mrs. Hutchinson says, that Colonel
Hutchinson, although he was very much confirmed
in his judgment concerning the cause, yet here,

being called to an extraordinary action, whereof
many were of several minds, he addressed himself
to God by prayer, desiring the Lord that if, through
any human frailty, he were led into any error or
false opinion in these great transactions, he would
open his eyes and not suffer him to proceed, but
that he would confirm his spirit in the truth, and
lead him by a right enlightened conscience: and
that finding no check, but a confirmation in his
conscience, that it was his duty to act as he did;
he, upon serious debate, both privately, and in his
addresses to God, and in conferences with conscientious, upright, and unbiassed persons, proceeded to sign the sentence against the King: that
though he did not then believe but it might one
day come to be again disputed among men, yet
both he and others thought they could not refuse
it without giving up the people of God, whom they
had led forth and engaged themselves unto by the
oath of God, into the hands of God's and their
enemies: and that therefore he cast himself upon
God's protection, acting according to the dictates
of a conscience which he had sought the Lord to
guide; and accordingly the Lord did signalise his
favour afterwards to him. Whitelock, who was no
fanatic or enthusiast, nor did he approve of the
trial of the King, speaking of the forementioned
meetings with Cromwell and others to consider of
the then critical affairs of the nation, and of their
reference to him and Sir Thomas Widdrington, to

prepare a declaration, &c. describes themselves as praying to God to direct them therein. All these circumstances do certainly prove the anxiety of these persons to do right, and that they were actuated by conscientious motives in all these their proceedings regarding the King, though they might be, and indeed it is conceived were, mistaken in their judgments of the legality of the action. All this is said to be hypocritical; but assertion is not proof; their consistency, sobriety, and regularity, show the falsehood of this charge. Supposing them to have been mistaken in their judgments respecting their legal right to bring the King to a trial, yet murderers they cannot properly be called, unless some premeditated malice could be proved against them, of which there is no appearance. The judges of the High Court of Justice (as it is called) were not answerable for their president's treatment of the King, which appears to have been harsh and unfeeling towards a fallen sovereign; nor were they answerable for the cruel and indecent behaviour of some of the soldiers and populace; and there is no evidence of their countenancing it; and they, the judges, except the president, appear to have been silent through the trial. The King was respectfully treated to his last moment, and his remains were carefully attended to. Dr. Bates, pursuing his then become favourite object, of blackening Cromwell's memory, represents him as causing the coffin to be opened, and curiously

viewing the body, and disturbing it; and that it
was delivered to a rascally quack physician for
embalming. Lord Clarendon, with his usual severity upon these occasions, describes his murderers
as causing his body to be opened, which he says,
they did, as if from mere cruel and wanton curiosity; when he must be well aware that the embalming, which he mentions a few lines afterwards,
rendered opening necessary. To cursory, willing
readers, loose assertions answer such writers' purposes. But Rushworth relates, that after having
been embalmed, the King's remains were delivered
to four of his servants, who removed them to
Windsor, where, in the Dean's hall, they lay in
state, and were then deposited in a royal vault, the
Duke of Richmond, the Marquis of Hertford, and
the Earls of Southampton and Lindsay attending
the funeral; for the expense whereof five hundred
pounds were voted by the Parliament, and the management thereof committed to the Duke of Richmond. This account agrees with the Journals of
the House of Commons. The House, it there appears, on the 8th of February, approved of Windsor
to be the place of interment, and the funeral to
be on the following day, and the above noblemen
and Dr. Juxon to attend the funeral with three
servants a-piece; and left it to the Duke of Richmond to take order for the place of the King's
burial, either in Henry the Eighth's Chapel, or the
choir there; the circumstances and manner of

the interment to be wholly left to the Duke of
Richmond; the committee to provide money for
defraying the charges of the funeral, not exceeding
five hundred pounds; and an order was given, on
the preceding 1st of February, to provide two
chambers to be hung with black for the Duke of
Gloucester.   This account of the attention of the
Parliament to the proper and respectful interment
of the remains of the King, is confirmed by a late
discovery of the place of interment.   It appears
that, in the month of April, 1813, on the day
before the interment of the Duchess of Brunswick,
sister of George III., in the new vault in St.
George's Chapel at Windsor, two ancient coffins
were found, the one of lead, the other of stone;
the leaden coffin was opened in the presence of
His present Majesty (then Prince Regent), and was
found to contain the body of the King in perfect
preservation.   The stone-coffin was also opened,
which, from its inscription, was found to contain
the remains of King Henry VIII., only the scull
and principal limb-bones.   A publication, in the
year 1792, entitled, The Secret History of the
Court and Reign of King Charles the Second,
perhaps of no great authority, attempts to account
for King Charles II. not interring these remains
with all solemnity at Westminster, before the state-
triumph on his own account, by alleging, that after
the strictest search, they could not be found, there
being no mark that might lead to the discovery of

the particular place of interment; all the wainscot, railing, and partitions in the church belonging to Windsor Castle having been broken down by the garrison during the civil wars, and all the monuments defaced before the royal body was conveyed thither by Cromwell's order: that this was the true reason of the solemnity not taking place, but that this not being made public, the omission of such a testimony of reverence for the late King was ascribed to a variety of other causes there assigned. Whether the words " by Cromwell's order" are meant to convey the idea of the King's remains being conveyed to this place of interment by his order, or to the destruction of the wainscot, and other articles in the church by him, does not certainly appear from the mode of expression used by this writer; but nothing can be more clear, than that Cromwell had no individual concern in the interment, nor is it probable, that he had any concern in the destruction of the church, if the fact of such destruction were true, because he never appears to have done any thing of the kind intentionally.

Lord Clarendon, in reference to the circumstances of the interment, describes the alterations and mutilations above mentioned, rendering it impossible to discover where our princes had used to be interred. That, at last, a fellow of the town undertook to tell them the place where, he said, there was a vault in which King Henry VIII. and

Queen Jane Seymour were interred; that as near that place as could conveniently be, they caused the grave to be made. That His Lordship had been thus particular, because the King (Charles II.) had not re-interred his father's remains, which was expected to have been done with great solemnity; and for the omission whereof the King and his ministers had been reflected on with some severity. His Lordship assigns the reason, that after the most diligent search, the place of interment could not be found. This account is not correct in every particular: the vault of Henry VIII. certainly was found, because the King's remains are now discovered in that vault, and not near it, as His Lordship describes. The forementioned order of the Commons rendered it certain, that the place of interment must have been in Henry the Eighth's chapel, or the choir there; and it seems impossible that those who, at the Restoration, searched for it, could have done it with due diligence, or with a very anxious desire to find it; for, by digging over the whole place, they could not have missed it. Whether for any of the reasons that have been surmised, or any others, the King did not wish to show this respect of re-interment to his father's remains, must continue matter of conjecture and uncertainty.

Mr. Hume, in addition to all the above misrepresentations, asserts, from Walker's History of Independency, that the King was placed in a situation

to be disturbed by the erection of the scaffold.
He says, the King slept sound as usual, though
the noise of the workmen employed in framing the
scaffold, and other preparations for his execution,
continually resounded in his ears. The writer of
the Lives of the Regicides implicitly follows him in
the same assertion. This. is a manifest misrepresentation in Mr. Hume·; for Rushworth says expressly, that the sentence was pronounced on Saturday the 27th of January; that the King remained at Whitehall all that day, and the whole
of the following day, Sunday the 28th: that he
was removed to St. James's Palace on Monday the
29th, and that not till that day was the place of
suffering determined on and ordered; consequently
the scaffold could not be begun till after the King's
removal to St. James's, which was probably early;
therefore his repose could not be thus disturbed,
nor his feelings violated by this, as it would have
been, most inhuman proceeding: it is probable he
was thus removed for the very purpose of avoiding
this distressing circumstance. In confirmation of
this removal, he (Rushworth) proceeds to state,
that on the following day, the 30th, the King was
conducted from St. James's to Whitehall, the place
determined on, walking through the Park, guarded
by a regiment of foot, his private guard of partizans,
with some of his gentlemen before and some behind,
bareheaded, and Bishop Juxon next him. And
both Whitelock and Ludlow, and also Lord Cla-

rendon, mention this latter circumstance of the King going from St. James's : so also does Colonel Tomlinson in his evidence on the trial of Colonel Hacker. Sir Philip Warwick says, the King was brought to St. James's on the Saturday noon, which, if correct, increases the proof of the impossibility of his being incommoded by the preparations, which could not, as has been shown, commence till Monday after determining the place of suffering. In either case, the King's nights' repose could not have been thus disturbed. Sir Philip says, the Bishop was not admitted to the King till Sunday evening ; Rushworth expressly says, the Bishop preached before the King in his private lodgings in Whitehall on the Sunday : he, or Sir Philip, must therefore be mistaken in the time of the King's removal, and of his admission to the King: but this is immaterial ; enough has been shown to prove the falsehood of the statement of the alleged inhuman disturbance of the King's repose in his approach to his last moments.

These circumstances, trivial as they may appear, show the small reliance to be placed on the statements of party writers, when misrepresentation best suits their purpose.

Lord Clarendon, at the conclusion of his account of the death of the King, says, that it was most certain, that in that very hour that he was thus wickedly murdered in the sight of the sun, he had as great a share in the hearts and affections of his subjects in general — was as much beloved, esteemed, and longed for by the people in general of the three nations, — as any of his predecessors had ever been. To conclude : — that he was the worthiest gentleman, the best master, the best friend, the best husband, the best father, and the best Christian that the age in which he lived produced: and that if he was not the greatest king, — if he were without some parts and qualities which have made some kings great and happy, — no other prince was ever unhappy, who was possessed of half his virtues and endowments, and so much without any kind of vice.

The King, says Bishop Burnet, showed a calm and composed firmness, which amazed all people; and that so much the more, because it was not natural to him : that it was imputed to a very extraordinary measure of supernatural assistance: that Bishop Juxon did the duty of his function honestly, but with a dry coldness that could not raise the King's thoughts; so that it was owing wholly to somewhat within himself that he went through so many indignities with so much true greatness, without disorder or any sort of affectation. Thus, adds the Bishop, he died greater than he had lived; and showed that which has been often observed of the whole race of the Stuarts, that they bore misfortunes better than prosperity: that his reign, both in peace and war, was a continual series of errors; so that it does not appear that he had a true judgment of things : that he was out of measure set on following his humour, but unreasonably feeble to those whom he trusted, chiefly to the Queen : that he had too high a notion of the regal power, and thought that every opposition to it was rebellion : that he minded little things too much, and was more concerned in drawing a paper than in fighting a battle : that he had a firm aversion to popery, but was much inclined to a middle way between Protestants and Papists, by which he lost the one without gaining the other.   In another place the Bishop says, he (the King) loved high and rough methods, but had neither the skill to conduct them, nor the height of genius to manage them : that he hated all that offered prudent and moderate counsels, which he thought flowed from a meanness of spirit and a care to preserve themselves by sacrificing his authority, or from republican principles ; and that even when he saw it was necessary to follow such advices, he hated those that gave them.

CHAPTER XIII.

CONSIDERATION OF THE PROOFS OF CROMWELL'S RELUCT-
ANCE TO BRING THE KING TO TRIAL. — OBSERVATIONS
UPON THE EVIDENCE UPON THE TRIAL OF THE KING'S
JUDGES BROUGHT FORWARD TO. PROVE THE CONTRARY.
— UPON LORD CLARENDON'S ACCOUNT OF CROMWELL'S
SUPPOSED CRUELTIES IN HIS CAPTURE OF DROGHEDA
(TREDAGH) BY STORM. — DEFENCE OF HIS CONDUCT IN
AND AFTER THE BATTLE OF WORCESTER. — DEFENCE OF
IRETON. — OBSERVATIONS UPON WHITELOCK'S ACCOUNT
OF MEETING TO CONSIDER OF A SETTLEMENT OF THE
NATION. — ALSO, OF CONVERSATION BETWEEN CROMWELL
AND HIMSELF, WHEREIN CROMWELL PROPOSES THE QUES-
TION, " WHAT, IF A MAN SHOULD TAKE UPON HIMSELF
TO BE A KING ?" — CONSIDERATION OF THE STATE OF
THE PARTIES, AND OF THE PUBLIC AFFAIRS OF THE
NATION AFTER THE CONCLUSION OF THE WAR BY THE
SURRENDER OF OXFORD AND OF OTHER THE KING'S
REMAINING GARRISONS, THE UNSUCCESSFUL TERMIN-
ATION OF THE TREATY OF NEWPORT, AND THE DEATH OF
THE KING, TO THE DEATH OF CROMWELL.

CROMWELL certainly very reluctantly concurred in
the measure of the trial of the King. His sincerity in the negotiation for his restoration upon
moderate terms, and his assistance in favouring the
King's escape from Hampton-court, and placing
him in a state of personal freedom to quit the
kingdom, cannot reasonably be doubted. The insincerity he discovered in the King in the treaty,

and the threats of the agitators, who appear to
have comprehended the greatest part of the army,
alarmed him, and satisfied him that he could be of
no further service to the King than to facilitate
his escape ; and it was the King's own fault that
he did not avail himself of the opportunity afforded
him.

Dr. Harris, in his anxiety to place Cromwell at
the bottom of all these proceedings of bringing the
King to a trial, takes upon himself to say, that
Cromwell had a principal hand in all these transactions ; and, in proof of his assertion, quotes
from Walker's History of Independency the following passage : — " When it was first moved in
the House of Commons to proceed capitally against
the King, Cromwell stood up and told them, that
if any man moved this upon design, he should
think him the greatest traitor in the world ; but
since Providence and necessity had cast them upon
it, he should pray God to bless their counsels,
though he were not provided on the sudden to
give them counsel." This speech does not appear
in Rushworth or Lord Clarendon, or in Ludlow,
Whitelock, or Mrs. Hutchinson ; and its authenticity is not to be relied on. But, supposing
Cromwell really to have thus said, it, instead of
supporting the Doctor's opinions, surely proves the
truth of what has been before said, — that the determination to bring the King to a trial did not
originate with Cromwell, and that he even then

had not made up his mind to it, or formed a decided opinion upon the measure : and Neal, in his History of the Puritans, gives the same passage from Dugdale, as a proof of Cromwell's indetermination, introducing it with these words :—"This unheard-of motion met with some opposition even in that packed assembly ; Oliver Cromwell was in doubt, and said, if any man, &c." These passages are probably taken the one from the other, and prove nothing in support of their veracity. He (Dr. Harris) allows that Bishop Burnet says, that Ireton was the person that drove it on ; for that Cromwell was all the while in some suspense about it : he (Burnet) adds, that Ireton had the principles and the temper of a Cassius in him ; he stuck at nothing that might have turned England to a commonwealth. Still, notwithstanding all this evidence in confutation of his assertion, he (Dr. Harris) persists in it : accordingly, he next produces the account the Bishop gives, communicated to him by Lieutenant-general Drummond, afterwards Lord Strathallan : the Bishop says, that the General served on the King's side, but had many friends amongst those who were for the covenant ; that the King's affairs being then ruined, he was recommended to Cromwell, who was then in treaty with the Spanish ambassador, respecting some regiments to be levied and sent over from Scotland to Flanders : that he happened to be with Cromwell when the commissioners, sent from Scotland to protest against the putting the King to death, came to argue the matter with him: that Cromwell bid the General stay and hear their conference : that they began in a heavy, languid style to lay indeed great loads upon the King, but that they still insisted on that clause in the covenant, by which they swore they would be faithful in the preservation of His Majesty's person; showing upon what terms Scotland, as well as the two Houses, had engaged in the war, and what solemn declarations of their zeal and duty to the King they had all along published, which would now appear to the scandal and reproach of the Christian name, to have been false pretences, if, when the King was in their power, they should proceed to extremities : that Cromwell thereupon entered into a long discourse of the nature of the regal power, according to the principles of Mariana and Buchanan : he thought a breach of trust ought to be punished more than any other crime whatsoever : he said, as to their covenant, they swore to the preservation of the King's person in defence of the true religion ; if, then, it appeared that the settlement of the true religion was obstructed by the King, so that they could not come at it but by putting him out of the way, then their oath could not bind them to the preserving him any longer: that their covenant did bind them to bring all malignants, incendiaries, and enemies to the cause to condign punishment ; and was not this to be executed impartially ? what were all those on whom public justice had been

done, especially those who suffered for joining
Montrose, but small offenders, acting by commission from the King, who was therefore the
principal, and so most guilty? The Bishop adds,
that Drummond said, Cromwell had plainly the
better of them at their own weapons, and upon
their own principles. The Bishop does not give
any date to this account; but this interview with
the Scots commissioners being before the King's
death, the above particulars must have been related more than twelve years afterwards, after the
Restoration in 1660; and having been given from
memory, its accuracy cannot be entirely relied on.
Nevertheless the substance may be true, and probably is so, but it does not support Dr. Harris's
assertion, that these transactions originated with
Cromwell, and that he had a principal hand
in them; it only proves that he, at the time of
the above interview, had determined upon the
part he should take in the King's trial.

Dr. Harris then proceeds with his proofs: he
says, from a publication called " The Exact and
Perfect Narrative of the Trial of the Regicides,"
that on the 21st January, 1648, Hugh Peters
preaching at Whitehall upon the passage, " Bind
your kings with chains, and your nobles in fetters
of iron," and talking in his bold manner concerning the King's being liable to the law, as well as
other men, Cromwell was observed to laugh.
From the same authority he says, — and when, on

the motion of Mr. Downes, on the last day of the
trial, the Court adjourned into the Court of Wards,
and was pressed in the most pathetic terms by him
to give the King liberty to make some proposition
to the Parliament for the settlement of the kingdom, as His Majesty had in court just before desired; that after Mr. Downes had urged this,
Cromwell did answer with a great deal of storm:
that he told the President, that now he saw what
great reason the gentlemen had to put such great
trouble upon them, saith he, Sure he doth not know
that he hath to do with the hardest-hearted man
that lives upon the earth : that however it was not
fit that the Court should be hindered from their
duty by one peevish man : that the bottom was
known, that he (meaning Downes) would fain save
his old master, and desired the Court would, without any more ado, go and do their duty. From
the same authority, he describes Mr. Wayte, another of the King's judges, as saying, that Cromwell laughed and jeered and smiled in the Court of
Wards on this occasion : that he (Wayte) being
told by the Lord Grey that the King would not die,
the next day he went to the House; they were
labouring to get hands for his execution, at the
door : I, says he, refused, and went into the House:
saith Cromwell, " Those that are gone in shall
set their hands : I will have their hands now."
He (Dr. Harris) proceeds, — Colonel Ingoldesby
was a relation of Cromwell, and named a judge ;

but disliking the action, he always absented himself; but that the day after the sentence was pronounced, having occasion to go to the Painted
Chamber, he saw Cromwell and the rest of those
who had sat upon the King, and were then, as he
found afterwards, assembled to sign the warrant
for the King's death : that as soon as Cromwell's
eyes were upon him, he ran to him, and taking
him by the hand, drew him by force to the table,
and said, though he had escaped him all the while
before, he should now sign that paper as well as
they; which he, seeing what it was, refused with
great passion, saying, he knew nothing of the
business, and offered to go away; but that Cromwell and others held him by violence; and Cromwell, with a loud laughter, taking his hand in his,
and putting the pen between his fingers with his
own hand, writ Richard Ingoldesby, he making all
the resistance he could. The same writer proceeds, — that Colonel Huncks (who was a witness
against Colonel Axtell) declared, at his (Axtell's)
trial, that a little before the King's execution he
was in Ireton's bed-chamber, where Ireton and
Harrison were in bed together; there was Cromwell, Colonel Hacker, Lieutenant-colonel Phayer,
Axtell, and himself, standing at the door : that the
warrant for the execution was there produced, and
Mr. Hacker was reading it, but Cromwell addressed himself to him (Huncks), commanding him,
by virtue of that warrant, to draw up an order for

the executioner. " I refused it," adds he ; " and upon refusing it, there happened some cross passages ; Cromwell would have no delay : there was a little table that stood by the door, and pen, ink, and paper being there, Cromwell stepped and writ ; (I conceive he wrote that which he would have had me to write;) as soon as he had done writing, he gives the pen over to Hacker ; Hacker, he stoops and did write, (I cannot say what he writ ;) away goes Cromwell, and then Axtell ; we all went out ; afterwards they went into another room; immediately the King came out, and was murdered." Then follows, in the same writer (Dr. Harris), the following relation, which, says he, (if it had not been contrary to Huncks's account), is of too doubtful an authority to be absolutely relied on, though in a work of this nature it cannot well be omitted. This relation appears to be taken from Perinchief's Life of Charles the First. It is as follows : — " While these things were acting, (the fitting the scaffold for the King's execution,) the Lord Fairfax, who had always forborne any public appearance in the practices of this murder, had taken up (as is credibly reported) some resolutions (either in abhorrency of the crime, or by the solicitations of others,) with his own regiment, though none else should follow him, to hinder the execution : that this being suspected or known, Cromwell, Ireton, and Harrison, coming to him, after their usual way of deceiving, endeavoured to persuade him that the Lord had rejected the King, and with such-like language as they knew had formerly prevailed upon him, concealing that they had, that very morning, signed the warrant for the assassination : they also desired him with them to seek the Lord by prayer, that they might know his mind in the thing; which he assenting to, Harrison was appointed for the duty, and by compact to draw out his prophane and blasphemous discourse to God in such a length as might give time for the execution, which they privately sent their instrument to hasten; of which, when they had notice that it was passed, they rose up, and persuaded the General that it was a full return of prayer; and God having so manifested his pleasure, they were to acquiesce in it. These passages," adds this writer (Dr. Harris), " are, I think, sufficient to show the part Cromwell had in this affair; though," says he, " after all, Burnet asserts, that Ireton was the person that drove it on; for that Cromwell was all the while in some suspense about it."

It is conceived that enough has been already said to prove, that the seclusion of the members, and the subsequent determination to bring the King to trial, did not originate with, or was pressed forward by Cromwell; and that he was, on the contrary, long undetermined. What induced him finally to concur with those who brought it forward, whether his conviction of the necessity of the measure, aided by, perhaps, some degree of personal apprehension from the army, or from what other cause, does not now appear.   The above further circumstances, brought forward by Dr. Harris in support of his persisted-in assertion of Cromwell having a principal hand in these transactions, must be considered.

The preceding relations respecting Peters, Downs, and Wayte, are from their respective trials, and from the trial of Colonel Axtel; and are to be found in the publication of the State Trials of those times.

The first, Cromwell's alleged laughing during Hugh Peters's sermon ; — this is considered good evidence of his approval of the measure : but it is, in the first place, hardly to be credited that such a trivial circumstance, if it did really happen, should be remembered twelve years afterwards : then, even supposing Cromwell to have then approved the measure, he must have considered it a grave and awful one, and not the subject of laughter : if he really smiled, it could be only at some of those quaint things that such an eccentric man as Peters was likely to say in the course of his sermon, or it might arise from some thought that might cross his own mind, not connected with the sermon : and then, admitting the truth of this laughter or smile, the particular moment is not, nor could be ascertained, to justify the application thereof to the particular parts of the sermon that immediately related to the King's then situation, and so in proof of Cromwell's approbation of the transaction: but any the most trifling circumstance, even a turn of his countenance, is to receive a construction favourable to the great object of these party writers, — the crimination of Cromwell. Then, upon what evidence rests the fact, that Peters did preach that sermon, or, if he did, that Cromwell was present at it: it rests wholly upon the credit of witnesses called to prove it, who relate, with incredible minuteness, the passages of sermons that had been preached more than twelve years before: and this is the more extraordinary, as they appear to be persons of ordinary conditions, and probably illiterate; also, to have been very willing and forward, and doubtless instructed and well-tutored witnesses: and Peters, at his trial, positively denies that he preached those things.

Downes, in his defence, endeavoured to convince the Court that he was an advocate for the King, but that he was violently over-ruled and intimidated by Cromwell. He describes himself as starting up, upon the clerk beginning to read the sentence, and declaring aloud his dissatisfaction, and desiring the adjournment of the Court to hear him: that the President declaring, that if any one of the Court were unsatisfied, the Court must adjourn: it accordingly did adjourn into the inner Court of Wards; and that he was there called upon by Cromwell to account for his putting the Court to this trouble and disturbance : that he thereupon declared he desired not the King's death, but his life ; and that the nation might be settled in peace : he then proceeded to state his reasonings with the Court thereon.   Then follows, in the State Trials, the passage cited by Harris, containing Cromwell's reply.   Then he (Downes) adds, he went into the Speaker's chamber, where he eased his heart with tears.   He concludes, saying, that he had an unhappy memory, and that he had slipped many things.   He seems to have remembered, at this distance of twelve years, very minutely, enough for his purpose, but to have forgotten a very material circumstance, his signing and sealing the warrant for the King's execution.   The Court reminding him of this circumstance, he said he did not know how to reconcile that with what he had before said ; he was totally at a loss, but he refers it to the violence of the soldiers, not a man daring either to disown or speak against them ; that he was threatened with his very life by one that had received his reward.   He was condemned, but his sentence was remitted, and he died in prison.   Not the least reliance can be had upon this account ; the whole of it must be a fabrication to save his own life : he brings forward no evidence to prove any part of it, or that he had at any time afterwards, during the twelve years that had since elapsed, expressed his contrition, or given this account to any one.

Wayte's account is equally improbable.   In addition to the part of his defence referring to the force he alledges to have been put upon him by Cromwell, he says, he came to London the day before the sentence was given; that he went to the House, (thought nothing,) some were sent to the Tower, and he was sent for to the House, and his name was in the act, unknown to him: that a note was sent to him in Lord Grey's name, that he would speak to him; that he went to him, and asked him what His Lordship would do with him; that His Lordship said he did not send for him, and that Cromwell and Ireton laid hold on him, saying, they sent for him, that he was one of the High Court; No, said he, not he, his judgment was against it: that they took him to the court. He adds, that when the King desired to speak with his Parliament, he (Wayte) rising up, one told him he must not be heard, for that the President was to give judgment, and that there was an order that none speak in court: that Mr. Downes moved, and the court was adjourned, and he was glad he got out: that Cromwell laughed and smiled, and jeered in the Court of Wards.

Instead of coming to town so late as only the day before the sentence was given, Mr. Noble says, he sat on the trial on the 25th, 26th, and 27th of January, in the Painted Chamber, and on the last of these days in Westminster Hall, when sentence was pronounced, and that he signed and sealed the warrant for the execution of the King; and so it appears, in the plate of that warrant published by the Antiquarian Society: these accounts are contradictory, and render the rest of them quite incredible.

Colonel Ingoldesby's account is perfectly ridiculous, and wholly unworthy of credit. Mr. Noble justly observes, that in describing the force he alleges to have been used upon him, in procuring his signature to the warrant, he forgot to say that his seal was also forced from him and used; — the hand-writing of his name in the above published plate-impression is steadily written, but could not have been so written had the violence he describes been really used. This falsehood, however, aided by his seizure of General Lambert shortly before and preparatory to the Restoration, probably saved him.

Huncks's story has the same appearance of inconsistency and falsehood: the warrant directed to Colonel Hacker himself, and Lieutenant-colonel Phayer, was a sufficient authority, for those to whom it was addressed, to act upon. This meeting is stated to have been immediately previous to the execution of the sentence: that Cromwell should have been present at such a meeting is quite improbable, and if any such order should have been thought necessary, it is not likely that it should have been deferred to the last moment of its being carried into execution. The whole is, upon the face of it, a gross falsehood, and Axtell in the most solemn manner denies the whole. Huncks was pardoned for the purpose of making him an evidence : and a most gross one must be the story of the prevention of Fairfax, by the contrivance of Cromwell, Ireton, and Harrison, from attempting the rescue of the King, Mr. Noble justly observes : so foolish a thing could not gain credit; for that he not only assisted in bringing the King to his mock trial and judgment, but knew that the warrant was signed; knew the hour appointed to put His Majesty to death, and sent the guard that was to see it done : and such was the fact. It is most extraordinary that such a writer as Mr. Hume should venture to state this story as a truth, without seeming to have examined into the probability of it, or expressing the least doubt of its authenticity. He gives it from Herbert, introducing it as a fresh instance of Cromwell's and his party's hypocrisy. It is completely falsified by the preceding accounts of Fairfax's conduct in this business; — he did every thing but sit upon the King's trial. He does not himself hint at any deception having been practised upon him.

But this story, and all the others of the like nature, are thrown out for the chance of their finding credit with those for whom they are intended; and they have had their designed effect; in stigmatising and transmitting to posterity Cromwell, and those who acted with him, or against the King, as unprincipled religious hypocrites, not to be trusted in any thing they said or did.

In further contradiction of all this supposed
force upon these persons, Mrs. Hutchinson says,
"Some of the King's judges, afterwards, to excuse,
belied themselves, and said they were under the
awe of the army, and over-persuaded by Cromwell,
and the like; but it is certain that all men herein
were left to their free liberty of acting; neither
persuaded nor compelled; and that as there were
some nominated to the commission who never sat,
and others who sat at first, but durst not hold on,
so all the rest might have declined it if they would;
when it is apparent they should have suffered
nothing by so doing: for those who then declined,
were afterwards, when they offered themselves,
received in again, and had places of more trust and
benefit than those who run the utmost hazard,
which they deserved not; for I know upon certain
knowledge that many, yea the most of them, re-
treated not for conscience, but for fear and worldly
prudence, foreseeing that the insolency of the army
might grow to that height as to ruin the cause and
reduce the kingdom into the hands of the enemy;
and then, those who had been most courageous in
their country's cause should be given up as victims."
Mrs. Hutchinson, in another part of this her work,
says, "That when it came to Ingoldesby's turn to
speak for himself in the Parliament that brought in
the King, he, with many tears, professed his repentance for that murder, and told a false tale how
Cromwell held his hand and forced him to sub-

scribe the sentence, and made a most whining re-
cantation." In another place, mentioning Colonel
Hutchinson's attendance upon the Attorney-general,
and his pressing the Colonel to own some of the
hands to the warrant, and to impart some circumstances of the sealing, because himself (the Colonel)
was present: he (the Colonel) answered, that in a
business transacted so many years ago, wherein
life was concerned, he durst not bear a testimony,
having been at that time so little an observer that
he could not remember the least tittle of that most
eminent circumstance of Cromwell's forcing Colonel Ingoldesby to set to his unwilling hand;
which, if his life had depended on that circumstance, he could not have affirmed. "And then,
Sir," said he, "if I have lost so great a thing as
that, it cannot be expected less eminent passages
remain with me." Mrs. Hutchinson appears to
consider this as meant sarcastically, to convey to the
Attorney-general his disbelief of the story, having
heard that Colonel Ingoldesby had put him upon
sending for the Colonel (Hutchinson), being in
distress for witnesses to some particular points.
Mr. Noble remarks, at the conclusion of his Life
of Ingoldesby, that it was singular that his regiment sent up to Parliament, previous to the King's
trial, a petition in the most determined language
against the Sovereign; so well had he tutored
them; but, he adds, in such times as these were, it
was laudable to purchase the most obnoxious

characters. The Journals of the House of Commons expressly state, that on the 80th October preceding the King's death, a petition was presented to the House by Colonel Ingoldesby's regiment, praying for justice upon the principal invaders of the liberties of the kingdom, naming the King and his party. Ingoldesby could not be a stranger to this petition, and must be considered a party to it. Ludlow says, that on account of his (Ingoldesby's) service in the suppression of the party that had followed General Lambert, he was not excepted from the act of indemnity. And it is certain that Ingoldesby continued in Cromwell's confidence; for we find him employed by him to watch and inform him of the proceedings of the Long Parliament, and his report determined Cromwell upon its immediate dissolution. These circumstances are alone sufficient to destroy the credibility of Ingoldesby's story of the force put upon him by Cromwell. It also does not appear that Ingoldesby ever, until the Restoration, mentioned to any one this supposed force, or his contrition for having signed the warrant; also acting with the subsequent ruling powers, many of them the causers and promoters of that transaction.

In Mr. Henry Marten's trial, a former servant of his describes himself as following him into the Painted Chamber, where the King's judges were signing the warrant, where he saw Cromwell mark Marten with the pen in the face, and Marten do the like to him. In the same trial, Sir Purbeck Temple describes himself as concealing himself in a hole in the wall, under the hangings of the room where the council was to meet for the purpose of determining the manner in which the King was to be tried: and that upon the conclusion of their usual prayer, there came news that the King was landed at Sir Robert Cotton's stairs; whereupon Cromwell ran to a window, looking on the King as he came up the garden; he returned as white as the wall: that, returning to the Board, he spoke to Bradshaw and Sir William Mildmay, how they and Sir William Brereton had concluded on such a business: that then turning to the Board, he said thus;—"My masters, he is come, he is come; and now we are doing that great work that the nation will be full of; therefore I desire you to let us resolve here, what answer we shall give the King when he comes before us: for the first question that he will ask us will be, by what authority and commission we do try him?" to which none answered presently: that then, after a little space, Henry Marten rose up, and said, "In the name of the Commons and Parliament assembled, and all the good people of England;" which none contradicted; so all rose up: and then adds this witness, "I saw every officer, that had waited in the room, sent out by Cromwell to call away my Lord Such-a-one, (whose name I have forgot,) who was in the Court of Wards' chamber, that he should send away the instrument, which came not; and so they adjourned themselves to Westminster Hall, going to the Court of Wards themselves as they went thither: and that, when they came to the court in Westminster Hall, he heard the King ask them the very same question that Cromwell had said to them. This witness accounts for this his hazardous curiosity, by acquainting the Court, that some persons of honour, servants to the King, had proposed to him, to engage with them to attempt the King's escape, to which nothing could so much tend as to endeavour to discover some part of their counsels; it having been resolved by Cromwell to have the King tried at the High Court of Justice the next day, desiring him (the witness), if possible, to be there to discover their counsels, whereby the King might have notice, and those that were to attempt his escape.

The circumstance of a servant (in the case of Mr. Marten) appearing to swear against his master much lessens the credit to his testimony, and which, not applying to the acts for which he was under trial, could only be brought forward for the purpose of prejudicing the minds of the jury against him. If exactly true, as represented, it would certainly be an act of gross levity, in both Cromwell and Marten, upon so solemn an occasion. It however does appear that upon one of the counsel for the prosecution saying, " We shall prove against the prisoner at the bar (because he would wipe off malice) he did this (his signing and sealing the warrant) very merrily and in great sport." Marten replied, " That does not imply malice." So far it appears that he did not deny the charge; but he does not, to excuse himself, charge Cromwell with the first marking him. Mr. Noble describes Marten to be a gay, licentious, debauched, abandoned man; and he might possibly wantonly and foolishly do this, and the other might so far forget himself at the moment as to return it; but both these stories bear strong marks of improbability, and of fabrication to answer a present purpose. The servant, probably a dismissed one, brought forward to accuse a, most likely, once kind master, a man not unlikely to be a debauched immoral character like himself; in a case that touched his life, minutely relating a trifling circumstance of more than twelve years' standing, happening in a place into which it is quite unlikely that a servant should be permitted to come. Sir Purbeck Temple's evidence, if true, certainly proves Marten's forwardness in this affair. His story, however, has much the appearance of improbability; his concealment is not credible; he could have no valuable object in this listening; no reason to expect to hear any thing at the very moment of the King's coming that could possibly assist the King's escape; nor is it conceivable that these principal members of the court should remain undetermined to this last moment on this supposed question of the King; their preparations for the trial show their expectation of his denial of the court's jurisdiction, and consequently their preparedness of the answer to that objection or question. But it appears also, in these preparatory proceedings, that they not only were aware of this objection, but that they had provided for the King's waver of it, and for his pleading to the charge, by proceeding to the examination of witnesses and the arrangement of the evidence in proof of the King's hostilities, &c. The circumstance of the presence in the room of consultation of the officers not members of the court, is another incredible circumstance. Sir Purbeck also appears to have done nothing towards the King's escape in consequence of what he then heard; nor does he account for the inactivity of himself and his friends in not making the attempt. The whole of his evidence has all the appearance of a fabrication of a very willing witness, making his court to the then ruling powers by blackening Cromwell's memory without fear of contradiction. But surely it goes very far to invalidate the servant's testimony respecting Cromwell; for if any part of this evidence of Sir Purbeck is to be credited, the whole of it must be taken as true; and to afford every reason to believe the gravity, instead of the levity, of his behaviour upon the whole of this solemn occasion; his change of countenance upon the King's approach, his hasty repetition of the words,

" He is come ;" his inability to advise the proper
answer to the King's supposed question ; also his
question to Bradshaw and Mildmay, how they had
concluded on such a business ; — these surely must
be deemed undeniable proofs of the solemn and
deep impression the whole of this transaction had
made upon his mind, and that some circumstances,
as has been said, had hurried or drawn him into
the measure.

Placed, as we of these happy times are, at so
great a distance from the scene of these troubles
and commotions, it is next to impossible for us to
form a correct judgment of the difficulties, and of
the hurry and confusion that must have attended
those great and important transactions ; and this
consideration alone should at least abate the harsh
and severe censures of subsequent times of the
actors therein, and their measures and motives ;
but the royalist historians, the one following the
other, condemn indiscriminately, and without
mercy or examination.

At the Restoration, every one endeavoured to
make his peace with the ruling powers, and found
the sincerity of their repentance to be best proved
by degrading the characters of those with whom
many of them had once acted ; and every idle tale
to their prejudice, however insignificant or improbable, was told with confidence and without
fear of contradiction, and received with avidity.
Hence the many ill-natured and ill-founded stories

that have reached our times, and which are now, without examination, received as settled truths.

Lord Clarendon describes the indifference of the neighbouring nations to the King's death : that there was scarce a murmur amongst any of them at it : that they made haste and sent over, that they might get shares in the spoils of a murdered monarch ; that Cardinal Mazarin, who, in the infancy of the French King, managed that sceptre, had long adored the conduct of Cromwell, and sought his friendship by a lower and viler application than was suitable to the purple of a cardinal, sent now to be admitted as a merchant to traffic in the purchase of the rich goods and jewels of the rifled crown, of which he purchased the rich beds, hangings, and carpets, which furnished his palace at Paris; and that so did the King of Spain, Christina Queen of Sweden, and other sovereigns : that in this manner did the neighbour-princes join to assist Cromwell with very great sums of money, whereby he was enabled to prosecute and finish his wicked victory over what yet remained unconquered, and to extinguish monarchy in this renowned kingdom ; whilst they enriched and adorned themselves with the ruins and spoils of the surviving heir, without applying any part thereof to his relief, in the greatest necessities which ever king was subject to : and that, adds His Lordship, which was stranger than all this, since most men, by recovering their fortunes, used to recover most of what they were before robbed of, many who joined in the robbery pretending that they took care to preserve it for their true owner; not one of all these princes ever restored any of their unlawful purchases to the King after his blessed restoration.

No other writer than His Lordship speaks of this disposition of the King's goods. Whitelock expressly states, that commissioners were appointed to inventory them, and those of the Queen and Prince, and apprise them for the use of the public: and that an act was passed to satisfy well-affected persons to whom they were indebted before the wars, out of the produce; only the first 30,000*l.* to be for the use of the navy: and the council of state to keep such of them as they should think fit, for the use of the commonwealth: and a subsequent order was made for preserving the library, medals, and statues, at St. James's. All which appears in the Journals of the House of Commons; and is sufficient evidence of the falsehood of the charge of Cromwell's deriving any benefit from the sale of these goods.

In reference to Lord Clarendon's observations upon Lord Capel's sentence, to the prejudice of Cromwell, the trial and sentence of His Lordship and the other prisoners, seem to have been a harsh construction of the Colchester articles of capitulation, where life was to be affected; but, it should be remembered, that Cromwell had no concern in this siege, or capitulation, or construction; nor does he appear to have been of the High Court of Justice. The speech attributed to him by Lord Clarendon does not appear in any other contemporary writers; nor does Ireton's any where else appear. The speech of Cromwell does not suit his generally allowed disposition to mercy : he is not represented in this speech as examining the justice of the sentence, but as advising its execution upon political motives, the prevention of his doing future mischief to the Parliament cause : this was very unlikely to be Cromwell's view of the question. Sir Philip Warwick alone, in his great anxiety to criminate Cromwell, describes him as (previously to his going to Ireland) giving directions for severely proceeding against Lord Capel and all others who had taken part with the late King. But this cannot be true of Lord Capel, who was Lord Fairfax's prisoner, and sent by him to the High Court of Justice for trial, under His Lordship's (Lord Fairfax) own construction of the capitulation; and Duke Hamilton was tried under very different circumstances.

His Lordship, in his account of his taking of Drogheda (or Tredagh) by storm, says, that not only the garrison, but all the citizens that were Irishmen, and women and children, were put to the sword, an that the army, upon entering the town, executed all manner of cruelty.

The letter, informing of this transaction, is given

by Whitelock *verbatim*, and is dated the 16th September (1649) ; the letter given by Dr. Harris is dated the 17th of the same month. If they be the same letters, they do not quite agree. Dr. Harris appears to give his letter from the Parliamentary history : he says, that Cromwell owns that he forbid to spare any that were in arms in the town, and that he thinks they put to the sword about two thousand men the first night they entered. This order does not appear in the letter given by Whitelock ; and the difference is so far important, that he appears, in Dr. Harris's letter, to have given the order not to spare, before he had summoned them to surrender; whereas, on the contrary, he had summoned them to surrender the day before and they had refused, and then quarter was refused. His Lordship, to aggravate the charge, says, that men not in arms, and women and children, were put to the sword ; but it is evident, from both letters, that only the garrison suffered. Cromwell evidently, in the letter given by Whitelock, regrets the necessity of the measure, but hopes it would save the future effusion of blood; and it appears to have had this effect, in the speedy reduction (in less than a year, Sir Philip Warwick observes,) of the rest of the country. Dr. Harris adds, as part of his quoted letter, that Cromwell expresses himself persuaded that it was a righteous judgment of God, upon those barbarous wretches who had imbrued their hands in so much innocent blood, and that it would tend to prevent the effusion of blood for the future; which, he adds, are the satisfactory grounds to such actions, which otherwise could not but work remorse and regret. This was saying enough in such a case.

In the Journals of the Commons, 2d October (1649), the House direct, that in the letter of thanks to be sent to the Lord-lieutenant of Ireland, and to be communicated to the officers there, the House's approbation is to be expressed of the execution done at Drogheda, as an act both of justice to them and mercy to others, who may be warned by it : and by a subsequent letter of 31st of January, Cromwell informs the House that several garrisons had surrendered in Munster, without blood or striking a stroke.

Ludlow says, that commissioners were appointed by Cromwell to take care of the goods that were found in the towns belonging to the rebels, that they might be improved to the best advantage of the public.

Respecting the appointment of the command of the army going against Scotland, Mrs. Hutchinson, who, it will be remembered, was no friend of Cromwell, referring to the General's (Fairfax) refusal to go, describing Scotland as having declared open war against the Parliament, says, that when they (the English army) were just marching out, the General, persuaded by his wife and her chaplain, threw up his commission at such a time, when it

could not have been done more spitefully and ruin-
ously· to the whole Parliament interest. That
Colonel Hutchinson and other Parliament men,
hearing of his intentions the night before, and
knowing that he would thus level the way to
Cromwell's ambitious designs, went to him, and
laboured to dissuade him ; which they had effected,
but that the presbyterian ministers wrought with
him to do it : that he expressed, that he believed
that God had laid him aside, as not being worthy
of more, nor of that glory which was already given
him.   To speak the truth of Cromwell, adds Mrs.
Hutchinson, whereas many said he undermined
Fairfax, it was false ; for, that in Colonel Hutchinson's presence, he most effectually importuned
him to keep his commission, lest it should discou-
rage the army and the people in that juncture of
time ; but could by no means prevail, although he
laboured it almost all the night with most earnest
endeavours : but that this great man (Fairfax)
was then as immoveable by his friends, as pertina-
cious in obeying his wife ; whereby he then died
to all his former glory, and became the monument
of his own name, which every day wore out. He
concludes, when his commission was given up,
Cromwell was made General, and new commissions
taken out by all the officers from him.

   Ludlow, referring to this transaction, says, he
laboured to persuade him (the General) of the
reasonableness and justice of our resolution to

march into Scotland, mentioning the several reasons that were urged to induce him to revoke his
determination. Finding him resolved, he says,
that Cromwell pressed, that notwithstanding the
General's unwillingness to command upon this
occasion, he might yet be continued General of the
army; professing, for himself, that he would rather
choose to serve under him in this post, than to
command the greatest army in Europe. He
(Ludlow) adds, but the council of state not approving that advice, appointed a committee of
themselves to confer further with the General in
order to his satisfaction. This committee, says he,
was appointed upon the motion of the Lieutenant-
general, who acted his part so to the life, that he
really thought him in earnest, which obliged him
(Ludlow) to step to him as he was withdrawing
with the rest of the committee out of the council-
chamber, and to desire him, that he would not
in compliment and humility obstruct the service
of the nation by his refusal : but, he adds, the
consequence made it sufficiently evident that he
had no such intention.

Nothing is unfavourable to Cromwell in all this
business. Mrs. Hutchinson is decidedly in favour
of his sincerity; Ludlow founds his opinion of his
insincerity only upon his acceptance of the commission upon the General's declining the service.
Cromwell's enemies wished it to be understood
that he never meant what he said. It is impos-

sible, in this instance, to determine what were his real wishes. The undertaking was hazardous, and unfavourably thought of by the presbyterian party attached to the Scots, by whom he must be sure that every obstacle would be thrown in his way, and the worst construction be put upon his conduct, whether successful or otherwise; and, if unsuccessful, he might lose the military reputation he had then acquired, and become the object of his enemies' vengeance: he might not therefore wish, under all these circumstances, to take upon himself the conduct of this important concern; his acceptance of the commission was no proof of his desire to succeed the General; he must feel it to be his duty so to do; and he must know he was the most fit person for the undertaking. Ludlow himself states, in the preceding passage, that he (Ludlow) pressed his acceptance for the service of the nation. He adds, that the success of this undertaking became very doubtful; for that the English army, through hard duty, scarcity of provisions, and the rigour of the season, became very sickly and diminished daily, obliging them to draw off to receive supplies from their shipping, which could not come nearer to them than Dunbar, distant from Edinburgh about twenty miles: that the Scots army followed them close to Dunbar, where, having shipped their heavy baggage and sick men, they designed to return to England: but that the Scots army had possessed themselves of all the passes

with 30,000 horse and foot, and the English army
was reduced to 10,000 at the most: that, therefore, there was no alternative but to yield themselves
prisoners, or to fight upon these unequal terms.
Under these disadvantages Cromwell, there can
be little doubt, reluctantly took the command; and
the battle of Dunbar was fought; and, had the
Scots army acted as they ought to have done in their
advantageous position, and with their great superiority of force, and as Cromwell expected they would
do, he and his army must have been destroyed.
Dr. Harris takes upon himself to say, that Cromwell urged him (Fairfax) to continue his command
with great vehemence, but in vain; and that being
sure that he was immoveably fixed in his determination, pressed him and the Parliament to continue him, with all that dexterity and dissimulation
I have elsewhere mentioned.   This is mere assertion, and unsupported by the preceding statements
of this transaction; but Cromwell's supposed
hypocrisy and dissimulation are this writer's
favourite theme.

  Ludlow, speaking of the battle of Worcester,
says, Cromwell called it the crowning victory; and
that he took upon him a more stately behavour, and
chose new friends; neither, adds he, must it be
omitted, that instead of acknowledging the services of those who came from all parts to assist
against the common enemy, though he knew they
had deserved as much honour as himself and the

standing army, he frowned upon them, and the very next day after the fight dismissed and sent them home, well knowing that a useful and expe‑rienced militia was more likely to obstruct than to second him in his ambitious designs. This is ill‑natured and illiberal. Whitelock simply says, the militia forces behaved themselves gallantly; five thousand, out of Norfolk and Suffolk, came in cheerfully the same night of the fight; the Lord General dismissed them all home. He (White‑lock) makes no comment upon this dismissal. Cromwell would not, probably, detain them from their homes when their service was no longer necessary. Ludlow, in the same ill-humoured, probably envious, strain, adds, that many members of Parliament, attended by the city, and great numbers of perons of all orders and conditions, went some miles out of the town to meet him, which, says he, tended not a little to heighten the spirit of this haughty gentleman. Lord Clarendon says, as this victory cost the enemy little blood, so, after it, there was not much cruelty used to the prisoners who were taken upon the spot; but that very many of those who ran away were every day knocked on the head by the country people, and used with barbarity. That towards the King's menial servants, whereof most were taken, there was nothing of severity; but that within a few days they were all discharged. This is surely in further favour of Cromwell's general lenity.

His Lordship, referring to General Ireton's death in Ireland, describes him of a melancholic, reserved, dark nature, who communicated his thoughts to very few, so that for the most part he resolved alone, but was never diverted from any resolution he had taken; and he was thought often, by his obstinacy, to prevail over Cromwell himself, and to extort his concurrence contrary to his own inclinations: but that that proceeded only from dissembling less, for that he was never reserved in the owning and communicating his worst and most barbarous purposes, which the other always concealed and disavowed. That hitherto their concurrence had been very natural, since they had the same ends and designs : that it was generally conceived by those who had the opportunity to know them both very well, that Ireton was a man radically averse from monarchy, and so fixed to a republican government, that if he had lived, he would, either by his council and credit, have prevented those excesses in Cromwell, or publicly opposed and declared against them, and carried the greatest part of the army with him; and that Cromwell, who best knew his nature and his temper, had therefore carried him into Ireland, and left him there, that he might be without his counsels, or importunities, when he should find it necessary to put off his mask, and to act that part which he foresaw it would be requisite to do: that others thought his parts lay more towards civil

affairs, and were fitter for the modelling that government which his heart was set upon, (being a
scholar conversant in the law, and in all those
authors who had expressed the greatest animosity
and malice against the regal government,) than
for the conduct of an army to support it; his
personal courage being never reckoned amongst
his other abilities.   His Lordship, in continuance,
referring to the deaths (by shooting) of Sir Charles
Lucas, and Sir George Lisle, who became Lord
Fairfax's prisoners upon the surrender of Colchester, imputes their deaths to Ireton, who, he
says, swayed the General, and who (Ireton), he
adds, was upon all occasions of an unmerciful
and bloody nature.

Lord Broghill, speaking of Ireton's supposed
cruelty, says, that soon after he (Ireton) had the
command of the army, he was informed that a certain barony had broken the articles, in consideration whereof they had been protected: that he
marched against the barony, and ordered every
man, woman, and child, to be killed; against the
cruelty of which, Lord Broghill expostulating with
him, Ireton, at first, persisted, representing of how
ill consequence it was to suffer villains so perfidious
to be spared: that His Lordship allowed the Irish
to be a perfidious people, but that it would be cruel
to make no distinction; that there were amongst
them many children, aged people, and women, who
perhaps had not broken the articles; and that it

would be a horrid villainy to slay the innocent with the guilty: that he (Lord Broghill) therefore recommended that the soldiers should kill none but those who should be found in arms, or made any opposition. His Lordship adds, that Ireton, at last, though reluctantly, followed this advice, and revoked his bloody orders.

Sir Philip Warwick mentioning the circumstance of Ireton's death, speaks of him as a man of blood (for, says he, he had deeply dyed himself in the King's); and adds, that he expired with that word in his mouth; for that in his raving, as he, Warwick, was told by one that was then there, he cried out, " I will have more blood, blood, blood!"

All this is highly improbable, and not reconcileable with the characters given him by Ludlow and Whitelock. Ludlow gives an instance of his (Ireton's) desire of doing justice, even to an enemy: he says that Colonel Axtell was accused of not performing some conditions said to have been promised to the enemy, who pretended that after they had surrendered upon assurance of mercy, they were all put to the sword, except a few who made their escape: that the Colonel endeavoured to prove that no conditions had been granted; that they were taken by force, and that they who had showed no mercy could not deserve to receive any. Though, continues Ludlow, the proof was not clear, that he had promised him their lives, yet because it appeared that some of the soldiers had thrown out some expressions tending that way, to the enemy, Ireton was so great a friend to justice, even where an enemy was concerned, that though Colonel Axtell was a person extraordinarily qualified for the service of that conjuncture, he, together with the council of war, at which the commissioners of the Parliament were also present, suspended him from his employment.

This was surely mercy as well as justice. He (Ludlow) gives another instance of his (Ireton's) disposition to mercy: that a daughter of the Earl of Thomond being accused of protecting the property of the enemy, under pretence that they belonged to her, and thereby abusing the favour of his safeguard, which he had granted to her, and being charged by him therewith, and told that he expected a more ingenuous carriage from her; she burst into tears, and requested his forgiveness, when Ludlow interceding with him for the continnance of his favour to her; he said, "As much a cynic as I am, the tears of this woman moved me;" and ordered his protection to be continued to her. These are surely no proofs of the cruelty or unmercifulness of Ireton's disposition.

But those who are so fond of loading Cromwell and Ireton with the imputations of cruelty and blood-thirstiness, would do well to recall to their remembrance the bloody scenes that gave rise to this war in Ireland, and rendered necessary the making some severe examples.

Lord Clarendon speaks slightingly of Ireton's personal courage. He produces no proof of the want of it, but the story before related by His Lordship, of his refusal of Holles's challenge, and of his subsequent submission to Holles's personal insult upon such refusal. But it has been before shown from other historians, that Ireton did accept that challenge. In Ireland there is no appearance of his defective courage or activity ; Ludlow says, that he accompanied him in his visiting, during the siege of Limerick, several garrisons, providing hospitals for the sick and wounded of his soldiers and for other objects of the war. And that he rode so hard that he spoiled many horses ; but that he was so diligent in the public service, and so careless of every thing that belonged to himself, that he never regarded what clothes or food he used, or what horse he mounted. Sir Philip Warwick in his account of the battle of Naseby, says, that Prince Rupert routed Fairfax's left wing commanded by Ireton, who made a soldierly and notable defence.

This gentleman (Colonel Ireton), says Whitelock, was a person very active, industrious, and stiff in his ways and purposes : that he was of good abilities for counsel, as well as action ; and made much use of his pen, and was very forward to reform the proceedings in law, wherein his having been bred a lawyer was an help to him. Dr. Bates says, he was initiated in the liberal arts in Trinity Col-

lege, Oxford, and made therein no contemptible
progress, and afterwards studied the common law
in the Temple. Whitelock adds, that he was stout
in the field, and wary and prudent in his counsel,
and exceedingly forward as to the business of
a commonwealth: that he married Cromwell's
daughter, who had a great opinion of him, and no
man could prevail so much, nor order him so much,
as Ireton could: that his death struck a great sadness into Cromwell; and indeed it was a great loss
to him, of so able and active, so faithful and so
near a relation and officer under him.

Ludlow, in mentioning the settlement of divers
annual sums upon several principal officers, particularly upon Cromwell, says, that an act was
ordered to be brought in, for settling two thousand
pounds per annum upon the Lord-deputy Ireton,
of which he being informed, was so unacceptable
to him, that he said, they had many just debts,
which he desired they would pay, before they
made any such presents: that he had no need of
their land, and therefore would not have it: and
that he should be more contented to see them doing
the service of the nation, than so liberal in disposing
of the public treasure. And, truly, adds Ludlow,
I believe he was in earnest, for as he was always
careful to husband those things that belonged to
the state, to the best advantage, so he was most
liberal in employing his own purse and person in
the public service. Afterwards mentioning his

death, he says, some of General Cromwell's relations, who were not ignorant of his vast designs then
on foot, caused his body to be transported into
England, and solemnly interred at Westminster, in a
magnificent monument, at the public charge, who,
if he could have foreseen what was done by them,
would certainly have made it his desire that his body
might have found a grave where his soul left it, so
much did he despise those pompous and expensive
vanities ; having erected for himself a more glorious
monument in the hearts of good men, by his affection to his country, his abilities of mind, his impartial justice, his diligence in the public service, and
his other virtues ; which were a far greater honour
to his memory, than a dormitory amongst the ashes
of kings, who, says he, for the most part, as they
had governed others by their passions, so were they
themselves as much governed by them.   He (Ludlow) adds, that his death was lamented by all good
men.   Referring, in another place, to his (Ireton's)
besieging and taking Carlow in Ireland, and the
surrender of the garrison upon articles, he adds,
" which he caused punctually to be executed, as
his constant manner was."   The above must be
deemed a sufficient confutation of all these loose and
unfounded assertions to the prejudice of Ireton.

Lord Clarendon says, that Scotland being subdued, and Ireland reduced to that obedience as
the Parliament could wish, nothing could be expected to be done in England for the King's

advantage : that from the time that Cromwell was
chosen General, he took all occasions to discountenance the Presbyterians, and put them out of all
trust and employment, as well in the country as in
the army : that when Cromwell returned to London,
he caused several high courts to be erected, by
which many gentlemen of quality were condemned
and executed in many parts of the kingdom.
Whitelock says the Parliament ordered the trials
of these persons.   Cromwell did not, and could not
order them : and so it appears ; for in the Journals
of the 6th of the same September in which the
battle of Worcester was fought (1651), being the
day on which the House received the intelligence
of the victory, and Cromwell not being then returned to London, is an order of reference to
the council of state, to take into consideration
which of the prisoners that were then taken, of the
Scots army, were fit to be brought up to London ;
and that they send for them accordingly : and that
they present their opinion to the Parliament how
the rest of the prisoners were fit to be disposed of :
and on the 9th of the same month, is an order (upon
report of a list of the prisoners taken at Worcester)
of a warrant from the Speaker to Lieutenant-
general Monk, to send up to London by shipping,
of the prisoners taken in Scotland, all the lords,
gentlemen of quality, and the ministers named in
the list of the prisoners then taken, together with
such of the country gentlemen as he should find

dangerous in their influence upon the people there : and referred to the council of state to consider of such prisoners, as well English as Scots, as were fit to be made examples of public justice, and all circumstances that they should think fit concerning it, and to present it to the Parliament: and to give direction for securing and disposing the rest as might be most for the safety of the·nation.   And on the 11th of the same month, it is reported from the council of state to be their opinion, that James Earl of Derby, Colonel Edward Massey, Duke Hamilton, John Earl of Lauderdale, the Earl of Cleveland, Captain Bendbow, Sir Timothy Fetherston Haugh, and the mayor and sheriffs of Worcestor, were fit persons to be brought to trial, and made examples of justice.   And resolved accordingly; and referred to the council of state to see those votes put in execution effectually and speedily.

Journals, 14th November (1651).   The House, according to former order, did this day take into debate, whether it be now a convenient time to declare a certain time for the continuance of this Parliament, beyond which it should not sit.   The question being propounded, and the previous question being put; the House was divided: tellers for the yeas, Lord-general, Lord Chief Justice, with the yeas, 50; tellers for the noes, Colonel Morley, Mr. Bond, with the noes, 46: so it passed in the affirmative : and the main question being put, the House was again divided: the same tellers, with the yeas, 49; the same tellers, with the noes, 47: therefore resolved to be now a convenient time to declare a certain time for the continuance of this Parliament, beyond which it shall not sit; and adjourned: and on the Tuesday following, being the 18th same November, it was resolved, that the time for the continuance of this Parliament, beyond which they resolve not to sit, shall be the third day of November, 1654.

About the 10th of December following (1651), says Whitelock, Cromwell desired a meeting with divers members of Parliament, and some chief officers of the army, at the Speaker's house; and a great many being there, he proposed to them, that now the King being dead, and his son being defeated, he held it necessary to come to a settlement of the nation; and that, in order thereunto, he had requested this meeting, that they might together consider and advise what was fit to be done, and to be presented to the Parliament.

Speaker. " My Lord; this company were very ready to attend Your Excellency; and the business you are pleased to propound to us is very necessary to be considered. God hath given marvellous success to our forces under your command; and if we do not improve these mercies to some settlement, such as may be to God's honour, and the good of this commonwealth, we shall be very much blameworthy."

Harrison. " I think that which my Lord-general hath propounded is to advise as to a settlement, both of our civil and spiritual liberties; and so that the mercies which the Lord hath given unto us may not be cast away: how this may be done is the great question."

Whitelock. " It is a great question, indeed, and not suddenly to be resolved; yet it were pity that a meeting of so many able and worthy persons as I see here should be fruitless. I should humbly offer, in the first place, whether it be not requisite to be understood in what way this settlement is desired, whether of an absolute republic, or with any mixture of monarchy."

Cromwell. " My Lord-commissioner Whitelock hath put us upon the right point, and indeed it is my meaning that we should consider whether a republic, or a mixed monarchical government will be best to be settled; and, if any thing monarchical, then in whom that power shall be placed."

Sir Thomas Widdrington. " I think a mixed monarchical government will be most suitable to the laws and people of the nation; and if any monarchical, I suppose we shall hold it most just to place that power in one of the sons of the late King."

Colonel Fleetwood. " I think that the question, whether an absolute republic, or a mixed monarchy, is best to be settled in this nation, will not be very easy to be determined."

Lord Chief Justice St. John. "It will be found that the government of this nation, without something of monarchical power, will be very difficult to be so settled as not to shake the foundation of our laws, and the liberties of the people."

Speaker. "It will breed a strange confusion to settle a government of this nation without something of monarchy."

Colonel Desborough. "I beseech you, my Lord, why may not this, as well as other nations, be governed in the way of a republic."

Whitelock. "The laws of England are so interwoven with the power and practice of monarchy, that to settle a government without something of monarchy would make so great an alteration in the procedings of our laws, that you have scarce time to rectify, nor can we well foresee the inconveniences which will arise thereby."

Colonel Whalley. "I do not well understand matters of law; but it seems to me the best way, not to have any thing of monarchical power in the settlement of our government; and, if we should resolve upon any, whom have we to pitch upon? The King's eldest son hath been in arms against us, and his second son is likewise our enemy."

Sir Thomas Widdrington. "But the late King's third son, the Duke of Gloucester, is still among us, and too young to have been in arms against us, or infected with the principles of our enemies."

Whitelock. "There may be a day given for the King's eldest son, or for the Duke of York his brother, to come into the Parliament, and upon such terms, as shall be thought fit and agreeable, both to our civil and spiritual liberties, a settlement may be made with them."

Cromwell. "That will be a business of more than ordinary difficulty; but really, I think, if it may be done with safety and preservation of our rights, both as Englishmen and as Christians, that a settlement with somewhat of monarchical power in it would be very effectual."

Much other discourse, adds Whitelock, was by divers gentlemen then present, upon several points, and too large to be here inserted; generally, the soldiers were against any thing of monarchy, though every one of them was a monarch in his own regiment or company: that the lawyers were generally for a mixed monarchical government; and many were for the Duke of Gloucester to be made king: but that Cromwell still put off that debate, and came off to some other point: and that, in conclusion, after a long debate, the company parted, without coming to any result, only Cromwell discovered by this meeting, the inclinations of the persons that spake, for which he fished, and made use of what he then discerned.

It was about this time, (November, 1652,) says Whitelock, that the Lord-general Cromwell, meeting with him, saluted him with more than ordinary courtesy, and desired him to walk aside with him, that they might have some private discourse together: that Whitelock waited on him, and he began the discourse, which was to the following effect:—

Cromwell. " My Lord Whitelock, I know your faithfulness, and engagement in the same good cause with myself and the rest of our friends, and I know your ability in judgment, and your particular friendship and affection for me; indeed, I am sufficiently satisfied in these things, and therefore I desire to advise with you in the main and most important affairs relative to our present condition."

Whitelock. " Your Excellency hath known me long, and, I think, will say, that you never knew any unfaithfulness or breach of trust by me; and, for my particular affection to your person, your favours to me, and your public services, have deserved more than I can manifest; only there is, with your favour, a mistake in this one thing, touching my weak judgment, which is incapable to do any considerable service for yourself or this commonwealth; yet, to the utmost of my power, I shall be ready to serve you, and that, with all diligence and faithfulness."

Cromwell. " I have cause to be, and am, without the least scruple of your faithfulness, and I know your kindness to me, your old friend, and your abilities to serve the commonwealth, and

there are enough besides me that can testify it:
and, I believe, our engagements for the commonwealth have been, and are, as deep as most men,
and there never was more need of advice and solid
hearty counsel than the present state of our affairs
doth require."

Whitelock.   " I suppose no man will mention
his particular engagement in this cause, at the
same time when Your Excellency's engagement is
remembered; yet, to my capacity, and in my station, few men have engaged further than I have
done, and that, besides the goodness of your own
nature and personal knowledge of me, will keep
you from any jealousy of my faithfulness."

Cromwell.   " I wish there were no more ground
of suspicion of others than of you; I can trust you
with my life and the most secret matters relating
to our business, and to that end I have now desired a little private discourse with you; and really,
my Lord, there is very great cause for us to consider the dangerous condition we are all in, and
how to make good our station, to improve the
mercies and successes which God hath given us,
and not to be fooled out of them again, nor to be
broken to pieces by our particular jarrings and
animosities one against another; but to unite our
counsels, and hands, and hearts, to make good
what we have so dearly bought with so much
hazard, blood, and treasure; and that the Lord
having given us an entire conquest over our ene-

mies, we should not now hazard all again by our private janglings, and bring those mischiefs upon ourselves which our enemies could never do."

Whitelock. "My Lord, I look upon our present danger as greater than ever it was in the field; and, as Your Excellency truly observes, our proneness to destroy ourselves when our enemies could not do it. It is no strange thing for a gallant army, as yours is, after full conquest of their enemies, to grow into factions and ambitious designs, and it is a wonder to me that they are not in high mutinies, their spirits being active, and few thinking their services to be duly rewarded: and the emulation of the officers breaking out daily more and more in this time of their vacancy from their employment; besides, the private soldiers, it is to be feared, will, in this time of their idleness, grow into disorder, and it is your excellent conduct, which, under God, hath kept them so long in discipline and free from mutinies."

Cromwell. "I have used, and shall use the utmost of my poor endeavours to keep them all in order and obedience."

Whitelock. "Your Excellency hath done it hitherto, even to admiration."

Cromwell. "Truly, God hath blessed me in it exceedingly, and I hope will do so still. Your Lordship hath observed, most truly, the inclinations of the officers of the army to particular factions and to murmurings, that they are not rewarded according to their deserts; that others, who have adventured least, have gained most; and they have neither profit nor preferment, nor place in government which others hold, who have undergone no hardships nor hazards for the commonwealth; and herein they have too much of truth; yet their insolency is very great, and their influence upon the private soldiers works them to the like discontents and murmurings. Then, as for the members of Parliament, the army begins to have a strange distaste against them, and I wish there were not too much cause for it; and really their pride, and ambition, and self-seeking, ingrossing all places of honour and profit to themselves and their friends, and their daily breaking forth into new and violent parties and factions: their delays of business, and design to perpetuate themselves, and to continue the power in their own hands; their meddling in private matters between party and party, contrary to the institution of parliaments, and their injustice and partiality in those matters, and the scandalous lives of some of the chief of them;—these things, my Lord, do give too much ground for people to open their mouths against them, and to dislike them. Nor can they be kept within the bounds of justice and law or reason, they themselves being the supreme power of the nation, liable to no account to any, nor to be controuled or regulated by any other power, there being none superior or co-ordinate with them. So that unless there be some authority

and power so full and so high as to restrain and
keep things in better order, and that may be a
check to these exorbitances, it will be impossible
in human reason to prevent our ruin."

Whitelock. "I confess, the danger we are in
by these extravagances and inordinate powers is
more than, I doubt, is generally apprehended;
yet, as to that part of it which concerns the soldiery, Your Excellency's power and commission
are sufficient already to restrain and keep them in
their due obedience; and, blessed be God, you
have done it hitherto; and I doubt not, but, by
your wisdom, you will be able still to do it. As
to the members of Parliament, I confess, the greatest difficulty lies there; your commission being
from them, and they being acknowledged the supreme power of the nation, subject to no controul,
nor allowing any appeal from them: yet I am sure
Your Excellency will not look upon them as generally depraved; too many of them are much to
to blame in those things you have mentioned, and
and many unfit things have passed amongst them;
but I hope well of the major part of them, when
great matters come to a decision."

Cromwell. "My Lord, there are little hopes
of a good settlement to be made by them, really
there is not, but a great deal of fear that they will
destroy again what the Lord hath done graciously
for them and us: we all forget God, and God will
forget us, and give us up to confusion, and these

men will help it on, if they be suffered to proceed
in their ways; some course must be thought on
to curb and restrain them, or we shall be ruined
by them."

Whitelock. "We ourselves have acknowledged
them the supreme power, and taken our commissions and authority, in the highest concernments,
from them; and how to restrain and curb them
after this, it will be hard to find out a way for it."

Cromwell. "What, if a man should take upon
him to be a king?"

Whitelock. "I think that remedy would be
worse than the disease."

Cromwell. "Why do you think so?"

Whitelock. "As to your own person, the title
of king would be of no advantage, because you
have the full kingly power in you already, concerning the militia, as you are General. As to the
nomination of civil officers, those whom you think
fittest are seldom refused; and although you have
no negative vote in the passing of laws, yet what
you dislike will not easily be carried; and the taxes
are already settled, and in your power to dispose
the money raised: and as to foreign affairs, though
the ceremonial application be made to the Parliament, yet the expectation of good or bad success
in it is from Your Excellency; and particular solicitations of foreign ministers are made to you only.
So that I apprehend, indeed, less envy, and danger,
and pomp, but not less power and real opportunities

of doing good, in your being General, than would be if you had assumed the title of king."

Cromwell. " I have heard some of your profession observe, that he who is actually king, whether by election or by descent, yet, being once king, all acts done by him as king are lawful and justifiable, as by any king who hath the crown by inheritance from his forefathers: and that by an act of Parliament in Henry the Seventh's time, it is safer for those who act under a king, be his title what it will, than for those who act under any other power; and surely the power of a king is so great and high, and so universally understood and reverenced by the people of this nation, that the title of it might not only indemnify, in a great measure, those that act under it, but likewise be of great use and advantage in such times as these, to curb the insolencies of those whom the present powers cannot controul, or at least are the persons themselves who are thus insolent."

Whitelock. " I agree in the general what you are pleased to observe as to this title of king; but whether for Your Excellency to take this title upon you, as things now are, will be for the good and advantage either of yourself and friends, or of the commonwealth, I do very much doubt, notwithstanding that act of parliament, 11 Hen. VII., which will be little regarded or observed to us by our enemies, if they should come to get the upper hand of us."

Cromwell. " What do you apprehend would be the danger of taking this title?"

Whitelock. " The danger, I think, would be this: one of the main points of controversy betwixt us and our adversaries is, whether the government of this nation shall be established in monarchy, or in a free state or commonwealth, and most of our friends have engaged with us upon the hopes of having the government settled in a free state, and to effect that, have undergone all their hazards and difficulties; they being persuaded, though I think much mistaken, that under the government of a commonwealth they shall enjoy more liberty and right, both as to their spiritual and civil concernments, than they shall under monarchy, the pressures and dislike whereof are so fresh in their memories and sufferings. Now if Your Excellency shall take upon you the title of King, this state of your cause will be thereby wholly determined, and monarchy established in your person; and the question will be no more, whether our government shall be by a monarch or by a free state, but whether Cromwell or Stuart shall be our king and monarch: and that question, whereinbefore so great parties of the nation were engaged, and which was universal, will by these means become in effect a private controversy only : before, it was national, what kind of government we should have; now it will become particular, who shall be our governor, whether of the family of the Stuarts or of the family of the Cromwells. Thus the state of our controversy being totally changed, all those who were for a commonwealth, (and they are a very great and considerable party,) having their hopes therein frustrate, will desert you, —your hands will be weakened, your interest straightened, and your cause in apparent danger to be ruined."

Cromwell. " I confess, you speak reason in this; but what other thing can you propound that may obviate the present dangers and difficulties wherein we are all engaged ?"

Whitelock. " It will be the greatest difficulty to find out such an expedient; I have had many things in my private thoughts upon this business, some of which perhaps are not fit or safe for me to communicate."

Cromwell. " I pray, my Lord, what are they? you may trust me with them; there shall no prejudice come to you by any private discourse betwixt us; I shall never betray my friend; you may be as free with me as with your own heart, and shall never suffer by it."

Whitelock. " I make no scruple to put my life and fortune in Your Excellency's hand, and so I shall if I impart these fancies to you, which are weak, and perhaps may prove offensive to Your Excellency; therefore, my best way will be to smother them."

Cromwell. " Nay, I prithee, my Lord Whitelock, let me know them; be they what they will, they cannot be offensive to me, but I shall take it

kindly from you; therefore, I pray, do not con-
ceal these thoughts of yours from your faithful
friend."

Whitelock. "Your Excellency honours me with
a title far above me; and, since you are pleased to
command it, I shall discover to you my thoughts
herein, and humbly desire you not to take in ill
part what I shall say to you."

Cromwell. "I shall not; but I shall take it, as
I said, very kindly from you."

Whitelock. "Give me leave, then, first to consider Your Excellency's condition. You are en-
vironed with secret enemies. Upon the subduing
of the public enemy, the officers of your army
account themselves all victors, and to have had an
equal share in the conquest with you. The success which God hath given us, hath not a little
elated their minds, and many of them are busy and
of turbulent spirits, and are not without their designs how they may dismount Your Excellency,
and some of themselves get up into the saddle;
— how they may bring you down, and set up themselves.

"They want no counsel and encouragement
herein: it may be from some members of Parliament who may be jealous of your power and greatness, lest you should grow to high for them, and
in time overmaster them; and they will plot to
bring you down first, or to clip your wings."

Cromwell. "I thank you that you so fully consider my condition; it is a testimony of your love to me and care of me; and you have rightly considered it; and I may say without vanity, that in my condition yours is involved and all our friends, and those that plot my ruin will hardly bear your continuance in any condition worthy of you. Besides this, the cause itself may possibly receive some disadvantage by the strugglings and contentions among yourselves. But what, Sir, are your thoughts for prevention of those mischiefs that hang over our heads?"

Whitelock. "Pardon me, Sir, in the next place a little to consider the condition of the King of Scots. This prince being now, by your valour, and the success which God hath given to the Parliament and to the army under your command, reduced to a very low condition, both he and all about him cannot but be very inclinable to hearken to any terms whereby their lost hopes may be revived of his being restored to the crown, and they to their fortunes and native country. By a private treaty with him, you may secure yourself and your friends and their fortunes; you may make yourself and your posterity as great and permanent to all human probability as ever any subject was, and provide for your friends. You may put such limits to monarchical power as will secure our spiritual and civil liberties, and you may secure the cause in which we are all engaged; and this may be effectually done by having the power of the militia

continued in yourself and whom you shall agree
upon after you. I propound therefore for Your
Excellency to send to the King of Scots, and to
have a private treaty with him for this purpose;
and I beseech you to pardon 'what I have said
upon the occasion; it is out of my affection and
service to Your Excellency and to all honest men;
and I humbly pray you not to have any jealousy
thereupon of my approved faithfulness to Your
Excellency and to this commonwealth."

Cromwell. " I have not, I assure you, the least
distrust of your faithfulness and friendship to me,
and to the cause of this commonwealth; and I
think you have much reason for what you propound; but it is a matter of so high importance
and difficulty that it deserves more time of consideration and debate than is at present allowed us.
We shall therefore take a further time to discourse
of it."

That with this, adds Whitelock, the General
brake off, and went into other company, and so
into Whitehall, seeming by his countenance and
carriage displeased with what had been said; yet
that he never objected against Whitelock in any
public meeting afterwards; only that his carriage
towards him from that time was altered, and his
advising with him not so frequent and intimate as
before : and that it was not long after, that he found
an occasion, by an honourable employment, to send
him out of the way; as some of his nearest rela-

tions, particularly his daughter Claypoole, confessed that he (Whitelock) might be no obstacle or impediment to his ambitious designs; as, he says, may appear by the process of this story.

The unsuccessful termination of the treaty of Newport left both the King and the nation in a most distressing dilemma. No hope could remain of an agreement between the King and the presbyterian party, whilst that party so obstinately persisted in the establishment of their own exclusive form of worship, and from which there remained no prospect of their receding; the independent party had ceased to treat with the King, when they found him dealing with others; and the republican party did not wish his return to power upon any terms, being determined upon another, a republican form of government. Indeed, all of them had reason to suspect the King's sincerity in his dealings with them; their discovery of his reluctant acknowledgment of the Parliament, and his recorded denial of its being one, for the purpose of supplying him with an excuse for disavowing at any future convenient opportunity its legal existence, and for thereby avoiding and nullifying his engagements with them, left no security upon which they could rely, for the performance of any treaties he might make with them. Nor can it be doubted, that in all his negotiations with the Parliament, subsequently to his going to the Scots army, he considered himself a prisoner, or under a degree of restraint, from which he could not extricate himself, otherwise than by acceding to their terms ; notwithstanding the Parliament's declaration, particularly in the treaty of Newport, that he should be in a state of freedom, safety, and honour. To have placed him really in that state, he should have been understood, in his several treaties with the Commons subsequently to his surrender of himself to the Scots army, to have been at liberty to quit the kingdom, in case of an unsuccessful termination of such treaties. Of the use he might make of this his situation of restraint he was evidently well aware, by his question to the Scots commissioners whilst with that army, when, as Whitelock says, he, at Newcastle, propounded to them, in what condition he stood, whether a freeman or under restraint ? adding, that if not a freeman, then his answer to their desires could not be valid. All the different parties being thus apprised, in their several treaties with the King, of the power he felt he had in himself of avoiding his obligations, and of the impossibility of securing themselves from the consequences of this possible, or rather probable, breach of faith, saw that there remained to them no encouragement for a renewal of treaties. The King appears to have retained to the end of his life the principles of passive obedience and non-resistance, and all the other high-prerogative principles of his education ; and, consequently, did always, from the commence-

ment of the opposition to his measures, consider
his opposing subjects rebels, and, as such, incapable of being dealt with in any other way than by
subjection to his will.   Therefore, all his treaties
were compulsory, and to be avoided when opportunity should offer.   For these sentiments, he is
perhaps more to be pitied than blamed.   It would
have been happy for his subjects could he have
fallen in with the advancing freer sentiments of the
times; but, in addition to his own prejudices, he
had the misfortune to have, in succession, three of
the most arbitrary ministers that a sovereign could
be cursed with; who, instead of advising him to
moderation, did every thing to inflame and insti-
gate him to those violent measures that terminated
in their own deserved destruction, and in the
King's unfortunate dethronement and death.
Quarrels between kings and their subjects are, of
all evils, to be deprecated: they can never be
amicably terminated; if they could forgive, they
never can again trust one another; and, if recourse
be had to arms, victory and defeat are equally
ruinous of all sides.   Mr. Hume observes, that
after the commencement of the war, it was very
difficult, if not impossible, to find security for both
parties, especially for that of the Parliament; that,
amidst such violent animosities, power alone could
ensure safety, and the power of one side was necessarily attended with danger to the other; and
that few or no instances occur in history, of an

equal, peaceful, and durable accommodation, that has been concluded between two factions which had been inflamed into civil war.

The war being terminated by the surrender of Oxford to the Parliament on the 24th June (1646), and the King in their hands, the disbanding of part of the army, and sending other part into Ireland, became the first object of the desire and consideration of the presbyterian party. It appears that this party considered the army as firmly attached to, and under the entire influence and controul of Fairfax and Cromwell and other the independent party in the House of Commons. By sending some to Ireland, and disbanding the remainder, this army would have been, in effect, annihilated; and Fairfax, and Cromwell, and Ireton, and the other leaders of the independent party, left at the mercy of their enemies. Cromwell was particularly and early marked out by Mr. Holles and his party, as an object of their vengeance, in the forementioned meeting at Essex-house, given by Whitelock, leaving no room for doubt of their intention to have declared him and other the obnoxious heads of the independent party public incendiaries, and, as such, to have sent them to the Tower, never more to be heard of. Well aware of these views of the presbyterian party, and probably having reason to suspect their intention to raise a new army that should be at their devotion, or to bring the Scots army into England to overpower this independent army, the leaders of that party would feel themselves fully justified in keeping together their own army, until it should become proper and safe to disband them.

Mr. May, in his Breviary, relating the King's arrival at Holmby-house, observes, that though the King's party, which had fought against the Parliament and liberties, were absolutely subdued, yet that a quiet liberty and security could not be suddenly obtained by the victory; for that the civil war being ended, a dissension more than civil arose amongst the conquerors, which seemed therefore more sad to all good men; because it was between those who before had, with most united affections and desires, thrown their lives and fortunes into hazard against a common enemy, and whom the same cause, the same fervour of reforming religion and restoring liberty, and the same prayers, had linked together in the nearest bonds of conscience; that by this division of the friends of liberty into two parties, under the names of Presbyterian and Independent, which was continually increasing, the minds of men came to be embittered against each other beyond all measure; one side complained that the covenant was broken; the other, that it was not rightly interpreted by them, nor so as that it could any way be a vindication of the cause undertaken for the public safety; that on both sides were men of great reputation; that yet they did not at first so far dissent, but that both sides seemed forward to vindicate the common cause against the King's party, who were called Malignants; that it must be longer time, that must by degrees so far work upon the consciences of that side, which seemed weakest, as to make them cleave to the malignants for a prop; that the malignants were ready to join with either side, that they might ruin both; that, though disarmed, they were now become the greatest number, especially by the inconstancy of many men, either upon particular grievances, or on account of the burden of taxations; that a great number of the citizens of London, not of the meanest, but highest rank, had revolted from their former principles, insomuch that the inhabitants of that city, (all the King's garrisons having been by Fairfax's bloodless victories emptied into it,) came to be in such a condition of strength, as that the Parliament, without the army's help, could not safely sit there; that these dissensions of Presbyterians and Independents (because the motions and intentions of men are not enough known) he meant to touch with brevity; that it were a work of too much length and difficulty to recite how many calumnies were raised by the other faction against the army, which they had before so much admired, as being maintainers of the independent faction; how divers petitions were drawn up, and subscriptions eagerly sought in the county of Essex against this army, (referring to the petition mentioned in Rushworth,) which was then quartered about Walden, in the month of April; and that, in the Parliament itself, it was so far and in that manner debated concerning the disbanding of the army, that the soldiers (being now taught to value their own merits) conceived themselves much injured, and in May presented a petition to their General, in which they desire to be satisfied, not only for their due pay as soldiers, but in things concerning the public liberties, which they had fought for, and which they said belonged to them as freeborn sons of the nation; of which petition, continues Mr. May, great complaint was made by those of the other faction; that these and some other alterations wrought at last so far, as that the soldiers, about the beginning of June, (upon what design or what jealousies he leaves his readers to judge,) took away the King from Holmby, out of the Parliament's commissioners' hands, and carried him along with them to the army, so that his person was to be in some town or palace near to their quarters.

The blame of these misunderstandings of the Parliament and the army have been very generally laid upon the army, as supposing them to have determined, after having subdued all their, the Parliament's enemies, to subdue the Parliament itself, and form a government more agreeable to their own views. A standing and deliberating army must always be dangerous to the government of a country, and should be disbanded or reduced, so soon as the objects for which it was raised shall have been accomplished. But the common soldiers of the Parliament army did not consider themselves of the usual description of common soldiers : — not, as they themselves say, a band of janizaries hired to fight the Parliament's battles, but voluntarily taking up arms for the liberty and defence of the nation of which they were a part. Whitelock describes Cromwell's regiment, as a brave regiment of horse of his countrymen, most of them freeholders and freeholders' sons, and who upon matter of conscience engaged in this quarrel ; and thus, adds he, being well armed within by the satisfaction of their own consciences, and without by good iron arms, they would, as one man, stand firmly and charge desperately. Of the same description was probably the majority of the Parliament army.

Of these two parties, thus dividing the Parliament, the Presbyterians were for uniformity in doctrine and discipline, without allowance to the tender consciences of those who differed from them in either. They were the inveterate foes of the Independents : — Neal, in his History of the Puritans, says, they, the Presbyterians, were now in the height of their power, the hierarchy being destroyed, the King their prisoner, and the best if not all the livings of the kingdom distributed amongst them ; but still, adds he, they were dissatisfied for want of the top-stone to their new building, which was church-power; the pulpits and conversation of the city were filled with invectives against the men in power, because they would not leave the church independent on the state; and that the presbyterian ministers were very troublesome, the Parliament being teased every week with church-grievances of one kind or another. He says, the presbyterian government was as narrow as the prelatical, not allowing liberty of conscience, but claiming a civil as well as ecclesiastical authority over men's persons and properties: in confirmation whereof he gives some extracts from a zealous presbyterian writer of that time against the sectaries; who, after giving a catalogue of many of the errors, heresies, and blasphemies of that, his time, calls down the vengeance of the higher powers upon these supposed deluded people; adding, that the great opinion of an universal toleration tends to the laying all waste, and dissolution of all religion and good manners; a connivance and suffering whereof without punishment provokes God to send judgments; that a toleration doth eclipse the glory of the most excellent reformation, and makes these sins to be the sins of the legislature that countenances them; that a magistrate should use coercive power to punish and suppress evils, as appears from the example of Eli. The same writer (Neal) adds, that this writer might have enlarged his catalogue with papists, prelates, deists, and others; but his business was to blacken the adversaries of presbyterian uniformity, that the Parliament might crush them by sanguinary methods. The Independents, he says, were put at the head of the sectaries, because they were for toleration of all Christians who agreed in the fundamentals of religion.

Mrs. Hutchinson, in her forementioned memoirs says, that upon Colonel Hutchinson her husband going to London upon the termination of the war, to attend his duty in the House of Commons, he found a very bitter spirit of discord and envy raging; and the presbyterian faction, of which were most of those lords and others that had been laid aside by the Self-denying Ordinance, endeavouring a violent persecution upon the account of conscience, against those who had, in so short a time, accomplished, by God's blessing, that victory which he was not pleased to bestow on them; that their directory of worship was at length sent forth for a three years' trial, and such as could not conform to it marked out with an evil eye, hated and persecuted under the name of Separatists; that the Colonel (Hutchinson), who abhorred that malicious zeal and imposing spirit which appeared in them, was soon taken notice of for one of the independent faction, whose heads were accounted Pierrepoint, Vane, St. John, and some few other grandees.

Whitelock, upon the same subject, says that that many complaints and cavils were made against the officers and soldiers of the army, as such who held erroneous and schismatical opinions, contrary to the true doctrine, and that they took upon them to preach and expound Scripture, not being learned or ordained; and, adds Whitelock, some of the King's party were not wanting to foment these things, and to raise an odium upon the army in the peoples' minds: and those, says he, who so lately were in their highest esteem and respect as freers of their country from servitude and oppression, are now by the same people looked upon as sectaries and oppressors themselves. Thus, continues he, we may see the inconstancy of the giddy multitude, and the uncertainty of worldly affairs. When their turns are served, their minds change, their best friends when they relieve them are counted their enemies when they are relieved: that the best course is to provide for such a condition as will always afford comfort, and will never change; not to trust in men, but in God alone.

The same writer observes that Mr. Holles, Sir Philip Stapleton, Recorder Glyn, and others of that party, did put on eagerly the business of disbanding the army. Some others declared their opinion against it, as that which might prove dangerous to them and to all the Parliament party if it should succeed: and withal that they believed the army would not submit to it, and ill consequences might follow if the votes should pass for the doing it. But they still, both in public and in private, pressed that point, having taken a pique against the army themselves, many of them having been left out by the Self-denying Ordinance, and Cromwell and Skippon and other members of the House, continuing officers of the army, and their great success did increase the envy against them: that they likewise apprehended the advantage in prosecuting this business, as that which would generally please the people, by ridding them of the soldiers, and easing of the taxes, and they would not consider the doubt of the army's mutiny and disobedience, being over-resolute in this temper: that the other party took occasion to have the more converse with Cromwell and that party, who entertained them with all respect and affection, and highly courted them. Yet it was observed, continues Whitelock, that this was not upon design or policy in them to come off to a new party who might be thought more growing into power than the other, but it was their clear judgment: but what they gained with the one party they lost with the other, neither continuing firm to them who were not thorough-paced in all things which they laboured to bring to pass. But, observes he, we shall find, in all sorts of business, that honesty is the best policy; and that a clear and sincere dealing, according to one's judgment and conscience, is seldom without a blessing accompanying it.

Ludlow in this place observes, that the party in the House that were betraying the cause of their country, became encouragers of such petitioners as came to them from the city of London and other places to that effect; very many of whom had been always for the King's interest, but their estates lying in the Parliament's quarters, they secured them by their presence in the House, and at the same time promoted his designs by their votes: that there was another sort of men who were contented to sacrifice all civil liberties to the ambition of the presbyterian clergy, and to vest them with a power as great or greater than that which had been declared intolerable in the bishops before: that to this end they encouraged the reduced officers of the Earl of Essex, such as Massey, Waller, Poyntz, and others, to press the Parliament for their arrears in a peremptory and seditious manner; that being furnished with money they might be enabled to stand by these their patrons in whatsoever design they had to carry on; and that the better to facilitate the disbanding of the army, which they so much desired, they resolved to draw off a considerable part of them for the service of Ireland; and, to render the work more acceptable, voted Major-general Skippon to command them, joining the Earl of Warwick and Sir William Waller in commission with Sir Thomas Fairfax, to draw out such forces as were willing to go, to continue such as should be thought necessary for the security of the nation, and to disband the rest : that the army being well informed of the design, began to consult how to prevent it; and though many of the officers were prevailed with to engage by advancement to higher commands, yet the major part absolutely refused : that the commissioners of the Parliament having done what they could in prosecution of their instructions, ordered those who had engaged in the Irish service to draw off from the army, which then lay at Saffron Walden, and about Newmarket, and to be quartered in the way to Ireland; which done, they returned to London with an account of their proceedings : that the Parliament being informed of what passed, were highly displeased with the carriage of the army; but the prudence and moderation of Major-general Skippon, in his report of that matter to the House, much abated the heat of their resentment; yet that some menacing expressions falling from some of them, Lieutenant-general Cromwell took the occasion to whisper him (Ludlow) in the ear, " these men will never leave till the army pull them out by the ears;" which expression, adds Ludlow, he should have resented, had the state of affairs permitted. He then proceeds to relate the choice of agitators, and their other proceedings as before related.

The foregoing accounts of the proceedings of the Parliament and army upon the conclusion of the war, leave no room for doubt that the object of the presbyterian party was to rid themselves of

the army. This measure would have given them
the complete ascendancy over the independent
party in Parliament, and would have placed in their
power all those individuals that obstructed their
progress to absolute sovereignty.

In prosecution of this object, it appears upon
the Journals of the House of Commons, that on
the 31st July, 1646, only about one month after
the surrender of Oxford, which terminated the war,
it was proposed that four regiments of foot and two
regiments of horse, of the army under General Fairfax's command, should be forthwith sent into Ireland for the relief of that kingdom : that upon
the previous question, (that this question be put,)
the House divided, when the numbers were,—
for the question, ninety, including the tellers,
Mr. Holles and Sir Philip Stapleton; against it,
ninety-one, including the tellers, Sir Arthur Heselrigge and Sir John Evelyn of Wilts. The
question being lost, this force was consequently
not then sent; but this division proves the then
equality of strength of the two parties in the
Commons. It appears, nevertheless, that in the
following month a considerable force from several
counties was ordered for Ireland, and that Cromwell was desired to inform the Colonel of one of
the regiments so ordered of its destination.

The army saw through these designs of the
Presbyterians, and, as might have been expected,
determined upon resistance; hence sprung the

agitators. They were, as described by Rushworth, to consist of committees to be chosen by the soldiers from amongst themselves, out of every troop and company, for the purpose of conferring together upon the votes of the House, for the satisfaction of the soldiers for arrears, and for indemnity, and for discovering the distempers of the army. The committees reported their proceedings to their officers, and they to the head-quarters, and from thence to be sent to the Parliament. The idea of forming these committees appears to have wholly originated with the soldiers, for the purpose of protecting their interests against the unfavourable designs of the presbyterian party in Parliament, and against the possibility of injury from the opposite views or inattention of their officers. They (the soldiers) refused to disband, or to go to Ireland, until the discharge of the arrears of their pay, and an indemnity for all their acts as soldiers during the late war; some of them appearing to have been prosecuted for these acts, as individuals, by the royalists in different parts of the kingdom. They assert their right of petitioning in common with their fellow-subjects: they also required, amongst other things, that the Houses should be purged of those members who, for delinquency or corruptions, or by undue elections, ought not to sit there; and that those who had abused the Parliament and the army, and endangered the kingdom, should be disabled from further mischief, particularly to the individuals of the army, when they

should be disbanded and dispersed, and in the condition of private men: and they required some
other things to be done for the settlement of the
King and kingdom in peace, disclaiming all intentions to overthrow presbytery, and to introduce
independency; only claiming the promise that had
been made of a provision for tender consciences,
in order that all who, upon conscientious grounds,
might differ from the established forms, might not
be debarred from the common rights belonging
equally to all, whilst they should live soberly and
inoffensively towards others, and peacefully and
faithfully towards the state. This was all very
reasonable; and the General and principal officers
openly countenanced the inferior officers and soldiers in their applications to Parliament for the
redress of these their grievances; and these applications, whether by petition or remonstrance, were
signed by the General (Fairfax) himself, or by his
secretary, Rushworth, by his order. But the Parliament gave them little attention, unless when
alarmed by the apprehension of their (the army's)
approach towards London, when they would order
them a little more of their pay, leaving still much
in arrear; nevertheless expecting they should disband, or go to Ireland. These proceedings of the
army therefore appear to have been self-defensive.
Finding, as they did, the tardiness of the Parliament
in the payment of their arrears, and in the redress
of their other grievances, whilst they continued

together, they had no reason to expect more attention from them when separated; and the principal officers of the army, and probably the greatest
part of the army itself, being of the independent
party, they were not likely to experience any
mercy from their inveterate enemies, the presbyterian party, when they should become defenceless
individuals. Under these circumstances, it would
have been the extreme of folly to have separated.

Lord Clarendon, with his usual ingenuity, has
worked up this simple transaction into a contrivance of the army to share with the Parliament
in the settlement of the kingdom; and, with his
accustomed acrimony, when speaking of Cromwell,
introduces him as having the sole influence over
the army, underhandedly, as he expresses it,
making them petition the Houses against any
thing that was done contrary to his opinion.

It appears to have been His Lordship's great
object throughout his history, to destroy the characters of all the leading men in the Parliament,
by attributing all their proceedings to a settled
design of raising themselves upon the ruins of the
late government. He could not do this more
effectually than by representing them as a set of
religious hypocrites, solemnly protesting one thing
and meaning another, introducing upon every occasion their fasts, and prayers, and preaching, in aid
of their deceptions. But Cromwell was the grand
object of his hatred; not an action of his public

conduct upon which he does not put an ill con-
construction; no faith or reliance is to be placed
in his most solemn promises or declarations; some
sinister design in every thing he does or says, to
serve the purposes of an inordinate ambition. He
represents him and his officers as taking upon
themselves to preach and to pray publicly to their
troops, and admitting few, or no chaplains in the
army, but such as bitterly inveighed against the
presbyterian government as more tyrannical than
episcopacy: also that the common soldiers, as well
as officers, did not only pray and preach among
themselves, but went up into the pulpits in all
churches and preached to the people; who quickly
became inspired with the same spirit; women as
well as men, taking upon them to pray and preach;
which made as great noise and confusions in all
opinions concerning religion as there was in the
civil government of the state; scarce any man
being suffered to be called in question for delivering
any opinion in religion by speaking or writing, how
profane, heretical, or blasphemous soever it was,
which they said was to restrain the spirit. His
Lordship adds, that liberty of conscience was
become the common argument and quarrel, whilst
the presbyterian party proceeded with equal bitterness against the several sects as enemies to all
godliness, as they had done, and still continued to
do, against the prelatical party: and that finding
themselves superior in the two Houses, little

doubted, by their authority and power there, to be
able to reform the army and to new-model it again,
which they would no doubt have attempted, if it
had not pleased God to have taken away the Earl
of Essex, some months before this, who died without being sensible of sickness. He insidiously
adds, that it was loudly said by many of his friends
that he was poisoned. Sure, says he, it is, that
Cromwell and his party (for he was now declared
the head of the army, though Fairfax continued General in name,) were wonderfully exalted with his
death, he being the only person whose credit and
interest they feared, without any esteem for his
person. He means this insinuation shall have the
effect of making it believed that Cromwell or some
of his party had poisoned him. Whatever might
be the imperfections of Cromwell's character, a
disposition to rid himself of his enemies by assassination was not one of them. Fortunately, in refutation of this unworthy aspersion, Ludlow, who
is no friend to Cromwell, says that he died from
overheating himself in the chase of a stag in
Windsor Forest. Dr. Bates attributes his death to
his lying on the ground in a sweat after hunting.
He adds, that his death was a great loss to his
party. His Lordship describes Cromwell and his
party as having introduced the principal officers of
the army and others of their friends to be elected
members of the House of Commons, in the room
of deceased members, or of those who had been

expelled by them for adhering to the King; by which means, he says, Fairfax, Ireton, Harrison, and many others of the Independents, officers and gentlemen of the several counties who were transported with new fancies in religion, and were called by a new name, fanatics, sat in the House of Commons: notwithstanding all which the Presbyterians carried it.

His Lordship's account of the presbyterian party's intention to reform and new-model the army, had the Earl of Essex lived, must surely be deemed a justification of the army's refusal to disband till they should have secured themselves against the undue exercise of the power that the presbyterian party would have then had over them, and which the heads of the army had sufficient reason to know would have been severely executed. Mrs. Hutchinson, referring to the King going to the Scots army, says, that the independent party had certain evidence that they (the Scots army) were prepared and had an intent to have cut off the English army who beleaguered (besieged) Newark; but that God changed their councils, and made them take another course, which was to carry the King to Newcastle. All that dissimulation and artifice, therefore, of which His Lordship so freely accuses Cromwell, amounts to no more than the prudent and vigilant exertions of a wise man to defeat the machinations of a powerful and vindictive party. He certainly was become apprehensive of the agitators in the army, who had become suspicious that he and some other principal officers were treating privately with the King: and this explains his complaint mentioned by His Lordship (if really made) of the licence that had got into the army, and of his having become odious to them. Ludlow mentions the circumstance referred to by His Lordship, of a determination of some in the House to secure Cromwell, and of his withdrawing to the army, upon his having intimation of it; adding, so they missed of him, and were not willing to show their teeth since they could do no more. The same writer, introductory of his account of the taking the King from Holmby, describes the agitators as aware of the perilous situation in which they were placed in consequence of a vote of the House brought about by Mr. Holles, declaring their petition to be seditious and themselves traitors: and that they must be at the mercy of the Parliament, unless they could secure themselves from their power by prosecuting what they had begun. The same writer, giving some instances of the army's respectful attention to the King after his removal from Holmby, says, that the King began to promise himself that his condition was altered for the better, and to look upon the independent interest as more consisting with episcopacy than the presbyterian interest; for that it would subsist under any form, which the other could not do: that he therefore largely promised liberty to the independent party, being fully persuaded how naturally his power would revive upon his restitution to the throne, and how easy it would be for him to break through all such promises and engagements, upon pretence that he was under a force.

This account, coming from one who was no friend to monarchy, and consequently was apprehensive of the King's restoration, and was likewise not well disposed towards Cromwell, of whom he repeatedly expresses himself suspicious of looking too much to his own aggrandisement, is good evidence of the reality of his (Cromwell's) serious apprehensions of the agitators' jealousy of his design to assist in the restoration, and of the reality and sincerity of that design. Had the King been, at that time, equally sincere, and had not trifled and balanced between the Parliament and the army under the delusion of an opinion that he held to the last, that neither of them could form a government without him; he might at that time, apparently, by adhering to the army, have been restored upon reasonable terms for the nation as well as for himself. One of the great obstacles to a successful treaty with the presbyterian party, the establishment of presbytery, would have been out of the way, when treating with the independent party: and some settlement of the question of religion might have been devised that might have removed the King's scruples, and accorded with the liberal religious sentiments of the Independents.

Lord Clarendon himself testifies the army's respectful treatment of the King after his removal from the Parliament's commissioners, where he describes him to have been, in various instances, much and rigidly restrained. The Parliament appear from His Lordship to have been very apprehensive of the army's agreement with the King, and used every endeavour to counteract them, by getting him again into their possession. The army with reason, according to His Lordship's own account, suspected the King's sincerity : nor does it afford any reason to doubt, and which is confirmed by Ludlow, Sir John Berkley, and other writers, of the sincere desire of Cromwell and Ireton to treat with the King, who, says His Lordship, doubted how to carry himself towards the different parties : instead of hesitating, he should have decidedly closed with the army, whose terms the King himself allowed to be much more liberal than those of the presbyterian party. But Cromwell and Ireton discerned, what His Lordship acknowledges, that he (the King) was balancing, as before observed, between the army and the Parliament, and playing off, if the expression may be allowed, one against the other, whereby he lost the confidence of both. For, says His Lordship, the King made use of the liberty allowed him at Hampton-court, by consulting the Lord Capel

and others of his friends that resorted to him, and
by forming the plan His Lordship describes, of
availing himself of the war which he expected
would shortly happen between the two nations of
England and Scotland, in which the Presbyterians
were expected to join the Scots against the army;
when his own party were to hold themselves in
readiness to act with their assistance in crushing
the army, and reinstating him without its assistance.

Cromwell and Ireton were not ignorant of these
proceedings; hence their sudden reserve towards
the King and those about him, and their resolution,
related by His Lordship, of their determination
never to trust the King, or to do any thing further
towards his restoration. His Lordship also says,
that Cromwell expostulated with Mr. Ashburnham,
and complained that the King could not be trusted,
and that he had no affection for, or confidence in
the army, but was jealous of them and of all the
officers, and that he had intrigues in the Parliament, and treaties with the Presbyterians in the
city to raise new troubles: that he had a treaty
concluded with the Scots commissioners to engage
the nation again in blood; and that therefore he
would not be answerable if any thing fell out
amiss, and contrary to expectation: their complaints appear to have been all well founded. His
Lordship, in another place, says, the Parliament
maintained no further contest with the army, but
tamely submitted to whatsoever they proposed; the

Presbyterians in both Houses, and in the city, being in a terrible agony lest some close correspondence they had held with the King, during his abode at Hampton-court, should be discovered, and therefore would have no further occasion of jealousy by any contradictions; leaving it to their clergy to keep the fire burning in the hearts of the people by their pulpit-inflammations; and that they stoutly discharged their trusts.

In a subsequent part of his history, His Lordship says, that when the Scots commissioners had, by various insinuations, gained new credit with the King, and had undertaken that their invading England with an army, equal to the undertaking, should be the foundation upon which all other hopes were to depend, they began to propose to him many conditions which would be necessary for His Majesty to engage himself to perform towards that nation; without which it would not be easy to induce it into so unanimous a consent and engagement as was necessary for such an enterprise; to which the King utterly refused to consent, and so the agreement was not concluded when the King left Hampton-court; but that, as soon as he was in the Isle of Wight, the Scots commissioners repaired to him at the same time with those who were sent to him from the Parliament for his royal assent to the four bills that they had sent to him: that then, in that season of despair, they prevailed with him to sign the propositions he had formerly refused; and having great apprehension from the jealousies they knew the army had of them, that they should be seized upon and searched in their return to London, they made up their precious contract in lead, and buried it in a garden in the Isle of Wight, from whence they easily found means afterwards to receive it. So constant, says His Lordship, were those men to their principles, and so wary to be sure to be no losers by returning to their allegiance; to which neither conscience nor honour did invite or dispose them: that so, after a stay of some months at London to adjust all accounts, and receive the remainder of those monies they had so dearly earned, or so much of it as they had hope would be paid, they returned to Scotland with the hatred and contempt of the army and of the Parliament, that was then governed by it; but with the veneration of the presbyterian party, which still had faith in them, and exceedingly depended upon their future negotiation, which was now incumbent upon them: and that, in order thereunto, a fast intercourse and correspondence was settled, as well by constant letters, as by frequent emissaries of their clergy, or other persons whose devotion to their combination was unquestionable.

Without having recourse to those supposed inventions and subtleties of Cromwell which His Lordship is so fond of discovering and dwelling upon, the above circumstances, given by His

Lordship himself, must surely be deemed cause sufficient for Cromwell's and Ireton's determination to have no more intercourse with the King.

Notwithstanding all His Lordship's assertions and insinuations to the contrary, the sincerity of Cromwell and of other the principal officers in treating with the King, and the reality of .their disposition to restore him upon reasonable terms, ought not, upon an impartial review of the authentic histories of those times, to be doubted: those engaged made no secret of it. Whitelock says, letters from Sir Thomas Fairfax to the Parliament, full of respect towards the King: and taking notice of some reports, as if he and his officers were upon some underhand contract with the King; and so, to slander their integrities, and endeavour a misunderstanding betwixt the Parliament and their army, which their enemies would fain effect, to hinder the settlement of the people's rights; but that a good accord between them was their design to preserve. He declares that they had not done, nor should do any thing which they should desire to hide from the Parliament and the world, and should not avow to the faces of their adversaries: that their desires to settle the King's rights, he first giving his concurrence to secure the rights of the kingdom, they had already declared publicly: that since their papers sent in to the Parliament, several officers were sent to the King, to satisfy him concerning those papers, and some

others sent to him about his removes; in which
addresses they bargained not, nor asked any thing
of the King, as to any private interest of their own;
but that they endeavoured only the settlement of
the public peace and rights of the nation; and
assured the King, that this being done with his
concurrence, the rights of His Majesty and his
family should be provided for; and in the mean
time His Majesty should find from them all personal
civilities and respects, and such freedom as
might stand with safety, and the trust lying upon
them: that they were no enemies to monarchy and
civil government: that upon His Majesty's importunity
(though with some reluctancy) they did
give way for the Duke of Richmond and the two
chaplains to come to His Majesty, as that which
they thought reasonable and just, and to make the
King less prejudiced against others: that they
conceived, to avoid all harshnesses, and afford all
kindnesses to His Majesty, consisting with the
peace and safety of the kingdom, was the most
Christian, honourable, and prudent way; and that
tender, equitable, and moderate dealing towards
His Majesty, his family, and party, was the most
hopeful course to take away the seeds of war and
feuds, and to procure a lasting peace; and that being
settled with the rights and liberties of the nation,
and propagation of the gospel of truth, and they,
honoured to be instrumental therein, they should
be willing to be dismissed, and be happy to be dis-

charged, not only from military employments, but from all matters of power whatsoever.

He (Whitelock) also, in an article in September (1647), says, letters from the commissioners with the King, — that he was willing to settle presbytery for three years, and the militia as he before offered, but others he was not satisfied to assent unto; but desired to put himself upon the proposals of the army, and that they might be taken into consideration. He adds, some private treaties are said to have been by some officers of the army with the King, and instructions given by Cromwell and others, that if he would assent to their proposals, lower than those of the Parliament, the army would settle him again in his throne. But, proceeds Whitelock, (unfortunate as to him,) his bishops persuaded him against what he was inclined in his own judgment to have agreed unto, and thereby ruined him and themselves at the present.

His Lordship says, that Cromwell's continuance in his northern progress was the reason that all they who wished ill to the treaty of Newport had used and interposed all the delays they could, that he might return before it began, as those who wished it might succeed were solicitous that it might be concluded before that time; which made them the less insist upon many particulars both in the propositions and in the instructions, which they hoped might be more capable of remedies in the treaty than before it.

This is wholly assertion, not founded in fact.
So far from precipitation, every article of the propositions was debated and disputed, and nothing
material on the part of the Parliament was con-
ceded. The article of religion was particularly
pressed upon the King in a most harsh and cruel
manner. Nothing but the establishment of the
presbyterian form of church-government and worship would satisfy the Parliament, without the
least allowance to the scruples of the King, or of
any of the sects. It appears in Rushworth, that
the King first consented to confirm for three years,
by act of Parliament, the presbyterian form of
church-goverment, but not to abolish episcopacy;
only he would agree to the alteration and regulation of the present hierarchy, so as that episcopacy,
reduced to its primitive state, might be continued.
And that he would confirm the public use of the
Directory in all churches and chapels, and would
consent to the repeal of so much of the statutes
as only concerned the book of Common Prayer,
and the taking the same away out of all churches
and chapels, provided that the use thereof might
be continued in His Majesty's chapel for himself
and his household. All this to be confirmed by
act of Parliament for three years; and in the mean
time a future form of church-government to be
considered of. He declared himself not satisfied
to take the covenant. He afterwards declared his
consent to abolish archbishops, deans, and chap-

ters, and the rest of the hierarchy, except bishops; and made some further concessions respecting bishops and ecclesiastical government. He also relinquished the continuance of the use of the Common Prayer in his own family and household, only reserving to himself the liberty to use therein some other set form of worship; and he declared the above concessions to be the farthest he could go in conscience: all these concessions were voted, not satisfactory.

More than this, says Whitelock, could not be obtained from His Majesty, though most earnestly begged of him by some of the commissioners (great persons) with tears, and on their knees; particularly as to the proposition touching religion, wherein the church-government and public worship, and chiefly the revenues of the church, swayed more with the King's chaplains then about him, and they more with His Majesty, (continually whispering matter of conscience to him,) than the Parliament and all their commissioners could prevail with him for an agreement, though possibly his own judgment, which was above all theirs, might not be so fully convinced by his eager divines about him; and thus terminated, unsuccessfully, this last treaty with the King.

The failure of this treaty must be deemed to be principally imputable to the obstinacy of the presbyterian party in thus pressing upon the King and upon the nation their own form of church-government and worship, without even allowing the King the use of the liturgy in his own private and family devotions.

Here is no appearance of haste, or independent interference: the presbyterian party, had, uninterruptedly, all the time they required; and it does appear most extraordinary, that a set of people, whose opposition to the measures of the King had been principally grounded upon their sufferings from religious intolerance, and who had so lately rescued themselves from the smart of it, should now be attempting religious uniformity: but they had entangled themselves in their engagement with Scotland, by the solemn league and covenant, which obliged them not only to assist the Scots in maintaining the reformed religion in the church of Scotland, but to endeavour the reformation of religion in England, according to the best reformed religion, so as to bring the churches in the three kingdoms as near together as possible. The similar attempt of the King in Scotland was one of the grounds of his quarrel with the Scots. What national and individual confusion and distress has this foolish attempt to bring about an impossibility, of no use to the state could it have been accomplished, caused in the world in all times! It might have been expected, that the number of sects into which the professors of Christianity are divided would present an insurmountable obstacle to the attempt. Not only the several different sects are separated by different modes of worship or religious sentiments from each other, but each of such sects are frequently divided amongst themselves; and even the clergy of our own establishment are not of one opinion upon the construction of many of its own articles. Had not the contrary appeared in all ages of the Christian church, religious persecution would not have been credible.

His Lordship says, the Independents were more learned and rational than the Presbyterians; who, though they had not so great congregations of the common people, yet infected and were followed by the most substantial and wealthy citizens, and by others of better condition: that to these men Cromwell and most of the officers of the army adhered with bitterness against the other. This bitterness of the Independents towards the Presbyterians is well accounted for by the intolerant persecuting spirit of the Presbyterians, who hated them for their tolerance of all religious opinions and modes of worship, and, could they have prevailed, would have persecuted the Independents to utter extirpation. Had the King sincerely and exclusively treated with the Independents instead of the Presbyterians, he would not probably have found any difficulty in the article of religion, which was the great obstacle in his treaties with the Presbyterians; they must, and would, no doubt, upon their own principles, have consented to his enjoyment of his own mode of worship, though not perhaps consenting to its re-establishment, reserving to the nation its liberty of adoption of the same, or any other mode each individual might for himself prefer.

Neal, in his History of the Puritans, observes, that the royal party being broken, and the King, as it were, a prisoner, had no prospect of recovering his throne, but by dividing his enemies, or making the best terms with them he could: that the Presbyterians being in league with the Scots nation were most numerous and powerful; but that that which rendered their agreement with the King impracticable was his belief that episcopal government was essential to Christianity, and that he was bound by his coronation-oath to maintain it; whereas the others held themselves equally bound by their solemn league and covenant to abolish episcopacy, and establish presbytery in its room: that both parties were immoveable, and upon this rock, says he, they split: that His Majesty's agreement with the army was more open and practicable, because they would have set aside the covenant, and obliged the Parliament to tolerate episcopal government as well as the sectaries: but, adds Neal, he affected to play the army and the Parliament against each other, hoping to take advantage of their divisions, and establish himself upon the ruins of both; for that it was His Majesty's maxim, which he did not scruple to avow, that neither party could subsist without him, and that those must be ruined whom he abandoned; by which conduct he lost his interest both in the Parliament and army, and laid the foundation of his own ruin.

. The Presbyterians, proceeds Neal, were no less unhappy; for the majority of the House of Commons, with the city of London and the whole Scots nation, being firmly in their interest, they imagined nothing could stand before them, and therefore would abate nothing of their demands, nor hearken to any other terms of accommodation with the King than those of the covenant, which were the entire abolishing of prelacy, and the establishing Presbyterian uniformity throughout both kingdoms, with an absolute extirpation of all sectaries whatsoever: that this embarrassed them, not only with the King, but awakened the jealousy of the army, who were thoroughly convinced, that when the presbyterians were in the legal possession of their demands, they would exercise equal tyranny over the consciences of men with the bishops of that reign; and that indeed nothing less was to be expected, considering their steady adherence to the covenant in all their treaties with the King, their efforts in Parliament to get the power of the keys into their hands, their frequent addresses for the suppressing all sectaries by the civil authority, and their declamations, both from the pulpit and the press, against toleration and liberty of conscience.

Neal adds, in another place, the Independents' principles might be too narrow and mistaken in some points, and their zeal for Christian liberty might betray them into some imprudencies; but on which side was the stiffness? on theirs who only desired a peaceable toleration; or on theirs who were determined to make the whole nation stoop to presbyterian uniformity? Were not these the men that kept open the church's wounds? Had their discipline been never so good, yet they might have had some regard to men of equal piety and virtue, that could not see with their eyes. Could they not be content with being the established religion, and having most of the livings of the kingdom divided amongst them, but they must subvert the religious rights of mankind, by enforcing an absolute uniformity, which can never be maintained but upon the ruins of a good conscience?

Ludlow's recollection of the part he took in the exclusion of the more than forty members of the House of Commons, for the purpose of carrying his and his party's point of procuring the votes of no more addresses to the King, and for bringing him to trial, should have moderated his wrath upon the occasion of Cromwell's dissolution of the Long Parliament. Had the exclusion of the whole House been necessary to the accomplishment of their object, they would not have scrupled it by the same means of military force. There is no difference between the two transactions, other than the extent; the principle upon which both acted was the same, the accomplishment of their respective particular purposes. Cromwell, notwithstanding the persistence of some writers to the contrary, had no concern in the exclusion of the above members; Ludlow takes the whole (as he conceives it) merit of this transaction to himself.

His (Cromwell's) dissolution of the Long Parliament, brought upon him the displeasure and resentment of Ludlow and his republican party, and of all others whose views were thereby frustrated. Ludlow presumes to dive into the thoughts and views of Cromwell, after the battle of Worcester. All he says is mere conjecture, arising probably out of a little-minded jealousy of Cromwell's superior talents and military renown. Even his moderation towards the royal party, of which Ludlow accuses him, and his magnanimity in procuring the act of oblivion, are unfavourably represented, and sinister motives applied to both.

The reasons for this dissolution are to be found in a declaration published a few days afterwards, and given at some length by Dr. Harris; and the substance by Whitelock. They are also fully entered into, and given in Cromwell's speech delivered in the council-chamber upon the 4th of July (1653) following the dissolution, which was, on the 20th of the preceding April, published in 1654 separately, by authority. It is stated to have been delivered to the persons then assembled and intrusted with the supreme authority of the nation. After giving a short history of the preceding times, concluding with the battle of Worcester, he proceeds to remind them of the passages that had been since transacted; whence coming, he says, with his fellow-officers and soldiers, they expected, and had some reasonable confidence that their expectations should not be frustrate. A few lines afterwards he says, that himself and those gentlemen that had been engaged in those military affairs, upon their return, came fully bent in their hearts and thoughts, to desire and use all fair and lawful means they could, to have had the nation to reap the fruit of all that blood and treasure that had been expended in the cause: that they were very tender for a long time so much as to petition; till August last they never offered to petition, but that some of their members and others having good acquaintance and relation to divers members of the Parliament, they did, from time to time, solicit that which they thought (if there had been nobody to prompt them, nobody to call upon them) would have been listened to, out of ingenuity and integrity in them that had opportunity to have answered their expectations: that when they saw nothing would be done they did, as they thought, according to their duty, remind them by a petition in July or August then last, to which they had no return: that finding the people dissatisfied, they had divers meetings, at

least ten or twelve, with divers members of Parliament; the first in October then last, whom they
besought, that they would, of their own accords,
do those good things that had been promised, that
so it might appear they did not do them by any
suggestion from the army, but of their own ingenuity; so tender were they (the army) to preserve
them in the reputation and opinion of the people
to the uttermost : that at last, when they saw that
things would not be laid to heart, they had a serious
consideration amongst themselves (the army) what
other way to have recourse unto : that when they
(the army) began to take those close considerations,
they (the Parliament) began to take the act of the
new representation to heart, and seemed exceeding
willing to put it on, the which, had it been done
with that integrity, with that caution, that would
have saved this cause, and the interest they (the
army) had been so long engaged in, there could
nothing have happened to their (the army's) judgments, more welcome than that would have been;
but that they found plainly that the intendment
of it was not to give the people their right of choice,
but only the appearance of it, and that their real
intention and design was to recruit the House, the
better to perpetuate themselves. "And truly having divers of us spoken to, to that end that we
should give way to it, a thing to which we had a
perpetual aversation, which we did abominate the
thoughts of, we always declared our judgments
16

against it, and our dissatisfaction; but yet they would not hear of a representative, before it lay three years before them, without proceeding with one line considerably in it; they that could not endure to hear of it then, when we came to our close considerations, then, instead of protracting, they did make as much preposterous haste, on the other hand, and ran into that extremity, and finding that this spirit was not according to God, and that the whole weight of this cause, which must needs have been very dear unto us who have so often adventured our lives for it, and we believe is so to you; when we saw plainly that there was not so much consideration how to assist it; or to provide security for it; and, indeed, to cross these, that they reckoned the most troublesome people they had to deal with, which was the army, which by this time was sufficiently their displeasure. When we saw this truly, that had power in our hands, to let the business go to such an issue as this, was to throw back the cause into the hands of them we first fought with; we came to this first conclusion amongst ourselves, that, if we had been fought out of it, necessity would have taught us patience; but, to be taken from us so unworthily, we should be rendered the worst people in the world," &c. In a subsequent part of this speech, that when they (the army) saw the Parliament's intendment to be, to perpetuate themselves, and that they could not endure to hear of being dissolved, they (the principal officers of

the army) did desire, once more, the night before
the dissolution, that they might speak with some
of the principal persons of the House, that they
might open their hearts to them, to the end that
they might be either convinced of the ground of
their principles and intentions to the good of the
nation, or that, if they (the officers) could not be
convinced, they (the Parliament) would hear their
(the officers') offer or expedient to prevent this
mischief: that they told the members they met,
that they desired to know from them what security
lay in the way of their proceedings, so hastily with
their representative, wherein they had made a few
qualifications (such as they were), and how the
whole business should be executed; and that if
they did proceed in honest ways, as might be safe
to the nation, they (the army) might acquiesce
therein: that, when pressed to give satisfaction in
this, the answer was that nothing could be good
to the nation, but the continuance of this Parliament: that "seeing they would not give us that
which might satisfy us that their way was honest
and safe, they would give us leave to make our
objections;—we did tell them, that we thought
that way they were going in would be impracticable; we could not tell them how it would be
brought to pass, to send out an act of Parliament
into the country, to have qualifications in an act
to be the rules of electors and elected, and not to
know who should execute this: desired to know

whether the next Parliament were not like to consist of all presbyters; whether those qualifications
would hinder them or neuters? and though it be
our desire to value and esteem of that judgment,
only they having, as we know, deserted this cause
and interest upon the King's account, and upon
that closure between them and the neighbour
nation, we do think we must profess, we had as
good have delivered up our cause into the hands
of any, as into the hands of interested and biassed
men; for it is one thing to live friendly and
brotherly, to bear with and love a person of
another judgment in religion, another thing to
have any so far set into the saddle upon that account, as that it should be in them to have all
the rest of their brethren at mercy : that having
had this discourse, making these objections of
bringing in neuters, or such as should impose
upon their brethren, or such as had given testimony
to the King's party, and objecting to the danger
of it, in drawing the concourse of all people, to
arraign every individual person, which indeed did
fall obviously in, and the issue would certainly
have been, the putting it into the hands of men
that had little affection to this cause: that the
answer again was made, and it was confessed by
some that these objections did lie, but answer was
made by a very eminent person at the same time
as before, that nothing would save the nation but
the continuance of this Parliament:" that this
being so, they (the army) proposed an expedient,

that the government being in that condition it was, and things being in so much ill sense abroad, and so likely to come to confusion if it went on, they (the Parliament) would devolve the trust over to persons of honour and integrity, well known, and well affected to religion and the interest of the nation, which they confessed was no new thing, when these nations had been under the like distractions : that to this it was answered, that nothing would save the nation but the continuance of that Parliament : that finding their endeavours did directly tend thereto, and they giving this answer, — that the things we had offered were of a tender and very weighty consideration, and making objections how we should raise money, and some other objections, we told them that we offered as an expedient, because we thought better than that for which no reason was or thought could be given. We desired them to lay the thing seriously to heart ; they told us they would take consideration of these till the morning, that they would sleep upon them : " and, I think," continues Cromwell, " there was scarce any day that there sat above 50, 52, or 53. That at the parting, two or three of the chief ones did tell us, that they would endeavour the suspending the proceedings of the representative the next day, till they had had a further conference, and we did acquiesce, and had hope, that if our expedient would take up a loving debate, the next day we should have some

such issue of it as would have given a satisfaction
to all. They went away late at night, and the
next morning, we, considering how to order that
which we had to offer to them, when they were to
meet in the evening, word was brought they were
proceeding with a representative with all the eagerness they could. We did not believe persons of
such quality could do it; a second and a third
messenger told us they had almost finished it, and
had brought it to that issue, with that haste that
had never been before; leaving out the things that
did necessarily relate to due qualifications, as we
have heard since, resolved to make it a paper bill;
not to engross it, that they might make the quicker
dispatch of it; thus to have thrown all the liberties of the nation into the hands that never bled
for it: upon this account we thought it our duty
not to suffer it; and upon this the House was dissolved." The speech then proceeds to exhort and
instruct the persons then assembled in the performance of their duties; and concludes with
ordering the instrument of government to be read;
which he (Cromwell) had signed by the advice of
his council of officers.

The cause of this apparently strong proceeding
of Cromwell's dissolution of the Long Parliament,
must be sought for in the circumstances in which
he found himself at the time. The forementioned
conversation at Essex-house, with the heads of the
presbyterian party, related by Whitelock, proves

the early dislike of the Scots and English Presbyterians to Cromwell, and their wish to get rid of him by the prosecution of him as an incendiary between the two nations. It appears also, from Lord Clarendon and Ludlow, that the presbyterian party in the House of Commons was the most powerful party, and that they made several attempts to impeach and send him to the Tower. They also repeatedly attempted to disband the army, for the generally understood purpose of depriving Cromwell and the other obnoxious chiefs of that support, and reducing them, as individuals, into their power, subjecting them also to a commonwealth form of government, with a presbyterian church-government and Directory, without the least allowance to the scruples of those who could not conscientiously submit to this church-government, or the use of such Directory : in opposition to the Independents' liberal indulgence of all religious denominations, in the exercise of their natural right of private judgment in matters of religion.

These considerations alone were sufficient to determine Cromwell and his party upon resistance to this, the presbyterian party's attempt of sovereignty.

The above speech expressly charges the presbyterian party in the House with the design of perpetuating themselves and their own power, by filling up the Parliament from their own party; thus having, as the speech expresses, the rest of their brethren at their mercy. It also appears from the speech, that the Parliament leaders deceived the army in the breach of their promise, to take the army's proposals into consideration the next morning, and to endeavour the suspending the Parliament's proceedings till they should have a further conference; instead of which, they were found proceeding with all eagerness with their proposed bill for their representative; which determined the army upon their dissolution, and which was effected by Cromwell, as before related, upon the 20th April, 1653.

This Parliament consisted, at the time of its dissolution, of not more (according to Cromwell's statement in his above speech) than 53 members. Referring to the Journals, the number upon the resolution to dissolve the House of Lords was only 73; the number upon the resolution of a commonwealth form of government, soon after the King's death, does not appear; but, upon the resolution of the act of oblivion in April (1649), the number was only 47: upon the appointment of the council of state in the same year it was 90; and, upon the vote shortly afterwards, for completing the number of the same council, the number then in the House was reported to be 108; upon the 24th November (1652), upon the election of a new council of state for the ensuing year, the number present was agreed to be 122; and on the 26th of the same month 97.

Thus the small numbers before stated took upon themselves to determine upon a commonwealth form of government, without King or House of Lords: but it is evident that this form had not been universally acquiesced in, or considered to be finally settled; for the consideration and determination of the form of government to be adopted was the express object of the meetings mentioned by Whitelock; upon which there was much difference of opinion.

Whitelock's observations upon this transaction are certainly very severe upon Cromwell and his party; they, however, confirm the impartiality of his memorials; notwithstanding his disapprobation of some parts of Cromwell's conduct, he continued to act with him during the remainder of his public life, and appears to have entertained a very favourable opinion of him. All other writers friendly to a commonwealth form of government, or for any other reason hostile to him, allow him no excuse.

It should be remembered, that the republican form of government was but an assumption upon the destruction of the monarchical form, to which the nation had always been accustomed, and might be supposed to have been generally partial: that it was certainly most tyrannical and oppressive, imposing upon the people an establishment and mode of public worship to which they had not been accustomed, framed by the presbyterian divines, under the sanction of the Parliament, without the·

least regard to the different religious opinions and scruples of those upon whom it was imposed, and subjecting the disobedient to the severest penalties. There cannot be a stronger proof of their intolerance, than their refusal, in their treaty in the Isle of Wight, to permit the King the use of the Liturgy, and of every other form of prayer in its stead, in his own household and family, insisting upon his use of the Directory only.

It is not therefore to be conceived, that Cromwell and his party would tamely submit themselves to the arbitrary domination of this assumed power; their inveterate enemies seeking every opportunity to rid themselves of such formidable opponents of their ambitious views. Cromwell's victories, and great endowments, had placed him and his party in the ability to determine upon this question; and they had, at least, as much right to deliberate upon and determine the form of the government of the country, as the party who had taken upon themselves so to do.

At the forementioned meeting, in December, 1651, of members of Parliament and chief officers of the army soon after the battle of Worcester, which was on the 3d of the preceding September, for the purpose of considering of a settlement of the nation, Whitelock describes Cromwell as proposing for consideration, whether a republic or a mixed monarchical government would be best; and, if any thing monarchical, then, in whom that power should be placed: that different opinions were given; some for a republic, others for a mixed monarchy, to be placed in one of the sons of the late King: that Cromwell thought this a business of more than ordinary difficulty; but that a settlement with somewhat of monarchical powers in it would be very effectual, if to be accomplished with safety and preservation of the nation's rights and privileges: but that the company parted without coming to any result, only that Cromwell thus discovered the inclinations of those present, for which he fished, and made use of what he then discerned.

A book or pamphlet is amongst the Cromwell family papers, appearing to have been published subsequent to Cromwell becoming Protector, entitled, " Animadversions upon a Letter and Paper subscribed and sent to him by certain Gentlemen and others in Wales," being, as described, " A Word for God, or a Testimony on Truth's Behalf; from several Churches, and divers Hundreds of Christians in Wales (and some few adjacent), against Wickedness in High Places."   This letter severely censures Cromwell for taking upon himself this office.

The animadversions are anonymous; they appear to be impartially written; favourable to Cromwell, but not to his becoming Protector.

Referring to the dissolution of the Long Parliament, the writer says, that it deserved to be mentioned with much honour by all honest men in

the nation that did adhere to it; for that it had in
it many sound and worthy men,. and was a long
time a bulwark that kept off slavery and destruction from breaking in upon us in many a hard
brunt and desperate assault; yet that the removing
of them at that time might be no injury to them
or us : that Parliament, as it then stood, was no
legal constitution, nor had they right to the government by our laws : what right had they to
take away the life and office of a king by whose
authority they were made a Parliament? or what
right had they to take away the House of Lords,
a constitution ancienter than themselves? when
this was done, what just power had they to constitute themselves a commonwealth? that there was
no act of the people that either made them so, or
gave them power to make themselves so; they had
no such power inherent in themselves, neither could
they ever manifest any such stamp of majesty set
upon them by God and his providence. Now,
proceeds the writer, the Parliament did assume the
government without any rule or authority, and
impose it and themselves upon the people, and so
upon the army; what law is broken in pulling
down that which stands not by law? that that
government, such a constitution as it had, was from
the army; the army urged them to do justice upon
the King, which they neither could nor durst do
themselves; for that they and every rational man
must confess, that were it not for the strength, .

honour, and success of the army, that which we
call Parliament, government, and commonwealth,
would have been made confederacy and rebellion:
that it is true the army did at least tolerate, and so
far consent, as to submit to this government; but
I (the writer) know not that they did, by any act,
ratify it, or ever intend to perpetuate it; and that
consent was not an act of judgment and righteous-
ness; for in all our affairs hitherto, we have not
had so much light and clearness as to produce any
work of true wisdom and understanding: but, as
in all other things, so in this, we are driven and
thrust forward from one thing to that which is
next, as the sense of danger and the hopes of ease
lead us, in the dark, without judgment: and so the
army set up or admit of this government, by a Parliament, without King or Lords being at hand,
knowing no better, finding some ease in being
freed from worse oppressors, and as a present conveniency: and, if they had power to admit it, or
set it up when they found it useful, why may they
not pull it down and reject it when they felt it
grievous and burthensome; that which you call
the government, as it never had a formal constitution, either from God or men, (that I know of,)
so, before it was taken down, it had quite lost the
nature and spirit of government,—a dry tree shrunk
into a private and selfish spirit: there were good
men and good things amongst them, but mingled
with a perverse and foolish spirit: that four or five

of the best of them could not agree in any one
proposition for public good, though they were wise
and honest men, yet (they themselves know) they
were absurdly and peevishly divided, in so great a
confusion, that there could be no reason of expecting any more fruit from them: they were a long
while a burthen to the nation, and the people very
sensible of it, and did, by a general dislike and
scorn of them, recall that choice that they had
made of them, and the honour they had put upon
them, and would, if the army had not guarded
them, have expressed their rejecting of them from
being their representatives, by pulling them out of
the House: they were indeed full ripe, and had
not the army done it, the rage of women, or some
base hand, would have gathered them.   I believe
they were self-condemned, and the more ingenuous
of them were sensible of an enlargement, by their
being discharged from their sore and unprofitable
travel; only having long enjoyed their places,
they lingered, and were loth to depart; and when
they saw they must go, they would provide for
their speedy return, and would have died to live
again; which was the great incivility done them
in their apprehensions; they were prevented in
their propagating their likeness and themselves
also in a new representative.

  Lord Clarendon, referring to this dissolution, observes, that there were many members of the House
who seemed to think it necessary for abating the

great envy which was confessedly against the Parliament throughout the kingdom, that they should
be dissolved, to the end that the people might
make a new election of such persons as they might
think fit to trust with their liberty and property,
and whatever was dearest to them ; but that it was
finally determined, that the Parliament would not
yet think of dissolving, nor would take it well, that
any persons should take the presumption any more
to make overtures to them of that nature, which
was not fit for private and particular persons to
meddle with : and that, to put a seasonable stop
to any farther presumption of that kind, they appointed a committee speedily to prepare an act of
Parliament for the filling up of their House; and
by which it should be declared to be high treason
for any man to propose or contrive the changing
of the present government settled and established :
that this bill being prepared by the committee,
they resolved to pass it with all possible expedition;
so, says His Lordship, Cromwell clearly discerned
that they would never be persuaded to part with
that authority and power which was so profitable
and so pleasant to them : that all things being thus
prepared, Cromwell thought this a good season to
expose those enemies to peace to the indignation
of the nation, which he knew was generally weary
of the war.   Then follows His Lordship's account
of the dissolution of that Parliament.

. Ludlow is vehemently indignant at Cromwell's

dissolution of the Long Parliament. He commences his account of this transaction upon the conclusion of his account of the Parliament's successes in Ireland; by observing that the enemy, by the blessing of God upon the counsels of the Parliament, and endeavours of their army, being every where dispersed and conquered, and the nation likely to attain in a short time that measure of happiness which human things were capable of, the hopes and expectations of all good men were disappointed by the ambition of one man. General Cromwell, says he, had long been suspected by wise and good men; but that he had taken such care to form and mould the army to his humour and interest that he had filled all places, either with his own creatures, or with such as hoped to share with him in the sovereignty, and removed those, who, foreseeing his designs, had either the courage or honesty to oppose him in it: that his pernicious intentions did not discover themselves till after the battle of Worcester, which, in one of his letters to the Parliament, he called the crowning victory. So much, continues Ludlow, was he elevated with that success, that Mr. Hugh Peters told him (Ludlow) that he took so much notice of it as to say in confidence to a friend upon the road, upon his return from Worcester, that Cromwell would make himself king; that he now began to despise divers members of the House, whom he had formerly courted, and grew most

familiar with those to whom he used to show most
aversion; endeavouring to oblige the royal party
by procuring for them more favourable conditions
than consisted with the justice of the Parliament
to grant, under colour of quieting the spirits of
many people, and keeping them from engaging in
new disturbances to rescue themselves out of those
fears, which many, who had acted for the King,
yet lay under; though at the same time, adds he,
he designed nothing, as by the success was most
manifest, but to advance himself, by all manner of
means, and to betray the great trust which the
Parliament and good people of England had reposed in him: that to this end he pressed the act
of oblivion with so much importunity, that though
some members earnestly opposed its bearing date
till after some months, as well in justice to those
of that party who had already fined for their delinquency, that others as guilty as themselves
might be upon an equal foot with them, as that
the state might thereby be supplied with money
which they wanted; and that such as had been
plundered by the enemy might receive some satisfaction from those who had ruined them: yet that
nothing could prevail upon the General, and so
the act was passed; the Parliament being unwilling
to deny him any thing for which there was the least
colour of reason.   But, proceeds Ludlow, though
he had gained this point, and eagerly coveted his
own advancement, he thought it not convenient

yet to unmask himself, but rather to make higher pretences to honesty than ever he had done before, thereby to engage Major-general Harrison, Colonel Rich, and their party to himself; and to this end he took all occasions, in their presence, to asperse the Parliament, as not designing to do those good things they pretended to, but rather intending to support the corrupt interests of the clergy and lawyers: and that, though he was convinced that they were hastening with all expedition to put a period to their sitting, having passed a vote that they would do it within the space of a year, and that they were making all possible preparations in order to it, yet did he industriously publish that they were so in love with their seats, that they would use all means to perpetuate themselves, which, and other calumnies, he had so artfully insinuated into the belief of many honest and well-meaning people, that they began to wish him prosperity in his undertaking. He (Ludlow) then gives the same account, in substance, as Whitelock, of the dissolution of the Parliament.

The same writer (Ludlow) says, that in the afternoon of the day on which he (Cromwell) had interrupted the Parliament, (the 20th April, 1653,) Cromwell came to the council of state, who were assembled to do their duty at the usual place, accompanied by Major-general Lambert and Colonel Harrison, and told them at his entrance, that if they were met there as private persons they should not be disturbed, but if as a council of state, that was no place for them, and that since they could not but know what was done at the House in the morning, so they were to take notice that the Parliament was dissolved: that to this, Sergeant Bradshaw answered, " Sir, we have heard what you did at the House in the morning, and, before many hours, all England will hear it ; but, Sir, you are mistaken to think that the Parliament is dissolved, for no power under Heaven can dissolve them but themselves; therefore take you notice of that :" that something more was said to the same purpose by Sir Arthur Haslerig, Mr. Love, and Mr. Scot: and then the council of state, perceiving themselves to be under the same violence, departed.

Ludlow proceeds ; — that soon after Cromwell had thus barbarously treated the Parliament, and effaced the civil authority, he sent for Major Salloway, and Mr. John Carew, to whom he complained of the great weight of affairs that by this undertaking was fallen upon him ; affirming that the thoughts of the consequences thereof made him to tremble, and therefore desired them to free him from the temptations that might be laid before him, and to that end to go immediately to the Chief Justice St. John, Mr. Selden, and some others, and endeavour to persuade them to draw up some instrument of government that might put

the power out of his hands: that to this was
answered, by Major Salloway, The way, Sir, to
free you from this temptation, is for you not to
look upon yourself to be under it, but to rest persuaded that the power of the nation is in the good
people of England, as formerly it was: that Cromwell, perceiving by this answer that he was better
understood than he would have wished, fell upon
another expedient before he could openly discover
himself, appointing a meeting of the chief officers
of the army to be at Whitehall, in order to consider what was to be done in this exigency. He
(Ludlow) then mentions the meeting and determination of Cromwell and his officers to settle the
representation of the nation referred to by Whitelock.

The above extracts from Ludlow are not in
Whitelock, and Ludlow being at the time in
Ireland must have had this information from
others: whether, therefore, true or false cannot
now be ascertained.

In Whitelock's forementioned conversation,
which, he says, passed between Cromwell and him
in November, (1652,) previous to this dissolution
of the Long Parliament, he says of its members,
that the army began to have a strange distaste
against them; and really, says he, their pride and ambition, and self-seeking, ingrossing all places of honour and profit to themselves and their friends, and
their daily breaking forth into new and violent parties

and factions; their delays of business, and design to perpetuate themselves, and to continue the power in their own hands; their meddling in private matters between party and party, contrary to the institution of parliaments; and their injustice and partiality in those matters, and the scandalous lives of some of the chiefs of them; these things do give too much ground for people to open their mouths against them, and to dislike them. Nor can they be kept within the bounds of justice, and law or reason; they themselves being the supreme power of the nation, liable to no account to any, nor to be controuled or regulated by any other power, there being none superior, or co-ordinate with them: so that, adds he, unless there be some authority and power so full and so high as to restrain and keep things in better order, and that may be a check to these exorbitances, it will be impossible in human reason to prevent our ruin. Whitelock acknowledges the danger to be feared from these extravagances and inordinate powers, both of the army and of the Parliament: those of the army he thinks might be corrected by his great powers; but that the greatest difficulty lay with the Parliament for the above reasons, that too many of them were much to blame in those he had mentioned, and many unfit things had passed; but that he hoped well of the major part of them when great matters should come to a decision.

Whitelock, in another part of his history, referring to the Parliament's arbitrary exercise of power,
relates, that they, upon hearing Sir Jacob Garrett's
business, (he does not describe it,) sentenced three
of his false accusers to stand in the pillory :—thus,
says he, they took upon them, and exercised all
manner of jurisdiction, and sentenced persons
secundum arbitrium.

After some further conversation with Whitelock
to the same effect, Cromwell puts the question,
" What, if a man should take upon him to be a
king ?" Whitelock thinks that remedy would be
worse than the disease ; for which he assigns his
reasons, to be found, with Cromwell's answers, in
the forementioned conversation. By the desire
of Cromwell, Whitelock states his sentiments of
the remedy to be found for the obviating the then
dangers and difficulties, wherein it was agreed all
were engaged. He tells Cromwell that he is en-
vironed with secret enemies in the army, who were
not without their designs how they might dismount
him ; how they might bring him down, and set up
themselves : and that they wanted no counsel and
encouragement from some members of Parliament,
jealous of his power and greatness, who would plot
to bring him down, or to clip his wings. Cromwell admits that Whitelock had rightly considered
his situation, and presses him to disclose his proposed remedy, which is the restoration of the King
(Charles the Second) by a private treaty, upon

certain terms. Cromwell, in answer, says, that he thought he had much reason in what he had propounded, but that it was a matter of so high importance and difficulty, that it deserved more time of consideration than at present allowed. Whitelock adds, that Cromwell seemed displeased, though he never afterwards objected it against him ; only that his carriage was, from that time, altered, and his advising with him not so frequent.

The preceding statements must, surely, be deemed fully to justify this act of Cromwell's dissolution of the Long Parliament.

The substance of Cromwell's speech of the 4th July, 1653, to the persons then assembled, and entrusted with the supreme power, (his reasons for dissolving the Long Parliament,) has been already given. The substance of the instrument of government therein referred to, will be found in the before-given extracts from Whitelock. The title of this assembly was determined to be, " The Parliament of the Commonwealth of England."

On the 12th of the following December (1653), this Parliament determined its longer sitting not to be for the good of the commonwealth, and delivered up to Cromwell the power they had received from him ; and on the 16th of the same month it was determined by Cromwell and a council of officers, that the government should be by a council of twenty-one persons, and by Cromwell as Lord Protector, who was thereupon invested with that office. The instrument of government consisted of forty-two articles; the proclamation of the council upon this occasion begins with relating, that this parliament dissolved itself.

Mr. Maidston, in his forementioned letter to Mr. Winthrop, of the 24th March, 1659, in Thurloe's State Papers, speaking of this parliament, says, they meet and accept it (the government), assume the title of Parliament, and sit in the House of Commons and enact sundry laws; but in a short time made it appear to all considering and unprejudiced men that they were *huic negotio impares, non obstante* their godliness; of which the more judicious of them being sensible, contrived the matter so as to dissolve themselves by an act of their own, and devolve their authority, whence they first derived it, upon the General.

Lord Clarendon, referring to this proceeding, says, that when they (this parliament) had tired and perplexed themselves some time in their debates, upon their meeting in the morning of the 12th December, and before many of them were come, who were likely to dissent from the motion, one of them stood up and declared, that he did believe they were not equal to the burthen that was laid upon them; and therefore that they might dissolve themselves, and deliver back their authority into their hands from whom they had received it, which being presently consented to, their Speaker, with those who were of that mind, went to White-

hall and redelivered to Cromwell the instrument
they had received from him, acknowledged their
own impotency, and besought him to take care of
the commonwealth ; and that, by this frank dona-
tion, he and his council of officers were once more
possessed of the supreme sovereign power of the
nation.

In the Parliament, held pursuant to the instrument of government on the 4th September (1654),
Cromwell made a speech, which Whitelock calls a
subtle one.   Describing the confusions, both civil
and religious, into which the nation had fallen, he
says, that it might not sink into confusion, a remedy must be applied: a remedy has been applied;
this government, a thing that is seen and read of
all, and which (let men say what they will, I can
speak with comfort before a greater than you all
as to my intention, and let men judge out of the
thing itself,) is calculated for the interest of the
people, for their interest alone, and for their good,
without respect had to any other interest.   It hath
endeavoured to reform the laws ; and for that end
hath joined persons (without reflection upon any)
of as great integrity and ability as any other, to
consider how the laws might be made plain, short,
and easy ; which may, in due time, be tendered.
It hath taken care to put into seats of justice men
of the most known integrity and ability.   The
chancery hath been reformed, and I hope, to the
satisfaction of all good men.   It hath put a stop to

that heady way for 'every man 'that will to make
himself a preacher; having endeavoured to settle .
a way for approbation of men of piety and fitness
for the work; and the business committed to
persons, both of the presbyterian and independent
judgment, men of as known ability and integrity
as (I suppose) any the nation hath; and who
(I believe) have laboured to approve themselves to
God, and their own consciences, in approving men
to that great function. One thing more, it hath
been instrumental to call a free parliament; blessed
be God, we see here, this day, a free parliament;
and that it may continue so, I hope, is in the heart
of every good man of England: for my own part,
as I desired it above my life, so to keep it free I
shall value it above my life. He then says, that a
peace has been made with Sweden; it being of
much importance to have a good understanding
with our Protestant neighbours: also with the
Danes, honourable, and to the satisfaction of the
merchants: the Sound open to us, from whence,
as from a fountain, our naval provisions are supplied: a peace with the Dutch. I beg that it may
be in your hearts to be zealous of the Protestant
interest abroad, which, if it be ever like to come
under a condition of suffering, it is now; many
being banished, and driven to seek refuge among
strangers. A peace is made with Portugal (though
it hung long) of great concernment to trade; and
the people that trade thither have freedom to

enjoy their consciences, without being subjected
to the bloody Inquisition : a treaty with France
now depending. He proceeds, it may be necessary, in the next place, for you to hear a little of
the sea-affairs, and to take notice of the great
expense of the forces and fleet; and yet 30,000*l*.
is now abated of the next three months' assess-
ment. These things are but entrances and doors
of hope; you are brought to the edge of Canaan
(into which many that have gone before could not
enter;) but if the blessing and presence of God
go along with you in the management of your
affairs, I make no question, but he will enable you
to lay the topstone of this work. But this is a
maxim not to be despised, — though peace be
made, yet that it is interest that keeps peace ; and
further than that, peace is not to be trusted. The
great end of calling this Parliament is, that the
work of God may go on, that the ship of this
commonwealth may be brought into a safe harbour. I. shall put you in mind, that you have a
great work upon you ; Ireland to look to, that the
beginning of that government may be settled· in
honour : that you have before you the considerations of those foreign states, with whom peace is
not made ; who, if they see we manage not our
affairs with prudence, as becomes men, will retain
hopes, that we may still, under the disadvantages
thereof, break into confusion. I shall conclude
with my persuasion to you, to have a sweet, gra-

cious, and holy understanding, one of another, and
put you in mind of the counsel you heard this day
in order thereunto. And I desire you to believe,
that I speak not to you as one that would be a
lord over you, but as one that is resolved to be a
fellow-servant with you to the interest of this great
affair.

It appears from the Journals of the House of
Commons, that one of the first subjects of debate
was, Whether the government should be in one
single person and a Parliament. This was evidently aimed personally at Cromwell. Whitelock
says the debates grew high, and that Cromwell,
apprehending that the Parliament would too far
invade, or endeavour to overthrow the new government, sent for the members to meet him in the
Painted Chamber, on the 12th of the same September, and addressed them to the effect given in
Whitelock. Amongst other things, he tells them,
that in informing them they were a free Parliament, he considered there was a reciprocation, for
that the same government that made them a Parliament made him Protector, and that, as they
were entrusted with some things, so was he with
all other things : that there were some things in
the government fundamental, and could not be
altered ; viz. that the government should be in one
person, and a Parliament ; that Parliament should
not be made perpetual, which would deprive the
people of their successive elections ; nor that the

Parliament should be always sitting, that is, as soon as one Parliament was up, another should come and sit in their places the very next day; that this could not be, without subjecting the nation to an arbitrary power in governing, because Parliaments, when they sit, are absolute and unlimited: that the militia was not to be entrusted in any one hand or power, but to be so disposed, that, as the Parliament ought to have a check upon the Protector to prevent excesses in him, so, on the other hand, the Protector ought to have a check upon the Parliament in the business of the militia, to prevent excesses in them; because if it were wholly in the Parliament, they might, when they would, perpetuate themselves; but that the militia being disposed of as it was, the one stood as a counterpoise to the other, and rendered the balance of government the more even, and the government itself, the more firm and stable : a due liberty of conscience in matters of religion, wherein bounds and limits ought to be set, so as to prevent persecution : and that the rest of the things in the government, were examinable and alterable, as the occasion and the state of affairs should require : that, as for a negative voice, he claimed it not, save only in the foresaid particulars: and that in all other things he had only a deliberative power ; and that if he did not pass such laws as were presented to him within twenty days after their presentment, they were to be laws without his consent : and concludes with requiring the members to sign the forementioned recognition, before they again went into the House. In his speech of the 22d January following (1654), upon dissolving this Parliament of the 4th of the preceding September, referring to the various favourable circumstances, affording good ground of hope that the nation had arrived at a safe port, and might reasonably look to a happy termination of all their difficulties; he proceeds to show by what means this favourable opportunity had been : is there not, says he, yet upon the spirits of men a strange itch? nothing will satisfy them, unless they can put their finger upon their brethren's consciences, to pinch them there. To do this, was no part of the contest we had with the common adversary ; for religion was not the thing at the first contested for; but God brought it to that issue, and gave it to us by way of redundancy, and at last it proved to be that which was most dear to us; and wherein consisted this, more than in obtaining that liberty from the tyranny of the bishops to all species of Protestants, to worship God according to their own light and consciences ; for want of which many of our brethren forsook their native countries, to seek their bread from strangers, and to live in howling wildernesses, and for which also many that remained here were imprisoned and otherwise abused and made the scorn of the nation : those that were sound in the faith, how proper was it for them to

labour for liberty, for a just liberty, that men
should not be trampled upon for their consciences.
Had not they laboured but lately under the weight
of persecutions, and was it fit for them to sit heavy
upon others?   Is it ingenuous to ask liberty, and
not to give it?   What greater hypocrisy than for
those who were oppressed by the bishops to become the greatest oppressors themselves so soon
as their yoke was removed?   I could wish that
they who call for liberty now, also had not too
much of that spirit, if the power were in their
hands.   As to profane persons,— blasphemers,
such as preach sedition, the contentious railers,
evil speakers, who seek by evil words to corrupt
good manners, persons of loose conversation,
punishment from the civil magistrate ought to
meet with them, because if these pretend conscience, yet walking disorderly, and not according
but contrary to the Gospel, and even to natural
light, they are judged of all, and their sins being
open make them subjects of the magistrates' sword,
who ought not to bear it in vain.   In another part
of this speech, he says, I will not presage what you
have been about ordering in all this time, nor do I
love to make conjectures; but I must tell you this,
that as I undertook this government in the simplicity of my heart, and as before God, and to do the
part of an honest man, and to be true to the interest which in my conscience is dear to many of
you, though it is not always understood what God

in his wisdom may hide from us as to peace and
settlement; so I can say, that no particular interest,
either of myself, estate, honour, or family, are, or
have been prevalent with me to this undertaking:
for if you had, upon the old government, offered
to me this one thing, (I speak as thus advised and
before God, as having been to this day of this
opinion, and this hath been my constant judgment, well known to many that hear me speak,) if
this one thing had been inserted that this government should have been and placed in my family
hereditary, I would have rejected it; and I could
have done no other, according to my present conscience and light. I will tell you my reason,
though I cannot tell what God will do with me,
nor you, nor the nation, for throwing away precious opportunities committed to us: this hath been
my principle, and I liked it when this government
came first to be proposed to me, that it put us off
that hereditary way, well looking that as God had
declared what government he had delivered to the
Jews, and placed it upon such persons as had been
instrumental for the conduct and deliverance of his
people; and considering that promise in Isaiah,
that God would give rulers as at the first, and
judges as at the beginning, I did not know but
that God might begin; and though at present
with a most unworthy person, yet as to the future
it might be after this manner, and I thought this
might usher it in. I am speaking as to my judg-

ment against making it hereditary, to have men
chosen for their love to God, and to truth and justice, and not to have it hereditary : for as it is in
Ecclesiastes, Who knoweth whether he may beget
fool or wise, honest or not? whatever they be,
must come in upon that account, because the
government is made a patrimony. And this I do,
perhaps, declare with too much earnestness, as
being my own concernment, and know not what
place it may have in your hearts, and of the good
people in the nation; but however it be, I have
comfort in this my truth and plainness. I have
thus told my thoughts, which truly I have declared
to you in the fear of God, as knowing he will not
be mocked, and in the strength of God, as knowing and rejoicing that I am kept in my speaking,
especially when I do not form or frame things
without the compass of integrity, and honesty, that
my own conscience gives me not the lie to what I
say, and then in what I say I can rejoice. In
another place, speaking of necessities to raise money
without parliamentary authority, and to do other
things for the benefit of the nation, he says, — But
if any man shall object; it is an easy thing to talk
of necessities, when men create necessities; would
not the Lord Protector make himself great and his
family great? Doth not he make these necessities?
and then he will come upon the people with this
argument of necessity. This were something hard
indeed; but I have not yet known what it is to

make necessities, whatsoever the judgments or thoughts of men are. And I say this, not only to this assembly, but to the world, that that man liveth not, that can come to me, and charge me that I have in these great revolutions made necessities. I challenge even all that fear God; and, as God hath said, My glory I will not give unto another, let men take heed and be twice advised how they call his revolutions, (the things of God,) and his working of things from one period to another, — how, I say, they call them necessities of man's creation; for, by so doing, they do vilify and lessen the works of God, and rob him of his glory, which he hath said he will not give unto another, nor suffer to be taken from him. It was, say some, the cunning of the Lord Protector, (I take it to myself,) it was the craft of such a man and his plot that hath brought it about: and, as they say in other countries, there are five or six cunning men in England that have skill; they do all these things. Oh! what blasphemy is this, because men that are without God in this world, and walk not with him, and know not what it is to pray or believe, and to receive returns from God, and to be spoken unto by the Spirit of God, who speaks without a written word sometimes, yet according to it. In another place he says, — They that shall attribute to this or that person the contrivances and productions of those mighty things God hath wrought in the midst of us, and that they have not been the revo-

lutions of Christ himself, upon whose shoulders the
government is laid, they speak against God, and
they fall under his hand without a Mediator; that
is, if we deny the Spirit of Jesus Christ the glory
of all his works in the world, by which he rules
kingdoms, and doth administer and is the rod of
his strength, we provoke the Mediator, and he
may say, I'll leave you to God, I'll not intercede
for you.   Therefore, whatsoever you may judge
men for, and say, This man is cunning, and politic, and subtle; take heed, again I say, how you
judge of his revolutions as the products of men's
inventions.   After censuring the Parliament for
neglecting to provide for the pay of the army, and
thereby obliging them to live upon free-quarter, he
concludes, I have troubled you with a long speech,
and I believe it may not have the same resentment
with all, that it hath with some; but because that
is unknown to me, I shall leave it to God, and conclude with that, that I think myself bound in my
duty to God, and the people of these nations to
their safety and good in every respect; I think it
my duty to tell you, that it is not for the profit
of these nations, nor for common and public good,
for you to continue here any longer; and therefore I do declare unto you, that I do dissolve this
Parliament.

Cromwell's speech to the Parliament of the 4th
September (1654), Whitelock calls a subtle one.
Wherein this subtlety lies is not very discernible:

he (Cromwell) describes the instrument of government as calculated for the interest of the people, and so it appears to be, in their then circumstances: it regulates the numbers and choice by each county and the places therein, of the members to be sent to Parliament, and the qualifications of the electors; and it declares the Parliaments triennial: it declares Cromwell to be the Protector, but the protectorship to be elective, not hereditary; also the free and unrestricted profession of religion. Lord Clarendon, in commendation of this mode of election, says, that though he (Cromwell) did not observe the old course in sending out writs to all the little boroughs, which used to send burgesses, (by which method some single counties sent more members than six other counties did,) he thought he took a more equal way, by appointing more knights for every shire to be chosen, and fewer burgesses; whereby the number of the whole was much lessened, and yet the people being left to their own election, it was not by him thought an ill temperament, and was then generally looked upon as an alteration fit to be more warrantably made, and in a better time.

This speech must surely be allowed to be a manly and able speech: no ambiguities, but a plain and interesting statement of the very advantageous and elevated situation in which his talents and exertions had placed the nation, both at home and abroad; and solid advice for their (the Parliament's) future proceedings.

The Parliament, instead of following the recommendations of this speech, began by disputing Cromwell's title to the Protectorship, and endeavouring to overthrow this new government. This Cromwell could not suffer, with justice or safety to himself; and, accordingly, in his before-given speech of the 12th of the same September, he remonstrates with them upon the irregularity of their proceedings, and states to them those things in the government, subject and not subject, to their alteration or controul: but the Parliament still persisting in these proceedings, he dissolves it on the 22d January following: religious intolerance is one of the causes assigned for this dissolution, which would have been of itself sufficient for this determination of Cromwell, whose great principle was, the right of private judgment in matters of religion: he disavows all private interest in his undertaking the government by aggrandizement of himself or his family: he positively denies creating necessities for his own purposes, with which he appears to have been charged, and defies any one to charge him therewith: he accuses them with not providing for the army, and thereby obliging them to live on free-quarter, and thus unintentionally rendering themselves odious and burdensome to the country: he deems these, and other circumstances, sufficient grounds for putting an end to this Parliament.

Cromwell's speech to the Parliament commencing Wednesday, 17th September, (1656,) is not in Whitelock, or in the Journals of the House of Commons.

It appears that a certificate was required of every member upon his entrance into the House, of his approbation by the council; and that those who had been excluded in consequence of the council's disapprobation, published a protest or remonstrance; which is given at length in Whitelock, and is signed by ninety-eight names.

In the Journals of the House of Commons is a resolution of the 20th same September; to desire the council to give to the House their reasons for disapproving the excluded members; and on the 22d of the same month their answer is reported,—That it being ordained by a clause in the government, that the persons elected to serve in Parliament should be such, and no other than such, as were persons of known integrity, fearing God, and of good conversation: that the council, in pursuance of their duty, and according to the trust reposed in them, had examined the said returns, and had not refused to approve any who had appeared to them to be persons of integrity to the government, fearing God, and of good conversation: and that those who were not approved, His

Highness had given order to some persons, to take
care that they do not come into the House.   And
the question for referring the excluded members
to the council for its approbation, and for the
House proceeding in the great affairs of the nation,
was carried by 125 to 29.

Mr. Whitelock observes, upon Cromwell's final
determination not to take upon himself the title of
King, which was the first object of the petition
and advice of the Commons, that he was satisfied
in his private judgment that he should do it, but
that afterwards, by the solicitation of the common-
wealthsmen, and fearing a mutiny and disaffection
of a great part of the army, his mind changed:
and that many of the officers of the army gave out
high threatenings against him, in case he should
do it; therefore, he thought best to attend some
better season and opportunity, and refused it at
this time with great seeming earnestness.

Lord Clarendon says, that it was reported, that
an officer of name, in the eclaircissement upon the
subject, told him resolutely and vehemently, that
if he ever took the title upon him, he would kill
him.   Certain it is, continues His Lordship, that
Cromwell was informed and gave credit to it, that
there were a number of men, who bound themselves by oath, to kill him within so many hours
after he should accept that title.

The title of King being laid aside, in consequence of Cromwell's declining it in his speech of

the 8th May (1657), and it being determined that
" Lord Protector" should be the title to be inserted in the petition and advice, Cromwell, upon
its presentment to the House with this, and some
other alterations, gave his assent in a short speech,
on the 25th of the same month.

Cromwell's speech at the meeting of the Commons, and of the other House, (the newly formed
House of Lords,) on the 20th January following
(1657), according to their adjournment, is in the
Journals. It is short, on account, Mr. Whitelock
says, of his indisposition of health. In Whitelock
is the speech of the Lord-commissioner Fiennes
immediately following it, which is very long. The
following passages refer to the persecuting spirit
by which these Parliaments appear to have been
throughout actuated:—There is another rock, says
he, and it is also a dangerous one; it is a rock
upon which many have split themselves in our
view; and it hath, lying right over against it, a
quicksand no less dangerous, which hath swallowed
up many in our sight: the rock is, a spirit of imposing upon men's consciences, where God leaves
them a latitude, and would have them free: the
quicksand is an abominable licentiousness to profess and practise any sort of detestable opinions
and principles: for the former, the prelates and all
their adherents, nay, and their master and sup-
porter too, with all his posterity, have split themselves upon it: the bloody rebels in Ireland, that

would endure no religion but their own amongst
them, have split themselves upon it: but as God
is no respecter of persons, so neither is he any respecter of forms, but in what form soever this
spirit appeareth he hath, he will testify his displeasure against it, though it be not of so deep a dye
as that I have spoken of before.   If men, though
otherwise good men, will turn ceremony into substance, and make the kingdom of Christ to consist
in circumstances, in disciplines, in forms, (though
these things also may have their use as to order
and decency, so they be strained no further, and
not carried beyond their line and measure,) but, I
say, if uniformity in these things shall dissolve
unity among brethren, and especially if it grow to
such a height of animosity, and so high a degree
of asperity, that if one say but Siboleth instead of
Shiboleth, it shall be accounted ground enough to
cut his throat, though one of his brethren. — If
any man shall account all as heathens and no
Christians that are not under such or such an ordinance; all men devils that are out of such a circle,
such a form; and all men the seed of the serpent,
that will not father such or such an opinion, (it may
be but fancies too when all is done,) such principles,
such practices, men cannot bear, God will not endure; and in vain do they protest against the
persecution of God's people, when, as eagerly persecuting all others, they make the definition of
God's people so narrow, that their persecution
becometh as broad as any others, and usually more

fierce, because ordinarily edged with a sharper temper of spirit. It may be, that many amongst these, shall, by God's mercy, meet together in heaven; but certainly, had they power at will, they would not suffer one another to live upon the earth. Therefore, blessed be God, who, in mercy to us and them, hath placed the power in such hands as make it their business to keep peace amongst them, and to hinder them from biting and devouring one another. In another part of this speech, there must be a voice, but it must be a small and still voice, enough to hold forth a certain and distinct sound, but not to make so great a noise, as to drown all other voices besides. It is good, it is useful, to hold forth a certain confession of the truth, but not so as thereby to exclude all those that cannot come up to it in all points, from the privileges which belong to them as Christians, much less which belong to them as men.

There is no speech on the dissolution of this Parliament on the 4th February following (1657), either in Whitelock or in the Journals.

Whitelock, referring to this dissolution and to the disagreement between the two Houses upon the Commons' disinclination to acknowledge the House of Lords, observes, all these passages tended to their own destruction, which was not difficult to foresee : that the Protector looked upon himself as aimed at by them, though with a side wind, and as

testimonies of their envy towards him, and he was
the more incensed, because, at this time, the Fifth
Monarchy-men began again their enterprises to
overthrow him and his government by force, whereof there were clear discoveries : that he therefore
took a resolution suddenly to dissolve the Parliament : that he was advised not to do it, and told
the danger of frequent dissolving of parliaments,
and the streights it would bring him into for
money, which he could not raise without the
highest discontent, except it were given by them ;
that a little time would cool their heats, and bring
the Parliament into a better temper ; but, contiuues
Whitelock, some fierce men and flatterers, to comply with him, advised the dissolution : that some
were troubled at this, others rejoiced at the troubles,
and were suspected to be assisters of the new designs of insurrection : that divers were imprisoned
upon the new plot, and the Protector and his
council were busy in the examination concerning
it ; and Thurloe did them good service : that General Harrison was deep in it : that he, Whitelock,
was much retired, and not satisfied with the public
transactions : that the Cavalier party were again
at work upon a new design, whereof the Protector
had intelligence from abroad, and from some of
the actors here : that about this he advised, and
sent for the lord mayor and aldermen of London,
and acquainted them therewith, and desired their
care to put the city into a posture of defence ; .

who presented to him a petition and representation
of their faithfulness and duty to him: and that
divers like addresses were made from General
Monk's and other regiments: and he answered
them with thanks.

Lord Clarendon, introductory of his account of
Cromwell's death, which happened on the 3d
September following (1658), says, it had been
observed in England, that though, from the dissolution of the last Parliament, all things seemed
to have succeeded both at home and abroad to the
Protector's wish, and his power and greatness to
be better established than ever it had been, yet,
that after he had refused the crown, he never had
the same serenity of mind he had been used to,
but was out of countenance and chagrin, as if he
were conscious of not having been true to himself,
and much more apprehensive of danger to his
person than he had used to be; insomuch, as he
was not easy of access, nor so much seen abroad,
and seemed to be in some disorder when his eyes
found any stranger in the room, upon whom they
were still fixed: that when he intended to go to
Hampton-court, which was his principal delight and
diversion, it was never known till he was in the
coach which way he would go; and he was still
hemmed in by his guards, both before and behind,
and the coach in which he was, was always thronged
as full as it could be with his servants, who were
armed; and he seldom returned the same way he

went, and scarcely lodged two nights together in
the same chamber; but had many furnished and
prepared to which his own key conveyed him and
those he would have with him, when he had a
mind to go to bed, which made his fears the more
taken notice of, and public, because he had never
been accustomed to those precautions: that he
seemed much afflicted at the death of his friend,
the Earl of Warwick, for whom he had a fast
friendship: that his domestic delights were lessened
every day. He plainly discovered that his son
Falconbridge's heart was set upon an interest that
was destructive to his, and grew to hate him perfectly: but that that which chiefly broke his peace,
was the death of his daughter Claypoole, who had
been always his greatest joy, and who, in her
sickness, which was of a nature the physicians
knew not how to deal with, had several conferences
with him, which exceedingly perplexed him:
though nobody was near enough to hear the particulars, yet her often mentioning, in the pain she
endured, the blood her father had spilt, made
people conclude that she had presented his worst
actions to his consideration; and that though he
never had the least show of remorse for any of
those actions, it is very certain that what she said,
or her death, affected him wonderfully: that whatever it was, about the middle of August he was
seized only by a common tertian ague, from which
he believed a little ease and divertisement at

Hampton-court would have freed him; but the fits grew stronger, and his spirits much abated, so that he returned again to Whitehall, when his physicians began to think him in danger, though the preachers who prayed always about him, and told God Almighty what great things he had done for him, and how much more need he had still of his service, declared, as from God, that he should recover; and he himself was of the same mind, and did not think he should die till even the time that his spirits failed him: that then he declared to them, that he did appoint his son to succeed him, his eldest son Richard, and so expired upon the 3d day of September, 1658, a day he thought always very propitious to him, and on which he had twice triumphed for two of his greatest victories: and this now, adds His Lordship, was a day very memorable for the greatest storm of wind that had been ever known, for some hours before and after his death, which overthrew trees, houses, and made great wrecks at sea; and the tempest was so universal, that the effects of it were terrible both in France and Flanders, where all people trembled at it; for that, besides the wrecks all along the sea-coast, many boats were cast away in the very rivers; and within a few days after, the circumstance of his death, that accompanied that storm, was universally known.

He was one of those men, continues His Lordship, *quos vituperare ne inimici quidem possunt, nisi ut*

simul laudent, whom his very enemies could not
condemn without commending him at the same
time; for he could never have done half that mischief without great parts of courage, industry, and
judgment. — That he must have had a wonderful
understanding in the natures and humours of men,
and as great a dexterity in applying them; who,
from a private and obscure birth (though of a good
family), without interest or estate, alliance or
friendship, could raise himself to such a height,
and compound and knead such opposite and contradictory tempers, humours, and interests into a
consistence that contributed to his designs and to
their own destruction; whilst himself grew in-
sensibly powerful enough to cut off those by whom
he had climbed, in the instant that they projected
to demolish their own building : that what was said
of Cinna might very justly be said of him, — *ausum
eum, quæ nemo auderet bonus ; perfecisse, quæ à
nullo, nisi fortissimo, perfici possent.* He attempted
those things which no good man durst have ventured on, and achieved those in which none but a
valiant and great man could have succeeded. —
That without doubt, no man with more wickedness
ever attempted any thing, or brought to pass what
he desired more wickedly, more in the face and
contempt of religion and moral honesty ; yet
wickedness as great as his could never have accomplished those designs without the assistance
of a great spirit, an admirable circumspection and

sagacity, and a most magnanimous resolution. — That when he appeared first in the Parliament, he seemed to have a person in no degree gracious, no ornament of discourse, none of those talents which use to conciliate the affections of the stander-by: yet, that as he grew into place and authority, his parts seemed to be raised, as if he had had concealed faculties till he had occasion to use them; and when he was to act the part of a great man, he did it without any indecency notwithstanding the want of custom. — That after he was confirmed and invested Protector by the humble petition and advice, he consulted with very few upon any action of importance, nor communicated any enterprise he resolved upon with more than those who were to have principal parts in the execution of it, nor with them sooner than was absolutely necessary. What he once resolved, in which he was not rash, he would not be dissuaded from, nor endure any contradiction of his power and authority; but extorted obedience from them who were not willing to yield it.

To reduce three nations, which perfectly hated him, to an entire obedience to all his dictates; to awe and govern those nations by an army that was indevoted to him, and wished his ruin, was an instance of a very prodigious address. But his greatness at home was but a shadow of the glory he had abroad. — It was hard to discover which feared him most, France, Spain, or the Low Countries, where his friendship was current at the value he put upon it: that as they did all sacrifice their honour and their interest to his pleasure, so there was nothing he could have demanded that either of them would have denied him. — To manifest which, there needs only to be mentioned one instance amongst many: — when those of the valley of Lucern had unwarily risen in arms against the Duke of Savoy, which gave occasion to the Pope and the neighbour princes of Italy to call and solicit for their extirpation, and their prince positively resolved upon it, Cromwell sent his agent to the Duke of Savoy, a prince with whom he had no correspondence or commerce, and so engaged the cardinal, and even terrified the Pope himself, without so much as doing any grace to the English Roman Catholics, (nothing being more usual than his saying, that his ships in the Mediterranean should visit Civita Vecchia, and that the sound of his cannon should be heard in Rome,) that the Duke of Savoy thought it necessary to restore all that he had taken from them, and did renew all those privileges they had formerly enjoyed, and newly forfeited.

That he would never suffer himself to be denied any thing he ever asked of the Cardinal, alleging that the people would not be otherwise satisfied; which the Cardinal bore very heavily, and complained of to those with whom he would be free. One day he visited Madame Turenne, and when he took his leave of her, she, according to her custom, besought him to continue gracious to the churches. — Whereupon the Cardinal told her, that he knew not how to behave himself; if he advised the King to punish and suppress their insolence, Cromwell threatened him to join with the Spaniard; and if he showed any favour to them at Rome, they accounted him an heretic. — That, contrary to all expectation both at home and abroad, this earthquake was attended with no signal alteration : that never monarch, after he had inherited a crown by many descents, died in more silence, nor with less alteration; and there was the same, or a greater calm in the kingdom than had been before. — That the next morning after the death of Oliver, Richard, his son, was proclamed his lawful successor; the army congratulate their new General, and renew their vows of fidelity to him; the navy doth the like; the city appear more unanimous for his service than they were for his father's; and most counties in England, by addresses under their hands, testified their obedience to their new sovereign without any hesitation. The dead is interred in the sepulchre of the kings, and with the obsequies due to such. His son inherits all his greatness and all his glory, without the public hate that visibly attended the other. Foreign princes addressed their condolences to him, and desired to renew their alliances; and nothing was heard in

England but the voice of joy, and large encomiums of their new Protector.

Sir Philip Warwick, referring to Cromwell's death, says, that agitated, some time before his death, by several untoward circumstances in his government, he seemed dispirited; and that by the acquaintance he had with an old gentlewoman, who made his broths and jellies, and other such cockering meats, he learnt, that for one, while he frequently used these, and for another, he took large draughts of wine, and that he seldom waked in the night, but with one or other of these he must be replenished. And sure, adds he, those were better comforts to him than the reflections on his successes. So, adds Sir Philip, at last falling into a fever, he soon fell into a delirium; and one of his physicians, with whom he (Sir Philip) was intimately acquainted, assured him that, during all his sickness, he was never master of so much reason as to determine any thing of his successor, or matters of state : and that though it was pretended at that time by Thurloe the secretary, and Goodwin the minister, that he gave them particular directions that his son Richard should be his successor, and they brought in others afterwards to testify the same; yet that this physician assured him that he never was in any such condition. And thus, says Sir Philip, on his beloved and victorious day, the 3d of September (1658),

he expired, ten years after he had spilt the innocent blood of the King; and that though he
had run through so many dangers, and had so
many plots against his life, and committed so
many wicked and flagitious acts, he yet breathed
out his last in his bed; but, adds Sir Philip, as
if the elements as well as men had waited ·for
this day, the day preceding, there was as loud
and great a tempest as was at any time ever
known.

Ludlow, referring to the same event, Cromwell's
death, says, that Mrs. Claypoole, Cromwell's
daughter and favourite, laboured earnestly with
her father to save Dr. Hewitt's life, who had been
tried and ·convicted of a conspiracy against Cromwell; but that having been unsuccessful, it so
affected her, that it was reported to have been one
cause of her death, which happened soon after,
with the concurrence of an ulcer in her womb. —
That, after her death, it was observed that ·Crom-
well grew melancholy, and also distempered with
divers infirmities, particularly a malignant humour
in his foot; which hindering him from the exercises
of walking or riding abroad, he obliged his physicians to endeavour to disperse it; which drove it
upwards to his heart: that, by these means, he
became desperately sick; and as some about him
had for a long time deceived others, so they now
endeavoured to impose upon God himself: for

that Dr. Goodwin, his creature and trencher chaplain, used this expression in his prayer during the time of his sicknes; "Lord, we beg not for his recovery; for that thou hast already granted and assured us of, but for his speedy recovery."

CHAPTER XIV.

CONSIDERATION OF MR. DENZIL HOLLES'S CHARGE OF COW-
ARDICE—OF THE CIRCUMSTANCES OF HIS LAST ILLNESS
AND DEATH; AND OF THE DEATH OF HIS DAUGHTER,
MRS. CLAYPOOLE—AND OF HIS APPOINTMENT OF HIS
SON RICHARD TO BE HIS SUCCESSOR.—OF THE DIF-
FERENT PARTS OF HIS CHARACTER AS GIVEN BY LORD
CLARENDON AND BY OTHER ROYALIST, AND BY REPUB-
LICAN WTITERS;—AS HIS SUPPOSED ENTHUSIASM—
HYPOCRISY—DEFECTIVE LEARNING AND ELOQUENCE—
INHUMANITY.—HIS REAL CHARACTER; AS, HIS AFFEC-
TIONATE ATTENTION TO HIS FAMILY—REALLY RELIGIOUS
—NO ENTHUSIAST OR HYPOCRITE—EXEMPLARY, MORAL,
AND REGULAR IN HIS PRIVATE CONDUCT, AND AN
ENEMY TO VICE IN OTHERS—KIND AND MERCIFUL TO
HIS ENEMIES AND TO THOSE WHO OCCASIONALLY OF-
FENDED HIM—COURTEOUS AND AFFABLE—INDULGENT
TO THE SEVERAL RELIGIOUS SECTS.—INTERPOSITION
IN FAVOUR OF THE PERSECUTED WALDENSES.—GENE-
ROUS AND PUBLIC SPIRITED.—HIS JUDGES UPRIGHT
AND LEARNED, AND JUSTICE IMPARTIALLY ADMINIS-
TERED.—AN ENCOURAGER OF LEARNING AND LEARNED
MEN.—NO ENEMY TO INNOCENT RECREATIONS.—
NATIONAL REPUTATION UNDER HIS ADMINISTRATION.—
COMPARISON OF HIS SUPPOSED RELIGIOUS ENTHUSIASM
AND HYPOCRISY, WITH THE RELIGIOUS CHARACTERS
OF WHITELOCK, LOCKART, AND OTHER EMINENT PUBLIC
CHARACTERS.

CROMWELL's great valour, industry, and judgment,
and wonderful understanding of men, and skill in

his application of that understanding, are acknowledged by Lord Clarendon in the last-cited passages
from his history, who describes him as a valiant
and great man, of a great spirit, admirable circumspection and sagacity, and 'a most magnanimous
resolution : that as he grew into place and authority, his parts seemed to be raised as if he had concealed faculties, till he had occasion to use them ;
and when he was to act the part of a great man,
he did it without any indecency, notwithstanding
the want of custom.   Sir Philip Warwick describes
him as of a great and majestic deportment and comely
presence.   These qualities appear to be allowed
him by the writers of all parties, except that his
courage, strange to tell, has been impeached by
one writer, whose charge of cowardice will be
hereafter considered.   His Lordship concludes,
that as he had been guilty of many crimes, against
which damnation was denounced, and for which
hell-fire was prepared, so he had some good qualities which had caused the memory of some men
in all ages to be celebrated ; and that he would
be looked upon by posterity as a brave wicked
man.

In the attainment, and in the possession and
exercise of the supposed objects of his ambition,
he is accused of every species of hypocrisy, tyranny,
cruelty, and oppression.

Previously to considering whether, and how far,
these charges are well founded, and thus to ascer-

tain his (Cromwell's) real character, it is desirable to examine and dispose of this charge of cowardice.

It is to be found in the Memoirs of Lord Holles, theretofore Mr. Denzil Holles: these Memoirs are addressed to the unparalleled couple, (as he calls them,) Mr. Oliver St. John, His Majesty's Solicitor-general, and Mr. Oliver Cromwell, the Parliament's Lieutenant-general, the two grand designers of the ruin of three kingdoms: they are written in the most abusive style, apparently in a transport of rage and disappointment: they were not published till after his death, when it might be supposed that there would be no danger of contradiction of any of his bold and unsupported assertions. It is a very discreditable performance to Mr. Holles's memory, and his living so long after his writing it, and not publishing it, afford good reason to believe that he determined that it should never see the light. The editor is aware of what he calls the vehemence of his style, which he is disposed to attribute to the supposed barbarous usage he had received, his concern for the presbyterian party, and his supposed displeasure at the King's misfortunes, to whom he says he was then an adherent and a friend; and which he seems to suspect has guided his pencil to draw the lines of Cromwell's face too strong, and the shades too many. The editor should have seen, that the publication of such a work must lower Mr. Holles's character, and should have

buried it in silence, which must have been Mr.
Holles's own determination, or he would have published it himself; and he determined wisely. There
cannot be a stronger proof of the extreme length
to which he carried his inveteracy to Cromwell,
than this charge of cowardice, which he founds
upon the following circumstances. — He says, that
he had several times heard from Crawford's own
mouth, (who was, he says, Major-general to the
Earl of Manchester's brigade,) and he thinks he
shall not be mistaken if he says that Cromwell himself has heard it from him; for that he once said it
aloud in Westminster Hall, when Cromwell passed
by him, with a design he might hear him : that
when the whole army at Marston Moor was in a
fair possibility to be utterly routed, and a great
part of it was running, he saw the body of horse
of that brigade standing still, and to his seeming,
doubtful which way to charge, backward or forward; when he came up to them in great passion,
reviling them with the name of poltroons and cow-
ards, and asked them if they would stand still and
see the day lost? whereupon Cromwell showed
himself, and, in a pitiful voice, said, " Major-general, what shall I do:" that he (Crawford), begging
pardon for what he had said, not knowing he was
there, towards whom he knew his distance as to
his superior officer, told him, " Sir, if you charge
not, all is lost:" that Cromwell answered, " that
he was wounded, and was not able to charge," (his

great wound being a little burn in the neck by the accidental going off behind him of one of his soldiers' pistols;) that when Crawford desired him to go off the field, and sending one away with him, (who very readily followed wholesome advice,) led them on himself; which was not the duty of his place, and as little for Cromwell's honour, as it proved to be much for the advancement of his and his party's pernicious designs. This, adds Mr. Holles, I had but from relation, but believe it upon the credit of the reporter, who was a man of honour, and that was not ashamed nor afraid to publish it in all places. Besides that he had a parallel story of his valour from a Colonel Dalbier, of his cowardly behaviour at the storming of Basinghouse: also, of his own knowledge, of his base keeping out of the field at Kineton (Edgehill) battle, where he with his troop of horse came not in, impudently and ridicuously affirming the day after, that he had been all that day seeking the army and place of fight, though his quarters were but at a village near hand; whence he could not find his way, nor be directed by his ear, though the ordnance was heard (as he, Mr. Holles had been credibly informed,) twenty or thirty miles off; so that, adds he, certainly he is far from being the man he is taken for: and that that man is as much a coward as he is notoriously perfidious, ambitious, and hypocritical. Mr. Holles adds, " that those who did the principal service that day were Major-general Leslie, who commanded the Scots horse, Major-general Crawford, and Sir Thomas Fairfax, who, under his father, commanded the northern brigade." But, says he, sarcastically, "My friend Cromwell had neither part nor lot in the business."

This cowardly General (Cromwell) had in the preceding year fought the battle of Horncastle, (or Winsby,) commanding (Lord Fairfax, in his memorial, says) the Earl of Manchester's forces, which had been previously joined by His Lordship and under the immediate eye of the Earl: that he (Cromwell) had the command of the van, the reserve of horse, and the Earl all the foot. The royalists were defeated. In this same battle, Rushworth says that the Earl's horse and foot came on to the attack, singing psalms: that Cromwell's horse was shot and fell upon him, and that, as he rose, he was knocked down by the gentleman that charged him, supposed to be Sir Ralph Hopton; but that he again rose and recovered a poor horse in a soldier's hand, which he mounted, and pursued his success. In favour of this same cowardly General was suspended, at the request of the same General Lord Fairfax, the operation of the Self-denying Ordinance, that he might be present and assist him in the then expected engagement with the royal army, and which shortly afterwards happened at Naseby; the total defeat of which was principally, if not wholly, attributed to Cromwell's courage and conduct. He afterwards subdued the

Welch royalists; defeated the Scots army, under Duke Hamilton, though very greatly superior in numbers to his own army; he defeated the Scots army at Dunbar, and reduced Edinburgh Castle; and finally defeated King Charles the Second's army at the battle of Worcester. These, with many other lesser engagements, were the successes of Cromwell's arms. To these Mr. Holles was no stranger: nevertheless, with his eyes open to all this, he could give implicit credit to this story of Crawford's. The quality of personal courage was one of the very few good ones left undenied to Cromwell: nor has it ever been doubted but in this single instance.

This story of Crawford's bears all the marks of falsehood upon the face of it; the hesitation about charging, and the pitiful voice of Cromwell's complaint of the slight burn in his neck does not belong to Cromwell's character. Nor, above all, is it possible to believe that Cromwell, the commander-in-chief of one of the wings of the army, should be led off the field attended by a single soldier, and no notice given to the General of so important a change. Crawford certainly intends it to be understood, that Cromwell remained in this inactive and cowardly state in the rear of the army during the remainder of the action, and that he (Crawford) took his place and was the cause of that wing obtaining the victory. How happened it that all these circumstances were not immediately made known ? Such a dereliction of duty, such cowardice, must immediately after the action have been noticed and censured by the General, and Cromwell's military character been for ever lost : Crawford must have been also publicly thanked ; but Crawford is silent upon this part of the subject; so is Lord Fairfax. None of the writers of those times, adverse to Cromwell, appear to have been aware of this extraordinary story, and it remains secreted amongst Mr. Holles's papers during his life : he died in 1658 ; Mr. Holles in 1679. These memoirs are addressed to him (Cromwell) as Lieutenant-general, and they were not made public untill 1699, forty years after Cromwell's death, and twenty years after Mr. Holles's death. The danger of contradiction had passed away.

Mr. Holles's blind partiality to the Scots gives them a share in this victory of Marston Moor; when, on the contrary, Rushworth, Lord Clarendon, and Whitelock, all agree in attributing it principally to Cromwell. Rushworth says expressly, that he was acknowledged by all to be a great agent therein; he notices his wound in the neck, but says, not dangerously. Lord Clarendon says, that the whole army of the Scots were totally routed and defeated, flying all ways for many miles together, and knocked on the head or taken prisoners by the country. Ludlow describes the left wing of the enemy as charging the right wing of the Parliament army, consisting of English and

Scots, and so totally routing them, that the Generals quitted the field and fled towards Cawood
Castle : and that the left wing, commanded by
Cromwell, after an obstinate dispute, obtained the
victory. — No notice of Crawford, who would have
been gladly brought forward by Ludlow, to Cromwell's disadvantage. Sir Philip Warwick also, who
cannot be suspected of partiality to Cromwell,
describes the Scots and English part of the army
under the command of General Leslie and the
Lord Fairfax as totally routed, and driven out of the
field, and as not returning to the army in two days:
but that Cromwell (who had experience of what
import a good reserve was in a day of battle) came
and turned the scale, and that though the Marquis
of Newcastle's foot stood like a wall, yet he mowed
them down like a meadow. — Still not a word of
the heroic Major-general Crawford.

But the General's (Lord Fairfax) account of this
battle, in his forementioned short memorials, must
be deemed to be a full confutation of this story of
Crawford's. His Lordship relates the advance of
Prince Rupert to relieve the city of York, then besieged by the Parliament forces under the command of His Lordship, General Leslie, and the
Earl of Manchester : that in consequence the siege
was raised ; Hessey-moor was, he says, appointed
the rendezvous; that the whole army drew thither;
that about a mile from thence lay the Prince (Rupert), the river Ouse being between them, which

he that night passed over at Poppleton : that the
next day he drew his army into the same moor,
which being joined by the Lord Newcastle's army,
made about 23,000 or 24,000 men, the Parliament's
army something more : that the Parliament Generals were divided in their opinions what to do ; the
English were for fighting, the Scots for retreating,
to gain, as they alleged, both time and place of
more advantage : that this being resolved on, they
marched to Tadcaster, which made the enemy
advance the faster : that Lieutenant-general Cromwell, Leslie, and himself (Lord Fairfax), were appointed to bring up the rear : that they sent word
to the Generals of the necessity of making a stand,
or else that the enemy, having this advantage,
might put them to some disorder ; but that, by the
advantage of the ground we were on, we hoped to
make it good till they came back to us, which
they did : that the place was Marston-fields, which
afterwards gave the name to this battle : that here
we drew up our army ; the enemy was drawn up
in battalia on the moor, a little below us ; that the
day being most part spent in preparations, we now
began to descend towards them : that Lieutenant-
general Cromwell commanded the left wing of the
horse, and was seconded by Major-general Leslie ;
I (Lord Fairfax) had the right wing, with some
Scots horse, and lances for my reserve ; the three
Generals were with the foot : that the left wing first
charged the enemy's right wing, which was per-

formed for a while with much resolution on both
sides, but the enemy at length was put to the
worst : that our right wing had not all so good
success, by reason of the furzes and ditches we
were to pass over before we could get to the
enemy, which put us into great disorder ; notwithstanding, proceeds His Lordship, I drew.up a body
of 400 horse ; but, because their intervals of horse
in this wing only was lined with musketeers, who
did us much hurt with their shot, I was necessitated
to charge them : that we were a long time engaged one with another, but at length we routed
that part of their wing which we charged, and
pursued them a good way towards York : myself
(Lord Fairfax) only returned presently to get to
the men I left behind me ; but that part of the
enemy which stood, perceiving the disorder they
were in, had charged and routed them before I
could get to them, so that the good success we
had at first was eclipsed by this bad conclusion :
our other wing (the left), and most of the foot,
went on prosperously till they had cleared the
field. Lord Fairfax, in that truly brave manly
spirit which characterised him, acknowledges the
defeat of his own wing, and most honestly declares
the victory to have been obtained by the left wing
under Cromwell's command, not making the slightest allusion to the Major, although he mentions his
own (Lord Fairfax) escape from different parties
of the enemy, upon his return from the pursuit of

the part of the left wing of the enemy that his right wing had defeated, to the Lord Manchester's horse in the other (the left) wing, which Cromwell commanded, which must have afforded him an immediate opportunity of knowing all that is alleged by Crawford to have passed, and which he could not have failed to have noticed in this his memorial, particularly as he had no intention of publishing it : but, unfortunately for this Major-general, or rather perhaps more correctly Colonel Crawford, His Lordship referring to approaches made in the siege of York, (prior to the battle,) to St. Mary's tower, which he mentions to have been in the Earl of Manchester's quarters, and the mining that tower, says, that Colonel Crawford, a Scotchman, who commanded that quarter, (he must be the same forementioned Crawford, it being unlikely there should be two of the same name in the Earl of Manchester's brigade,) sprung the mine, being ambitious to have the honour alone of it, without acquainting the other two Generals, for their advice and concurrence, which proved very prejudicial ; for that having engaged his party against the whole strength of the town, without more forces to second him, he was repulsed with the loss of 300 men ; for which, says His Lordship, he had surely been called to an account, but escaped the better by reason of the triumviral government. No allusion to his alleged great service at Marston-moor, a few days afterwards.

A passage given by Rushworth, from the life of the Duke of Newcastle, (who must have been related to Mr. Holles,) said to be written by his Duchess, describing this battle of Marston-moor, says, that the left wing of the Parliament horse was commanded by the Earl of Manchester and his Lieutenant-general, Cromwell: " That the first division of Prince Rupert's horse advanced, and with them His Highness in person, charged Cromwell's division of 300 horse, in which he was in person, and very hard put to it, being charged by Prince Rupert's bravest men, both in front and flank, and stood at sword's point a pretty while, hacking one another; but at last Cromwell broke through, and at the same time the rest of his horse of that wing." That the royalists' left wing was more successful against the Parliament's right wing, which they defeated, and pursuing their success, and being just ready to seize all the carriages, " Cromwell with his horse and Manchester's foot, came back from the chase of the Prince's right wing, and perceiving their friends in the mean time thus worsted, advanced in good order to a second charge with all the Prince's horse and foot that had thus disordered their right wing and main battle; who seeing their approach, gave over the pursuit, and prepared to receive them, both sides being not a little surprised to see they must fight it over again for that victory which each thought they had already gained: that the battle, thus renewed, grew very desperate; but that, at length, after the utmost efforts of strength and courage on either side, victory wholly inclined to the Parliament forces.

Considering the undisputed (except in this instance) character of Cromwell's personal courage and military skill, it may be thought that too much consequence has been attached to this story of Crawford's; and unnecessary pains bestowed upon the confutation of it. But Mr. Holles's positive charge of general cowardice is founded upon his belief of this (Crawford's) story, and upon two other proofs, as he calls them, coming nearly within his own knowledge, but which, when told, appear to be merely conjectural, and the indulgence of a prejudiced mind, open to the admission of every ill-founded charge to the injury of Cromwell's character and hardly-earned fame. His inveterate party-rancour against Cromwell must have prevailed over his understanding and better knowledge, to believe these improbable stories, without examination, and against the conviction of his own mind, aware, as he was, of the great victories obtained, confessedly by all parties, by Cromwell's personal valour and able conduct in the command of the Parliament forces.

This supposed cowardly Cromwell, is, nevertheless, the man of whom Mr. May, in his parliamentary history, says, that he contributed, by his great wisdom and indefatigable industry, to crush, in the beginning, all the endeavours of the King's party in several counties to raise a force for the King: and, in a subsequent part of such history, he describes the successful services of this one gentleman, whose wisdom, valour, and vigilancy, he says, were no less available in those important businesses than remarkable afterwards, in the highest services and greatest battles of the whole war: that it pleased God to raise him afterwards into the greatest commands, and prosper in so high a measure all his undertakings, that he became within a few years one of the chief props on which the Parliament leaned.

Bishop Burnet says of Mr. Holles, that he was a man of great courage and of as great pride; that he was counted for many years the head of the presbyterian party; that he engaged in a particular opposition to Cromwell in the time of the war; that they hated one another equally; that Holles seemed to carry this too far, for that he would not allow Cromwell to be either wise or brave, but often applied Solomon's observation to him, " that the battle was not to the strong, nor favour to the man of understanding, but that time and chance happened to all men;" that he was well versed in the records of Parliament, and argued well, but too vehemently, for he could not bear contradiction; that he had the soul of an old stubborn Roman in him; that he was a faithful but a rough friend, and a severe but fair enemy;

that he had a true sense of religion, and was a man of an unblamable course of life, and of a sound judgment, when it was not biassed by passion ; and that he was made a lord for his merits in bringing about the Restoration.

Lord Clarendon's confinement of Cromwell's character to the terms of " brave and wicked," does not include all that it was incumbent upon His Lordship to say, consistently with his preceding account of him : he should have added to his bravery, his great ability of understanding, and his magnanimity of resolution, which he there acknowledges in the strongest terms. His alleged wickedness and contempt of religion and of moral honesty, in the accomplishment of his ambitious designs, rest upon unproved assertions, very much the offspring of His Lordship's own imagination, and of his inveterate hatred of Cromwell. He seems to feel an awkwardness in summing up Cromwell's character, in the conviction that he is not doing it justice; and that his history does not support the severity with which he treats his memory.

The unimpeachableness of his (Cromwell's) private character, and his sobriety and morality, and religious deportment, in all his different situations and circumstances, also his bravery and personal courage, and his great abilities, are allowed on all hands : except his courage in the above solitary feeble attempt of Mr. Holles, they are indisputable : but he is described by His Lordship, and all other his enemies of the then, and even of the present times, as hypocritical and tyrannical, cruel and blood-thirsty; as obtaining his elevation by deceit and violence, and generally, as a most wicked and depraved character, destitute of every valuable quality and worthy motive in any of his seemingly best actions. The justness of these parts of his character remain to be considered.

But it will not be amiss, first to dispose of His Lordship's assertions respecting the Earl of Warwick and Lord Fauconberg. Mentioning the Earl's death, His Lordship describes him, Lord Warwick, as one for whom he, Cromwell, had a fast friendship, though neither their humours or their natures alike : that upon the death of the heir of that house, who had married his youngest daughter, all his relation or confidence in that family was at an end, the other branches of it abhorring his alliance. The truth of this abhorrence, and how His Lordship acquired the knowledge of it, does not appear. Certain it is, that from the letters with the Cromwell family-papers (hereafter given), the Earl himself and his family, and the Cromwell family, appear to have had the most affectionate regard for each other.

Mr. Rich, the Earl's grandson, was married to Cromwell's daughter Frances, 11th November, 1657 ; Lord Clarendon says at Whitehall, but it was at the parish-church of St. Martin-in-the

Fields, according to the certificate of the marriage in Mr. Noble's memoirs. He died 16th February following. The Earl of Warwick died 19th April following, suddenly, as Lord Fauconberg, in a postscript of a letter upon other subjects, informs Mr. Thurloe. A letter is to be found in Thurloe's State Papers from Henry Cromwell, then Lord Deputy of Ireland, to Lord Broghill, dated 24th of the same month of February in which Mr. Rich died, in which he writes, — " I am sending over to my Lord of Warwick and my Lady Devonshire, to condole our loss of dear Robin Rich; indeed I am much affected with that Providence, which I desire you to let them know as there is occasion."

Accordingly follows a letter of the same date from Henry Cromwell to the Earl of Warwick: — " My Lord; I am ashamed to have been so negligent of my obligations to Your Lordship, that nothing but so sad an occasion as the death of my dear brother, Mr. Rich, should mind me of it; and I am sorry that I cannot say what is just, in honour to his memory, without a kind of cruelty to Your Lordship; and truly, my Lord, but that I know religion is more prevalent with Your Lordship than other worldly consideration; that you do not so much look upon your own loss as our dear friend's gain, nor upon your own disappointment as the fulfilling of that will to which we must all submit, I should almost despair of Your Lordship's patience under so searching and proving a triall, but I know Your Lordship has learnt to mourn, as not without hope, and to read the mind of God in these characters of his Providence ; and withall to believe, that all things shall work for the best to those that feare him. Upon these grounds I do the more presume upon Your Lordship's courage under this dispensation. For my own part, I am cut very short in my expectations : for I placed much happiness, even in thinking, upon the fruits of those seeds which I understood to be in Mr. Rich, both as to the honour of our whole family and the advantage of my own particular concernments.

" But I hereby learn, that even these best things are but frail, not knowing but that this stroke may be a reproof, particular unto myself, for placing (if it were possible) too much upon the consequences of this alliance. Upon these considerations I need not tell Your Lordship how I and my wife resent (feel) this Providence, and sympathise with Your Lordship's just sorrow; the fuller accompt whereof I leave to the bearer. In the mean time, praying the Lord to sanctify this affliction to all concerned in it, giving us to make due use of it to his glory; and withall, that God would help Your Lordship to moderate the sense of this rebuke, and to recompense this loss unto us by some more durable good than this world can afford. In which affections I remayne, My Lord, Your Lordship's, &c.

" H. CROMWELL."

Then follows his, Henry Cromwell's, letter of
the same date, to the Countess of Devonshire : —
" Madam ; I know not how seasonable it would
be to tell Your Ladyship my thoughts of my brother Rich, nor what honour and support his virtues
promised to both our families, lest I should aggravate Your Ladyship's grief, already too great.
There be many reasons why our family, and particularly myself, should be affected with this stroke ;
yet there is none more prevalent with me than my
concernment for Your Ladyship's own person ;
for, considering my obligations, I must be very
ill-natured if I should not grieve because Your
Ladyship is grieved ; and I am sure the loss of the
only son of an only daughter, and the hopes which,
Madam, you had of that now blessed person, cannot but grieve Your Ladyship. I am confident
Your Ladyship has so learned Christ, the world,
and the use of these dispensations, as to be enabled to bear this crosse even beyond what might
be expected from flesh and blood, and that tenderness of affection so eminent in Your Ladyship :
and truly, Madam, this consideration only wipes
my eyes ; for truly I am assured the Lord will
bring you safe out of this affliction. This occasion
calls for your best thoughts ; nor would I willingly
interrupt them, the end of this expresse being to
express how much my wife, myself, and indeed all
good people, are affected with this Providence ; and
to assure Your Ladyship, that although God hath

seem'd to break the bond that men think would
have held our familys together, yet I desire Your
Ladyship to believe that nothing shall be wanting
in me to strengthen this knott, whereof I was ever
ambitious. I hope the bearer will bring me a good
accompt of the Lord's supporting Your Ladyship
under this visitation, the happy newes whereof
would be most welcome to, Madam, Your Ladyship's, &c.

" H. Cr."

Then follows a letter to Henry Cromwell from
the Earl of Warwick, in answer to the above letter
to him : it has only the day of the month (the 11th
March,) and the place from whence it was written,
but not the year; it must be the March of the year
1657, in which Mr. Rich died, because the Earl's
death was (as before mentioned) in the April following (1658). It is indorsed " The Earl of
Warwick to my father on the death of the Earl's
grandson, Mr. Rich. — My Lord ; My penne &
my heart were ever Y^r Lo$^{p^{ss}}$ servants, now they are
become y^r debtors. This paper cannot enough
confesse my obligation, & much lesse discharge it,
for your seasonable and sympathizing letters, w^{ch}
(besides the value they derive from soe worthy a
hand) expresse such faithfull affections, and administer such Christian advice, as render them beyond
measure welcome and deare to mee. And although
my heavinesse and distraction of thoughts persuades

mee rather to peruse those excellent lines thn to answer them, and to take releife from them rather then make a return to them, yet I must not be so indulgent to myne own sorrowes, as to lose this opportunitie of being thankfull to Y^r Lo^p for so greate a favoure.   My L^d, I dare not be insensible of that hand wch hath lay'd a verie sharpe & awakeing affliction upon mee ; but wee may not bee so presumptuous as to make choise of our own Rodde, or so much as in thought to detract from, or diminish, the justice & wisdom and goodness of God in those harde events, wch must all stand invioliable when millions of such worms as I am are gone to dust.   I must needs say I have lost a deare and comfortable relation, one in whom I had much determined my affections & lodged my hopes, wch are now rebuked & withered by a hasty and earely death; but my propertie in him was inferior to his who hath taken him, and I must reste my hearte in his proceedings, making it my care and suite, that those evills wch cannot be averted may be sanctifyed.   In order to wch I desire from this one sadde instance to argue the whole worlde of vanitie and variablenesse.   Alas! what a staffe of reed are .... these things, wch have noe stay in themselves, and therefore canne give none to us.   They witnesse their own impotencie, & themselves admonish us to pitch our rest above this sphere of changeable mortalitie, and to caste anchor in heaven, while we canne finde noe holde at all on earth.   Assuredly, hee that will have & holde a right tranquilitie, must found it in a sweete fruitio⁰ of God, wch whosoever wants may be secure, but cannot be quiet. That this breach therefore may be filled upp wth the presence & communicatiõs of God, shall be my daylie desire and prayer. My Lord, all this is but a broken echo of your pious counsell, wch gives such ease to my oppressed minde, that I canne scarse forbidd my Penne being tedious. Onely it remembers Your Lo^{ps} many weighty & noble employm^{ts}, w^{ch} (together wth your prudent, heroique, and honourable managery of them) I doe heere congratulate as well as my griefe will give me leave. Others goodnes is their owne, yours is a whole countries, yea, three kingdomes, for wch you justly possesse interest and renowne wth wise and good men: vertue is a thousand escushions. Goe on, my Lord, goe on happily to love religion, to exemplify it. May Your Lo^{p} longe continue an instrum^{t} of use, a patterne of vertue, & a precedent of glory. This is the inward & affectionate prayer of, My Lord,

Your Lo^{ps} most affectionate Servant,

" WARWICKE."

" I desire my humble service may bee presented to y^{r} good Lady.

" Beddinto', this 11th of March."

The above first three letters are stated, in the margin of Thurloe, to have been in the possession of William Cromwell, Esq., (one of Henry Cromwell's grandsons,) but are not to be now found with the family-papers. They must have been lent by this Mr. Cromwell with many others also missing, for publication, and not returned. The letter to the Earl of Warwick is still with the family-papers.

Of Lord Fauconberg's and Cromwell's supposed mutual hatred nothing appears but in the above (Lord Clarendon's) account. His character is given in a letter of Lockhart to Cromwell through Thurloe, dated Paris, 21–31. March, 1657. It begins, — " May it please Your Highnesse, since my last I have had the opportunity of seeing my Lord Falconbridge, who, in my humble opinion, is a person of extraordinary parts, and hath (appearingly) all those qualities in a high measure that can fitt one for His Highnesse and countrie's service, for both of which he owns a particular zeale. He seemed to be much troubled for a report he heard, that the enemys gave him out to be a Catholic; and did purge himself from having any inclinations that way. He desyres His Highnesse may cause 'make exact enquiry after his carriage in England, and hopes by that means his innocency will be vindicated, and the malice of his accusers discovered. 'He is of opinion that the intended settlement will be very acceptable to all the nobility and gentry of his country, save a few who may be biassed by the interests of their relations."

, Thurloe, in a letter to Henry Cromwell, dated 23d November following (1657), says, "This week hath in a great part been taken up in solemnizeinge the marriage of my Lady Mary with my Lord Falconbridge. They were marryed at Hamptoncourt upon Thursday. He is a person of very great parts and sobrietye, and I hope His Highnesse and his family will have comfort in hym." Lord Clarendon says, this, and Mr. Rich's marriage, were at Whitehall; but it has been shown not to be true, as to either of them. He adds, that though these marriages were performed in public view according to the rites and ceremonies then in use, they were presently afterwards in private married by ministers ordained by bishops, and according to the form in the Book of Common Prayer; and this with the privity of Cromwell, who pretended to yield to it in compliance with the importunity and folly of his daughters. This is mere assertion; it may, or may not be true.

Henry Cromwell, in a letter to Lord Fauconberg, dated 9th December following, stated in Thurloe to be in the possession of the above Mr. William Cromwell, and a copy in his hand-writing, yet in the family, says, — " My Lord; Your Lordship's letter was very welcome to me, as bringing demonstration of His Highnesse's wisdom, and my sister's happiness. I wish His Highness may make as happy a choice of members for the other House of Parliament, as he hath done of a husband for his daughter. But I hope that God, who assisted him in the one will also continue his goodness for the other. I may repeat Your Lordship's words, — ' This near degree of alliance, united with the satisfaction I have received of Your Lordshipp's personal meritt, affords me a double happiness;' only I must confess, that this contentment (great as it is) doth not so much satisfy me as fill me with new desires; for now I am longing to have a nearer converse with Your Lordship; being apt to think my absence the ill husbandry of so great a talent. I will not wish Your Lordship in Ireland (although our barbarisms here, by giving Your Lordship a greater lustre, might be some advantage, if Your Lordship could be pleased with such airs) but rather wish myself in England, where I might in that measure which becomes Your Lordship's meritt, express myself, My Lord, Your Lordship's most affectionate brother, and humble and faithfull servant,   " H. CROMWELL."

The following is a letter from Thurloe's State Papers, dated Whitehall, 9th February, 1657, from Lord Fauconberg to Henry Cromwell: — " My Lord; After the liberty Your Lordship has given me, there cannot ought of concerne happen in this place which I shall not endeavour to give you the perfectest account of, and, if possible, outstrip all others in it. But those great things expected in order to the nation's settlement, from the two

Houses meeting, it has pleased God to dash all of a sodaine.—For, my Lord, two days after my last, H. H. (His Highness) surprised us all, not only us of the lower orbe, but those, I mean of his councell, most (I am sure) of them, if not all, by putting an end to boath the Houses of Parliament that Thursday morning. This, we now see, he was forced to doe, least some turbulent spirits amongst them should have put an end to the peace of this nation, by embroyling it as farre in blood and confusions as ever.

" Major-General Packer, who commands H. H. (His Highness's) owne regiment, is now with H. H., (His Highness,) and I have some reason to think his commission will be taken from him ere they part. It is believed some others too must follow; but I dare not say who, being resolved to give Your Lordship all the truth of matters I can, without the least mixture of my owne or others' conjectures.

" I cannot at all perceive H. H. disposed to that of Your Lordship's coming into England, tho' for never so small a time; and the truth is, I do not marvell att all as things now stand; for the troblers of our quiet will, no doubt, be watching all advantages there, as well as heere, and a greater then Your Lordship's absence I am sure they do not wish, whose actions stirre up as much dread in them, as wonder in all us that love you. This, my Lord, is the language of my judgment only, for my affection runnes quite counter, and would perswade that for a few months Your Lordship might be dispensed with, there being no person alive so impatiently longing for the honour to kisse Your Lordship's hands as, My Lord, Your Lordship's most faithfull and obedient servant,

"FAUCONBERG."

The following is a letter from Thurloe's State Papers, dated 20th February, in the same year (1657), from Henry Cromwell to Lord Fauconberg (stated to have been in the possession of the above William Cromwell, Esq.): " My Lord; When Your Lordship had any communication to impart unto me, I was always made sensible of your liberality therein; wherefore now I must attribute as much to Your Lordship's prudent tenderness of me, in that when the sad news of poor Robin Riche's death must be written, Your Lordship was but sparing in your mention of that sad story. My Lord, these providences are singly in themselves no miracles; yet when they happen so thick as of late upon Sir John Reynolds, (who was shipwrecked in his return to England from his service in assisting the French in their war against Spain,) and now upon this gentleman, I cannot think but that God intends them for our instruction. I desire Your Lordship, on my behalf, to condole with my poor sister. Your Lordship is able to say whatever is materiall upon this occasion: wherefore,

for me to venture upon any particulars, were to
put Your Lordship upon a kind of pennance, in
observing my impertinencies, and to endanger the
end of comforting myself, which cannot miscarry
upon Your Lordship's single management. I hope
Your Lordship's being called to succour my dear
sister, your lady, tends but to repair our family,
of the late loss it hath sustained; and I hope
that the sad apprehensions occasioned by this late
stroke, will not frustrate our hopest herein. I believe Your Lordship may by this time repent of
the liberty you have given me, and see the inconvenience of good nature and civility. My dear
Lord, I will be at present more moderate in
troubling Your Lordship, begging at this time
only the leave not to omitt declaring myself, My
Lord, Your Lordship's, &c.

" H. CROMWELL."

A letter in Thurloe's State Papers, by Lord
Fauconberg to Lockhart, the ambassador in France,
dated Whitehall, January 25—February 4. 1657-8,
which was after Cromwell's ·death, and during
Richard Cromwell's protectorate, proves His Lordship's continued confidential connection with
him. The last passage in this letter is as follows :—
" Last of all as to newes, I shall tell you, that the
House of Commons appeare yett a little pettish,
refusing on Saturday last, upon a message, sent
them from the House of Lords, to owne them for
such. This afternoone, both Houses, by command

from H. H. mett him in the Banquetting-house, where (His Highness Richard) he made a very pious and eloquent speech to them, tending to unity among themselves, and provision against the common enimyes of this nation. The Lord Lambert appeared this day in the Lower House, as did Sir Arthur Haselrig, notwithstanding his writ of summons to the other, and without ever wayting on H. H. to excuse itt. What these things will produce, God Almighty only knows: to whose protection I committ you, subscribing myselfe with all sincere affection, yours,

"FAUCONBERG."

A letter from Lord Fauconberg to Henry Cromwell, dated Whitehall, 8th June, 1658, informs of his return from his embassy at the French court, where, he says, he had the honourablest reception imaginable, which he particularly describes. He adds, — "In summe, through all their actions, not the least circumstance was omitted that might witnesse the truth of these respects they beare His Highnesse, and the English nation. The Cardinal admires Your Lordship very much, as all the world must needs doe."

The following letter is in Thurloe, from Lord Fauconberg to Henry Cromwell, dated 7th September, 1658, N. S., informing him of the death of Cromwell: — "Deare my Lord; This bearer, Mr. Underwood, brings Your Lordshipp the sad newes of our general losse in your incomparable father's death, by which these poore nations are deprived of the greatest personage and instrument of happinesse, not only our owne, but indeed any age else ever produced. The preceding night, and not before, in presence of four or five of the councell, he declared my Lord Richard his successor; the next morning grew speechlesse, and departed betwixt three and four in the evening. A hard dispensation itt was, but so itt has seemed good to the Allwise God; and what remaines to poore creatures, but to lay our hands upon our mouthes to the declaration of his pleasure? Some three houres after his decease (a time spent only in framing the draught, not in any doubtfull dispute) was Your Lordshipp's brother, His now Highnesse, declared Protector of these nations, with full consent of councell, soldier, and city. The next day he was proclaimed in the usuall places. All the time His late Highnesse was drawing on to his end, the consternation and astonishment of people is unexpressible: their harts seemed as sunke within them. And if this abroad, in the family Your Lordship may imagine what it was in Her Highness, and other neer relations. My poor wife, I knowe not what in the earth to doe with her; when seemingly quieted she bursts out again into passion, that tears hir very hart in pieces; nor can I blame her, considering what she has lost. It fares little better with others. God, I trust, will sanctifye this bitter cup to us all. His mercy is extraordinary, as to the quiet face of things among us, which I hope the Lord will continue. Your Lordshipp's most affectionately faithfull and very humble servant,   · · " FAUCONBERG."

In additional proof of the continuance of this affectionate intercourse between these families, is brought forward the following letters from Lady Fauconberg, remaining in the Cromwell family. The first is addressed " To my dear bro. Henry Cromwell, att Speny." It has no date of time or place; but from the address to him at Spinney Abbey, in Cambridgeshire, the place of his residence after the Restoration, it must have been subsequently to his quitting Ireland. " Dear brother; I have sent this bearer on porpos to se you and my sister, fearing I shall not se you befor I go from hence. My poor mother (she must mean the late Protectress) is so affecting a spectacle as I scars know how to writ, she continuing much the same as she was when you wer hear: the Lord knows best what is fit for us to sufer, and therfor I desir we may willingly submit to his will; but the condishon she is in is very sad; the Lord help her and us to bear it. I am now able to say no mor, my hart being so opprest; but that I am your dear wiff's and yours most afec. sister,

" M. FAUCONBERG."

" My stay hear, unles somthing extrordynary hapen, will be till Munday next."

The next letter is dated the 29th January, the

year not mentioned, addressed to her (Lady Fauconberg's) nephew, Henry Cromwell, at Spinney Abbey, who was her late brother the forenamed Henry Cromwell's eldest son. It is an affectionate letter upon his wife's recovery from a lying-in, and death of the child; adding, " that my Lord as well as self return thanks" (for a present), " and charges me to assure you both of his humble service"—" Most affectionate aunt and servant,

" M. FAUCONBERG."

And the third letter is dated August the 10th, and upon the back is written " 1689."—It is addressed to the same nephew, Henry Cromwell:— " Dear Nephew ; I receaved y" which this comes in answer to: my Lord was one Thursday at Hampton-court, when he spoke to the King (must be King William) againe as for your concern and your cosens ; but all the answer he could gitt was that he wanted money, and att present did not think of raising any more men, which for your sakes I am concerned for." Then follows some public news from Ireland.

Many other letters, to be found in Thurloe, many of them theretofore in the Cromwell family's possession, and lent, but probably not returned, show the same affectionate attention of the two families to each other.

These letters may perhaps appear tedious and uninteresting; but they cannot but have the effect of proving the unfoundedness of His Lordship's (Lord Clarendon's) assertion of Lord Fauconberg's and Cromwell's mutual aversion ; His Lordship is upon all occasions too well disposed to credit every improbable, unsupported tale to the injury of Cromwell's good name.

So soon after writing the above letter of 10th August, 1689, as February, 1693–4, King William, no doubt through the same interest of Lord and Lady Fauconberg, gave the above Henry Cromwell a captain's commission in the Earl of Denbigh's regiment of dragoons. And Queen Anne, in the first year of her reign, gave him a captain's commission in Lord Mohun's regiment of foot. And in the seventh year of her reign, gave him a major's commission in Colonel Kilner Brasier's regiment of foot. He died in Spain in 1711, in the British army under the command of Lord Galway.

Mr. Noble attributes these appointments to the exertions of the Duke of Ormond, in acknowledgement, as Mr. Noble says he always declared, of the great service and benefit his family received from Henry Cromwell while he was Lord Lieutenant of Ireland. He might have added, in acknowledgement also of the kind and generous treatment both the Duke and his Duchess experienced from Henry Cromwell's father (the Protector) heretofore related, when they were both wholly in his power, and were secretly serving the royal party. The Duke might support the Fauconberg efforts in his favour.

By the same interest (it is presumed), he, Lady Fauconberg's nephew, the same Henry Cromwell, was in the year 1690 appointed one of the gentlemen of King William's privy chamber.

Whitelock in his mention of his (Cromwell's) daughter Claypoole's death, says nothing to induce a supposition of the reality of the alleged perplexing conferences with her father, or of her allusion, in her bodily sufferings, to the blood she is asserted by His Lordship to have accused him of having shed. He speaks highly of her, and says her death did much grieve her father. His Lordship acknowledges he (Cromwell) had not the least appearance, upon his approaching death, of remorse for any of his actions; and concludes with only saying, that either what she said or her death affected him wonderfully.

Ludlow, referring to her's and Cromwell's death, says, that it had been reported that her ill success in her application to her father for the sparing Dr. Hewitt's life had so afflicted her, that it had been one cause of her death: he is silent as to these her supposed accusations of him during her last illness. But he describes him as manifesting no remorse of conscience for betraying (as he calls it) the public cause, and sacrificing it to his own ambition; and that some of his last words were rather becoming a mediator than a sinner; recommending to God the condition of the nation that he had so infamously cheated; and expressing a great care of the people, whom he had so manifestly despised. He adds, he seemed above all concerned for the reproaches he said men would cast upon his name, in trampling upon his ashes when dead; and that in this temper of mind he died about two in the afternoon.

Mrs. Hutchinson only says, that before he could accomplish his design (which she supposes he intended) of imprisoning the Colonel her husband, death imprisoned himself, and confined all his vast ambition, and all his cruel designs, into the narrow compass of a grave.

Mr. Noble says, that it is allowed by our historians, that in the repeated conferences she (Lady Claypoole) had with Cromwell just before her death, she painted the guilt of his ambition in the most dreadful colours: he gives Lord Clarendon as his authority. He adds, that she was particular in mentioning the death of her pious pastor, Dr. Hewitt; the near approach of her dissolution giving her, she supposed, liberty to say what formerly she thought, yet durst not then express. Dr. Bates says, in her hysterical fits she much disquieted him, by upbraiding him, sometimes with one of his crimes, and sometimes with another, according to the furious distractions of her disease, which, he says, was an inward imposthume in her loins.

Who the historians are, besides Lord Clarendon and Dr. Bates, that have said all this, does not appear. His Lordship could know nothing but from report; and the subsequent writers have probably implicitly followed him, and perhaps also Dr. Bates; but his testimony to Cromwell's prejudice is not to be relied on, when he is seen turning round at the Restoration, and recommending himself to the ruling powers by disclosing and probably misrepresenting the professional secrets of Cromwell's family, and abusing and vilifying the memory of his late patron.

The probable falsehood of these accounts and assertions will best appear from the following circumstances.

In Thurloe's State Papers is a letter, appearing to be supplied by the forenamed Mr. William Cromwell, dated so near her death as 12th June, 1658, from her (Lady Claypoole) " to the Lady of Henry Cromwell," in which she begs her pardon for not writing oftener, " but in earnist, I have bin so extreme sickly of late that it has made mee unfitt for any thing. Truly the Lord has bin very gratius to us, in doeing for us abofe whot we could expect; and now has shewed himself more extraordinary in delivering my father out of the hands of his enymise, which wee have all reson to be sensible of in a very particular manner; for sertingly, not ondly his family would have bin ruined, but in all probabillyti the hol nation would have bin invold in blod. The Lord grant it maye never be forgot by us, but that it may cause us to depend upon him from hom wee have reseved all

good, and that it may cose us to se the muttable-
nes of thise things, and to yuse them accordingly.
I am suer wee have nede to bag that sperrit from
God."

General Fleetwood, in a letter to Henry Cromwell, dated July, 1658, says, — " Deare brother; I
have received yours, whearin you desire to understand the condicion of my Lady Elizabeth, who
was in a very hopefull condicion till within this
3 or 4 dayes, shee hath bine exceeding ill, and
very much weakned, and brought low, but hoped
she is agayn upon the mending hand. Shee hath
bin troubled with great paynes in her bowells, and
vapours in the heade. The truth is, its beleeved
the physitians do not understand thoroughly hir
case. She is now advised to tak Tunbridge waters.
It hath bin a very sore and sharpe tryall ; yet being
a Father's hand, I hope we shall have all of us
advantage by it, for sure it is a voyce to all of the
relations. I neade not tell you the great sence
both Their Highnesses have of this dispensation.
There is nothing wanting of care or skill : but the
blessing of the Lord must make all effectuall.
She hath many prayers going for hir, a return of
which will make the mercy double. Both Their
Highnesses and family are at Hampton-court.
His Highness takes the waters, and they agree
pritty well."

In a letter to Henry Cromwell, dated 3d August
following, he writes, — that it hath pleased the

Lord, when all hopes were even at an end, and the doctors did believe Her Ladyship's condition was desperate and near expiring, beyond all expectation to give hir a composure of spirits by sleepe : and that since Friday last, she had bin dayly upon the recovery, and so continued in a very hopefull way : that His Highness had bin for this 4 or 5 days very indisposed and ill ; but that night had had a very good refreshment by sleep, and was much revived, his paynes and distemper abated and much amended, &c.

The next letter is from Secretary Thurloe to Henry Cromwell, dated 17th same August, informing of the interment in Westminster Abbey, of the Lady Claypoole (she died 6th same August). He adds, " Your Lordship is a very sensible judge how great an affliction this was to both Their Highnesses, and how sadd a familye she left behind her, which saddnesse was truly very much increased by the sicknesse of His Highnesse, who at the same tyme lay very ill of the gout and other distempers, contracted by the long sicknesse of my Lady Elizabeth, which made great impressions upon hym ; and since that, whither it were the retireinge of the gout out of his foot into his body, or from some other cause, I am not able to say, he hath been very dangerousely sicke ; the violence whereof lasted 4 or 5 dayes ; but, blessed be God, he is now reasonable well recovered, and this day he went abroad for an houre, and findes himselfe much refreshed by it; soe that this recovery of His Highness doth much allay the sorrow for my Lady Elizabeth's death," &c.   A letter from Dr. Clarges to Henry Cromwell, of the 10th same August, says, " His Highness, by the blessing of God, is much amended, and will, with his whole traine, be this evening at Whitehall."

None of the above letters afford the slightest ground for the belief of the truth of these assertions of the Lady Claypoole's accusations of her father. Although her letter of the 12th June, 1658, is dated only four days after the execution of Sir Henry Slingsby and Dr. Hewitt, which, according to a letter from Dr. Clarges, (also in Thurloe's State Papers,) was on the 8th of the same month of June, she expresses no concern for their deaths; but on the contrary, much thankfulness for the deliverance of her father from what she considers a most destructive plot.   Dr. Clarges only relates the fact of the execution, adding that the court was to meet again on Thursday, for the trial of the other conspirators.

The circumstances of Cromwell's last illness and death, in addition to those already mentioned in the preceding letters, will be best collected from the following letters in Thurloe's State Papers.

In a letter to Henry Cromwell, dated 24th August, 1658, Thurloe says, " His Highness continuing ill, hath given a stopp to all buissines : he was soe well upon Friday, that wee hoped that the

worst of his sicknesse was over; but it pleased
God, that upon Saterday morninge he fell into a fitt
of an ague, and by its course ever since it appeares
to be a tertian. The fitts were longe and somewhat sharpe; but yet the last was not soe badd as
the former. This being the intervall day, he came
from Hampton-court hither, all the doctors judge-
inge this to be much the better place, besides the
advantage which the change of aire usually gives
for the recovery out of agues; and although it be
an ill tyme of the year to have an ague in, yet itt
beinge a tertian, and His Highness being pretty
well in the intervalls, the doctors do not conceive
there is any danger as to his life. However, Your
Excellency will easily ymagine how much trouble
we are all under here; and though it shall please
the Lord to recover him againe, yet, certeinely,
considering the tyme that this visitation is in, and
other circumstances relating thereunto, it cannot
but greatly affect us all towards God, and make us
deepely sensible how much our dependence is
upon him, in whose hands is the life and breath of
this his old servant; and if he should take him
away from amongst us, how terrible a blow it
would be to all the good people of the land; and
that therefore we should be carefull how wee walke
towards God, least wee provoke him to depart
from us, and bringe upon us this great evil," &c.
A postscript—"His Highness is just now enteringe
into his fitt. I beseech the Lord to be favourable
to him."

In a letter from Dr. Clarges, of the same date, to Henry Cromwell, he says, that the calling of a parliament had been lately delayed by reason of His Highness's sickness; but that his recovery, which was in a good measure advanced, would draw on consideration about it.

In a letter dated, 27th of the same August, Whitehall, two in the morning, Thurloe to Henry Cromwell, describes his (Cromwell's) fit upon the Tuesday night as somewhat more favourable than the former; and that the good interval after it gave great hopes that his ague was very much upon the decrease, especially the fit which he then was in beginning very favourably, the cold part of it slipping over without any observation; but that the hot fit had been very long and terrible, insomuch, that the doctors feared he would not get through it; that he was then fallen into a breathing sweat, which, it was hoped, he would come well out of. He adds, that he durst not to inform him (Henry Cromwell) that the last fit had rendered His Highness's condition very dangerous, and doubts their fears were more than their hopes.

On the 30th of the same month, he writes that lest the last-mentioned letter should miscarry, he had sent an express that he (Henry Cromwell) might fully understand how it was with His Highness: that on the 13th day, since his ague took him, having been sick a fortnight before, of a general distemper of body : that it continued a good while to be a tertian ague and the burning fits very violent: that upon Saturday it fell to a double tertian, having two fits in twenty-four hours, one upon the heels of another, which had extremely weakened him, and endangered his life: and that since Saturday morning he had scarce been perfectly out of his fits: that the doctors were yet hopeful that he might struggle through it, though their hopes were mingled with much fear. But truly, adds he (Thurloe), wee have cause to put our hope in the Lord, and to expect mercy from him in this case, hee haveinge stirr'd up the saints to pray for hym in all places, &c. " And that which is some ground of hope is, that the Lord, as in some former occasions, hath given to himself (Cromwell) a perticuler assurance, that he shall yet live to serve hym, and to carry on the worke which he hath put into his hands." He proceeds: — That " he fears our own divisions may be great, if His Highness should not settle and fix his successor before he dies; which truly I believe he hath not yet done. He did by himselfe declare one in a paper before he was installed by the Parliament, and sealed it up in the forme of a letter, directing it to me, but kept both the name of the person and the paper to himselfe. After he fell sicke at Hampton-court, he sent Mr. John Barrington to London for it, telling hym it lay on his study table at Whitehall; but it was not to be found there, nor elsewhere, though it hath beene

very narrowly looked for.   And in this condition
matters stand, His Highness having been too ill to
be troubled with a buissiness of this importance.
This day he hath had some discourse about it, but
his illness disenabled hym to conclude it fully.
And if it should please the Lord not to give hym
tyme to settle his succession before his death, the
judgment would be the soarer, and our condition
the more dangerous ; but trust he will have com-
passion on us, and not leave us as a prey to our
enemies, or to one another."

Lord Fauconberg in a letter to Henry Cromwell,
dated the same 30th August, says, — " It is with
unspeakable grief I now give Your Lordship the
sad account of His Highness's condition, which all
the physicians have for some days judged dangerous, and now, more than ever.   Though his loss
must needs carry weight ynough in itselfe, yet the
consideration of the miserable posture hee leaves
these nations in, is stupendious.   My Lord, I hold
it my duty to acquaint you how wee stand at present, and then leave the further proceed of things
to God's direction and Your Lordship's wisdom.
A successor, there is none named that I can
learn ; T. (Thurloe) has seemed to be resolved to
press him, in his intervals, to such a nomination :
but whether out of apprehensions to displease him,
if recovering, or others hereafter, if it should not
succeed, he has not yet done it, nor doe I believe

wil." Tuesday, August 31. " His Highness is beyond al possibility of recovery."

Thurloe, in a letter dated 4th September, (Saturday,) 1658, informs Henry Cromwell of Cromwell's death. " He died yesterday, (Friday, 3d,) about four of the clocke in the afternoone. I am not able to speake or write ; this stroake is so soare, soe unexpected, the providence of God in it so stupendious, consideringe the person that is fallen, the tyme and season wherein God tooke hym away, with other circumstances, I can doe nothinge but put my mouthe in the dust and say, It is the Lord; and though his wayes be not alwayes knowne, yet they are alwayes righteous, and we must submitt to his will, and resigne up ourselves to him with all our concernements. His Highness was pleased before his death to declare my Lord Richard successor. He did it upon Munday (the 30th), and the Lord hath so ordered it, that the council and army have received him with all manner of affection."

In a subsequent letter, of the 7th of the same September, he (Thurloe) refers to the bearer, Mr. Underwood, " a very sober gentleman, who was of the bedchamber to His late Highness, and attended him in all his sicknesse, for a full account of all that passed on this sadd occasion, to which purpose His Highness (Richard) hath sent him over to Your Excellency, that you might fully understand the perticulars of God's dealinge with

His Highness, your father, through his whole visitation."

Thurloe, in the forementioned letter of the 4th September, says, he (Cromwell) appointed his son Richard his successor on the Monday preceding his decease; on which day Lord Fauconberg says in his letter, he had not then done it, nor did he believe he would. Sir Philip Warwick says, that, from the information of one of his physicians, he was never during his last illness in a state of mind to determine any thing of his successor, referring to Thurloe's declaration of his appointment of his son Richard to the Protectorate. Nevertheless, it is undeniable, that on the evening before his death, (Thursday the 2d September,) he was sufficiently himself to compose and utter the following prayer, which remains with the Cromwell family-papers, and is probably the one mentioned in a letter of Thurloe's, to be then sent to Henry: it is described, " His Highness's prayer, Sept. 2d, being the night before he departed."—Lord, although I am a wretched and miserable creature, I am in covenant with thee through grace, and I may, I will come unto thee for my people: Thou hast made me a mean instrument to doe them some good and thee sarves, and many of them have sett too high a vallue upon me though others wishe and would be glad of my death, but, Lord, however thou shalt dispose of me, continue and goe on to doe good for them ; give them consistancy of judgment,

mutual love, and one harte, goe one to deliver
them, and with the worke of reformation, and
make the nam of Christ glorious in the world;
teach those who looke too much upon thy instruments to depend more upon thyselfe. Pardon
such as desire to trample upon the dust of a poore
worme; for they are thy people too, and pardon
the folly of this short prayer, for Jesus Christ
his sake, and give us a good night if it be thy
pleasure."

Neal, in his History of the Puritans, says, from
Baxter's Life, — " About twelve hours before he
died, he lay very quiet, when Major Butler, being
in his chamber, says he heard him make his last
prayer to this purpose :— " Lord, I am a poor
foolish creature ; this people would fain have me
live ; they think it best for them and that it will
redound much to thy glory, and all the stir is
about this. Others would fain have me die ; Lord,
pardon them, and pardon thy foolish people ; forgive their sins and do not forsake them, but love and
bless and give them rest, and bring them to a consistency, and give me rest for Jesus Christ's sake,
to whom, with thee and thy Holy Spirit, be all
honour and glory, now and for ever. Amen."
Dr. Harris gives the above first-mentioned prayer,
with some variations, and concluding with the
above word " too " from a collection of several
passages concerning His late Highness, in the time
of his sickness, by one that was groom of his bed-

chamber, published in the year 1659. He (Dr.
Harris) adds, this was all in character : and that,
two or three more of his expressions, when death
was in his view, will show us in what temper he
left the world. These are quoted from the forementioned collection of passages :— " Lord, thou
knowest if I do desire to live, it is to shew forth
thy praise and declare thy works :" that again he
said, " I would be willing to live to be further serviceable to God and his people, but my work is
done; yet God be with his people." He then
refers to a passage from Dr. Bates, " But all his
distemper was not in his mind alone ; for shortly
after he was taken with a slow fever, that at length
degenerated into a bastard tertian ague. — For a
week's time the disease so continued without any
dangerous symptoms, (as appearing sometimes one
and sometimes another kind of distemper,) that
every other day he walked abroad : but that after
dinner his five physicians coming to wait upon
him, one of them having felt his pulse, said that
it intermitted : at which, suddenly startled, he
looked pale, fell into a cold sweat, almost fainted
away, and orders himself to be carried to bed,
where, being refreshed with cordials, he made his
will, but only about his private and domestic
affairs. That next morning early, when one of his
physicians came to visit him, he asked him why he
looked so sad ? and when he made answer, that so
it becomes any one who had the weighty care of

his life and health upon him : ye physicians (said he) think I shall die.   Then the company being removed, holding his wife by the hand, to this purpose he spoke to him ; I tell you, I shall not die this bout ; I am sure of it.   And because he observed him to look more attentively upon him at these words, Don't think, said he, that I am mad ; I speak the words of truth, upon surer grounds than your Galen or Hippocrates furnish you with. God Almighty himself hath given that answer, not to my prayers alone, but also to the prayers of those who entertain a stricter commerce and greater intimacy with him.   Go on, cheerfully banishing all sadness from your looks, and deal with me as you would with a serving man.   Ye may have skill in the nature of things, yet nature can do more than all physicians put together ; and God is far more above nature.

These several circumstances, however they may be deemed by some to prove Cromwell's enthusiasm, which will be considered hereafter, are surely sufficient to prove the assertion of his physicians, to Sir Philip Warwick, not to be true, — that he was in a constant state of delirium till his death.

It is remarked by Lord Clarendon, that he showed no remorse in his last illness, for the blood he states his daughter to have accused him of having spilled, nor for any other of his supposed wicked actions. Sir Philip Warwick also allows that he died quietly in his bed.   Ludlow, with his usual malignity

towards Cromwell, says, he showed so little remorse of conscience for betraying the public cause,
and sacrificing to the idol of his own ambition,
that some of his last words (probably alluding to
his before-given prayers) were rather becoming a
mediator than a sinner, recommending to God the
condition of the nation whom he had so manifestly
despised. But that he seemed, above all, concerned for the reproaches, he said, men would cast
upon his ashes when dead. And that in this temper of mind he departed this life about two in the
afternoon.

Dr. Harris describes him a professor of religion,
even to a degree of enthusiasm. — He allows him
really religious, which he thinks appears from a
religious letter to a Mr. Storie, dated St. Ives, 11th
January, 1635, which he gives at length, from the
original letter in the British Museum. This letter
respects the erection of a lecture by a Mr. Storie,
in some part of Huntingdonshire, commending him
for it, and strongly urging its support. It proves
nothing more than outward profession, which is
not disputed; the sincerity and reality of that
profession can only be ascertained by the uniformity and consistency of his religious and moral
conduct, both public and private. He (Dr. Harris)
says very truly, that real inward religion appears
not to men but by its fruits. He says, he not only
practised the external duties of religion, but that
he was carried away into enthusiasm : that he

fancied himself favoured and distinguished by Heaven: that God, in answer to his prayers, afforded him supernatural illumination and assistance. He then, in proof of this supposed enthusiasm, quotes the before-given conversation of Sir Philip Warwick with Dr. Simcott, and, from Thurloe, the forementioned letter from Cromwell to his cousin Mr. St. John ; also, from Thurloe, a passage in a letter to Lord Wharton, dated 2d September, 1648. In Thurloe, this letter begins, — "My Lord ; You know how untoward I am att this businesse of writinge ; yet a word" — it proceeds as in Dr. Harris — " I beseech the Lord make us sensible of this great mercye heere, (the victory, the Doctor supposes, over the Scots under Duke Hamilton ; it must be so ; it was towards the end of the preceding August,) which surelye was much more then . . . . . the House expresseth. I trust . . . . . . the goodnesse of our God, time and opportunitye to speak of itt with you face to face. When we think of our God, what are wee ! oh ! his mercye to the whole societye of saincts, despised, jeered saincts. Let them mocke onn. Would we were all saincts ; the best of us are (God knows) poore weake saincts, yet saincts ; if not sheepe, yet lambes, and must bee fed. We have daily bread, and shall have itt in spite of all enemies. There's enough in our Father's house, and he dispenseth itt as our eyes . . . . behind, then wee can . . . . we for him. I think thorough these outward mercyes (as we call them), faith, patience, love, hope, all are exercised and perfected, yea Christ formed, and grows to a perfect man within us. I knowe not how well to distinguish; the difference is only in the subject, to a worldly man they are outward; to a sainct, Christian; but I dispute not. My Lord, I rejoice in your particular mercye. I hope that is soe to you; if soe, it shall not hurt you, nor make you plott or shift for the younge baron to make him great. You will say hee is God's to dispose of and guide for, and there you will leave him." Thurloe continues, " My love to the deare little ladye, better then the child. The Lord bless you both. My love to all friendes, high and low; if you will, my Lord and Lady Moulgrave and Will. Hill. Your faithfull friend and humblest servant,

" O. CROMWELL."

In further proof of this supposed enthusiasm, he (Dr. Harris) gives, from Thurloe, a letter to the governor of the castle of Edinburgh, dated 9th September, 1650. Whitelock introduces this letter; — " That Cromwell sent to the governor of the castle (Dundas), that the ministers with him might return to their churches, and be at liberty to preach there, and commanded that none of the army should molest them :" that the ministers sent answer, that they found nothing expressed (in Cromwell's letter) whereby to build any security for

their persons, and for their return, they resolved
to reserve themselves for better times, and to wait
upon him, who had hidden his face for a while
from the sons of Jacob: that the General (Cromwell) replied in the following letter: — " Our
kindness offered to the ministers with you was
done with ingenuity, thinking to have met with
the like ; but I am satisfied to tell those with you,
that if their Master's service (as they call it) were
chiefly in their eye, imagination of suffering would
not have caused such a return; much less the practices of our party, as they are pleased to say, upon
the ministers of Christ in England, have been an
argument of personal persecution. The ministers
of England are supported, and have liberty to
preach the Gospel, though not to rail, nor, under
pretence thereof, to overtop the civil power, or
debase it as they please. No man hath been troubled in England or Ireland for preaching the
Gospel, nor has any minister been molested in
Scotland since the coming of the army hither.
The speaking truth becomes the ministers of Christ.
When ministers pretend to a glorious reformation,
and lay the foundation thereof, in getting to themselves worldly power, and can make worldly mix-
tures to accomplish the same, such as their late
agreement with their King, and hopes by him
to carry on their designs, they may know that
the Sion promised and hoped for, will not be
built with such untempered mortar. As for the

unjust invasion they mention, time was, when an army of Scotland came into England, not called by the supreme authority." (So far is from Whitelock and Thurloe, omitted by Dr. Harris.) "We have said in our papers, with what hearts, and upon what account we came, and the Lord hath heard us, though you would not, upon as solemn an appeal as any experience can parallel." (An immaterial passage is also here omitted.) "When they trust purely to the sword of the Spirit, which is the word of God, which is powerful to bring down strong-holds, and every imagination that exalts itself, which alone is able to square and fit the stones for the New Jerusalem; then, and not before, and by that means and no other, shall Jerusalem, which is to be the praise of the whole earth, the city of the Lord, be built, the Sion of the Holy One of Israel. I have nothing to say to you more, but that I am, Sir, your humble servant,

" O. CROMWELL."

The Scots ministers sent an answer to this letter by the governor (which is in Thurloe), the substance whereof Dr. Harris gives shortly,—that they had not so learned Christ as to hang the equity of their cause upon events; and Cromwell another letter in answer to them, wherein he says,— "We look upon ministers as helpers of, not lords over the faith of God's people. I appeal to their consciences, whether any, denying their doctrines, and dissenting, shall not incur the censure of sectary. And what is this but to deny Christians their liberty, and assume the infallible chair? Where do you find in Scripture, that preaching is included in your function? Though an approbation from men hath order in it, and may do well, yet he that hath not a better than that, he hath none at all. I hope He that ascended up on high may give his gifts to whom he pleaseth, and if those gifts be the seal of mission, be not envious, though Eldad and Medad prophesy; you know who bids us covet earnestly the best gifts, but chiefly that we may prophesy; which the Apostle explains there, to be a speaking to instruction, and edification, and comfort, which the instructed, edified, and comforted, can best tell the energy and effect of. If such evidence be, I say again, take heed you envy not, for your own sakes, lest you be guilty of a greater fault than Moses reproved in Joshua; for envying for his sake. Indeed you err through mistake of the Scriptures. Approbation is an act of conveniency in respect of order, not of necessity, to give faculty to preach the Gospel. Your pretended fear lest error should step in, is like the man that would keep all the wine out of the country lest men should be drunk; it will be found an unjust and unwise jealousy to deny a man the liberty he hath by nature, upon a supposition he may abuse it; when he doth abuse it, judge.

Dr. Harris makes use of the following passage in the same letter, in support of his assertion of Cromwell's enthusiasm. He (Cromwell), says he, re-assumed his pen on the same subject, and writes as follows: — "In answer to the witnesse of God upon our solemn appeal, you say you have not so learned Christ to hang the equity of your cause upon events. We could wish blindnesse hath not been upon your eyes to all those marvellous dispensations, which God hath wrought lately in England. But did not you solemnly appeal and pray? Did not we do so too? and ought not you and we to think with feare and tremblinge of the hand of the great God in this strange and mighty appearance of his? but can slightly call it an event. Were not both yours and our expectations renewed from time to time, whilst we waited upon God, to see which way he would manifest himself upon our appeals? And shall we, after all these our prayers, fastings, tears, expectations, and solemn appeals, call these base events? The Lord pitye you. Surely we fear, because it hath been a merciful and gracious deliverance to us. I beseech you, in the bowels of Christ, search after the mind of the Lord in it towards you, and we shall help you by our prayers, that you may find it out; for yet (if we know our hearts at all) our bowels do in Christ Jesus earn after the godly in Scotland."

In further proof, Dr. Harris gives the following passage from Bishop Burnet: — That when Cromwell was in the greatest streights and perplexities, just before the battle of Dunbar, (3d September, 1650,) he called his officers to a day of seeking the Lord. He loved to talk much of that matter all his life long afterwards. He said he felt such an enlargement of heart in prayer, and such quiet upon it, that he bade all about him take heart; for God had certainly heard them, and would appear for them. Atter prayer they walked in the Earl of Roxburgh's gardens that lay under the hill; and by prospective glasses they discerned a great motion in the Scottish camp: upon which Cromwell said, God is delivering them into our hands; they are coming down to us." This event, adds Dr. Harris, was conformable to his expectations.

Also the before-mentioned passage from Whitelock, (who, he says, well knew the man,) describing Cromwell and Ireton supping with Whitelock, and relating to him wonderful observations of God's providence in the affairs of the war.

The above passages he (Dr. Harris) thinks abundantly sufficient to establish the enthusiasm of Cromwell.

Nevertheless, in addition to the above proofs, the Doctor adds, from Calamy's Life of Howe, — Cromwell's real opinion concerning returns of prayer, will clearly show his enthusiasm. What

follows, he says, he believes may be depended on :
" I (presume he means Calamy) had heard from
several, and it had been confirmed to me by Mr.
Jeremy White, who lived at Whitehall at the very
same time with Mr. Howe, that the notion of a
particular faith in prayer prevailed much in Cromwell's court; and that it was a common opinion
among them, that such as were in a special manner
favoured of God, when they offered up prayers and
supplications to him for his mercies, either for
themselves or others, often had such impressions
made on their minds and spirits by a Divine hand,
as signified to them, not only in the general, that
their prayers would be heard, and graciously answered, but that the particular mercies that were
sought for, would be certainly bestowed ; nay, and
sometimes also intimated to them in what way and
manner they would be afforded ; and pointed
out to them future events beforehand, which, in
reality, is the same as inspiration. Having heard
of mischief done by the prevalence of this notion,
I took the opportunity that offered, when there was
nothing to hinder the utmost freedom, to enquire
of Mr. Howe what he had known about this matter, and what were his apprehensions concerning
it. He told me the prevalence of the notion that
I mentioned at Whitehall, at the time when he
lived there, was too notorious to be called in question, and that not a little pains were taken to
cultivate and support it, and that he once heard a

sermon there, from a person of note, the avowed
design of which was to maintain and defend it.
He said he was so fully convinced of the ill-ten-
dency of such a principle, that after hearing this
sermon, he thought himself bound in conscience,
when it came next to his turn to preach before
Cromwell, to set himself industriously to oppose it,
and to beat down that spiritual pride and confidence which such fancied impulses and impressions were apt to produce and cherish. He told
me he observed, that while he was in the pulpit,
Cromwell heard him with great attention, but would
sometimes knit his brows, and discover great un-
easiness. When the sermon was over, he told me,
a person of distinction came to him, and asked
him if he knew what he had done? and signified
it to him as his apprehension that Cromwell would
be so incensed upon that discourse, that he would
find it very difficult ever to make his peace with
him, or secure his favour for the future. Mr.
Howe replied, that he had but discharged his conscience, and could leave the event with God. He
told me, he afterwards observed Cromwell was
cooler in his carriage to him than before; and
sometimes he thought he would have spoken to
him of the matter, but he never did, and rather
chose to forbear."

The Doctor (Harris) is also of opinion, that the
forementioned discourse, in his last sickness, to
his wife, also plainly manifests enthusiasm. He

concludes, that he would rest the evidence of Cromwell's enthusiasm here, (though, he says, many more proofs could be brought of it,) not doubting but it will appear strong and convincing, and account, in some degree, for those actions and expressions to be met with in the succeeding part of his (Dr. Harris's) work; account, he says, in some degree; for that whoever thinks him wholly under the power of this principle, will be greatly mistaken ; for that Cromwell ranks in this respect with Mahomet and Aurengzebe, who were great masters of themselves, though by nature strongly tinctured with enthusiasm.

Bishop Burnet says, that his (Cromwell's) beloved notion was, that once a child of God, was always a child of God: that having led a very strict life for above eight years together before the war, he comforted himself much with his reflections on that time, and on the certainty of perseverance. Mr. Neal says, from Baxter's Life, that he (Cromwell) once asked Dr. Goodwin, who attended at his bed-side, and is said to have expressed an unbecoming assurance to Almighty God, in prayer, of his recovery; whether a man could fall from grace ? which the Doctor answering in the negative, the Protector replied, " Then I am safe ; for I am sure I was once in a state of grace."

After giving the forementioned passages in proof of Cromwell's supposed enthusiasm, he (Dr.

Harris), in order to enable the reader better to determine between his hypocrisy and enthusiasm, gives the following anecdotes, which seem, he says, to indicate him a hypocrite. The following is from Waller's Life : — " His rude cant and spiritual simplicity were," says the Doctor, " downright affectation ; than which, nothing can be more evident, from Mr. Waller's observation, and his confession to him. Mr. Waller often took notice, that in the midst of their discourse a servant has come in to tell them such and such attended ; upon which Cromwell would rise and stop them talking at the door, where he would overhear them say, The Lord will reveal, the Lord will help, and several such expressions ; which, when he returned to Mr. Waller, he excused, saying, Cousin Waller, I must talk to these men after their own way ; and would then go on where they left off." This created in Mr. Waller an opinion that he secretly despised those whom he seemed to court. Also the following anecdote, appearing to be taken from the Monthly Review for August, 1757. The author, says the Doctor, of the political history of the age, thinks " the enthusiasm of Cromwell entirely assumed and politic ; quoting the following anecdote, from Oliver St. John, in proof of it ; viz. " That being one day at table with his friends, and looking for the cork of a bottle of champaign which he had opened, on being informed that some person attended for admittance to see him, tell him, says Cromwell, we are in search of the Holy Spirit."

The Doctor adds—" These are the passages which seem to destroy the enthusiasm of Oliver; seem, I say, seem to destroy it; for, allowing their truth, in my opinion, they do not in reality do it. For what do they prove but that Cromwell sometimes talked inconsistenly with his principles; or being at times less under their power, he indulged himself in jesting and raillery, to which he was naturally prone? If, says the Doctor, two or three casual expressions are to determine a man's character, in opposition to his whole speech and behaviour, woe be to those who think themselves virtuous and good. Whoever will consider the times in which Oliver lived; the part he bore in the transactions of them; his real principles, with respect to returns of prayer, and his opinion, expressed in his last moments, will not be long at a loss to determine about his real enthusiasm.

Bishop Burnet gives the following instance of this supposed hypocrisy of Cromwell.—That Sir Harbottle Grimston told him a few weeks before his death, that when the House of Commons were quarrelling (the particular time the Bishop could not tell), at a meeting of the officers, it was proposed to purge the army better, that they might know who to depend on: that Cromwell said he was sure of the army; but that there was another body that had more need of purging, naming the

House of Commons, and he thought the army only
could do that : that two officers that were present
brought an account of this to Grimston, who carried them with him to the lobby of the House of
Commons, they being resolved to justify it to the
House : that there was another debate then on
foot, but Grimston diverted it, and said he had a
matter of privilege of the highest sort to lay before
them ; it was about the being and freedom of the
House : so he charged Cromwell with the design
of putting a force on the House ; he had his witnesses at the door, and desired they might be
examined ; they were brought to the bar, and
justified all that they had said to him, and gave a
full relation of all that had passed at their meetings : that when they withdrew, Cromwell fell
down on his knees, and made a solemn prayer to
God, attesting his innocence, and zeal for the service of the House ; he submitted himself to the
providence of God, who it seems thought fit to
exercise him with calumny and slander, but he
committed his cause to Him ; this he did with
with great vehemence, and with many tears : that
after this strange and bold preamble, he made so
long a speech, justifying both himself and the rest
of the officers, except a few that seemed inclined
to return back to Egypt, that he wearied out the
House, and wrought so much on his party, that
what the witnesses had said was so little believed,
that, had it been moved, Grimston thought that

both he and they would have been sent to the Tower. But whether their guilt made them modest, or that they had no mind to have the matter much talked of, they let it fall ; and there was no strength on the other side to carry it farther : that, to complete the scene, as soon as ever Cromwell got out of the House, he resolved to trust himself no more among them, but went to the army, and in a few days he brought them up, and forced a great many from the House.

The Bishop adds, that he had much discourse with one who knew Cromwell well, and all that set of men ; and asked him how they would excuse all the prevarications, and other ill things of which they were visibly guilty, in the conduct of their affairs : that he told him (the Bishop) they believed there were great occasions in which some men were called to great services, in the doing of which they were excused from the common rules of morality ; such were the practices of Ehud and Jael, Samson and David ; and by this they fancied they had a privilege from observing the standing rules. It is very obvious, says the Bishop, how far this principle may be carried, and how all justice and mercy may be laid aside on this pretence, by every bold enthusiast. The Bishop concludes, — He (Cromwell) never could shake off the roughness of his education and temper : that he spoke always long and very ungracefully : that the enthusiast and the dissembler mixed so equally in a great part of his deportment, that it was not easy to tell which was the prevailing character : that he was a true enthusiast, but with the principle formerly mentioned, from which he might be easily led into all the practices, both of falsehood and cruelty ; which was, that he thought moral laws were only binding on ordinary occasions, but that upon extraordinary ones these might be superseded : that when his own designs did not lead him out of the way, he was a lover of justice and virtue, and even of learning, though much decried at that time.

Lord Clarendon, relating the appointment of Cromwell to go to Ireland, as General, and the circumstances he supposes to have led to it, and describing his reception of it, and behaviour thereon in the House, says, that Cromwell, how little surprised soever with the design of this appointment, appeared the next day in the House full of confusion and irresolution, which the natural temper and composure of his understanding could hardly avoid when he least desired it ; and that, therefore, when it was now to his purpose, he could act it to the life ; and that, after much hesitation, and many expressions of his own unworthiness and inability to support so great a charge, &c. he submitted to their good will and pleasure. His Lordship adds, that with incredible expedition he raised money, provided shipping, and drew forces together for this enterprise.

Another extraordinary instance of Cromwell's supposed hypocrisy is given by His Lordship, — That Cromwell, though the greatest dissembler living, always made his hypocrisy of singular use and benefit to himself; and never did any thing, how ungracious or imprudent soever it seemed to be, but what was necessary to the design : that even his roughness and unpolishedness, which in the beginning of the Parliament he affected, contrary to the smoothness and complacency which his cousin and bosom friend, Mr. Hampden, practised towards all men, was necessary ; and his first public declaration in the beginning of the war, to his troop when it was first mustered, that he would not deceive or cozen them by the perplexed and involved expressions in his commission, to fight for King and Parliament, and therefore told them, that if the King chanced to be in the body of the enemy that he was to charge, he would as soon discharge his pistol upon him as any other private person ; and that if their conscience would not permit them to do the like, he advised them not to list themselves in his troop, or under his command. This, His Lordship adds, was generally looked upon as imprudent and malicious, and might, by the professions the Parliament then made, have proved dangerous to him ; yet that it served his turn, and severed from others and united among themselves all the furious and incensed men against the government, whether ecclesiastical or civil, to look upon him as a man for their turn, upon whom they might depend.

Another instance of Cromwell's supposed hypocrisy and insincerity, is to be found in Mrs. Hutchinson's before-mentioned Life of Colonel Hutchinson. She states, that upon the death of Colonel Thornhaugh, his regiment, in the reduction of the garrison forces, had one Major Saunders (a Derbyshire man, who was a very godly honest country gentleman, but had not many things requisite to a great soldier,) assigned them for their major, and that with him he brought in about a troop of Derbyshire horse ; but that the Nottinghamshire horse were not satisfied in serving under a less man than their late colonel ; and that remembering their successes under Colonel Hutchinson, they applied to Cromwell to send to Lord Fairfax to request him not to dispose of the command of the regiment till they should know whether the Colonel would accept of it : that Cromwell, with all the assentation imaginable, seemed to rejoice they had made so worthy a choice, and promised them to take care the regiment should not be disposed of till they received Colonel Hutchinson's answer ; and that thereupon the captains severally wrote to him, to request him to permit them to procure a commission for him to conduct them, which she (Mrs. Hutchinson) says, the Lieutenant-general (Cromwell) had already promised to send for, if he pleased to accept it : that the Colonel did accept it; but that Cromwell, as soon as the Nottinghamshire men had imparted to him their desires, sent for Saunders, and cajoling him, told him that none was so fit as himself to command the regiment; but that the regiment thought not all of them so, but were designing to procure themselves another colonel, which he advised him to prevent by sending speedily to the General, to whom Cromwell also wrote to further the request; and that before the messenger returned from Colonel Hutchinson, he procured the commision for Saunders, which, she says, was highly resented by the troops of the regiment. Mrs. Hutchinson assigns two reasons for this proceeding; that he had found that Colonel Hutchinson understood him, and was too generous either to fear or flatter him; and that he carried, though under a false face of friendship, a deep resentment of the Colonel's plain dealing with him at Nottingham: and that the other reason was, that he had a design, by insinuating himself into Saunders, to flatter him into the sale of a town of his called Ireton, which he wished to purchase for Major-general Ireton, his son-in-law; and that when he could not obtain it, he, in process of time, took the regiment away from him.

Respecting his supposed enthusiasm, it will be proper, first, to consider the meaning of the term enthusiasm.

It has been described to be — A vain belief of private revelation; a vain confidence of Divine favour, or communication; heat of imagination; violence of passion; confidence of opinion; elevation of fancy; exaltation of ideas. Mr. Locke has been quoted, as saying, that enthusiasm is founded neither on reason nor Divine revelation, but rises from the conceits of a warmed or overweening brain.

This may be a correct definition of the term; but its individual application is not so easy or admissible. Enthusiasm, in its common use and acceptation, seems to be a phrase upon the tongue of every one who wishes to describe a warmer and more energetic character than his own, either in civil or religious life; but it is generally confined to religious characters professing a greater degree of zeal and strictness of religious faith and practice, than those that use this phrase think necessary, or choose, perhaps for worldly reasons, to adopt. It is a phrase expressive of the contempt and dislike of those that use it, of those to whom it is applied — of the falsehood or absurdity of their eligious opinions, and of their supposed immodeat e and unnecessary strictness, and of their con - sequent unsociableness in their commerce with the world. Whether in or out of the church, this description of persons, in the sixteenth century called Puritans, have been in later days generally denominated Methodists.

For the purpose of determining upon this supposed enthusiasm of Cromwell, it becomes necessary to ascertain the state of religion in the
sixteenth century.

The religion of this country, as has been observed, had not been well settled in Queen Elizabeth's reign; a very large portion of the nation,
both Catholics and Protestants, had been then left
greatly dissatisfied, and had suffered in that reign
severe persecutions on account of their conscientious
inability to conform to the ruling religion. Afterwards the protestant part of the nation became
greatly apprehensive of the introduction of the
Roman Catholic religion, upon their discovering
the determination, (both of King James and of his
son, afterwards King Charles the First,) upon the
latter's marriage of a Princess of that religion, and
by his, accordingly, subsequent marriage : and
these apprehensions were not a little heightened
by the high principles and violent proceedings of
Archbishop Laud, who was become a great favourite, and the ruling ecclesiastical minister of
both reigns; and was thought to be favourably
disposed towards that religion.

Thus impressed, it should not excite surprise that
the conduct and language of the nation, both in
public and in private, should strongly partake of
a religious nature, and that, consequently, Scripture phrases should have been so much used, not
only by the particularly religious of those time, but

in the speeches of the members of both Houses of
Parliament; and even in those of both both these
Kings, James and Charles. So much in use do
they appear to have been from the time of the
Reformation, that a reservation was made in the
statute of the thirty-fourth and thirty-fifth of King
Henry the Eighth, in favour of the chancellors in
Parliament, judges, recorders, and all others who
had been accustomed, on public occasions, to make
speeches, and commonly took a place of Scripture
for their text, to continue that practice.

Religion had a large share of the animosities
and heart-burning disputes of those reigns of King
James, and his son King Charles the First, very
much resulting from the intemperate and indiscreet
zeal of the Archbishop in matters of rites and
ceremonies, and other things of no real consequence or value to the church, or tendency to the
increase of its stability. These he pressed on all,
both clergy and laity, with the most unrelenting
severity, not making the least allowance for conscientious nonconformity, or difference of opinion,
respecting what he determined in his arrogant and
impetuous, and fatally mistaken zeal, to impose.

This misguiding favourite and counsellor originated the war with Scotland in pursuit of the same
objects there, which soon spread itself over
England, and proved fatal to its religious establishment.

The destruction of the national establishment,

and the consequent termination of all ecclesiastical restrictions, left the nation at liberty to adopt and profess different articles of religious faith, and modes and forms of worship, according to their several opinions and fancies; which necessarily divided it into divers sects or bodies of religious professors. Each of these sects or bodies bore a a name allusive to the natures and forms of their respective religious tenets and church-govern- ments.

Mr. Neal, in his History of the Puritans, gives the following account of these different sects or parties: he says, that the friends of the Parlia- ment, who were agreed in the cause of civil liberty, were far from being of one mind in points of church- discipline; the major part were for episcopacy, and desired no more than to secure the constitution, and reform a few exorbitances of the bishops; some were Erastians, and would be content with any form of government the magistrate should appoint; that the real Presbyterians, who were for an entire change of the hierachy, upon the foot of divine right, were as yet (1642) but few, and could carry nothing in the House.

The same writer, in a subsequent part of this history, says, the state of the controversy about ecclesiastical discipline was then (1644) changed; for that whereas before the entrance of the Scots, the Parliament insisted only upon a reformation of the hierarchy: now they were obliged to attempt

the total extirpation of it, and to establish another
scheme for both kingdoms in its room; but that
it was a considerable time before this could be
perfected.

He then proceeds to distinguish the several parties of which the assembly of divines, then about
to meet upon the business of religion, was composed. — That the episcopal clergy had entirely
deserted it before the bringing in of the covenant;
so that the establishment had not a single advocate
in that assembly: all who remained were for
taking down the main pillars of the hierarchy,
before they had agreed what sort of building to
erect in its room. — That the majority at first intended only the reducing episcopacy to the stan-
dard of the first or second age, but, for the sake
of the Scots alliance, they were prevailed with
to lay aside the name and function of bishops, and
to attempt the establishing a presbyterial form upon
the ruins of all others; which they at length advanced into *jus divinum*, or divine institution, derived
expressly from Christ and his apostles: but that
this engaged them in so many controversies, as
prevented their laying the top-stones to their building, so that it fell to pieces before it was perfected. — That the chief patrons of presbytery in the
House of Commons were Mr. Denzil Holles, Sir
William Walker, Sir Philip Stapleton, Sir John Clot-
worthy, Sir Benjamin Rudyard, Sergeant Maynard,
Colonel Massey, Colonel Harley, Mr. John Glyn,

and a few others. — That the Erastians (so called from Erastus, a German divine of the sixteenth
century) formed another branch of the assembly
of divines : and that the pastoral office, according
to him, was only persuasive, like a professor of
the sciences over his students, without any power
of the keys annexed. — That the chief patrons of
this scheme in the assembly were Dr. Lightfoot,
Mr. Colman, Mr. Selden, Mr. Whitelock ; and, in
the House of Commons, besides Mr. Selden and
Mr. Whitelock, Mr. Oliver St. John, Sir Thomas
Widdrington, Mr. John Crew, Sir John Hipsley,
and others of the greatest names. — That the Independents, or congregational brethren, composed
a third party, and made a bold stand against the
proceedings of the high Presbyterians : that their
numbers were small at first, but increased pro-
digiously in a few years, and grew to a considerable figure under the protectorship of Oliver
Cromwell : that the scheme they embraced was,
that every particular congregation of Christians
had an entire and complete power of judrisdiction
over its members, to be exercised by the elders
thereof within itself : that this they were sure
must have been the form of government in the
primitive church, before the numbers of Christians
in any city were multiplied so far as to divide into
many congregations, which it was dubious, whether
it was the fact in the apostles' time : that their
mode of public worship was the same with other

Protestants, reading the Scriptures in their assemblies, and expounding them on proper occasions, offering up public and solemn prayers for kings and all in authority : and that though they did not approve of a prescribed form, they admitted that public prayer in their assemblies ought to be framed by the meditations and study of their ministers, as well as their sermons : that the word of God was constantly preached; the two sacraments, of baptism of infants, and of the Lord's supper, were frequently administered, to which was added singing of psalms and a collection for the poor every Sabbath-day : that they professed their agreement in doctrine with the articles of the church of England, and other reformed churches: that their officers and public rulers in their churches were pastors, teachers, ruling-elders, (not lay but ecclesiastical persons, separated to that service,) and deacons: that they practised no church censures but admonition, and excommunication upon obstinate and impenitent offenders, which latter they apprehended should not be pronounced but for crimes of the last importance, and which might reasonably be supposed to be committed contrary to the light and conviction of the person's conscience. And in their apologetical narration, given in this history, (in which are contained the preceding account of their tenets,) and presented to the House of Commons, and published at this time, of the meeting of the assembly of divines, they call God and man to witness, that out of regard to the public peace, they had forbore to publish their peculiar opinions either from the pulpit or press, or to improve the present disposition of the people to the increase of their party; nor should they have published that apology to the world, had not their silence been interpreted as an acknowledgment of those reproaches and calumnies that had been cast upon them by their adversaries; but should have waited for a free and open debate of their sentiments in the then assembly o divines, though they were sensible they should have the disadvantage with regard to numbers, learning, and the stream of public interest: that, however, they were determined in all debates to yield to the utmost latitude of their consciences, professing it to be as high a point of religion to acknowledge their mistakes, when they should be convinced of them, as to hold fast the truth; and when matters should be brought to the nearest agreement, to promote such a temper as might tend to union as well as truth: they therefore besought the Houses not to look upon them as disturbers of the public peace, but to consider them as persons that differed but little from their brethren.

The same writer (Neal) adds, that there was nothing in the principles of the Presbyterians, Independents, or Anabaptists, (as far as he could learn,) inconsistent with monarchy, or that had a

natural tendency to put the kingdom into a flame :
and that Mr. Baxter, the nonconformist minister,
and who was no friend to the Independents, and
knew them well, admits that most of them were
zealous, and very many learned, discreet, and
pious, capable of being very serviceable to the
church, and searchers into Scripture and antiquity ;
though he blames them on other occasions for
making too light of ordination, for their too great
strictness in the qualification of church-members,
for their popular form of church-government, and
their too much exploding of synods and councils.
But adds, that he (Baxter) saw a commendable
care of serious holiness and discipline in most of
the independent churches, and found that some
episcopal men, of whom Archbishop Usher was
one, agreed with them, that every bishop was independent, and that synods and councils were not
so much for government as concord. Neal proceeds, — that the Anabaptists, joining with the Independents in the point of discipline and toleration,
made them the more considerable, and encouraged
their opposition to the Presbyterians, who were for
establishing their own discipline without regard to
such as differed from them.

If the preceding account from Neal, of the Independents, be correct, and there is no reason to
believe it is not, Mr. Hume's history of them is
surely much otherwise. His idea of a secret distinction having long prevailed in the House of

Commons between the presbyterian and independent parties, and beginning to discover itself in
proportion to the increase of their hopes of success
against the King, must be the work of his own
imagination.   The existence of these distinctions
was well known, and that the two parties held
different sentiments respecting church-government;
nor had the Independents probably ever been confounded with the presbyterian party, but must,
from their respective commencements, have been
separate and distinct.   The Presbyterians must
have been the prevalent party at the time of their
procuring the establishment of the Directory,
which was, even according to Mr. Hume, directly
opposite to the liberal sentiments of the Independents.   Mr. Hume becomes perfectly unintelligible in his endeavour to explain the genius of
the Independents, and to talk of their enthusiastic
spirit, as the mean of their distinction and preferment, and of their holy fervours, and habits of
hypocrisy and saintship : and in describing their
becoming dangerous and destructive by their
fanaticism, and going a note higher than the
Presbyterians, thereby becoming less likely to be
restrained within the bounds of temper and moderation.   He tells us, that the Catholics, pretending to an infallible guide, had justified, upon
that principle, their doctrine and practice of persecution : that the Presbyterians, imagining that
such clear and certain tenets as themselves adopted

could be rejected only from a criminal and perti-
nacious obstinacy, had hitherto gratified, to the
full, their bigotted zeal in a like doctrine and
practice : that the Independents, from the extremity of the same zeal, were led into the milder
principles of toleration ; their mind, set afloat in
the wide sea of inspiration, could confine itself
within no certain limits. After all these heavy
charges against the Independents, he finally tells
us, that they were the first of the Christian sects
which, during its prosperity, always adopted the
principle of toleration ; and that it was remarkable
so reasonable a doctrine owed its origin not to
reasoning, but to the height of extravagance and
fanaticism. Were it true, it would indeed be extraordinary ; but this doctrine could only originate
in large and liberal minds, and could not have
been the production of fanaticism and enthusisasm.
He makes this extraordinary observation, — that
the variations in which an enthusiast indulged
himself, he was apt, by a natural train of thinking,
to permit in others. The contrary of this proposition seems to be true, — that an enthusiast
must be so assured of his own infallibility, that he
must conclude all others to be in error and not to
be indulged, and therefore must surely be likely to
be intolerant : enthusiasm and bigotry will be found
to differ little from each other. Mr. Hume describes Sir Harry Vane, Oliver Cromwell, Na-
thaniel Fiennes, and Oliver St. John, as the leaders

of the Independents.   The truth seems to be, that
Mr. Hume, being an unbeliever in Divine Revelation, it suited him to consider as fanaticism and
enthusiasm every the slightest expression of religious feeling.   It is most unreasonable to deny
to religious characters their fervours in the pursuit
of their great object, and to indulge the worldly in
all their ardours and extravagances, in the com-
paratively trifling objects of their pursuits.   By
the men of the world, the arduous, persevering
Christian of the parliament party was, in those
times, deemed an enthusiast and an hypocrite, and
his best actions represented as influenced by the
most sinister and mischievous motives : all was
resolved into hypocrisy or enthusiasm.   Hence,
that cry against the Independents, who happened
to become finally the ruling party : their principles
are represented as inimical to peace and to kingly
government; but nothing appears in the above
statement to warrant that opinion : the fear of the
King's vengeance, should he overcome them, and
the difficulty of finding security against it, there is
every reason to believe, was the great obstacle with
both Presbyterians and Independents, to the successful conclusion of their several treaties with him.
The fasts so much in use in the parliaments of this
reign, in those times of national discord and
dreadful apprehension, Lord Clarendon thinks
proper to characterise as hypocritical instruments
for the service of worldly and political purposes ;

he should have remembered that fasts in troublesome times were not new things: that in those
times, particularly, they had been frequently
ordered, or consented to by the King, who had at
that very time monthly fasts for the purpose of
imploring success to his arms, and for the restoration of peace to the country; and that upon all
solemn national occasions he had fasts: he had one
preparatory to entering upon the treaty of the
Isle of Wight. His Lordship would not venture
to say they were hypocritically meant on his part.
The King himself was a religious character, and
the thinking part of the country were also seriously religious. Mr. Hume says, the war itself
was theological, or religious; which had been, he
thinks, improperly blended with civil questions;
but though this is not strictly true, the war being,
certainly, both civil and religious, yet religious
grievances were always deemed, and determined to
be, the object of first consideration and redress.

Mr. Hume takes upon himself to describe these
monthly fasts on the part of the King to have
been instituted by him for the purpose of com-
bating the Parliament with their own weapons, and
to afford the opportunity of instructing the people
in the duties of loyalty and submission to the
higher powers. If the Parliament fasts must be
deemed political and not religious, the King's fasts
then must, upon this statement of Mr. Hume,
surely be so; but it is not to be believed that

either were other than they appeared to be, solemn religious observances.

Lord Clarendon speaks contemptuously of the expression, "seeking God," which, he says, was a new phrase brought from Scotland with their covenant. It might have been a new phrase in England; but it is perfectly expressive of the thing meant, namely, a devout and humble application by prayer to the Almighty, by a nation or individuals, to avert impending public or private calamities, or to remove them if incurred, or for direction and assistance in concerns of importance too great for human accomplishment. In religious language, perhaps, it may be generally best to avoid what may be called technical phraseology, particular words frequently used, expressive (for brevity sake) of any particular religious act or observance, are liable to be catched at by the world, and used for the purpose of turning into ridicule every thing serious. In the succeeding licentious reign of King Charles the Second, all semblance of religion was studiously put out of sight; it was become quite unfashionable; and the ridicule of its professors, and of all the religious language and acts of the preceding times, was considered a kind of test of loyalty to the then sovereign and government. This phrase of "seeking God," then used as expressive of the act of prayer, public or private, became, after the Restoration, with other religious phrases or expressions, subjects of ridicule. Lightly,

or contemptuously, however, the men of the world,
when in health or prosperity, may treat this application to, and reliance upon, Divine Providence,
the religious part of the Christian world are in the
constant and habitual practice of it, and thence,
there can be no doubt, derive the greatest comfort
and assurance. Independently of prayer being a
commanded duty, it is surely a reasonable service,
inasmuch as it is an acknowledgment of our dependence upon the Supreme Being, to whom,
feeble and insufficient as we are, we must be
constantly looking for the support of our existence
and for the continuance of all our comforts and
enjoyments. Prayer is universal in public practice,
although perhaps partial and occasional in individuals, according to their momentary dispositions
and feelings : and the very use of it implies an expectation or hope of receiving a favourable answer ;
and every attentive observer of the circumstances
of his own life must have good reason to believe
that his prayers have been frequently answered,
and he preserved in a manner for which he cannot
account, otherwise than by the conviction of an
interposition more than human. All look up to
some superior being : the heathen to deities of his
own creation ; whom they think capable of reliev-
ing in their various necessities, beyond the succour
of mortal power. The most thoughtless and pro-
fligate are found ready to pray sincerely and fer-
vently enough when in bodily danger, or in the

immediate view of a future state. Our holy religion teaches us to expect this assistance through
and by the means of the Holy Spirit; for which
assistance, and for whose influence we all ask in
the most expressive terms in our attendance upon
the public worship of our established church, and
in the prayers of our Liturgy. Strange, then, to
tell how all these acts of devotion, and all the
religious professors of the above times, were afterwards, in this succeeding reign of King Charles
the Second, held up to ridicule and contempt as
the vilest of canting, enthusiastical hypocrites and
knaves, and as masking their political, ambitious
designs under the show and pretence of religion.
And in this light it is to be lamented that the more
than common strict religious professor in succeeding times hath been too often viewed by the less
religious part of the community; nothing appearing
to afford them more pleasure than the real or imagined detection of any of these professors in any
sin or folly; seeming to presume that the crimes or
failings of these persons extenuate and supply
them with an excuse for their own perpetual and
repeated unrepented errors; whereas they should
remember that the best of the human race are imperfect, and ever liable to occasional failure. In
this unfavourable light do Lord Clarendon and all
other the writers for the royal cause represent the
Parliament and its adherents, allowing them no
good motive for any of their proceedings, but at-

tributing them solely to concealed ambition and
sinister views; and thus stigmatised, they have
been handed down to the present day.

Cromwell was certainly a religious professor, and
nothing has hitherto appeared to prove him other
than also a really religious character. But this
will not answer these writers' purpose; he must be
imperfect and faulty in every thing; even his religion, if its sincerity be admitted, must be excessive; he must then be deemed righteous over-
much, by those who call themselves Christians,
but who deny every principal fact and doctrine of
the Scriptures, believed to be most unequivocally
therein stated, and declared by those of Cromwell's
faith and profession, and who, with him, hold
them to be the fundamentals of religion and the
guides of their faith and practice : — also, probably,
by the lukewarm believers of these facts and doctrines, either wholly or partially, he, Cromwell,
will be deemed an enthusiast. His faith in prayer
has been much condemned, as tending to, and
producing spiritual pride and confidence. He
might carry it to excess; but who shall say where
this reliance, this confidence, shall stop? Cromwell
appears much, and justly, offended by Mr. Howe's
rude public attack upon his well-known opinion
upon this subject, which he resented very properly
in becoming more cool in his carriage towards him,
and not condescending to notice his sermon.
Deeming, as he, Mr. Howe, did, the correction of

this opinion of importance, he should rather have availed himself of an opportunity of conversing and reasoning with Cromwell in private, than have thus brought him forward to the attention and animadversion of probably a numerous and observing audience.   The continuance of him in his office of chaplain was one, amongst many other instances, of the kindness and forbearance of his temper.   A less ardent and feelingly religious mind than Cromwell's, would have been sensibly impressed and confirmed in his reliance upon the efficacy of prayer by his forementioned extraordinary and most unlooked-for deliverance in the battle of Dunbar, on the third of September, 1650, related by Bishop Burnet.   He is described, as having felt himself in the greatest streights and perplexities. Whitelock's account is, that he was greatly outnumbered by the Scots army commanded by Lesley, one of the ablest of their Generals, advantageously posted upon the hills ; which, had it kept its post, must have obliged his (Cromwell's) army, greatly reduced and weakened by sickness, to surrender in a very few days.   Of so experienced a General as Lesley, quitting so advantageous a position, and descending the hill to attack Cromwell, there could be no prospect, and his army's ascent to attack the Scots army would have been sure defeat : seeing no resource in human means, he is described as applying himself to prayer, or seeking the Lord, as prayer was at that time generally called, and he is represented as having thought he felt in his mind, strong assurance of a favourable issue: that, immediately afterwards, he observed the Scots army most unexpectedly and most unadvisedly coming down the hill, which he considered as the deliverance of them into his hands, and which happened accordingly by their total defeat. The above is related by the bishop, but is not remembered to have been given by any other writer.

Who, that every prays, will take upon himself to deny this extraordinary and unlooked-for, and utterly improbable event, to be an immediate answer to that prayer of Cromwell's? It is, then, not surprising that he should be thus deeply impressed with the efficacy of prayer, and feel strongly assured of favourable answers, having been in the constant use of it preparatory to all the important actions of his life, and probably never fighting a battle without previous prayer of himself and his army for the success of it; and it has been observed that he never was defeated. He may have yielded too far to these assurances and favourable answers; and others may have availed themselves of this tendency, to impose upon him by pretences of like assurances; but it is not wonderful, favoured so extraordinarily as he had been in all his undertakings, that he should feel an unusual assurance of more than human support.

The above may be considered to be the whole
amount of this charge of enthusiasm. There is
no crime in a heated imagination ; it may lead men
into error, and if the effects of their error be mischievous, or inconvenient to others, those effects
become punishable ; the thing is innocent in itself:
but what to some may appear a heated imagination may be found to be no more than the degree
of warmth and energy properly belonging to the
subject.

In answer to the objections to Cromwell's party's
admission of lay-preachers, he declares, in his foregiven letters to the Scots ministers, his approbation of a regular ministry, as having, he says,
order in it, but not to the exclusion of lay-preachers,
capable of the undertaking.

The above-given letters and circumstances would
not probaby be considered by the religious of the
then, or of the present times, as enthusiastic or
extravagant ; their correspondence with each other
would probably be generally found to be expressed
in some such terms. The frame and temper of
his (Cromwell's) mind in his last moments were
truly christian ; his prayer, notwithstanding Ludlow's ill-tempered observation, was truly affectionate and benevolent ; supplicating, not only for
himself, but for the nation, and even for his
enemies.

Dr. Harris says, this was all in character, meaning his character of enthusiasm. With some

persons, every thing is enthusiasm that has in it
the least degree of zeal or warmth. Mr. Fox,
upon another occasion, says of enthusiasm, in his
James II., — " We are accused of enthusiasm! are
we then fanatics? are we enthusiasts, because we
do not rob — abstain from murder? If by enthusiasm be meant zeal and warmth, I freely
acknowledge it; I glory in it. Enthusiasm, when
it arises out of a just cause, is that which makes
men act in it with energy; it is that, without which,
nothing was ever done great, since the creation
of the world. Enthusiasm of this sort, I hope,
therefore, I shall always possess."

He, Cromwell, died in the full possession of his
faculties, and perfectly calm and composed, which,
no doubt, arose from an unconsciousness of those
crimes with which his enemies have so heavily
loaded him.

Respecting his alleged beloved notion of final
perseverance, that once a child of God always so;
and his supposed question, whether a man could
fall from grace, and the supposed answers of Dr.
Goodwin and himself; such a conversation might
or might not pass, but is conceived to mean no
more than Cromwell's, perhaps, belief of the doctrine of predestination and election, which many
wise and good persons of the then and present
times, both in and out of the church, have believed
and do still believe to be contained in the articles
of our established church. Mr. Neal, as before

said, describes the Independents as agreeing in doctrine with the articles of the church; and Cromwell might believe this doctrine, with the rest of the doctrines of those articles. In the Scriptures may be found some passages that may seem to countenance, but surely their general spirit is perfectly contradictory of it, enjoining, as they do, the preaching them to the whole world and calling all to repentance. This opinion of predestination and election seems to be wholly speculative; it should have no influence upon our conduct, and probably rarely, if ever, has. Cromwell's question to Goodwin certainly does not determine his belief of the doctrine of final perservance; nor does his answer to Goodwin imply his acquiescence in Goodwin's explanation; it can only be considered as a confidence in his safety, supposing Goodwin's explanation to be true, but not an admission of its truth; on the contrary, remaining doubt.

In proof of the supposed enthusiasm of Cromwell not being wholly and exclusively his own, the religious conduct and conversation of Whitelock may be successfully brought forward. Although the confidential friend and counsellor of Cromwell, he is no where charged with enthusiasm or hypocrisy. He did not concur in the trial of the King, and wholly disapproved it; and was for the restoration of the royal family. He was, as Cromwell was, in favour of religious toleration. He was allowedly of great talents and learning. Mr. Hume says, he was a man of great abilities and merit.

Whitelock being informed that he had been named by the council of state to go ambassador to Sweden in 1653, and whilst it was in suspense, he not having heard directly from the council, he, in his journal of this embassy, says, that the Lord's day, after public exercises of religious worship, he retired himself to his private meditations upon the holy Word of Truth, the greatest and highest comfort to a soul; he considered the vanity of earthly honours and preferments in this world, the uncertainty, toil, and danger in them; he consulted his own heart, and found not the least inclination to accept of the high employment and honour.

He says, that Cromwell's secretary, by his direction, prepared the draft of a letter to him, which Cromwell disapproving, undertook to write himself, which he did in his own hand, as followeth :—
" My Lord ; The Council of State having thoughts of putting Your Lordship to the trouble of being extraordinary ambassador to the Queen of Swizland, did think fit not to impose that service upon you without first knowing your own freedom thereunto ; wherefore they were pleased to command our service to make this addsess to Your Lordship ; and hereby we can assure you of a very large con-

fidence in your honour and abilities for this employment; to which we, begging your answer, do
rest,

> " My Lord, your humble Servant,
>> " O. CROMWELL,
>> " GIL. PICKERING."

2d September, 1653.

Whitelock, in a subsequent passage, says, a principal care of Whitelock, as to those of his retinue,
was to get able and fit chaplains, such as were of
a pious life and conversation, and of good abilities and learning, for example and instruction of
his company.

That, September 25., after public exercises of
devotion on this (the Lord's) day, he retired himself from the continual discourses of his Swedish
business, unto his private meditations upon the
Holy Scriptures.

That, October 25., besides his private and particular seeking to God for his counsel and blessing
in this undertaking, he had the joint prayers of
his friends; with him, divers of them met in the
evening at his brother Wilson's house, several
members of Mr. Cokayne's church, and, among
them, Mr. Taylor expounded a place of Scripture
very pertinently, and several of them prayed very
affectionately for him (Whitelock), and the good
success of his business; and divers expounded
places of Scripture suitable to the occasion. That

then, he (Whitelock) addressed his friends as follows in the narrative, — an address full of devout
sentiments and expressions : he says therein, he
has taken much comfort from Genesis, xxviii. 15.,
God's promise to Jacob in his journey to Padan-
Aram.

That, by his appointment, all the company met
in the chapel at Whitehall to seek God for his
protection and blessing on them in their intended
journey. The doors were open: Mr. Cokayne,
Mr. Peters, and Mr. Ingelo, prayed, and expounded several texts of Scripture, giving good
exhortations to all the company with great fer-
vency and pertinence on the occasion, so that many
affirmed they never were at any meeting of this
nature which appeared more spiritual and comfortable to their souls than this was : that Whitelock himself concluded, by speaking to the company
to this effect ; — he informed them of great hardships to be expected in their voyage and journey,
but adopts the language of Gideon and Judas
Maccabæus to the fearful : acquaints them that he
shall endeavour strictly to observe the decree of
Joshua, " As for me and my house, we will serve
the Lord;" and that, through God's grace, he
should resolve to keep a strict discipline and order
in the government of his house, not permitting any
debauchery, prophaneness, licentiousness, swearing, cursing, quarrelling, or the like, so far as
God should enable him to hinder it; therefore, as

Joshua said to his people, " If it seem evil unto you to serve the Lord, choose you this day whom you will serve."

That when on board the ships, he ordered prayers to be said night and morning.

That Cromwell sent one of his gentlemen with a present to Whitelock before his departure, of a sword and a pair of spurs, richly inlaid with gold of a noble work and fashion.

In Whitelock's first interview with the Queen (Christina), on the 26th December, 1653, the Queen says, — " I have been told that many officers of your army do themselves pray and preach to their soldiers: is that true?" Whitelock. "Yes, Madam, it is very true : when their enemies are swearing, or debauching, or pillaging, the officers and soldiers of the Parliament army used to be encouraging and exhorting one another out of the word of God, and praying together to the Lord of Hosts for his blessing to be with them ; who hath shewed his approbation of this military preaching by the success he has given them."—Queen. " That's well ; do you use to do so too?" Whitelock. " Yes, upon some occasions, in my own family, and think it as proper for me, being the master of it, to admonish and speak to my people when there is cause, as to be beholden to another to do it for me, which sometimes brings the chaplain into more credit than his Lord."—Queen. " Doth your General, and other great officers, do so ?" Whitelock. " Yes, Madam, very often, and very well; nevertheless they maintain chaplains and ministers in their houses and regiments; and such as are godly and worthy ministers, have as good provision in England as in any place of Christendom; yet it is the opinion of many good men with us, that a long cassake with a silk girdle, and a great beard, do not make a learned or good preacher, without gifts of the Spirit of God, and labouring in his vineyard; and whosoever studies the Holy Scriptures, and is enabled to do good to the souls of others, and endeavours the same, is no where forbidden by that word; nor is it blameable. The officers and soldiers of the Parliament held it not unlawful, when they carried their lives in their hands, and were going to adventure them in the high places of the field, to encourage one another out of His word who commands over all; and this had more weight and impression with it than any other word could have, and was never denied to be made use of, but by the popish prelates, who by no means would admit lay people (as they call them) to gather from thence that instruction and comfort which can no where else be found." — Queen. " Methinks you preach very well, and have now made a good sermon; I assure you, I like it very well; but, I pray you tell me, where did your General and you, his officers, learn this way of praying and preaching yourselves?" Whitelock. " We learnt it from a near friend of

Your Majesty, whose memory all the protestant interest hath cause to honour."—Queen. " My friend! who was that?" Whitelock. " It was your father, the great King Gustavus Adolphus, who, upon his first landing in Germany, did himself, in person, upon the shore, on his knees, give thanks to God for his safe landing; and before his soldiers, himself prayed to God for his blessing upon that undertaking; and he would frequently exhort his people out of God's word; and God testified his good liking thereof by the wonderful successes he was pleased to vouchsafe to that gallant King." To this the Queen made no further reply.

In answer to a question by the Queen, whether dancing was prohibited in England, he takes the opportunity of expressing his disapprobation of balls and other amusements on the Lord's day, and recommends to her, as an act of piety and most becoming a Christian Queen, to restrain and punish the sin of prophanation of the Lord's day, as likewise swearing and debauchery, too much used and countenanced in those parts; and pardon me, Madam, if I say I think God requires this at your hands.

This, and much other to the like effect, says Whitelock, he spake with plainness, yet fitting respect and apologies to the Queen, hoping that God did put it into his heart to speak thus freely to her, in a matter wherein the honour of God was so much concerned: and it took, adds he, so good effect, that after that, the Queen had no more balls in her court on the Lord's day.

At Whitelock's first interview with the Chancellor (Oxenstièrne), he (the chancellor) describes himself in his retirement, as under a cloud, his chief study to be the Bible, wherein is all wisdom and the greatest delight to be found, and much more in the practice of that Divine wisdom; and counsels Whitelock, as a younger man, to make the practice and study of the word of God his chief contentment and delight, as it would be to every such that savours the truths of God, which do infinitely excel all worldly things,

29th January. The Lord's day; a day usually with them (the Swedes) a day of travaile; and it being the time of a fair, the shops were open all the day, as they had been the preceding Sunday, so little regard have they of this day, or of the observance of it, but perform the ordinary works of their callings, buying and selling, carting and travelling upon this, as upon any other day; and, which is yet worse, acting commonly and openly their debaucheries, and appointing their drinking meetings on the Lord's day. Visits were made to Whitelock on this day, and to let him know of the Queen's return to this place; but he staid in his own house, not going abroad himself, nor suffering his people to roam abroad this day; but all of them joined together in the worship of God; and, according to his custom, he had two good sermons

this opinion of importance, he should rather have availed himself of an opportunity of conversing and reasoning with Cromwell in private, than have thus brought him forward to the attention and animadversion of probably a numerous and observing audience. The continuance of him in his office of chaplain was one, amongst many other instances, of the kindness and forbearance of his temper. A less ardent and feelingly religious mind than Cromwell's, would have been sensibly impressed and confirmed in his reliance upon the efficacy of prayer by his forementioned extraordinary and most unlooked-for deliverance in the battle of Dunbar, on the third of September, 1650, related by Bishop Burnet. He is described, as having felt himself in the greatest streights and perplexities. Whitelock's account is, that he was greatly outnumbered by the Scots army commanded by Lesley, one of the ablest of their Generals, advantageously posted upon the hills ; which, had it kept its post, must have obliged his (Cromwell's) army, greatly reduced and weakened by sickness, to surrender in a very few days. Of so experienced a General as Lesley, quitting so advantageous a position, and descending the hill to attack Cromwell, there could be no prospect, and his army's ascent to attack the Scots army would have been sure defeat : seeing no resource in human means, he is described as applying himself to prayer, or seeking the Lord, as prayer was at that time gene-

barking for Lubec, he called his company into his cabin, where they gave thanks to God for their safe arrival at this place, and humbly prayed for the continuance of his blessing and presence with them the rest of their journey yet to come: and, on the 1st of July, he arrived safe with all his company, 100 in number.

July 5. By Whitelock's appointment, all his company who were with him in Sweden came this day to his house at Chelsey, where divers others of his good friends met them, to the intent they might all join together in returning humble and hearty thanks to God for his great mercy and goodness to them in their preservation and wonderful deliverance in their voyage, in blessing them with health and with success in their business, and bringing all of them in safety and comfort to their native country and most dear relations: he then relates the religious services performed in a large room prepared for the purpose; and his address to them at the conclusion, which was very solemn and impressive, reciting their many preservations and deliverances in the course of their journies and voyages to and from Sweden, with quotations of many apposite texts of Scripture.

If Cromwell is to be deemed an enthusiast, surely Whitelock must share the charge with him: he seems to have been equally impressed by the necessity of seeking God (as he also calls prayer), by himself and his friends, for his counsel and blessing

in his intended embassy; he justifies, as Cromwell
does, the officers' preaching, and considers the
army's successes as favourable answers: he obliges
his household, whilst in Sweden, to a strict observance of the Sabbath, notwithstanding the Queen's
and her subjects' ill observance of it; he appears
to have been as strictly a religious professor as
Cromwell; but he has never, it is believed, been
called an enthusiast or an impostor.

Perhaps the following circumstance may determine, in the estimation of these denouncers of
enthusiasm and hypocrisy, Lockhart to be one or
other of these characters. Lockhart was ambassador from Cromwell to the court of France: he
married his niece; and Bishop Burnet says of
him, that he was in high favour with Cromwell, as
he well deserved to be; that he was both a wise
and a gallant man; calm and virtuous, and one
that carried the generosity of friendship very far:
that he was, after the Restoration, sent ambassador to the court of France by the King. In Thurloe's State Papers is a letter from Lockhart to
Thurloe, dated Paris, 7th February (1656–7): he
says, that the Cardinal (Mazarin) prevailed on him
(Lockhart) to see the King's ball this night *in-
cognito:* " I have been twice invited before, and
was so pressed in it, that I was forced to own my
scruple of being there upon the Lord's day, upon
which it hath been always danced hitherto:. I have
not the vanity to imagine that this night is in con-

sidereration of me, and yet I know the King did interest himself in my seeing it, so as to offer to cause to make me a place behind the theatre, where nobody should see me. As I thought the exposing myself to be too great libertine, by seeing it upon the Lord's day would offend God, and be against your service, so I hope the appearing not to be over-nice and scrupulous, will not be construed to be for your disservice."

A writer, speaking of the Protectress, describes her amusements, when unbending her mind from the superintendence of her family, as partaking in a great measure of the religious enthusiam of the age; instancing Cromwell's entertainment of Jongestall the Dutch ambassador, at dinner, upon the conclusion of the peace between the two nations; communicated in a letter dated 28th April (1654), from the ambassador to William Frederick, Earl of Nassau, to be found in Thurloe's State Papers. He says, — " Yesterday, at noon, we were invited to dinner to His Highness the Lord Protector, where we were nobly entertained : Mr. Strickland and the master of the ceremonies came to fetch us in two coaches of His Highness, about half an hour past one, and brought us to Whitehall, where twelve trumpeters were ready sounding against our coming : my Lady Nieuport and my wife were brought to His Highness presently, the one by Mr. Strickland, and the other by the master of the ceremonies, who received us with great demonstration of amity : after we staid a little, we were conducted into another room, where we found a table ready covered : His Highness sat on one side of it alone ; my Lord Beverning, Nieuport, and myself, at the upper end ; and the Lord-president Laurence, and others, next to us : there was in the same room another table covered for other lords of the council and others : at the table of my Lady Protectrice dined my Lady Nieuport, my wife, my Lady Lambert, my Lord Protector's daughter and mine : the music played all the while we were at dinner ; the Lord Protector had us into another room, where the Lady Protectrice and others came to us, where we had also music and voices and a psalm sung, which His Highness gave us, and told us, that it was yet the best paper that had been exchanged between us ; and from thence we were had into a gallery next the river, where we walked with His Highness about half an hour, and then took our leaves, and were conducted back again to our houses after the same manner as we were brought," &c.

But the religious part of this entertainment was not confined to Cromwell and his family. Whitelock says, that on the 7th of June (1649), an entertainment was given on the day of thanksgiving for the suppression of the levellers, by the city to the House of Commons, the General (Fairfax) and other officers of the army, council of state, &c. at Grocer's Hall, after the hearing of two sermons, that the music was only drums and trumpets, the feast sumptuous, no toasts drank, and besides the overplus of the victuals left at dinner, a sum of 400*l.* was given to the poor of London : he (Whitelock) in his journal of the Swedish embassy, referring to this entertainment, says, that the Swedish ambassador was present : that before dinner, Mr. Peters prayed and expounded a place of Scripture, and a psalm was sung; the ambassador very attentive : that he observed to Whitelock, with much surprise, the civility and good order of so great a company; who (Whitelock) told him that it was their constant demeanour, which the ambassador highly commended. But by these fastidious writers, all must be resolved into enthusiasm and hypocrisy.

The grand charge against Cromwell is his supposed hypocrisy, in which all the writers hostile to his memory seem, without examination, implicitly to have followed Lord Clarendon, and one another. His Lordship's object seems to have been, to charge him with all the real and imaginary misdeeds of the times whereof he wrote ; the truth in favour of Cromwell, nevertheless, sometimes involuntarily escaping him ; unintentionally praising him where he means to dishonour him. This, his insincerity, taken for granted, exposes him to all the obloquy with which his memory is loaded. No obstacle then remains to the representation of him, as the grand secret spring and mover of all the anti-royalist transactions of those times. Lord Clarendon's history is made up, in what relates to Cromwell, of these his supposed machinations. However distinct from the scene of action, he is made answerable; all the actors are represented to be mere instruments in his hands, to carry on his secret arts and designs; nor are his most solemn declarations of ignorance of those various proceedings to be relied on; his whole language is to be considered as that of gross falsehood and deception, under the cloak and mask of religion and moral honesty. Having thus destroyed his credit, without fear of contradiction from his family or friends, who durst say nothing in his defence after the Restoration, not only his enemies of the different parties, but also many who had received great favours from him, and had acted with him to the last, were the forwardest in relating every trifling circumstance they could pick up, or had invented to blacken and insult his memory, in the hope, no doubt, of obliterating the remembrance of past transgressions and recommending themselves to the new powers. Hence, amongst others, the stories and anecdotes to be found in Bishop Burnet's History of his Own Times, Mr. Waller, and other writers subsequent to the Restoration.

Those who remember Mr. Waller's share in the conspiracy of 1643, with Tomkins and Challoner, and others, to surprise the city militia, and some members of Parliament, and to let in the King's

forces and disturb the Parliament; and of which
Whitelock says, he (Waller) being a very ingenious
man, was the principal actor and contriver, and
for which Tomkins and Challoner suffered death;
and of which Waller was also convicted, and
escaped the same punishment by paying a large
fine, and going into exile. Also those who attend
to his high panegyric in his verses addressed to
Cromwell, and upon his death, wherein he describes
him as giving in private life a just pattern how
fathers, husbands, pious sons, should live; and then
observes how he turns round in his high-flown
complimentary verses to King Charles the Second,
upon his restoration, where he talks of offenders
beginning to strive for grace, and expiation of their
sin, comparing the King to our Saviour; those
persons will surely not readily believe his (Waller's)
forementioned story of Cromwell's acknowledged
hypocrisy. Were it true, it would have been in
Waller a most dishonourable and inexcusable betrayal of an inadvertent confidence in an unguarded
moment; but it is utterly improbable: the religious language he is there represented as using,
was his constant mode of expression on religious
subjects, and in no other part of his history, except
in this instance, and in the next, related from
Oliver St. John's Life, does he appear to have
treated ludicrously or lightly those subjects; the
whole tenour of his life was strictly religious and
circumspect, and render these stories highly im-

probable and unworthy of credit. Had Cromwell been so great a dissembler as it became the fashion to consider him, he would not surely have thus committed himself, even with his nearest friend and greatest confidant. We have none of these stories from Whitelock; he gives instances of his unbending himself with his friends, but they are wholly cheerful and innocent. It was not likely that Cromwell should be in habits of intimacy and confidence with Waller, whose former treacherous conduct he could not but remember. Dr. Johnson, in his Life of Waller, says, that he solicited and obtained Cromwell's permission to return; and adds, that Cromwell received him, as his kinsman, to a familiar conversation. This supposed reception is only founded upon Waller's own account, from the writer of his Life, to introduce the forementioned story. Cromwell could not have been the man of wisdom and penetration he is allowed to be, had he trusted such a character as Waller with so important a secret. Dr. Johnson observes, that it is not possible to read without some contempt and indignation, poems of the same author, ascribing the highest degree of power and piety to Charles the First, then transferring the same power and piety to Oliver Cromwell; now inviting him to take the crown, and then congratulating Charles the Second on his recovered right. Lord Clarendon's character of Waller is given by the Doctor, from his history. His Lordship says,

the excellency and power of his wit, and pleasant-
ness of his conversation, was of sufficient magnitude
to cover a world of very great faults; that is, so
to cover them, that they were not taken notice of
to his reproach, viz. a narrowness in his nature to
the lowest degree; an abjectness and want of courage to support him in any virtuous undertaking;
an insinuation and servile flattery to the height
the vainest and most imperious nature could be
contented with: that it preserved and won his
life from those who most resolved to take it, and
in an occasion in which he ought to have been
ambitious to have lost it; and then preserved him
again from the reproach and contempt that was
due to him for so preserving it, and for vindicating
it at such a price: that it had power to reconcile
him to those whom he had most offended and provoked, and continued to his age with that rare
felicity, that his company was acceptable where
his spirit was odious; and he was at least pitied
where he was most detested. This was not the
man likely to be trusted by Cromwell, who knew
men as well as most.

The anecdote said to be from Oliver St. John
rests on no foundation to be relied on; it is not
consistent with Cromwell's whole deportment.
Dr. Bates, who does not spare him in his betrayal
of the confidence of the Cromwell family, does
not hint at any expressions like the above, even in
his account of Cromwell's entertainments of his
officers and soldiers.

Dr. Johnson, giving, in his Life of Waller, a sharp reply to a question of King James the Second, observes,—" Such is the story which I once heard of some other man.   Pointed axioms and acute replies fly loose about the world, and are assigned succesively to those whom it may be the fashion to celebrate."   This observation applies forcibly to the many stories applied to Cromwell.

The instance of this hypocrisy, given by Bishop Burnet from Sir Harbottle Grimston's relation, does not amount to any thing like a proof of it. Sir Harbottle knew of it, no otherwise than from the account of the two officers, of whom he seemed to have had no previous knowledge.   No time is ascertained; Sir Harbottle was, no doubt, delighted with this opportunity of attacking Cromwell; he takes them immediately to the House of Commons, at the bar whereof they told their story, in the presence of Cromwell.   He solemnly denies the charge, and the House believed him: and Sir Harbottle adds, that had it been moved, he thought, that both he and the officers would have been sent to the Tower; and probably they deserved it, for this attempt to ruin Cromwell by false accusation, to which they were probably instigated by some of his enemies.   He very prudently withdrew himself from the House to the army, resolving not longer to trust himself amongst them.   This charge was similar to the forementioned charge of Major Huntingdon, which has been shown to have been a like fabrication to ruin Cromwell.

. The confusion and irresolution of Cromwell, described by Lord Clarendon, upon his appointment to the chief command in Ireland, and inability to command his temper and countenance, ill describe an hypocritical character. Nor is his supposed declaration to his troop (which is not remembered to be mentioned by any other writer), of the conditions of permission to enlist under his command, a very well chosen instance of this hypocrisy.

Mrs. Hutchinson's account of Cromwell's conduct towards Colonel Hutchinson, in the appointment of Major Saunders to the command of the late Colonel Thornhaugh's regiment, if told correctly, has certainly the appearance of insincerity. But great allowance must be made for Mrs. Hutchinson's affectionate partiality for her husband, who appears, from her narrative, to have been a most amiable and excellent man. She describes Cromwell as having assented to the appointment, and as having promised to send to the General for a commission, and then procuring it for Major Saunders. It is impossible, now, to come at the knowledge of the real circumstances of this transaction. Although Cromwell might have, and probably had, a very favourable opinion of the Colonel, as a person of integrity and ability, and great personal worth, he might not, upon consi-

deration, think him qualified to take the command
of a regiment, nor might he think it consistent
with strict discipline to permit the subaltern officers
and privates to take upon themselves to dictate to
their commanders. He (Cromwell) has been universally allowed to excel in deep knowledge of
men, appointing those only of ability to fill the
stations to which he appointed them. The situation of men in power must be very trying: the
insincerity of courtiers is a favourite subject of
declamation with disappointed expectants; they
are apt to construe into promise a civil speech or a
smile, from a dislike, in a feeling, kind disposition,
to distress by an absolute denial. This may have
been Cromwell's situation, he might have been
taken by surprise to think and speak favourably
of the Colonel's appointment; but finally, upon
further consideration, determine Major Saunders
to be the most proper person for the situation. It
was very important that Cromwell should have a
man at the head of a regiment upon whom, in
arduous situations, he could rely. Saunders was a
tried man, and had, according to Mrs. Hutchinson's own account, brought into the regiment a
troop of Derbyshire horse : he might think this,
and his then command of Major in the regiment, a
good ground of superior claim to the Colonel's.
Mrs. Hutchinson speaks favourably of his private
character, but not so of his abilities as a soldier.
Cromwell thought otherwise of him, and therefore

gave him the command of the regiment; for which
Mrs. Hutchinson and the Colonel appear never to
have forgiven him, and expresses herself disre-
spectfully of his family, though not of him, other
than upon this occasion.

Little need be said upon Bishop Burnet's account of the principle upon which Cromwell is
alleged to have acted, by some who pretended to
know Cromwell well: that great occasions would
excuse from the common rules of morality; from
which, the Bishop says, he might be easily led into
all the practices, both of falsehood and cruelty.
This principle is certainly a most mischievous one,
and is an opening to all crime : but Cromwell's
actions have not yet appeared to have been influenced by it, or to need this iniquitous apology.
Who were the Bishop's informers, he does not say.
Cromwell has not thought it necessary thus to
defend his actions ; they needed no such defence.
Where the Bishop speaks from his own knowledge,
there can be no doubt of his veracity; but he
seems to lend too ready an ear to others' information, particularly as relating to Cromwell.   He
appears to receive and relate every story told him
without examination ; not considering the person
and the circumstances by and under which they
are related.   He does not seem to recollect that
these stories are told immediately after the Restoration, by persons, in many instances, implicated in
the occurrences they relate, and in the hope to re-

commend themselves to the then powers by defaming Cromwell's memory, by stories and anecdotes, whether true or false, of no consequence, having no fear of contradiction or confutation. Of this description is the following passage : — the Bishop says, that, during Cromwell's absence in Scotland, the treaty of the Isle of Wight was set on foot by the Parliament, who, seeing the army at such a distance, took that occasion of treating with the King: that Sir Henry Vane and others, who were for a change of government, had no mind to treat any more ; but that both city and country were so desirous of a personal treaty, that it could not be resisted : that Vane, Pierpoint, and some others, went to the treaty on purpose to delay matters till the army could be brought to London : that all that wished well to the treaty prayed the King, at their first coming, to dispatch the business with all possible haste, and to grant the first day all that he could bring himself to grant on the last : that Holles and Grimston told him (Burnet) that they had both on their knees begged this of the King: they said they knew Vane would study to draw out the treaty to a great length, and that he who declared for an unbounded liberty of conscience, would try to gain on the King's party by the offer of a toleration for the Common Prayer, and the episcopal clergy : that his design in that was to gain time till Cromwell should settle Scotland and the North : but that they (Holles and Grimston)

said, if the King would come frankly in, without
the formality of papers backward and forward, and
send them back next day with the concessions that
were absolutely necessary, they did not doubt but
he should in a very few days be brought up with
honour, freedom, and safety to the Parliament,
and that matters should be brought to a present
settlement: that Titus, who was then much trusted
by the King, and employed in a negotiation with
the Presbyterian party, told him (the Bishop) that
he had spoke often and earnestly to him in the
same strain; but that the King could not come to
a resolution; still fancying that in the struggle
between the House of Commons and the army,
both saw they needed him so much, to give them
the superior strength, that he imagined, by balancing them, he would bring both sides into a greater
dependence on himself, and force them to better
terms : that, in this, Vane flattered the episcopal
party to the King's ruin as well as their own : but
that they still hated the Presbyterians as the first
authors of the war, and seemed unwilling to think
well of them, or to be beholden to them: that thus
the treaty went on with a fatal slowness, and by
the time it was come to some maturity, Cromwell
came up with his army and overturned all.

All the Bishop says respecting the Parliament's
motive for setting on foot the Isle of Wight treaty,
namely, Cromwell's and the army's absence in
Scotland, and Sir Henry Vane's and Mr. Pier-

point's object in attending the treaty, is conjectural; he brings no proof.   It is not meant to dispute the veracity of Mr. Holles's or Sir Harbottle Grimston's relation of their endeavours to prevail on the King to accede to the terms of the treaty; but their recollection of their then deemed former delinquencies, and their wonderful escape from their consequences, and anxious desire to prove to the then powers the sincerity of their conversion, would be very likely to give a favourable colouring to their narrative.   Nevertheless, it was not very creditable to them, or to the other commissioners of the Presbyterian party who might join them, to request His Majesty to accede to the articles of the treaty, many of them highly unreasonable, under an implied, to say the least, undertaking for the softening or rather riddance of those that might be disagreeable to him, when restored to power ; to which, greatly to the King's honour, he would not consent.   Lord Clarendon says, that such of the commissioners who were known to wish well to the King, found means to advertise him that they were of His Majesty's judgment with reference to the government, which they hoped might yet be preserved : that all the reasonable hope of preserving the crown was in dividing the Parliament from the army, which could be only done by his giving satisfaction in what was demanded with reference to the church, which would unite the Parliament in itself, some few persons excepted, and the city to the Parliament where the Presbyterians were most powerful; and this being done, the Parliament would immediately have power to reform their army, and to disband those who would not be re-formed : that then the King would be removed to London, to perfect that by his own presence in Parliament which should be prepared by this treaty; and that then the wording those bills, and the formality of passing them, would give oppor-tunity for many alterations, which being now at-tempted would destroy all, and reconcile the Parliament to the army; which would destroy the King.   But, that then, what the King should urge as matter of conscience in himself, would find re-spect, reverence, and concurrence.

The above passages leave no room for doubt of the duplicity of Mr. Holles, and of the other com-missioners of the Presbyterian party. They certainly deceived their employers in the temptation they held out to the King, of his evasion of the treaty upon his return to power; and it is not certain that they did not intend to deceive the King by the same temptation, to prevail upon him to assent to it; the articles whereof were most severe and unjust, the fabrication of the Presbyterian party, and with which, these commissioners must know, from the experience of the failure of former treaties, that the King would not nor could comply.   Pursuing the same object, they endeavour to intimidate the King to a compliance by the insinuation of Vane's supposed procrastination of the treaty till Cromwell's return. His Lordship describes the Presbyterians as the most powerful party in the Parliament, and their object to be, upon the King's return, to (what they call) reform the army; or, in other words, to dissolve it, and thereby to get into their power obnoxious individuals; dreading, above all things, the union of the Parliament and the army.

Mrs. Hutchinson, in confirmation of this statement, gives the account before given of Colonel Hutchinson's (upon his return to health) attendance in the House, and finding the Presbyterian party's prevalence there, and their resolution to close with the common enemy, that they might thereby compass the destruction of their Independent brethren; and for that purpose, their strengthening their faction, by restoring to their seats the late suspended members. Mr. Holles, during his secession, having been in France, and having there pieced up with the Queen an ungodly accommodation; notwithstanding his declaration at the beginning, openly in the House, of his abhorrence of the word " accommodation."

It is not true, as above stated, and as has been before observed, that Cromwell came up with his army and spoiled all. The design of the exclusion of the members was wholly Ludlow's, who relates

the circumstances with considerable exultation
and self-applause. Cromwell was not consulted
upon it, being absent and not returning to town
from his northern expedition, till after the exclusion, as already related. The treaty was not
precipitated; it was defeated only by the unreason-
ableness of its terms, and terminated unsuccessfully before Cromwell's return.

Whitelock, in his Swedish embassy, giving a
conversation between the Queen and him, describes her as, with some earnestness, saying, "You
are hypocrites and dissemblers." To which
Whitelock answers, " For myself, I can have little
of design (especially in your country) to dissemble. I always hated hypocrisy, as a thing
unworthy a Christian or a gentleman; and my
General hath not been charged with that odious
crime."—Queen. " I do not mean either your
General or yourself; but I think that in England
there are many who make profession of more holiness than is in them, hoping for advantage by
it." Whitelock. " I doubt there may be some
such in England, especially in this time, when
(through the goodness of God) religion is become
the chief interest of the nation; and there are of
these likewise in other countries; but when they
come to be found out with us, (as such cannot be
long undiscovered,) they lose their aim and credit,
and their dissembling is scorned and punished."

Here may be observed Whitelock's declaration, that Cromwell had not been then charged with the odious (as Whitelock justly calls it) crime of hypocrisy; nor, had he and his family continued in power, would it ever have been heard of.

If Lord Clarendon is to be credited, Cromwell must be the most inhuman of characters. His Lordship describes him the sole instigator and cause, immediately or mediately, of the sufferings of all the royalists under the sentences of the several high and other courts of justice, from the commencement of the Republic, succeeding the King's death.

This is a harsh and unfounded assertion. Cromwell must not be responsible for the results of any of the trials of the royalists, until the commencement of his protectorate. The executions in Cromwell's protectorate were few in number, compared with the number convicted of conspiracies against his life, either by the high courts of justice, or in other courts, very many of whom were afterwards pardoned and released, as has been before and are hereafter related, and the instances given.

Neal, in his History of the Puritans, observes upon this charge of cruelty, — that it has been brought against him (Cromwell), for having put some men to death for conspiring against his person and government, deserves no confutation, unless they would have had him sit still, till some conspiracy had succeeded, — that cruelty was not

in his nature; he was not for unnecessary effusion
of blood. He quotes in proof,. the before-given
passage from Lord Clarendon; that when a general massacre of the royalists was proposed by
the officers in council, he (Cromwell) warmly
opposed and prevented it. And Bishop Burnet
says, he was afraid of the cavalier party's assassination and other plottings; and that he took a
· method to prevent assassinations, that proved very
effectual; saying often and openly, that in a war
it was necessary to return upon any side all the
violent things that any of the one side did to the
other: that this was done for preventing greater
mischief, and for bringing men to fair war : that
assassinations were such detestable things, that he
would never begin them; but that, if any of the
King's party should endeavour to assassinate him,
and fail in it, he would make an assassinating war
of it, and destroy the whole family: that he pretended he had instruments to execute it, whenso-
ever he should give order for it. The terror of
this, says the Bishop, was a better security to him
than his guards. The Bishop adds, that he had
this and other information from the Earls of Carlisle and Orrery, the one having been the captain
of his guards, (then Colonel Howard,) and the
other, then Lord Broghill, had been the president
of his council in Scotland.

Cromwell's great mind could never stoop to put
this threat into execution, notwithstanding the

provocations to it he met with, in the various attempts that were made upon his life; nor has he ever been charged with any thing of the kind. Not so King Charles the First, as has been before shown, nor King Charles the Second; for in Thurloe is to be found a proclamation by King Charles the Second, in 1654, giving free liberty to destroy his (Cromwell's) life by pistol, sword, or poison, or otherwise, promising a reward of five hundred pounds *per annum*, and knighthood.

Thurloe's State Papers abound with instances of these plots of assassination. Amongst many others, in 1653–4, a person of the name of Corker informs Thurloe, that Colonel Deane had told him, Corker, that he was informed that Cromwell would dine in the city on the next Wednesday, when he, Deane, would assassinate him. The same Corker informs Secretary Morland that Dr. Hewitt was more a Tully than a Catiline, and had been more prevalent with his tongue than his brains: that he had great influence over ordinary capacities, both in the city and country, and had pursued it to the utmost of his power. A letter dated Paris, 14th May, 1655, from the Duke of York to Charles the Second, decyphered by the King's own hand, informing that a proposition had been made to him: four Roman Catholics had bound themselves in a solemn oath to kill Cromwell and then to raise all the Catholics in the city and in the army to rise for the King's restoration; but that they demanded a

sum of money.   The Duke appears to approve the
assassination.   A letter dated Paris, 10th June,
1654, from Monsieur Riviere, to Colonel Dis-
browe, informing of a proposal by a Thomas
Henshaw and others to King Charles II., to
murder Cromwell, which had been accepted, and
they went to England for that purpose.   Thurloe,
in a letter to Henry Cromwell in Ireland, dated
9th December, 1656, says, the levellers are very
busy, and are in perfect conjunction with the King
of Spain ; that the part they had first undertaken
was to assassinate my Lord Protector, and have
laid the way of doing it.   He adds, " this I know
with as much certainty as that Your Lordship is
in Ireland : I trust the Lord will disappoint them
as he hath done ; but we see hereby the spirit of
these men."   Lord Broghill, in his memoirs, says,
that he observed Cromwell, some time before his
death, to grow melancholy and pensive, and to be
afraid of every body : that at one particular time,
when he was with Cromwell in his coach, going
from Westminster to Whitehall, the crowd of
people was so great, that the coach could not go
forward, and the place was so narrow, that all the
halberdiers were either before the coach or behind
it, none of them having room to stand by the side :
that while they were in this posture, His Lordship
observed the door of a cobbler's stall to open and
shut a little ; and at every opening of it, he saw
something bright, like a drawn sword or a pistol ;

that thereupon His Lordship drew out his sword with the scabbard on it, and struck upon the stall, asking who was there : that this was no sooner done, but a tall man burst out with a sword by his side; and that Cromwell was so much frightened, that he called his guard to seize him ; but the man got away in the crowd. His Lordship adds, that he thought him to be an officer in the army of Ireland, whom he remembered Cromwell had disgusted, and supposes he laid there in wait to kill him : that Cromwell forbore to come any more that way; but, in a little time after, sickened and died. Mrs. Hutchinson, referring to these assassination plots, says that the cavaliers were every day forming designs, and plotting for the murder of Cromwell, and other insurrections, which being contrived in drink, and managed by false and cowardly fellows, were still revealed to Cromwell who had most excellent intelligence of all things that passed. And that, to speak the truth, Cromwell's personal courage and magnanimity upheld him against all enemies and malecontents. She adds, that some of the Lambertonians (General Lambert's party) had at that time a plot to come with a petition to Cromwell, and while he was reading it, certain of them had undertaken to cast him out of a window at Whitehall, that looked upon the Thames, where others should be ready to catch him up in a blanket, if he escaped breaking his neck, and carry him away in a boat prepared for the purpose, to kill or keep him alive, as they saw occasion, and then set up Lambert: that this was so carried on, that it was near the execution, before the Protector knew any thing of it: that Colonel Hutchinson, accidentally becoming acquainted of this plot, apprised him of it through General Fleetwood; not from his good-will towards Cromwell, but to prevent Lambert from succeeding him, whom he suspected would be the worst tyrant of the two.

Many more instances might be brought forward of these plots of assassination; but nothing could provoke Cromwell to retaliation. A few of the most dangerous of these conspirators were tried and executed, but mercy shown to many. Amongst other instances of mercy : — The Dutch ambassador in England in a letter to the States-general, dated 23d July, 1655, in Thurloe, says, that divers lords and gentlemen who had been secured in sundry places, were dismissed to their houses and habitations, and proclamation, that those that had headed the King's party, or assisted them, were to withdraw from London and Westminster, and all places twenty miles round, and to repair to their birth-places. — In January, 1657, Whitelock says, that Lord Willoughby, upon his petition to the Protector, had leave to go into the country to dispatch some necessary business respecting his estate, upon his promise to return to prison when required. — Also, Sir Roger Martyn released from prison upon his parol not to disturb the government.

In a letter of intelligence in Thurloe, dated Paris, 29th May, 1655, the writer says, — " Sir; Yours of the 24th instant I received, by which I see the Protector is merciful to the late risers, contrary to the expectations of most here ; but now they find it otherwise, and some highly commend him for it."

In a letter, also in Thurloe, from Major-general Whalley to Cromwell, dated Warwick, 31st March, 1656, Whalley says, — " After the assizes at Warwick be over, which is the last of Judge Hale's circuit, I shall acquaint Your Highness, by Mr. Secretary, what we have done, and what is desired, in reference to public good : and indeed, My Lord, I cannot but inform you, that Judge Hale hath so demeaned himself in the counties under my charge, both in reference to Your Highness's interest, as also for his justice to all ; and in a special manner taking care of poor men in their causes, without which some had suffered ; as that I desire when he shall wait upon Your Highness, you would be pleased to take notice of it, and if it seem good to you, to give him more than ordinary thanks." And, in a subsequent letter from the same Major-general Whalley to Thurloe, dated Nottingham, the 9th of the following April, he says, " I have hitherto forborne to write to you, that I might give you the better account of our transactions in these five counties, after the circuit. And in the first place, I must let you know, I am persuaded there never was any Judge in this circuit got more applause, more the affections of honest men, than Judge Hale; who, as he is unquestionably an able, so upon good grounds I judge him a godly, man. I hope His Highness, as I have humbly desired in a letter to him, will give him more than ordinary thanks upon his waiting of him." — " The Judge hath not been free to execute any for horse-stealing, but hath reprieved them, and two for robbery; hath continued divers other notorious wicked fellows in the gaol, in order to be sent out of the nation, if His Highness and the council think well of it." These letters prove that he, Cromwell, permitted justice to take its course. Had he not been both just and merciful, he would not have confided the administration of justice and mercy to so exalted a character as Judge Hale; nor would the Judge have accepted the office under any restraints in these respects.

Dr. Harris allows he was humane and benevolent, instancing some of the evidences thereof before given and hereafter referred to. Mr. Maidston, in his forementioned letter to Governor Winthorp, describes him as naturally compassionate towards objects in distress, though God had made him a heart, wherein was left little room for any fear, but what was due to himself; yet did he exceed in tenderness towards sufferers.

The instances of his humane and honourable treatment of the royalists are many. Mr. Maidston, in his above letter, referring to the execution of the Reverend Christopher Love for high treason against the commonwealth, in 1651, says, that many of his brethren were endangered, being detained prisoners till General Cromwell came home, and procured their release.—His procuring the Act of Oblivion in 1651;—his kindness in endeavouring to free the Countess of Arundel's estate from sequestration;—his attention to the Marchioness of Ormond's application for his assistance in the recovery and management of her estate in Ireland, for the subsistence of herself and family;—his lenity towards the Marquis of Ormond, in directing Lord Broghill to inform him of his knowledge of his being in London, thereby enabling him to escape;—his direction of the discharge of Mrs. Lucy Barlow and her young son from their imprisonment in the Tower of London, whom she had declared to be King Charles the Second's son, and herself to be his wife;—his letter to his son Henry, recommending lenity towards those opposing his government in Ireland;—his conduct in Scotland. Whitelock says, that, upon his arrival with his army in Scotland, he published a proclamation through his army, stating that several soldiers had strayed from their colours, and enforced victuals from the Scots without paying for them, and frightened some of the people from

their habitations; and commanding all officers and
soldiers of his army that none should, without
leave, go half a mile from their quarters, upon
pain of death, nor offer any violence or injury to
the person or goods of any in Scotland, not in
arms: that upon his entry into Glasgow, many Scots
appeared to see him march, but no violence was
offered to any of them; the General having given
a strict command for that purpose, and that none
of the soldiers entered till he and his soldiers were
first in their quarters; and that on the Lord's day
a Scots minister railed foully against the General
and his army; and that though many soldiers
heard it, no violence was offered; and that the
General was returned to the siege of Edinburgh
Castle: and he (Whitelock) adds, that he published
a proclamation for free and safe trading by the
Scots at Edinburgh, who were not in arms, and
liberty to sell their commodities, and to be free
from violence of the soldiery, and to be protected
in their habitations. This lenity and forbearance
towards the Scots was at the head of a victorious
and, as above appears, an insulted General and
army. Bishop Burnet describes the state of Scotland during Cromwell's time.— He says, the country was kept in great order during Cromwell's
government: that some castles in the Highlands
had garrisons put in them, that were so careful in
their discipline, and so exact to their rules, that in
no time the Highlands were kept in better order:

good justice was done, and vice suppressed and
punished ; so that it was always reckoned a time
of great peace and prosperity. Whitelock says,
that letters from Scotland informed of the Scots
being full of compliance with the government,
established there by the Protector ; which, adds
he, was more conformity than ever they yielded
before. The anecdote given by the Bishop, describing Cromwell, by the means of Sir Richard
Willis's treachery, as having all the party in a net,
in which, says he, he let them dance at pleasure,
and occasionally clapt them up for a short time,
but did not hurt them. His (Cromwell's) moderation is further seen in his very indulgent terms of
the various capitulations of the several places taken
by him, and his severity in the punishment of any
of his soldiers guilty of plundering, or of other
breaches of those capitulations ; and his very liberal proposal and procurement of the release of the
Duke of Gloucester, the King's son. The magnanimity of his mind, in the confidence he reposed
in those he deemed honourable men, and, as such,
worthy of his confidence, is very strikingly evidenced in his gaining Lord Broghill, who appears
to have been ever afterwards the firm friend of
himself and his family. It is related in His Lordship's memoirs, that under pretence of going to
the Spa waters in Germany, he intended to cross
the seas, and apply himself to His Majesty (Charles
the Second) for a commission to raise what forces

he could, to restore His Majesty in Ireland, and
to recover his own estate then given for lost; for
which purpose he had applied for a licence to go
to the Spa, communicating his real design only to
some friends, whom he imagined to be loyal and
secret: that he had already made up a considerable sum of money, and was arrived in London in
order to the prosecution of his voyage, when a
gentleman belonging to Cromwell (who had then
been made General in Sir Thomas Fairfax's place)
came to his lodging to inform him that the General, his master, intended to wait upon him, if he
knew the hour when he would be at leisure to receive him: that His Lordship was much surprised
at this message, because he never had any acquaintance with Cromwell, nor had ever exchanged one
word with him : that, therefore, he told the gentleman he presumed he was mistaken, and that he
was not the person to whom the General had sent
him with that message.   The gentlemen answered,
he was sent to the Lord Broghill ; and therefore if
he was that Lord, he was sent to him : that His
Lordship finding there was no mistake in the gentleman, owned that he was the Lord Broghill ; but
desired the gentleman to present his humble service to the General, and to inform him that he
would not give him the trouble to come to him,
but that he would wait upon the General if he
knew where he was, and when he might ; and to
that end would immediately make himself ready

for it. The gentleman said, he would acquaint
His Excellency with it, and so took his leave: that,
in the mean time, His Lordship was mightily concerned, what Cromwell's business with him should
be; and while he was thus musing, Cromwell came
to him; and after mutual salutations, told him, he
had a great kindness and respect for His Lordship;
and that, therefore, he was come to acquaint him
with something that did very nearly concern him,
and to give him his advice in the matter: that he
then proceeded to inform him, that the council of
state was acquainted with his designs, in coming to
town in order to his passing beyond sea; and that,
instead of going to the Spa for his gout, he was
going to the King for a commission to raise men,
and oppose their government in Ireland; and that,
under this pretence, the Earl of Warwick had got
him a licence from the state to pass the seas: that
as Cromwell was proceeding, His Lordship interrupted him, and told him, he presumed His Excellency was mistaken in the matter; for that he was
not capable of doing any thing that way, and therefore desired him to believe no such thing. But
Cromwell told him he had good proof for what he
said, and could show copies of his letters to that
purpose, and therefore desired him not to deceive
himself, for that the council had ordered him to be
clapped up in the Tower upon his arrival in town,
which had been executed accordingly, had not he
himself interposed in his behalf, and procured some

time to confer with him to see whether he might not be drawn off from his design.—That upon this and other circumstances, His Lordship, finding that he was discovered, begged Cromwell's pardon, and thanked him for his kindness, and desired him to advise him what to do: that Cromwell told him, that neither he nor the council were strangers to his actions in the Irish war; and that, therefore, the subduing of the Irish rebels being now left to his care, he had obtained leave from the council to make an offer to Lord Brogbill, that if he would serve in the wars against the Irish, he should have a general officer's command, and should have no oaths nor engagements laid upon him, nor should be obliged to fight against any but the Irish: that His Lordship did not a little wonder at this large offer, and would have excused himself, desiring some time to consider of it; but Cromwell told him, he must resolve presently, for that there was no time to deliberate; because the council, from whom he came, were resolved to send His Lordship to the Tower, as soon as ever Cromwell should return to them, in case this offer was not readily accepted.—That His Lordship seeing no subterfuges could any longer be made use of, and finding his liberty and life in danger, whereby he might be rendered utterly incapable of serving His Majesty, and not knowing but by accepting this offer he might afterwards be serviceable to the royal party, he resolved to accept

of it, upon the conditions which Cromwell mentioned; promising, upon his word and honour, he
would faithfully assist Cromwell in subduing the
Irish rebellion.   Whereupon Cromwell assured
him he should have those conditions performed to
a tittle; and desired him to haste down to Bristol,
where men should be sent to him, and ships wait for
his transportation, and that he himself would follow him with another army; all which was accordingly done.

The preface to these Memoirs of Lord Broghill,
referring to this transaction, observes, that nothing
could more strongly evidence Cromwell's deep
penetration into mankind, nor show plainer the
wisdom and niceness with which he made choice
of his friends than this his behaviour to Lord
Broghill.

Ludlow says, that Cromwell gave directions to
the judges who were ready to go their several cir-
cuits, to take especial care to extend all favour and
kindness to the cavalier party, and gives some instances of his personal kindness to them; adding,
however, with his usual bitterness towards Cromwell, his motive to be, endeavouring to fix himself
in his throne by all ways imaginable.

To show Cromwell's contempt of the assassin-
ation-plots against him, Whitelock gives the following anecdote:— That in the month of May,
1657, the Sieur Phillipi Passinni being sent by the
Queen of Sweden to the Protector, with letters

credential, and to inform His Highness of some secret affairs, he, by the Queen's instructions, addressed himself first to Whitelock, with letters to him from the Queen, desiring him to bring his secretary (this gentleman) to the presence of His Highness, and to promote his business : that Whitelock acquainted the Protector therewith, and read to him the Queen's letters to Whitelock, which were in French : the Protector desired him to read them again, in English, which he did, and the Protector said he would consider of the business. That upon advice with his council about it, some of them to show their extraordinary care of his person, suggested to him, that this messenger, being an Italian, (who were skilful in the art of poisoning, and ready to be hired for such a purpose,) might bring poison with his letters, to the danger of His Highness; and therefore endeavoured to dissuade him from receiving him, or permitting him to come into his presence : that the Protector, smiling, acquainted Whitelock with this cautious counsel, who convinced him of the folly of it, and the high distaste that would be taken by the Queen, in case her secretary should be denied audience : that the Protector replied, that the messenger desired to deliver his errand in private to him (the Protector), and none to be present but one more, whom the Protector should appoint, and that person, His Highness said, he intended should be Whitelock, who said that if he should be present when the gentleman delivered his letter, he would receive it of the gentleman, and hazard the danger of being poisoned by it, at which the Protector laughed, and appointed a day for the gentleman's audience. That at that time Whitelock only was present with the Protector, and the gentleman offering to deliver the letter to His Highness, Whitelock took it first from the gentleman, and then he delivered his secret message to His Highness, which Whitelock interpreted from the French; and it was a particular account of the causes why she ordered her servant, the Italian marquis, to be put to death in France. That he (this gentleman) also propounded to His Highness several matters, in order to alliances with foreign princes, which were of great consequence, and probable advantage to England; with which the Protector seemed well pleased: that Whitelock procured a civil treatment of the gentleman whilst he was here, and a respectful answer to his business, and dismission of him; wherein Her Majesty had satisfaction as well as her secretary.

Dr. Harris allows, that bigotry made no part of Cromwell's character, and that he had a mind superior to it; that he had a fixed opinion concerning liberty of conscience in matters of religion. The Doctor justly observes, that no bigot ever had sense sufficient to see the plain and just right that every man has, to think and act for himself in matters purely of a religious nature; or to be convinced, that unless men freely and voluntarily choose their religion, they can have no merit in the eyes of God or reasonable men; and consequently that they ought never to be debarred from acting according to their own choice. The bigot, proceeds the Doctor, is always in the right, every man of a different belief is in the wrong; heaven is his own portion, but hell and damnation attend those who think and act opposite to him : that Cromwell was not of this cast; he always professed it to be his belief, that men had a right to think and act for themselves in matters of religion, and that as long as they behaved peaceably, they were free to dissent from the magistrate and the priest. The Doctor quotes a passage from Ludlow, that "the liberty that was to be extended to tender consciences was an engine by which Cromwell did most of his work;" and a saying of Baxter, from a passage in his life, "that liberty of conscience he (Cromwell) pretended to be most zealous for." These are in Ludlow's and Baxter's usual ill-natured style, when speaking of Cromwell. The Doctor then gives passages to prove that he was of the opinions he professed, respecting this liberty of conscience, from a sonnet by Milton; his speeches upon the dissolution of the Long Parliament, and to the Parliament of 1657, respecting the provision made for liberty of conscience in the humble petition and advice. These extracts, the Doctor observes, fully evince Cromwell's judgment con-

fidence in your honour and abilities for this employment; to which we, begging your answer, do
rest,

"My Lord, your humble Servant,

"O. Cromwell,

"Gil. Pickering."

2d September, 1653.

Whitelock, in a subsequent passage, says, a principal care of Whitelock, as to those of his retinue,
was to get able and fit chaplains, such as were of
a pious life and conversation, and of good abili-
lities and learning, for example and instruction of
his company.

That, September 25., after public exercises of
devotion on this (the Lord's) day, he retired himself from the continual discourses of his Swedish
business, unto his private meditations upon the
Holy Scriptures.

That, October 25., besides his private and particular seeking to God for his counsel and blessing
in this undertaking, he had the joint prayers of
his friends; with him, divers of them met in the
evening at his brother Wilson's house, several
members of Mr. Cokayne's church, and, among
them, Mr. Taylor expounded a place of Scripture
very pertinently, and several of them prayed very
affectionately for him (Whitelock), and the good
success of his business; and divers expounded
places of Scripture suitable to the occasion. That

humane to such as professed opinions uncountenanced by the many in Britain; in the instance of John Biddle, who was a Unitarian, and the father of the English Unitarians, in his banishment into Scilly, (on account of his religious opinions,) he allowed him a pension of an hundred crowns a year. Neal says, he was committed to the Gatehouse by the Parliament; but that Cromwell, upon its dissolution, gave him his liberty; and that afterwards he was committed for a like offence by the council to Newgate, but that Cromwell thought it best to send him out of the way, and accordingly transported him to Scilly, and allowed him this one hundred crowns. A letter upon this subject to Secretary Thurloe, is in his State Papers: it is dated 24th July, 1658. He (Biddle) says, His Highness was pleased, when I was under restraint in the Isle of Scilly, by his letters of privy seal, to allow me ten shillings per week towards my maintenance; but since I have been restored to my liberty, as I do with many thanks acknowledge His Highness's bounty towards me, so I should be very loath that the intention thereof should be perverted, and therefore I beseech Your Honour to certify His Highness, that my hope is that I shall be now otherwise sufficiently provided for. That he admitted Jeremiah White and Peter Sterry into the number of his chaplains, though few speculated more freely on the ends and designs of Providence, or more out of the then road; and John Goodwin, though hated by the fashionable ecclesiastics, continued constantly in his favour: nor, adds the Doctor, were even the Romanists, that behaved well, destitute of his protection and favour.—He gives the following passage in a letter from Sir Kenelm Digby, a man of quality, a philosopher, and a Catholic, to Thurloe, (to be found in Thurloe,) dated Paris, March 18. 1656:—" My obligations to His Highness are so great, that it would be a crime in me to behave myself so negligently as to give cause for any shadow of the least suspicion, or to do any thing that might require an excuse or apology. I make it my business every where, to have all the world take notice how highly I esteem myself obliged to His Highness, and how passionate I am for his service, and for his honour and interest, even to the exposing of my life for them. I should think my heart were not an honest one, if the blood about it were not warmed with any, the least imputation upon my respects and my duty to His Highness, to whom I owe so much." The Doctor adds, " Mr. Prynne informs us (in a work quoted in the margin), that Sir Kenelm was lodged by Cromwell at Whitehall; that he suspended the penal laws against Romish priests, and protected several of them under his hand and seal: and adds, as certain, that he wrote to the governor of Virginia in favour of Lord Baltimore, proprietor of Maryland, who was of the Catholic persuasion. This letter is to be found in Thurloe.

Mrs. Hutchinson says that the Papists wanted not patrons in Cromwell's time.

Dr. Harris adds, that it was well known that Cromwell (though a believer in the prophecies of the Old Testament, equally, to say the least, with our modern controversists,) was willing to harbour the Jews in England; that he appointed an assembly of men of several professions to consider of the expediency of it, and that it was not owing to him or his council that it proved lost labour. He adds, " All these considerations will, if I mistake not, abundantly make appear the truth of the text, that bigotry made no part of Cromwell's character."

Mr. Neal gives a more particular account of this favourable disposition towards the Jews. He says, that such was the Protector's latitude, that he was for indulging the Jews, who petitioned for liberty of their religion, and for carrying on a trade in London: that Manasseh Ben Israel, one of their chief rabbis, with some others, came from Amsterdam to Whitehall for this purpose, whom the Protector treated with respect, and summoned an assembly of divines, lawyers, and merchants, to consult upon the affair; that the divines were to consider it as a case of conscience, the lawyers to report how far it was consistent with the laws of England, and the merchants whether it was for the advantage of trade and commerce: but that the assembly not agreeing in their opinions, the affair was dropped.

Whitelock says, that the Protector ordered two hundred pounds to be paid out of the treasury to Manasseh Ben Israel, the Jewish rabbi.

Dr. Harris says, his (Cromwell's) edict against the episcopal clergy was very cruel: that he was by nature, as before observed, generous and humane, kind and compassionate; but that when he was provoked, he showed his resentment, and made his enemies feel the weight of it: that, with respect to religion, he was no bigot; and that yet, exasperated by the conduct of the cavaliers, who had so foolishly risen against him under Wagstaff, Penruddock, and Grave in the west, he treated the clergy of that party very rigorously; for that, in a declaration, dated 4th October, (Neal says, published November 24th,) 1655, are found the following prohibitions, which are given by the Doctor verbatim; the substance of which is, to prohibit all persons, whose estates had been sequestered for delinquency, or who had been in arms against the Parliament, from keeping in their houses and families as chaplains, or schoolmasters for the education of their children, any sequestered or ejected minister, fellow of any college, or schoolmaster, or permitting any of their children to be taught by such, upon pain of being proceeded against in such sort, as thereby directed in such cases: also prohibiting all persons who had been sequestered or ejected out of any benefice, college, or school for delinquency or scandal, from keeping any school, public or private : also prohibiting all persons who, for delinquency or scandal, had been sequestered or ejected, from preaching in any public place, or at any private meeting of any other persons than those of his own family, or administering baptism or the Lord's supper, or marrying any persons, or using the book of Common Prayer or the forms of prayer therein contained, under certain penalties. Nevertheless, it is added, that " His Highness doth declare, that towards such of the said persons as have since their ejection or sequestration given, or shall hereafter give a real testimony of their godliness and good affection to the present government, so much tenderness shall be used as may consist with the safety and good of the nation."

The Doctor (Harris) is unmercifully severe upon this declaration; he says it would be useless to spend words in exposing the cruelty of it; persecution is written upon the face of it, nor is it capable of a vindication. He then quotes a passage from the Life of Archbishop Usher, relating an application of some of the most considerable episcopal clergy through the Archbishop, requesting him to use his interest with the Protector to take off this restraint, which at last he promised (though with some difficulty) that they should not be molested, provided they meddled not with any matters relating to his government, but that when the Lord Primate went to him a second time to

get this promise ratified and put into writing,
Cromwell told him that he had better considered it,
having advised with his council about it, and that
they thought it not safe for him to grant liberty of
conscience to those sort of men, who were restless
and implacable enemies to him and his government; and so took his leave of him, though with
good words and outward civility; and the Archbishop is represented as greatly dissatisfied, and as
accusing Cromwell as having broken his word.
The Doctor thinks the Archbishop had reason to
be out of humour; for that whatever might have
been the practices of many of the episcopal clergy,
certainly there were amongst them wise, pious,
learned, and peaceable men who merited a very
different treatment from this which was given them
by Cromwell. He nevertheless allows, he says,
in justice to the Protector, that, notwithstanding
this declaration, he winked at, or permitted, some
worthy Episcopalians to officiate in the public
places of worship; nor do we, says he, find that
they suffered any inconveniences on account of it.

The Doctor might have spared much of his censure, had he considered this act, or order, as not
meant to be executed in the strictness of its terms,
not intending to disturb those who did not disturb
the government; and towards these, the Doctor
allows he, Cromwell, performed his promise.

Mr. Neal, in his forementioned History of the
Puritans, appears to consider this measure in its

true light. He describes it as a severe and terrible
order upon the Episcopalians, and unjustifiable in
itself, but that the title of the act, which was an
ordinance for securing the peace of the commonwealth, as well as the last clause, shows it was
made for the safety of the government, against a
number of men that were undermining it : and
was published chiefly *in terrorem ;* for that no
person was prosecuted upon it; nor did the Par.
liament that met the next year confirm it, which
made it absolutely void. He says, that Doctor
Gauden presented a petitionary remonstrance to
the Protector against this order. He also mentions
the Archbishop's above application, and he adds,
from the Archbishop's Life, probably written by
another hand, that the Protector promised either
to recall his declaration, or to prevent its being put
in execution, provided the clergy were inoffensive
in their language and sermons, and stood clear in
meddling with matters of state : that Cromwell
accordingly laid the matter before his council, who
were of opinion that it was not safe for him to
recall his declaration, and give open liberty to men
who were declared enemies to his government, but
that he should suspend the execution of it as far
as their behaviour should deserve; so that, says
Neal, there was no great reason of complaint; for
that, notwithstanding this ordinance, the sober
episcopal clergy preached publickly in the churches
at London and in the country, as Doctor Hall,

afterwards Bishop of Chester, Doctor Ball, Doctor Wild, Doctor Hardy, Doctor Griffith, Doctor Pearson, Bishop of Chester, and others.   Remarkable, says Neal, 'are the words of Bishop Kennet to this purpose; — " It is certain, says His Lordship, that the Protector was for liberty, and the utmost latitude to all parties, so far as consisted with the peace and safety of his person and government, and therefore he was never jealous of any cause or sect, on the account of heresy or falsehood, but on his wiser accounts of political peace and quiet; and even the prejudice he had against the episcopal party was more for their being royalists than for being of the good old church : that Dr. Gunning, afterwards Bishop of Ely, kept a conventicle in London, in as open a manner as the dissenters did after the toleration ; and so did several other episcopal divines."

For the same reason, adds Neal, His Highness girt the laws close upon the Papists, not upon account of their religion, but because they were enemies to his government; for that, in the month of May, (1655,) a proclamation was published for the better executing the laws against Jesuits and Papists, and for the conviction of popish recusants; the reason of which the Protector gives in his declaration of October 31st, published with advice of his council, in these words: " Because it was not only commonly observed, but there remains with us somewhat of proof, that Jesuits have been

found among discontented parties of this nation,
who are observed to quarrel, and fall out with
every form of administration in church and state."
That the Protector, continues Neal, gave notice
of the like kind to the Republicans, Fifth-monarchy-
men, Levellers, and to the Presbyterians, that they
should stand upon the same foot with the royalists,
in case of any future delinquencies.

Bishop Burnet, in reference to Cromwell's lenity
to the Episcopalians, and moderation in government, has the following passage: — " He studied
to seek out able and honest men, and to employ
them, and having heard that his (the Bishop's)
father had a very great reputation in Scotland for
piety and integrity, though he knew him to be a
royalist, he sent to him, desiring him to accept
of a judge's place, and to do justice in his own
country; hoping only, that he would not act
against his government, but that he would not
press him to subscribe or swear to it: that his (the
Bishop's) father refused it in a pleasant way, desiring no other favour of him but leave to live privately without the imposition of oaths and subscriptions; and," adds the Bishop, "he ever lived in
great quiet;" of which he gives the following instance.—Overton, one of Cromwell's Major-ge-
nerals, who was a high republican, being for some
time at Aberdeen, where the Bishop's father and
family then lived, his father and he (Overton) were
often together: that, in particular, they were shut

up alone for about two hours the night after the order came from Cromwell, to take away Overton's commissions, and to put him in arrest: that Colonel Howard, afterwards Earl of Carlisle, being sent down to enquire into all the plots that those men had been in, heard of this long privacy, but that when, with that, he heard what his (the Bishop's) father's character was, he made no farther enquiry into it, but said, Cromwell was very uneasy when any good man was questioned for any thing.

The Bishop relates, that Dr. Wilkins, afterwards bishop of Chester, who married Cromwell's sister, told him, that when Cromwell was designing to make himself king, he had often said to him (Dr. Wilkins), that no temporal government could have a sure support without a national church that adhered to it; and that he thought that England was capable of no constitution but Episcopacy; to which, the Doctor told him (the Bishop), he did not doubt but Cromwell would have turned, as soon as the design of his kingship should have been settled.

It appears from Whitelock, that he very reluctantly consented to the prevention of the celebration, by some congregations, of a Christmas-day, being advised, and being sensible, it was contrary to the liberty of conscience, so much owned, says Whitelock, and pleaded for by him and his friends; but that he, finding it to be contrary to ordinances of Parliament, that those days should be solemnized, felt himself obliged to consent to the suppression of these meetings, though much against his inclination.

Neal observes, that the Protector and his council were in large sentiments upon these religious rights : that Mr. Baxter says, that the Protector and his friends gave out, that they could not understand what the magistrates had to do in matters of religion; that they thought that all men should be left to the liberty of their own consciences, and that the magistrate could not interpose without ensnaring himself in the guilt of persecution : and, adds Neal, were not these noble and generous sentiments, though the Parliament could not be brought into them, and upon which the Protector reproaches them in his speech at their dissolution?

That, continues Neal, agreeable to these principles, Dr. George Bates, (the forementioned Dr. Bates,) an eminent royalist, and, as before observed, become a great enemy to Cromwell's memory upon the Restoration, writes, " that the Protector indulged the use of the Common Prayer in families, and in private conventicles ; and that though the condition of the church of England was but melancholy, yet it cannot be denied, but they had a great deal more favour and indulgence than under the Parliament ; which would never have been interrupted, had they not insulted the Protector, and forfeited their liberty by their seditious practices and plottings against his person and government."

-. Cromwell's settled disapprobation of religious persecution adds no inconsiderable proof of the extraordinary greatness and comprehensiveness of his mind and understanding.. He appears to have early and forcibly. seen and adopted the great principle of the right of private judgment in matters of religion, contrary to, it is conceived, may be said, the universal, opposite principle and practice of those times: none of the religious sects and parties of those days had an idea of toleration; their contest was for power, which should be uppermost and rule the rest, without an apprehension of the justice of allowing their opponents their right of judging for themselves in a matter so highly important to their present and future interests; each sect had its uniformity act, and its consequent persecuting principle, which they enforced with the most rigid severity. This principle Cromwell opposed with all his power; and there is not an instance in his whole history, of his voluntary disturbance of merely religious opinions.

Hence, from this principle of disapprobation of religious persecution, would naturally arise his determination to interpose in behalf of the oppressed Vaudois. Neal observes, that the Protector's zeal for the reformed religion made him the refuge of persecuted Protestants in all parts of the world.

Dr. Newton, in his Dissertation on the Prophecies, referring to this persecution of the Vaudois

by their sovereign, the Duke of Savoy, calls them
Waldenses and Albigenses; and says, that their
first and proper name seems to have been Vallenses,
because living in the valleys of Piedmont; that
they were also called Albigenses, from Alby, a
city in the southern parts of France, where great
numbers where situated; that they were afterwards denominated Valdenses or Waldenses, from
Peter Valdo or Waldo, a rich citizen of Lyons,
and considerable leader of the sect; that from
Lyons, they were also called Leonists, and Cathari,
from the professed purity of their lives and doctrines, as others since had the name of Puritans;
that they fled for refuge into foreign nations,
some into Germany, and some into Britain; that
in Germany, they multiplied so fast, notwithstanding the violence and rage of the Croisaders and
Inquisition, that it was computed, that at the beginning of the seventeenth century there were
80,000 of them in Bohemia, Austria, and the
neighbouring territories; that among a variety of
other names they were called Lollards, from one
Walter Lollard, who preached in Germany about
1315, against the authority of the Pope and super-
stitions of the church of Rome, and was buried
alive at Cologne in 1322; that in England they
were also called Lollards, though, says the Doctor,
there was a man more worthy to have given a name
to the sect, namely, John Wickliffe.

Bishop Burnet, referring to this interposition of Cromwell, observes, that he had two signal occasions given him to show his zeal in protecting the Protestants abroad : that the Duke of Savoy raised a new persecution of the Vaudois; so Cromwell sent to Mazarin, desiring him to put a stop to that, adding that he knew well, that they had that Duke in their power, and could restrain him as they pleased; and that if they did not, he must presently break with them : that Mazarin objected to this as unreasonable. He promised to do good offices, but that he could not be obliged to answer for the effects they might have : that this did not satisfy Cromwell; so they obliged the Duke of Savoy to put a stop to that unjust fury: and that Cromwell raised a great sum for the Vaudois, and sent over Morland to settle all their concerns, and to supply all their losses : that there was also a tumult in Nismes, in which some disorder had been committed by the Huguenots, and they apprehending severe proceedings upon it, sent one over, with great expedition, to Cromwell, who sent him back to Paris in an hour's time, with a very effectual letter to his ambassador, requiring him either to prevail that the matter might be passed over, or to come away immediately : that Mazarin complained of this way of proceeding as too imperious, but that the necessity of his affairs made him yield. These things, adds the Bishop, raised Cromwell's character abroad, and made him be much depended on.

. Dr. Harris, in his account of this interposition of Cromwell on behalf of the Vaudois, refers to Mr. (afterwards Sir Samuel) Morland's History of the Evangelical Churches of the Vallies of Piedmont. Mr. Morland was Secretary of State under Thurloe. This history is in the Cromwell family : it is, in the title-page, described to be an exact geographical description of the place, and a faithful account of the doctrine, life, and persecutions of the ancient inhabitants, together with a most naked and punctual relation of the late bloudy massacre (1655), and a narrative of all the following transactions to the year of our Lord 1658 ; collected and compiled with much pains and industry by Samuel Morland, Esq., during his abode in Geneva, in quality of His Highness's Commissioner-extraordinary for the affairs of the said Vallies ; and particularly for the distribution of the collected monies among the remnant of those poor distressed people. It is dedicated to Cromwell.

In this history it appears that in the year 1654 the Duke of Savoy confirmed to his Protestant subjects, the Piedmontese, by divers articles proposed by them, and assented to by him, all their religious and civil privileges. Notwithstanding, and in gross violation of these articles, these same subjects, without being charged with any crime, were, by an order, dated 25th January following (1655), directed to quit their estates and property within three days from its publication, and to be, with their families, transported to other places at the pleasure of the Duke, upon pain of death and confiscation of houses and goods, in case they did not make it appear, within twenty days, that they were become Catholics.

Morland proceeds: that these oppressed people having unsuccessfully represented to the Duke and his ministers the cruelty and injustice of this measure, so contrary also to the Duke's late concessions, quitted their houses and goods, and retired with their wives and children, the young and old, whole and sick, halt, lame, and blind, dragging all those that were infirm, either by sickness or age, through the rain, snow, ice, and a thousand difficulties: that in April of the year 1655, a great army arrived, who pillaged and devastated the country, which the people in many places resisted for a time with success, defeating the Duke's troops. Then follows an authenticated account of some part of those extraordinary cruelties that were exercised upon this oppressed people, the particulars whereof are too shocking to relate. — That the Swiss Protestant Cantons, alarmed at these proceedings, applied to the Duke of Savoy in their favour, to which the Duke replied in a complimental, but cold answer, little better than a plain denial to their request and mediation: — that upon information of this dreadful massacre, they, the Cantons, ordered a day of public humiliation, and for the making a collection for their relief, and for communicating the doleful news to their Protestant neighbours : — that the Protector being informed of these proceedings, recommended a free and liberal contribution towards their relief and support, and also awakened all his Protestant neighbours professing the same faith and religion with himself to join him in this work. He also sent a person (Mr. Morland) expressly in quality of his envoy, to the King of France and to the Duke of Savoy, to mediate on their behalf, whose mission was, for the present, successful.

The amount of the contribution so recommended by Cromwell, amounted, as stated by Morland, to 38,097*l.* 7*s.* 3*d.*, towards which Cromwell appears to have contributed 2000*l.* ; the cities of London and Westminster, 9384*l.* 6*s.* 11*d.* ; and the several parishes in England and Wales different sums.

Dr. Harris, in a note, says, that Cromwell's adversaries, who stuck at nothing to blacken him, had the boldness to affirm, in the following passage, in a publication entitled " A Letter from a true and lawful Member of Parliament," " That most of the money which was collected for this purpose was returned, and applied to the levying of a body of Swiss, to be brought over to controul the army, and reduce the people to an implicit

in his intended embassy; he justifies, as Cromwell
does, the officers' preaching, and considers the
army's successes as favourable answers: he obliges
his household, whilst in Sweden, to a strict observance of the Sabbath, notwithstanding the Queen's
and her subjects' ill observance of it; he appears
to have been as strictly a religious professor as
Cromwell; but he has never, it is believed, been
called an enthusiast or an impostor.

Perhaps the following circumstance may determine, in the estimation of these denouncers of
enthusiasm and hypocrisy, Lockhart to be one or
other of these characters. Lockhart was ambassador from Cromwell to the court of France: he
married his niece; and Bishop Burnet says of
him, that he was in high favour with Cromwell, as
he well deserved to be; that he was both a wise
and a gallant man; calm and virtuous, and one
that carried the generosity of friendship very far:
that he was, after the Restoration, sent ambassador to the court of France by the King. In Thurloe's State Papers is a letter from Lockhart to
Thurloe, dated Paris, 7th February (1656–7): he
says, that the Cardinal (Mazarin) prevailed on him
(Lockhart) to see the King's ball this night *in-
cognito:* " I have been twice invited before, and
was so pressed in it, that I was forced to own my
scruple of being there upon the Lord's day, upon
which it hath been always danced hitherto: I have
not the vanity to imagine that this night is in con-

fidelity ; so likewise it shall be his constant endeavour that what yet remains, or shall hereafter be collected and laid up in the hands of the treasurers, (who are as ready now as ever to receive what shall be further collected,) shall be improved for the best advantage of those for whom it was, or shall be, solely intended. For which end and purpose, His Highness, after mature consideration, both with his commissioners at home, and his public ministers abroad, hath already caused some part thereof to be put out to interest in sure hands, (but so that it may be called in upon urgent occasion,) and for the future will take such resolutions as the necessities of those poor people and the circumstances of their condition shall require, which (the Lord knows) is now as sad as ever in many respects, and without the same miraculous hand of Providence that hath hitherto preserved them, must in a short time inevitably perish."

In the Cromwell family are the original written accounts of this sum (part of the above collection) remitted from England. " Not only the manner of its remission, with all the circumstances belonging, but also the actual distribution amongst those poor people, with all the original acquittances," &c.

Neal says, that about 30,000l. were remitted to their (the Piedmontese) deputies, in that (1655) and the following year, at several payments : but that the confusions which followed upon the Protector's death prevented the clearing the whole account till the Convention Parliament at the Restoration, who ordered the remaining 7000*l.* to be paid.

The above passages will, it is presumed, be admitted to be a complete refutation of the forementioned charge of Cromwell's misapplication of the produce of this contribution. But it probably had its effect at the time, with those for whom it was intended, to blacken Cromwell's memory.

Bishop Burnet relates, that a person of the name of Stoupe, a foreigner, who was much trusted by Cromwell in foreign affairs, informed him of a great design Cromwell had intended to begin his kingship with, if he had assumed it; that he resolved to set up a council for the Protestant religion, in opposition to the congregation *De Propaganda Fide* at Rome : that he intended it should consist of seven counsellors and four secretaries for different provinces : these were the first, — France, Switzerland, and the Vallies; the Palatinate and the other Calvinists were the second ; Germany, the North, and Turkey, were the third ; and the East and West Indies were the fourth. The secretaries were to have 500*l.* salary a-piece, and to keep a correspondence every where, to know the state of religion all over the world, that so all good designs might be by their means protected and assisted : that Stoupe was to have the first province ; to have a fund of 10,000*l.* a-year at their disposal, for ordinary emergencies, but to be farther supplied as occasions should require : that Chelsea College was to be made up for them, which was then an old decayed building, that had been at first raised to be a college for writers of controversy. The Bishop adds, that he thought it was not fit to let such a project as this be quite lost ; it was certainly a noble one, but how far he would have pursued it must be left to conjecture. These, referring to some other passages besides the above, not immediately applicable to the present object, are, says the Bishop, all the memorable things that I have learnt concerning Cromwell, of whom so few have spoken with any temper ; some commending, and others condemning him, and both out of measure.

Dr. Harris observes, the following wish of a very modern writer will be deemed highly honourable to the memory of Cromwell. It is, he says, put into the mouth of Bishop Burnet, by the writer of a work, entitled " Moral and Political Dialogues," just after the Revolution. " Oh !" says he, " that I might see the day when our deliverer (William III.) shall become what a bold Usurper nobly figured to himself in the middle of this century, the soul and conductor of the Protestant cause through all Europe ! and that, as Rome has hitherto been the centre of slavish impositions and antichristian politics, the court of England may henceforth be the constant refuge and asylum of fainting liberty and religion."

In Thurloe's State Papers, is a letter from Burrning, the Dutch ambassador to the States-general, dated 8–18th February, 1658, wherein he says, — " My Lords, I am informed by a very good hand, that the Lord Protector doth take a great deal of pains, and hath already spent much time about the affairs of the churches of England, to bring the same, by some toleration and connivance, into a considerable and peaceable condition, to the content of all differing parties ; and that the business is already so far advanced, that a meeting is, upon certain conditions, agreed on, not under the name of a synod, but of a loving and Christian-like reception, where every one may propound for a mutual toleration. It is also firmly agreed, that to that end the Bishops and the Anabaptists shall be admitted into it, as well as the Independents and Presbyterians ; but yet with this proviso, that they shall not dispute one another's principia, but labour to agree in union ; and it is believed that the effects thereof will be to be seen in a short time."

Dr. Harris says, — he (Cromwell) was courteous and affable, and inclined to buffoonery. In proof of his courteousness and affability, he quotes the before-given passage from Sir Philip Warwick's Memoirs, in which he says, that in his conversation towards him (Sir Philip) he was ever friendly : that Whitelock, even under a sense of an injury done him by him (Cromwell), (referring to the taking from him the Great Seal,) owns he was good-natured; adding the account already given from Whitelock, of him (Cromwell) and Ireton being stopped in their way from the supping with White-lock, as a further proof of his affability and conde-scension. Also the forementioned passage from the same writer, of his affability and cheerful re-laxation, when advising with Lord Broghill, White-lock, and others of his council, upon great busi-nesses of state. Dr. Harris observes, " These passages, simply and artlessly told, strongly indicate the cheerfulness and pleasantry of Cromwell, and show how well qualified he was to conciliate the affection and regard of those whom he thought it worth his while to court." ' The Doctor adds, that this condescension sometimes inclined him to prac-tise some little arts of buffoonery. He gives the following instances : from Waller, — " That he lived mostly at Beaconsfield, where his mother dwelt in her widowhood, and often entertained Oliver Cromwell there during his usurpation, he being related to her. But notwithstanding her relation to the Usurper and Colonel Hampden, she was a royalist in her principles; and when Oliver visited her at Beaconsfield, she would frankly tell him how his pretensions would end. The Usurper used merrily to throw a napkin at her in return, and said, he would not enter into further disputes with his aunt, for so he used to call her, though not quite so nearly related." That Mr.

Cowley speaks of his flinging of cushions, and playing at snowballs with his servants. Another instance given, is the forementioned account from
Ludlow, of his (Cromwell's) termination of the
meeting of those called the Grandees of the House
and Army, to consider of a form of government,
by his throwing a cushion at Ludlow, which he
returned, by throwing another at Cromwell. Another instance is, Cromwell with his pen marking
Henry Martin in the face, and Martin doing the
like to him, at the time of signing the warrant for
the King's execution. Also Cromwell's alleged
laughing, at the time of Hugh Peters's showing, in
his sermon, the lawfulness of the execution. And,
lastly, a passage from the forementioned Dr. Bates,
— " That he would often make feasts for the inferior officers, and whilst they were feeding, before
they had satisfied their hunger, cause the drums to
beat, and let in the private soldiers, to fall on and
snatch away the half-eaten dishes. The robust
and sturdy soldiers he loved to divert with violent
and hazardous exercises, as, by making them sometimes throw a burning coal into one another's
boots, or cushion at one another's heads. When
the officers had sufficiently laughed and tired themselves with these preludes, he would wheedle them
to open their hearts freely, and by that means he
drew some secrets from the unwary, which afterwards they wished might have been wrapped up
in everlasting darkness; whilst he, in the mean

time, pumping the opinion of all others, concealed his own."

Of Cromwell's courtesy and affability there can be no doubt. The term " buffoonery" is grossly misapplied to the instances given; there is surely nothing of buffoonery in his terminating Mrs. Waller's observations upon his public conduct; it was a serious subject, which he could not think proper for their discussion; but wishing not to offend her by gravely telling her so, he laughingly and good-naturedly put an end to it. The other instances seem to be misapprehended: Cromwell's termination of the meeting, by flinging the cushion at Ludlow, seems, as related, too ludicrous for the occasion; but having learnt, as Ludlow says, the principles and inclination of those present, he might not wish a continuance of the conversation, and might think this the easiest way of getting rid of the business; it was probably a sudden thought, and it was not worth mentioning. It does not, however, come very well from Ludlow, who, instead of gravely checking this supposed levity, pursues and encourages it, following Cromwell down stairs with another cushion, and throwing it at him in his flight: but this relation seems to be given with a view, principally, of complimenting himself upon his supposed prowess, in putting to flight the victorious and hitherto invincible Cromwell. Ludlow is not defective in egotism. The highly improbable stories of his marking Henry

Martin in the face, when signing the warrant for the King's execution, and his laughing at some passages in Hugh Peters's sermon, have been already noticed. His object, in his amusements with his inferior officers and soldiers, if truly related, could be only for the keeping up of the discipline of his army, by inuring them to vigilance and privation, and athletic exercises. Similar various amusements and exercises would probably be found with the greatest commanders of all times, with the same views. The discovery of the secrets of inferior officers and private soldiers could not be Cromwell's object; they could have nothing to disclose worthy of notice. Dr. Harris gives a passage from, he says, more than one writer, relating a stratagem of Cromwell, to try the courage of his troopers in the beginning of the war: that upon the first muster of his troop, having privately placed twelve resolute men in an ambuscade, (it being near some of the King's garrisons,) upon a signal, on the appointed time, the said ambush, with a trumpet sounding, galloped furiously to the body, out of which some twenty instantly fled out of fear and dismay, and were glad the forfeiture was so cheap and easy; and ashamed of their childish and disgraceful deserting of their station and colours, had not the confidence to request their continuance in his service, or deny or scruple the rendering their horses to them who should fight the Lord's battle in their stead.

Mr. Hume says, that Cromwell, though himself
a barbarian, was not insensible to literary merit.
He mentions the foregiven instance of his attention
to Archbishop Usher, notwithstanding, he says,
being a bishop, receiving a pension from him ; that
Marvel and Milton were in his service; that Waller, who was his relation, was caressed by him;
that other eminent writers flourished in his time,
as Cowley, Sir John Denham, Hobbes, Harring-
ton, and Harvey the physician. He adds, from
Whitelock, that Sir John Davenant in the year
1658 published an opera, notwithstanding the
nicety of the times : also the circumstance of his
giving one hundred pounds a-year to the divinity-
professor at Oxford, and of his intention of erecting a college at Durham for the benefit of the
northern counties. In Thurloe is a letter from Dr.
Ralph Cudworth to Thurloe, dated 20th January,
1658, informing him of his intention to publish
some discourses in Latin, in defence of Christianity
against Judaism, which task, he says, he the rather
undertook, not only because it was suitable to his
Hebrew profession, but also because he conceived
it to be a work proper and suitable to the then
present age : that it was his purpose to dedicate
these fruits of his studies to His Highness (Richard),
to whose noble father he was much obliged, if he
might have leave, or presume so to do, &c. Mr.
Neal observes of Dr. Cudworth, that he was
universally known in the learned world for his

great learning, which he discovered in his intellec-
tual system; he should only observe, he conformed
at the Restoration, and a little before, resigned
his mastership of Clare-hall into the hands of Dr.
Dillingham, who continued it to his death. To
which instances may be added, from different writers
buoted by Dr. Harris, Dr. John Pell, eminent for
his skill in the mathematics, in the Latin, Greek,
Hebrew, Arabic, Italian, French, Spanish, and
High and Low Dutch languages, and who was
appointed envoy from the Protector to the Protestant cantons in Switzerland. Mr. (afterwards
Sir) William Petty was ordered by Cromwell to
take a survey, and make maps of the kingdom of
Ireland, for which he had a salary of 365*l.* *per
annum*, besides many other advantages, which enabled him to raise a great estate. His (Cromwell's)
presentment of the Greek manuscripts to the Bod-
leian Library; also the permission of the import-
ation duty-free, of the paper intended for Dr.
Walton's Polyglot Bible; also his preventing the
sale of Archbishop Usher's valuable library to
foreigners, by causing it to be purchased and sent
to Dublin; and many other instances might be
added of his patronage of learning and learned
men. Mr. Neal relates, that in order to secure
the education of youth, he took care to regulate
both Universities, and the public schools, by appointing new visitors; the former ceasing with the
dissolution of the Long Parliament. He (Neal)

then gives their names, and adds, that by their proper and diligent discharge of their duty, learning revived, and the Muses returned to their seats, as appeared by the number of learned men who adorned the reign of King Charles the Second, and owed their education to those times. Notwithstanding all these instances to the contrary, Mr. Hume ventures to assert, that gaiety and wit were in those times proscribed; human learning despised; freedom of enquiry detested; cant and hypocrisy alone encouraged.

Nothing appears in Cromwell's character to justify this epithet of barbarian. He, Mr. Hume, referring to the offer to him of the crown, describes the members of the committee appointed to confer with him, and to endeavour to overcome his supposed scruples, as discovering judgment, knowledge, elocution; Lord Broghill, in particular, exerting himself on this occasion: then contrasting them with Cromwell's replies. After, continues Mr. Hume, so singular a manner, does nature distribute her talents, that, in a nation abounding with sense and learning, a man who, by superior personal merit alone, had made his way to supreme dignity, and had even obliged the Parliament to make him a tender of the crown, was yet incapable of expressing himself on this occasion, but in a manner which a peasant of the most ordinary capacity, would justly be ashamed of. He (Mr. Hume) then says, "We shall produce any passage at random, for his discourse is all of a piece:" he then gives a passage from the account of the conferrence at Whitehall upon this occasion. The great defect in Oliver's speeches, continues Mr. Hume, consists, not in his want of elocution, but in his want of ideas; that the sagacity of his actions, and the absurdity of his discourse, form the most prodigious contrast that ever was known. He, however, in contradiction of his own description of Cromwell's want of ideas, but not of elocution, describes him, a few pages afterwards, as not defective in any talent except that of elocution. These passages are irreconcileable; both cannot be true.

Dr. Harris describes his speeches as generally long-winded, obscure, flat, and ambiguous, referring to his speeches at the dissolution of his first Parliament and at the above-mentioned conference at Whitehall: that the reason of these defects seems to be, sometimes the enthusiasm of his temper, which produced a kind of expression favouring of cant; other times his being necessitated to find excuses for refusing what he was desirous of; and most times a willingness to hide his real intentions. To which, continues the Doctor, probably may be added, his having been little used to speak in public assemblies on public occasions, before he seized the supreme power. But, adds he, design, I am persuaded, had the greatest share in producing some of his oddest compositions. Nevertheless, says the Doctor, he had seen and should produce copies of original letters written by him, which show that he well knew how to express himself: also, referring to his foregiven letter to the governor of Edinburgh Castle, and his speech to the Swedish ambassador; a better turned answer than which, he says, is not to be found in England, in Cromwell's age; it shows what he could do, though he seldom equalled it.

It is difficult to reconcile these vague conjectures with the contradictory facts produced by the same writers. It is not necessary, however, to the lustre of his character, to show him to have been the greatest orator of his time. Nevertheless, to prove that he was not quite so deficient in elocution as these writers represent him; to the above letters to the governor of Edinburgh Castle, and speech to the Swedish ambassador, may be added his forementioned speech upon the Self-denying Ordinance; his speech, wherein he assigns his reasons for dissolving the Long Parliament, delivered 4th July, 1653;—of the 4th September, 1654, upon the meeting of his first Parliament, which is given at length in Whitelock, and which he calls a large and subtle one; and of the 12th same September, of advice and caution to the same Parliament; upon his dissolution of that Parliament on the 22d January following. It is very long, but does not appear ambiguous, and is much to the purpose.

The following letter is given as a specimen of
Cromwell's nice sense of honour, and of his gen-
tlemanly attention to the feelings of others; and
of his abhorrence of falsehood. It is copied from
a copy taken by one of the Cromwell family from
the original letter then at Farley Castle, in Somer-
setshire, late the seat of the Hungerfords. The
address is, "For my honored friend Anthonie
Hungerford, Esq. — Sir; I understand by my
cozen Dunce, of soe much trouble of yours, and
soe much unhandsomnesse (at least seeminge so)
on my part, as doth not a little afflict me, untill I
give you this account of my innocencye. She was
pleased to tell my wife of your often resorts to my
house to visit me, and of your disappointments.
Truly S^r, had I but once known of your beinge
there, and have concealed myselfe, it had been an
action soe belowe a gentleman, or an honest man,
soe full of ingratitude for ye civillityes I have receaved from you, as w^d have rendred mee unworthy
of human societye. Believe me, S^r, I am much
ashamed that ye least color of ye appearance of
such a thinge should have happened, and could
not take satisfaction but by y^t plaine dealinge for
my justification, wch I ingeniously offer you, and
although Providence did not dispose other matters
to our mutual satisfaction, yet your noblenesse in
that overture obligeth me (and I hope shall whilst
I live) to studye upon all occasions to approve

myselfe your families and your most affectionate
and humble servant,   " O. Cromwell.
     " My wife and I desire our service bee presented
to y^r lady and family.
     " Cockpitt, Dec. 10th, 1652."

Another instance of his high sense of honour is
to be found in Whitelock, who says that a proposal
was made to the Protector to betray Dunkirk to
him for money, by its then Spanish governor,
which he refused, as a dishonourable action.

His generosity and disinterested public spirit appears in the Journals of the House of Commons of
the 24th March, 1647; — Sir John Evelyn reported from the committee of Lords and Commons
for the affairs of Ireland, sitting at Derby House,
the offer of Lieutenant-general Cromwell, for the
service of Ireland. Which was read, and was in
these words following: — " The two Houses of
Parliament, having lately bestowed 1680*l.* *per
annum* upon me and my heirs out of the Earl of
Worcester's estate; the necessity of affairs requiring assistance, I do hereby offer 1000*l.* annually,
to be paid out of the rents of the said lands; that
is to say 500*l.* out of the next Michaelmas rent,
and so on by the half years, for the space of five
years, if the war in Ireland shall so long continue,
or that I live so long; to be employed for the
service of Ireland, as the Parliament shall please to
appoint, provided the said yearly rent of 1680*l.*

become not to be suspended by war or other accident. And whereas there is an arrear of pay due unto me whilst I was Lieutenant-general unto the Earl of Manchester, of about 1500*l.*, audited and stated ; as also a great arrear due for about two years being Governor of the Isle of Ely ; I do hereby discharge the State from all or any claim to be made by me thereunto, 21° Martii, 1647." Subscribed with his name. — Ordered ; That this House doth accept of the free offer of Lieutenant-general Cromwell, testifying his zeal and good affections to the service of Ireland, and the relief of the distressed Protestants there : and that Mr. Speaker do return the hearty thanks of this House to the said Lieutenant-general Cromwell for his so free and liberal offer, to the good example and encouragement of others, liberally to contribute to so good a work. Which were given accordingly.

It is not remembered that this noble act of Cromwell is noticed in any of the histories of those times, though it must have been well known. His enemies were interested in the suppression of it.

Mr. Neal says, from the writer of his Life (Carrington) that it had been computed that he distributed forty thousand pounds a-year out of his privy purse, to charitable uses.

He had not (as has been said) been unaccustomed to speak in public assemblies : he is found frequently speaking in Parliament; and Mr. Hume acknowledges that the speeches of the parliamentary orators, during the period of the civil wars, were of a strain much superior to what any former age had produced in England; and the force and compass of our tongue were then, he says, first put to trial. And yet Sir Philip Warwick acknowledges, as before mentioned, the attention with which he was heard by the House, upon what he chooses to consider a trifling subject. These instances must surely be admitted to prove, that Cromwell does not deserve the above severe strictures upon his supposed defective elocution.

Civil wars, observes Mr. Hume, especially when founded on principles of liberty, are not commonly unfavourable to the arts of eloquence and composition; or rather, by presenting nobler and more interesting objects, they amply compensate that tranquillity of which they bereave the Muses.

Whatever ambiguity may be found in Cromwell's speeches at the conference, and upon his refusal of the crown, is no proof of his general inability of expression upon other public occasions; for, as Mr. Hume observes, while the Protector argued so much in contradiction, both to his judgment and inclination, it is no wonder that his elocution, always (he is pleased to say) confused and unintelligible, should be involved in tenfold darkness, and discover no glimmering of common sense or reasoning. The passage in this speech, given by Mr. Hume, is certainly not so well expressed as others of his speeches, and has much the appearance of confusion of mind; but it is unfair to consider this as a specimen of Cromwell's general mode of expressing himself. His mind was disturbed : he was, as the same writer observes, convinced of the solidity of the committee's reasons for urging his acceptance of the crown, and his own inclination, as well as judgment, was entirely on the side of the committee. But he was deterred, as is said by Whitelock, by some of his own family, and commonwealth's men, and part of the army; they could not bear the thought of any thing like monarchical government.

Mr. Hume, after his account of the Restoration, thinks it proper to stop a moment and take a general survey of the age, so far as regarded manners, finances, arms, commerce, arts, and sciences. — Of manners, he observes, that the gloomy enthusiasm that prevailed amongst the parliamentary party is surely the most curious spectacle presented by any history, and the most instructive and entertaining to a philosophical mind : that all recreations were in a manner suspended by the rigid severity of the Presbyterians and Independents : that horse-races and cock-matches were prohibited as the greatest enormities: that even bear-baiting was esteemed heathenish and unchristian; the sport of it, not the inhumanity, giving offence : that the manners of the two factions were as opposite as those of the most distant nations. " Your friends, the cavaliers," said a parliamentarian to a royalist, " are very dissolute and debauched." " True," replied the royalist; " they have the infirmities of men; but your friends, the roundheads, have the vices of devils, —tyranny, rebellion, and spiritual pride." It was an article, continues Hume, positively insisted on in the preliminaries to the treaty of Uxbridge, that all playhouses should for ever be abolished.

Religious profession, without regard to the sincerity or insincerity of its professors, seems to be, with Mr. Hume, a great crime : he appears to treat very lightly the licentiousness of the reign of Charles the Second, deeming excesses to be less pernicious to men of birth and fortune than to the vulgar; the contrary must surely be true : the licentiousness of the great is not only equally pernicious to themselves with the inferior orders, destroying their healths, and fortunes, and characters; but the evil consequences of their bad example spread far and wide amongst their inferiors, who are too prone to imitate them, even in vice and folly; whence that wickedness and depravity so obvious in the lower orders of every people, where this bad example prevails.

However lightly Mr. Hume may hold cock-matches and bear-baiting, they are, certainly, as is also bull-baiting and prize-fighting, or pugilism, as it is now gently termed, inhuman and unmanly, degrading amusements; and, notwithstanding Mr. Hume's contemptuous manner of expressing himself of the rigid severity of their abolition, they are, surely, both heathenish and unchristian, and ought not to be admitted amongst a people calling themselves Christians.

' The abolition of theatrical amusements was certainly an article in the treaty of Uxbridge; but the ordinance of the 2d September, 1642, given in Rushworth, only suspends them during the continuance of the sad causes and set times of humiliation therein enumerated, which are described to be the distressed estate of Ireland steeped in her own blood, and the distressed estate of England threatened with a cloud of blood by a civil war, which, says the ordinance, call for all possible means to appease and avert the wrath of God appearing in these judgments; amongst which, fasting and prayer having been often tried to be very effectual, had been lately, and were still enjoined: also, that public sports did not well agree with public calamities, nor public stage-plays with seasons of humiliation; they being exercises of sad and pious solemnity, and the other being spectacles of pleasure, too commonly expressing lascivious mirth and levity. Instead of these are recommended the profitable and seasonable considerations of repentance, reconciliation, and peace with God, which probably might produce outward peace and prosperity, and bring again times of joy and gladness to these nations.

The ordinance prohibiting cock-matches is dated

31st March, 1654: it states that public meetings and assemblies of people together in divers parts of the nation, under pretence of matches for cock-fighting, were found to tend many times to the disturbance of the public peace, and were commonly accompanied with gaming, drinking, swearing, quarrelling, and other dissolute practices, to the dishonour of God; and did often produce the ruin of persons and their families: this ordinance prohibits such meetings.

The most fastidious can surely see no gloomy enthusiasm, or fanaticism, or rigid severity in this suspension of theatrical amusements during these awful times; which, it should be observed, were not wholly done away, but only suspended to the return of better times of joy and gladness. Cock-matches are, on the contrary, wholly prohibited; and so they should be, for every reason, as one of the most vile and cruel amusements.

So far as concerns Cromwell, the following instances will be sufficient to prove that he, or those who served him, had no dislike to innocent amusements and recreations. In Thurloe is a letter, dated Lincoln, 12th March, 1655, from Major-general Whalley to Cromwell, in which he says, that he met with the Earl of Exeter at Stamford, in his way to Lincoln, who, he supposes, came on purpose to know of him, whether he (Whalley) would permit the Lady Grantham's cup to be run for at Lincoln. "If I would give way to it, he (the Earl of Exeter) should put in a horse. I assured him, it was not Your Highness's intention, in the suppressing of horse-races, to abridge gentlemen of that sport, but to prevent the great confluences of irreconcileable enemies : that he having therefore timeously advertised me of it, I should presume to give way to it; and what Your Highness, at my last waiting upon you, spoke to me, gave me encouragement thereunto. If it stand not with Your Highness's pleasure, I humbly beg it may be made known to me by Mr. Secretary."

Dr. Bates says, (from whom Dr. Harris quotes the passage,) that the nobles and great men, (for with some few of them he says he had an intimacy,) he delighted with raillery and jesting, contended with them in mimical gestures, and entertained them with many collations, music, hunting, and hawking : that when he was in the country, he used once or oftener a year to give the neighbours a buck, to be run down in his park, and money to buy wine to make merry with.

Mr. Noble says, from Heath's Flagellum, that the Protector (Oliver) was a great lover of music, and entertained those that were most skilled in it, as well as the proficients in every other science.

Whitelock, in his forementioned conversation with the Queen of Sweden, in answer to her question, whether dancing was prohibited in England, replies, that there were some who did not approve it; but that it was not prohibited by any law, and many there were that used it: but he condemns the use of it on Sundays, as in Sweden: he speaks of the Queen's fondness for balls, dancing, and music; which, adds Whitelock, being modestly and moderately used, he held indifferent things, and not unlawful in themselves; and therefore accepts the Queen's invitation to be present at a ball given by her: that about twelve o'clock at night the meeting broke up.

He (Whitelock) describes himself present, by invitation from the Queen, at a masque, at which the Queen danced in different characters, and at which he tells the Queen that any of his countrymen might have been present without offence, the whole design being to show the vanity and folly of all professions and worldly things.

That at a wedding at court of one of the Queen's nobles, the Queen, with whom Whitelock appears to have been highly in favour, came to him to take him out to dance with her, who excused himself. —"Madam" says he, "I am fearful that I shall dishonour Your Majesty, as well as shame myself, by dancing with you."—Queen. "I will try whether you can dance."—Whitelock. "I assure Your Majesty, I cannot in any measure be worthy to have you by the hand."—Queen. "I esteem you worthy, and therefore make choice of you to dance with me."—Whitelock. "I shall not so much undervalue Your Majesty's judgment, as not to obey you herein, and I wish I could remember

as much of this, as when I was a young man."—
That after they had done dancing, and Whitelock
had waited upon the Queen to her chair of state,
she said to him "*Par Dieu*, these Hollanders are
lying fellows."—Whitelock. "I wonder how the
Hollanders should come into your mind upon such
an occasion as this is, who are not usually thought
upon in such solemnities, nor much acquainted
with them."—Queen. "I will tell you all: the
Hollanders reported to me, a great while since,
that all the noblesse of England are of the King's
party; and none but mechanics of the Parliament
party, and not a gentleman among them; now, I
thought to try you and to shame you, if you could
not dance; but I see.that you are a gentleman,
and have been bred a gentleman, and that makes
me say the Hollanders are lying fellows, to report
that there were no gentlemen of the Parliament
party, when I see, by you chiefly, and many of
your company, that you are gentlemen."—Whitelock. "Truly, in this they told a great untruth to
Your Majesty, as I believe they have done in
several other particulars: I do confess that the
greatest part of our nobility and gentry were of
the King's party, but many of them likewise were
of the Parliament party; and I, who am sent to
wait upon Your Majesty, can, without vanity,
derive to myself an ancient pedigree of a gentleman: they would not have given the honour to
any but a gentleman to kiss Your Majesty's hand;

and you are pleased to do your servant right and his company, by acknowledging that our superiors have commanded gentlemen to wait on you." —Queen. "I assure you, that I esteem it the greatest honour done to me, and you are the more welcome to me because you are a gentleman; and, had I not known and found you to be so, your business would not have been so well dispatched as it is: I see you have all the qualities of a gentleman, and I believe that you were excellent in your music and dancing in your younger days."—Whitelock. "I was bred up in the qualities of a gentleman, and in my youth was accounted not inferior to others in the practice of them; but, it is so long since I used this of dancing, especially after we learned to march, that had it not been to obey Your Majesty, I should hardly have been drawn to discover my deficiencies."— Queen. "You have discovered nothing but what tends to your honour and to my contentment; and I take it as a favour that you were willing to lay aside your gravity, and play the courtier, upon my request, which I see you can do so well when you please."

The Queen, in an interview with Whitelock, said, "Your General is one of the gallantest men in the world; never were such things done as by the English in your war: your General hath done the greatest things of any man in the world; the Prince of Condé is next to him, but short of him: I have as great a respect and honour for your General as for any man alive, and I pray let him know as much from me."

The Chancellor (Oxenstierne) enquired much of Cromwell's age, health, children, family, temper, &c.; and said that Cromwell was one of the gallantest men that this age had brought forth, and that the things which he had done argued as much courage and wisdom in him, as any actions that the world had seen for many years.

Whitelock continues:—In an interview with Cromwell upon the subject and proceedings of his embassy, Cromwell asks him many very pertinent questions: as how he and his company passed over their very long wintry nights: Whitelock says, in answer, " I kept my people together, and in action and recreation, by having music in my house, and encouraging that and the exercise of dancing, which held them by the ears and eyes, and gave them diversion without any offence; and I caused the gentlemen to have disputations in Latin, and declamations upon words, which I gave them."—Protector. " These were very good diversions, and made your home a little academy."—Whitelock. " I thought these recreations better than gaming for money, or going forth to places of debauchery."—Protector. " It was much better; and I am glad you had so good an issue of your treaty."

Whitelock, in conclusion, says, " After my return into England, I often waited on the Protector, who seemed to take much contentment in discoursing me about my negotiation, and the particular passages between the Queen and me, and between the Chancellor Oxenstierne and the other great lords and senators, and officers of the army, and of the court and me, relating to the Protector's person and to the treaty. He was very inquisitive also to learn of me the polity and government of the kingdom, as well in spiritual as in civil and military matters, and of their laws and supreme councils and judicatories, and of the administration of public justice in all causes: wherein I endeavoured to give him the best satisfaction I could. The Protector seemed so well pleased with the account I gave him in this business, that he desired me to give him some notes in writing of my observations touching that matter, and of what I had related to him in my discourse on this subject: I laboured much to excuse myself from this task; but he was earnest with me to have it done, and was not to be denied, whereupon I collected the following notes," &c.

Cromwell's moral character, as has been before observed, was never seriously impeached, although surrounded by inveterate and vigilant enemies, eager to take advantage of every false step; and his strictly religious deportment is allowed, even by those who much disliked him on other accounts.

Mr. Hume says, — If we survey the moral character of Cromwell with that indulgence which is

due to the blindness and infirmities of the human
species, we shall not be inclined to load his memory
with such violent reproaches as those which his enemies usually throw upon it: that the private deportment of Cromwell, as a son, a husband, a father, a
friend, is exposed to no considerable censure, if it
does not rather merit praise: and that, upon the
whole, his character does not appear more extraordinary and unusual by the mixture of so much
absurdity with so much penetration, than by his
tempering such violent ambition and such enraged
fanaticism with so much regard to justice and
humanity.

It is difficult to common understandings to conceive the meaning of the latter part of this passage;
the terms, " absurdity and enraged fanaticism,"
do not seem intelligible, as applicable to Cromwell;
but it is curious to observe the caution and re-
luctance of his praise of his private deportment in
his several different characters: he knew that he
was in these respects irreproachable, and he should
in candour have said so.

Dr. Bates, an apostate enemy, as has been before
observed, describes his court as regulated according to severe discipline ; no drunkard, nor whore-
master, nor any guilty of bribery, to be found
there.

Mr. Neal quotes Dr. Welwood, an adversary, as
admitting that he was not addicted to swearing,
gluttony, drunkenness, gaming, avarice, or the love

of women, but kept close to his marriage-bed: that he promoted virtuous men, and was inflexible in his punishment of ill actions. He likewise quotes Mr. Eachard, also an adversary, as saying, that his court was regulated according to a most strict discipline, where every vice was banished, or severely punished: that he maintained a constant appearance of piety, and was regular in his public and private devotions: that he retired constantly every day to read the Scriptures, and prayer; and that some who watched him narrowly have reported, that after he had read and expounded a chapter, he prostrated himself with his face on the ground, and with tears poured out his soul to God for a quarter of an hour: that he was a strict observer of the Sabbath, and an encourager of goodness and austerity of life. Mr. Neal adds, that Mr. Baxter, also unfriendly to him, admits that he kept as much honesty and godliness as his cause and interest would allow; that he had a zeal for religion, meant honestly in the main, and was pious in the main course of his life, till prosperity corrupted him. This is as much as could be expected from a sour party man. He certainly praises, but most unwillingly: had he had the good fortune to please Mr. Baxter, we should have seen a juster character; but, from an enemy, it is quite sufficiently favourable to Cromwell.

In farther proof of Cromwell's regularity in his private as well as public devotions, the following anecdote is given in the Gentleman's Magazine. The letter communicating it is dated Knaresborough, March 6., but the year is omitted to be mentioned, the article having been cut out from the Magazine. This letter states that the late Sir John Goodricke, who died in the year 1789, used to relate an anecdote of Oliver Cromwell, told him when a boy, by a very old woman who had formerly attended his mother, Lady Goodricke, in the capacity of midwife, and who spent most of her latter days at Ribstone-hall: that Sir John used to give it thus in her own words: — " When Cromwell came to lodge at our house in Knaresborough, I was then but a young girl. Having heard much talk about the man, I looked at him with wonder: being ordered to take a pan of coals and air his bed, I could not, during the operation, forbear peeping over my shoulder several times to observe this extraordinary person, who was seated at the far side of the room untying his garters. Having aired the bed, I went out, and shutting the door after me, stopped and peeped through the key-hole, when I saw him rise from his seat, advance to the bed and fall on his knees, in which attitude I left him for some time; when returning again, I found him still at prayer; and this was his custom every night, so long as he stayed at our house; from which I concluded he must be a good man; and this opinion I always maintained afterwards, though I heard him very much blamed and exceedingly abused." The writer observes, " Surely no one will say, this was a parade of piety, or a pha-risaical intention to be seen of men." How far ambition might alter those sentiments afterwards, is left to the historian of those turbulent times: that the person's name who related this to Sir John Goodricke was Ellenor Ellis, whose father owned the house before mentioned: that she was born, as appears by the parish register, June 30. 1632, and was therefore twelve years old, at the siege of Knaresborough Castle: that she afterwards mar-ried a Mr. Fishwick, had several children, and died in the year 1714, aged eighty-two: that the house, which stood near the place where the Crown Inn now stands, in the High Street of Knaresborough, was taken down and rebuilt in the year 1764; but that care was taken to preserve the floor of the room where Cromwell lay.   (Signed)   " E. H."

In a letter in Thurloe, from the Countess of Ranelagh to the Lord Broghill, her brother, dated 17th September, 1658, she thus expresses her-self upon Cromwell's death :— " My dear, dear brother; I must owne not to have received the news of His Highness's death unmovedly; though, when I consider, I find it's no more than a repe-tition of that lesson that I have often binn taught, of the vanity of man in his best and highest estate. And sure he, that shall think, that that very person, who a few days before shooke all Europe

by his fame and forces, should not be able to
keepe an ague from shakeing him, nor to keepe
himselfe from being shaken into his grave by a
few fitts thereoff, even in the midest of victorys
and successes, that had raised both great féares and
great expectations of him in both his enemys and
allyes, can't but see, how wise a council that is,
which bid us cease from man whose breath is in
his nostrils; for wherein is he to be accompted of?
And how mortifying a consideration may it justly
be to all the greatnes in this world, to think that
he, who kept such a bustle in the world, should
not now be able to keep himself from crumbling
into dust, nor after he had commanded so many
vast armys and fleetes, have power to lift a finger
to remove those wormes, that his designeing
braines corrupt into. Certainly he may justly be
esteemed improvident, that after such a warneing,
shal make noe better provision for himselfe, than
the greatest stock of such vanishing greatnes
comes too, of which we have had express mani-
festations, both of his coming into and going out
of his government. And if the common charity
allowed to dead men be exersised towards him, in
burying his faults in the grave with himselfe, and
keepeing alive the memory of his vertues and
great aymes and actions, he will be allowed to
have his place amongst the worthyest of men;
and that's but a poore place neither; for though
fame be not too ayreie for opinnion to live in, it's

too little substantial for an immortal soule in the exercise of it's rational faculties to find satisfaction in. I doubt his loss will be a growing affliction upon these nations, and that we shall learne to value him more by missing him, than we did when we enjoyed him; a perverseness of our nature, that teaches us in every condition wherein we are, therewith to be discontent, by undervaluing what we have, and overvaluing what we have lost. I confes his performances reached not the makeing good of his professions; but I doubt his performances may goe beyond the professions of those, who may come after him. Al this, I say, not as grumbleing at that wise and good hand, that has taken him away, but as laying before you why I think we should not receive soe smart a blow from that hand, without haveing such a sence thereof, as may really humble us under it, and cause us soe to sett upon mending our ways by this judgement that we may prevent the worse that are yet to come, if this produce not that effect upon particular persons, and these nations in general. And now at the foote of this great accompt of loss upon publick score, I must come in with the penny-halfe-penny of my owne particular, who can, thorough the goodnes of God, say truely, I did even, when I sought his assistance, consider what has now happened, and many other accidents that might have happened, as very possible to intervene betweene my seeking and obtaineing of it," &c. This passage refers to an

application she (Lady Ranelagh) appears, in a subsequent part of her letter, to have made to Cromwell for his assistance in respect to some property
in Ireland, who appears to have written a letter
in her favour, which she considers as rendered
useless by his death.

Mr. Neal, observing upon his (Cromwell's)
government, gives a passage from the forementioned Mr. Eachard: " That the Protector having
waded through all these difficulties to the supreme
government of these nations, appeared on a sudden
like a comet or blazing star, raised up by Providence to exalt this nation to a distinguished pitch
of glory, and to strike terror into the rest of
Europe : that his management, for the little time
he survived, was the admiration of all mankind;
for though he would never suffer his title to the
supreme government to be disputed, yet his
greatest enemies have confessed, that in all other
cases distributive justice was restored to its ancient
splendour: that the judges did their duty according to equity, without covetousness or bribery;
the laws had their full and free course without
impediment or delay: men's manners were wonderfully reformed, and the Protector's court was
under an exact discipline: that trade flourished,
and the arts of peace were cultivated throughout
the whole nation, the public money was managed
with frugality, and to the best advantage ; the army
and navy were well paid, and served accordingly: that
as the Protector proceeded with great steadiness and

resolution against the enemies of his government, he was no less generous and bountiful to those of all parties who submitted to it; for as he would not declare himself of any particular sect, he gave out that it was his only wish that all would gather into one sheep-fold, under one Shepherd, Jesus Christ, and love one another: that he respected the clergy in their places, but confined them to their spiritual function.   Nor was he jealous of any that did not meddle in politics, and endeavour to raise disturbances in the state : that even the prejudice he had against the episcopal party (says Bishop Kennet) was more for their being royalists than being of the church of England ; but that when one party of the clergy began to lift up their heads above their brethren, or to act out of their sphere, he always found means to take them down : that he had a watchful eye over the royalists and republicans, who were always plotting against his person and government; but that this erecting a House of Lords, or Upper House, so quickly after his instalment, roused the malecontents, and had like to have subverted his government in the infancy of it."

Mr. Neal, in continuation, observes, that the forenamed Dr. Welwood compares the Protector to an unusual meteor, which, with its surprising influences, overawed not only three kingdoms, but the most powerful princes and states about us. A great man he was, (says he, Dr. Welwood,) and posterity might have paid a just homage to his memory, if he had not imbrued his hands in the blood of his prince, and trampled upon the liberties of his country.

That, upon the whole, adds Neal, it is not to be wondered at, that the character of this great man has been transmitted down to posterity with some disadvantage, by the several factions of royalists, presbyterians, and republicans: because each were disappointed and enraged, to see the supreme power wrested from them; but that his management was a convincing proof of his great abilities: that he was at the helm in the most stormy and tempestuous season that England ever saw; but by his consummate wisdom and valour, he disconcerted the measures and designs of his enemies, and preserved both himself and the Commonwealth from shipwreck: and that after his death, his great achievements were celebrated in verse, by the greatest wits of the age, as Dr. Sprat, afterwards Bishop of Rochester, Waller, Dryden, and others, who, in their panegyrics, outdid every thing which till that time had been seen in the English language.

Mr. Hume observes, that, amidst the passions and prejudices of that period, Cromwell should prefer the parliamentary to the royal cause, will not appear extraordinary; since, even at present, some men of sense and knowledge are disposed to think that the question, with regard to the justice of the quarrel, may be regarded as doubtful and

uncertain : that the murder of the King, the most
atrocious of all his actions, was, to him, covered
under a mighty cloud of republican and fanatical
illusions ; and it is not impossible but he might
believe it, as many others did, the most meritorious
action that he could perform : that his subsequent
usurpation was the effect of necessity, as well as of
ambition, nor was it easy to see how the various
factions could, at that time, have been restrained,
without a mixture of military and arbitrary authority.

The same writer also observes, — that it must
be acknowledged that the Protector, in his civil
and domestic administration, displayed as great
regard both to justice and clemency, as his usurped
authority, derived from no law, and founded only
on the sword, could possibly permit : that all the
chief offices in the courts of judicature were filled
with men of integrity : that amidst the virulence
of faction, the decrees of the judges were upright
and impartial ; and that to every man but himself,
and to himself, except where necessity required
the contrary, the law was the great rule of his
conduct and behaviour; and that though often
urged by his officers, as was pretended, to attempt
a general massacre of the royalists, he always with
horror rejected such sanguinary counsels.

Bishop Burnet, referring to the gentleness of
Cromwell in the instances he had given, says, —
this gentleness had, in a great measure, quieted

people's minds with relation to him; and his maintaining the honour of the nation in all foreign countries gratified the vanity which is very natural to Englishmen; of which he was so careful, that though he was not a crowned head, yet his ambassadors had all the respects paid them which our King's ambassadors ever had. He said, the dignity of the crown was upon the account of the nation, of which the King was only the representative head; so the nation being still the same, he would have the same regards paid to his ministers. He adds, that all Italy trembled at the name of Cromwell, and seemed under a panic fear as long as he lived: that his fleet scoured the Mediterranean, and the Turks durst not offend him, but delivered up Hide, who kept up the character of an ambassador from the King there, and was brought over and executed for it: that the putting the brother of the King of Portugal's ambassador to death for murder, was the carrying justice very far; since, though in the strictness of the law of nations, it is only the ambassador's own person that is exempted from any authority but his master's that sends him, yet that the practice had gone in favour of all that the ambassador owned to belong to him. Cromwell, continues the Bishop, showed his good understanding in nothing more than in seeking out capable and worthy men for all employments, but most particularly for the courts of law, which gave a general satisfaction.

Thurloe, in one of his dispatches to Whitelock, writes, — " His Highness is much resolved upon a good and solid reformation of the law, and proceedings in the courts of equity and law; the matter of law he hath committed unto Mr. Justice Hale and Mr. John Vaughan; the reformation of the Chancery to Lord Widrington, Mr. Attorney-general, and Mr. Chute, being resolved to give the learned of the robe the honour of reforming their own profession; and hopes that God will give them hearts to do it; and that no time may be lost, the next term is adjourned."

The same writer (the Bishop) relates, that the States of Holland were in such dread of him, that they took care to give him no sort of umbrage, and that, when at any time the King or his brothers came to see their sister, the Princess Royal, within a day or two after, they used to send a deputation to let them know that Cromwell had required of the States that they should give them no harbour: that King Charles, when he was seeking for colour for the war with the Dutch, in the year 1672, urged it for one, that they suffered some of his rebels to live in their provinces; Borel, then their ambassador, answered, that it was a maxim of long standing among them, not to enquire upon what account strangers came to live in their country, but to receive them all, unless they had been concerned in conspiracies against the persons of princes: that the King told him upon that, how

they had used both himself and his brother : Borel
in great simplicity answered, *Ha ! Sire, c'estoit
une autre chose ; Cromwell estoit un grand homme,
et il se faisoit craindre et par terre et par mer.*
This, says the Bishop, was very rough.   That the
King's answer was, *Je me feray craindre aussi a mon
tour ;* but that he was scarce as good as his word.

The following are the only serious charges against
Cromwell : —

The share he is alleged to have had in bringing
about the Self-denying Ordinance ; the removal of
the King from Holmby-house ; his concurrence in
the measure of bringing the King to trial ; his
determination of the Long Parliament, and, in
consequence, the republican form of government ;
and his assumption of the supreme power.

' All these charges have been before considered ;
but it may be proper, in conclusion, to add a few
words upon each of them.

The grand reliance of Cromwell's enemies was,
upon their denial of all faith in his veracity. This
Lord Clarendon, and all other the adverse writers,
endeavour to establish as a principle ; no doubt
of great use to them, in their designed misrepresentations of his actions, and the motives of those
actions ; they accordingly use this instrument very
freely. This impeachment of his veracity, necessarily, as intended, increases the difficulty of the
part of his defence depending upon his own declarations ; nevertheless, it should be remembered

that these declarations are only opposed by mere assertion on the other side.

Upon the subject of the Self-denying Ordinance, and the removal of the King from Holmby, so far as concerns Cromwell, nothing need be added to the account already given of those transactions, and to the observations thereon. To those who disbelieve the sincerity and veracity of Cromwell, and of those who acted with him, or affect so to do, nothing that can be offered will prevail upon them to acknowledge their conviction that Cromwell had not a thought of the suspension of the act in his favour; and that he came to Windsor for the express purpose (as Rushworth relates) of taking leave of the General Fairfax. It being impossible to dive into the secret motives and minds of men, the sincerity of Cromwell, and of those acting with him in this transaction, must necessarily be incapable of absolute proof: it must rest upon the several circumstances before stated, which ought to leave no doubt of Cromwell's innocence in this matter. It is, however, certain that the consequences, the speedy termination of the war, prove the necessity and wisdom of the Ordinance and of its suspension in favour of Cromwell, to whose valour and military abilities must principally, if not wholly, be attributed all the future successes of the Parliament army. And in like manner Cromwell's solemnly-repeated declarations of his ignorance of the removal, by Cornet Joyce, of the King from Holmby, must rest upon the belief of the sincerity of those declarations, and the several before-stated circumstances attending that transaction; which, to unprejudiced minds, will surely be accepted as sufficient evidence that Cromwell was not privy to it, and that it was solely the act of the agitators, for the reasons assigned by them in their foregiven narration.

Cromwell's concurrence in the measure of bringing the King to trial is not, nor can be, denied. But it is perfectly clear, from the forestated facts, that he once wished to save and restore him; and had he dealt ingenuously and sincerely with Cromwell and the other principal officers, he would have been restored (or at least the attempt would have been made) upon more favourable terms than offered by the Parliament, particularly as to religion. Ludlow expressly charges upon Cromwell as a crime this treating with the King, calling it a driving on a bargain for the people's liberty by Oliver alone.

There remains no reasonable ground of doubt that Cromwell assisted the King in his escape from Hampton-court, and that he arrived upon the coast of Hampshire in a state of perfect liberty to quit the kingdom; and that his going to the Isle of Wight was wholly his own act: that the Parliament commissioners had all the time they could wish for the negotiation with the King, of the treaty of Newport; and that it was defeated solely

by their own obstinacy in adhering to their unreasonable terms of the King's religious conformity
and other conditions, with which they might have
well dispensed, and have concluded the treaty long
before Cromwell's arrival, had that been likely to
be an obstacle to such conclusion; but it was
much more probable that Cromwell was sent out
of the way to Scotland, that he might not impede
the design of the republicans of bringing the
King to trial.

The exclusion of the members, previous and
preparatory to bringing the King to trial, has been
also attributed to Cromwell: he declares he did
not know of the design; and it was certainly determined on, and executed before his arrival in
London: and Ludlow takes to himself the whole
merit, as he deems it, of that transaction; nevertheless, severely condemning Cromwell for his subsequent dismissal of the rest of them, in his dissolution of the Long Parliament.

Nothing more need be said upon the subject
than what has been already said, to prove that
Cromwell very reluctantly came into the determination of bringing the King to trial. His
arguments with the Scots commissioners, given by
Bishop Burnet from the relation of Colonel Drummond, afterwards Lord Strathallan, so far as it
may be relied on, certainly show that he (Cromwell) had then apparently become convinced of
the necessity and justice of the determination:

whether this alteration of his conduct towards the King originated in fear of the republican party, who were hurrying on the measure, and who were jealous of him (Cromwell), does not certainly appear; but there is much reason to believe it did. The measure itself did not want defenders, upon various principles: it was certainly a very bold, though not seemingly a politic, surely not a legal one.　But it may be contended, on behalf of those concerned in it, that they deemed it to be so, in their consciences and judgments; which though no proof of the legality or rightness of the action, should moderate the severity of their adversaries' language, when speaking of those persons, and of this action.　And considering the confusions and distractions, and various opinions of those times, it should seem that it would have been honourable in the King to have extended his Act of Oblivion to those persons, and all others, without exception; but he was driven on by the Parliament, many of whom had equally contributed to the King's death and to much of the subsequent proceedings, with those that sat in judgment upon him, only they had the good fortune to escape punishment by turning round in time.

This measure has been considered, by its defenders, as an awful and useful lesson to sovereigns, of the danger of offending their subjects by illegal or violent treatment; but it may surely also be equally useful as a caution to subjects, not, by intemperate language, to provoke or irritate their sovereigns in their seeking redress of real or imaginary grievances: both carried beyond a certain point must produce irreconcileableness, terminating in intestine commotion and war, and in final revolution and confusion.

His (Cromwell's) reasons for his determination of the Long Parliament, and, in consequence, the republican form of government, and the circumstances that led to it, are before given. The measure was self-defensive; he had no alternative but to submit to the government of the Presbyterian republic, which, both civil and religious, he detested, and who certainly would have availed themselves of the first opportunity to rid themselves of him and the other chiefs of the independent party; or to take upon himself the government of the country, which he had an equal right with them to do, in the absence of monarchy.

The republican government itself was, as has been observed, an usurpation upon the monarchy; the House of Commons, immediately after the King's death, took upon themselves to determine the House of Peers to be useless and dangerous, and upon the abolition of the kingly office, as unnecessary, burdensome, and dangerous to the liberty, safety, and public interest of the nation; and reduced the government to a commonwealth. All this appears to have been accomplished by a small number of the Commons' House. The whole House, had all the members been present, even with the concurrence of the House of Lords, had no right to change the form of government; they came together as one branch only, of a constitution composed of the three estates, of King, Lords, and Commons; and it is conceived they could not alter that form without resorting to the people for fresh specific powers. It is very generally admitted, that they had greatly abused their power, and which they were in the act of continuing and perpetuating at the moment of their dissolution. Cromwell felt himself of sufficient strength to put an end to this tyrannical government; and to the satisfaction of the nation, who were tired of them, accomplished it with no more force than was necessary to the occasion, and without bloodshed.

The writer of the " Modest Vindication of Oliver Cromwell from the unjust Accusations of Lieutenant-general Ludlow," observing upon this dissolution, says, that no man was higher extolled, no man more basely vilified; no man worse, no man better spoken of, as interest led the judgments of men: that the Presbyterians, with Baxter at their head, affirm it was an act of rebellion, perjury, perfidiousness, and impudence, to turn so many of their members out of the House at once. The republican party say, No; that was no crime at all, but it was a villainous, barbarous, perfidious act to dissolve the Rump. Whence, continues this writer, it is naturally concluded, that until both parties can make out their diametrical infallibility in these points, Cromwell's reputation stands irreproachable as to those acts with which they charge him, committed against themselves.   And there is a passage in Whitelock's Swedish embassy, mentioning that at a meeting in 1658, of the King's chief agents, one of them asked what would be their advantage when they should have taken off Cromwell and Lambert, seeing that the present men in power were but a company of giddy-headed men; that some of the old men, as Bradshaw, St. John, Whitelock, Rolles, Vane, &c., would take the opportunity to bring themselves into power again, and that if one of those got it into their hands, we should never get it out again; they being the men that turned the whole of the nation formerly; and that what Cromwell did, was by force to take it out of their hands, lest he should be turned out himself.

Cromwell's assumption of the supreme power (upon the surrender to him by the Parliament that succeeded the Long Parliament, of its power, which was derived from him,) was the natural consequence of such surrender.   A new form of government became necessary.   At the time of the meeting, mentioned by Whitelock, in 1651, of divers members of Parliament, and chief officers of the army, soon after the battle of Worcester, it is evident that the form of the government of the country was not considered as finally settled and acquiesced in, although the republican form had been declared, the nation had not been accustomed to that form, and it appears to have been arbitrarily exercised. The meeting was for. the express purpose of considering of a settlement of the government of the nation, whether republican, or mixed monarchical, upon which there were different opinions: Cromwell declared himself in favour of some mixture of monarchy. It is unfair to say that his preference of monarchy arose from his design of assumption of the supreme power; he certainly greatly disliked the lately dissolved republic, as a tyranny, both in its form and exercise, and had always felt that it had been his inveterate enemy, jealous of his growing greatness, and watching for every opportunity of crushing him, to whom they owed all their own power and consequence. If his negotiations with the King for his restoration were sincere, and there is no reason for doubt of his sincerity, he could not then have had a thought of his own elevation. In anwer to Whitelock's proposal to Cromwell to restore the King (Charles the Second) in the foregiven conversation, wherein he had proposed himself to be King, he acknowledges Whitelock's proposition to be reasonable, but defers its consideration, as a matter of high importance and difficulty, to a future time. Experiencing, as he had, the difficulties attending his treaty with the late King, and the ill success of it, he must surely consider the proposed treaty with his son as a matter of at least as high importance and difficulty. Lord Broghill, to show that Cromwell did not, even after the King's death, appear to be averse to the restoration of the royal family, relates, in his Memoirs, the following passage : — That after the wars of Ireland were finished, that kingdom settled, (Cromwell being made Lord Protector,) a parliament was called; the members of which were taken out of the three kingdoms, whereof Lord Broghill was one : that His Lordship had now and then opportunities of a secret correspondence with some persons about the King, by whom he had sounded the King's inclinations, which were favourable to a design of making a match between His Majesty and one of Cromwell's daughters, (the Lady Frances, as I remember,) to promote which he had orders to do whatsoever lay in his power : and that, having His Majesty's leave, he took a fit occasion to move it to Cromwell, which he did in the following manner : — He first acquainted Cromwell's wife and daughter with his design, and then caused a rumour of it to be spread abroad in the town; and one day coming out of the city, and going to Cromwell's closet, Cromwell immediately came to him, and walking with him alone, he asked where he had been? My Lord answered, in the city: Cromwell asked him, what news there? My Lord answered, very strange news: Crom-

well earnestly enquiring what it was, My Lord
detained him awhile, only by repeating it was
strange news, and smiling at the same time.
Cromwell, by the delay, became more earnest to
know it. My Lord at last replied, that perhaps
he would be offended to hear it. Cromwell,
not well enduring any longer delay, assured
him he would not, and therefore conjured him to
tell it. Upon that, in a jocular way, My Lord told
him all the news in the city was, that he was going
to marry his daughter Frances to the King. Cromwell, then, with a merry countenance, asked him
— And what do the fools think of it? My Lord
then replied, All liked it, and thought it the wisest
thing he could do, if he could accomplish it. Upon
that, Cromwell made a stand; and looking stead-
fastly in my Lord's face, asked him — And do you
believe so too? His Lordship seeing him a little
moved, answered, he did believe it was the best
thing he could do to secure himself. Cromwell
then walked up and down the room with his hands
behind him in a very thoughtful manner; and at
last asked My Lord, what reason he had to be of
that belief? His Lordship represented to him,
how little he could confide in those of his own
party, being upon every occasion subject to murmur and repine; how unlikely it was for him to
continue long in that grandeur, the very same persons who set him up being willing to pull him
down; and, on the other hand, the King, in his

great exigencies, would be ready enough to hearken
to any proposition rather than live in exile; so
that he might make his own terms with him, and
be General of all the forces during life; the loyal
party would readily join with him in the work;
and if his daughter had children by the King
(which was likely enough), he would thereby be
endeared to King and country, and would have
such interest in the crown, that nobody could ever
attempt any thing against him; having a King his
son-in-law, an heir-apparent to the crown his
grandson, and the whole power of the nation in his
own hands; by all which his greatness would be
for ever established: whereas if he neglected these
means, he could not expect to transmit his greatness to his next heir, and, perhaps, would hardly
be able to preserve it during his own life: that
Cromwell gave great attention to these reasons;
but, walking two or three times, and pondering
with himself, he told Lord Broghill the King
would never forgive him the death of his father.
His Lordship desired him to employ somebody to
sound the King in this matter, to see how he would
take it, and offered himself to mediate it for him;
but Cromwell would not consent, but again repeated, — the King cannot, and will not forgive
the death of his father; and so he left His Lordship,
who durst not tell him he had already dealt with
His Majesty on that affair. — That upon this, My
Lord withdrew, and meeting with Cromwell's wife

and daughter, they enquired how he had succeeded; of which having given them an account, he added, they must try their interest in him; but none could prevail. Bishop Burnet gives this conversation as from Lord Broghill himself, with some variations, and with this addition, — that Cromwell replied, in the course of the conversation, that the " King (Charles II.) was so damnably debauched he would undo us all." And so turned, says the Bishop, to another discourse, without any emotion, which made Orrery (Broghill) conclude he had often thought of that expedient. This phrase, " damnably," is not Cromwell's language.

He (Cromwell) here assigns his reasons for deeming a treaty with the King impracticable; which, after experience of the King, did not prove to be incorrect.

Cromwell, thus circumstanced, had no other alternative than to assume the supreme power, or to let the nation return to its republican government; and, surely, his mixed monarchical form was most consonant to the habits and dispositions of the nation, which suffered no inconvenience from it; on the contrary, was, by his great talents and magnanimity, raised to the highest point of prosperity and renown, both at home and abroad, as universally allowed by his greatest enemies. He is aware that he is accused of creating necessities for the purpose of bringing about his various designs; but in one of his speeches to his Parliament before-given, he solemnly declares, not only to that assembly, but to the world, that the man lived not that could come to him and charge him, that he had, in those great revolutions, made necessities.

Rapin, at the conclusion of his history of Cromwell's protectorate, observes, that to form a just and rational idea of his character, his conduct and actions in themselves must be examined, and joined to the juncture of the time, independently of the opinions of his enemies.

Cromwell had no want of panegyrists to celebrate his memory; but they meanly and contemptibly turned round with the times, and then, most disgracefully to themselves, equally vilified and abused it.

No one, after the Restoration, durst come forward to do justice to his character, of the many who, though his enemies, had experienced his lenity and kindness, nor any one of those who owed to him all their consequence: and he was not present to answer for himself. Every circumstance and anecdote of his life, both public and private, has been, without examination of its truth or falsehood, assiduously brought forward, uncontradicted or unexplained, and implicitly received and distorted in every imaginable way, for the purpose of defaming his memory: whence originated all the obloquy under which it has been handed down, in some degree, even to the present times.

But it is hoped and presumed, that the preeeding account of him will have placed his character in its just light; and that he will be found to have been a good, as well as a great man, undeserving of the virulent and uncharitable denunciations of Lord Clarendon, and others implicitly following him in his bitter invectives.

Richard Cromwell

eldest son of Oliver Cromwell.

Drawn and Engraved by W. Bond, from a three
quarter Portrait, in the Possession of Oliver Cromwell Esq.

Published by Longman, Hurst, Rees, Orme, & Brown, London, Jan.ᵉ 1ˢᵗ 1820.

CHAPTER XV.

In continuation, from the death of Oliver Cromwell to the abdication of Richard Cromwell —

Whitelock proceeds. — Immediately upon his
(Oliver Cromwell's) death the council assembled,
and being satisfied that the Protector, in his life-
time, according to the petition and advice, had
declared his son (Richard Cromwell) to be his
successor, caused the same to be proclaimed, in
a solemn manner, in London and Westminster,

and they went the same day to him (Richard Cromwell) to acquaint him with it, and sent a committee of the council into the city to inform them thereof.   Then there follows the proclamation.

The council gave the oath to Richard; and, with his consent, another proclamation was published for all, that were officers in his father's time, to continue in their places.

10th September, 1658.   Richard and his council kept a day of humiliation, and ordered the keeping of it another time in London.

Several addresses came to the new Protector, declaring satisfaction in his succession, and resolution to adhere to him; also, an address from the sea-officers, acknowledging Richard, and promising to stand by him; and from General Monck and his officers in Scotland: also, an address from the gentlemen and freeholders of the county of Buckingham, to which Richard made very good and prudent answers.

18th October.   Audience given by Richard to the French ambassador;   when he carried himself discreetly.

16th November.   Addresses from the officers of the army, presented by General Desborough; and the officers of the army attended, and made large professions of their obedience and faithfulness; and he courted them at a high rate.

23d November.   The funeral of the late Protector was celebrated with great solemnity.

26th November.   Richard knighted General
Morgan, a very gallant person.

Several audiences were given by Richard to
foreign ministers, sent to him from neighbouring
princes and states, to condole the death of his
father, and to congratulate his succession to the
government.

December.   Richard, by advice of his council,
determined to call a Parliament, to meet on the
27th day of January then next.

January.   Whitelock met about the business of
the Great Seal, whereof he was then again made
a commissioner: that Richard had a particular
respect for him; and upon the 22d of this month,
by advice of some near to him, without any seeking for it by Whitelock, he was sent for to Whitehall, where he met the two Lords Commissioners
of the Seal, Fiennes and L'Isle, and they together
being called into the council-chamber, the Great
Seal was delivered to His Highness, sitting in
council, who presently delivered it to the three,
as Keepers of the Great Seal of England.

Journals of the House of Commons, 27th January.   The Parliament met; and the oath appointed by the humble additional and explanatory
petition and advice, to be taken by every member,
of either House of Parliament, before he sit in
Parliament, was administered accordingly; the
substance of which was, — to maintain the true
reformed Protestant Christian religion in the purity

thereof, as contained in the Holy Scriptures of the Old and New Testament; and to be true to the Lord Protector of the commonwealth of England, Scotland, and Ireland, as chief magistrate thereof.

Same day. Mr. Chaloner Chute was chosen Speaker of this Parliament: an excellent orator, says Whitelock, and of great parts and generosity; whom many doubted that he would not join with the Protector's party; but he did heartily.

The members of the House of Lords, says Whitelock, took their places, being summoned by the like writ as they had before, according to the petition and advice.

Journals, January 28. A fast was appointed for humiliation and seeking of God for his special assistance and blessing upon the endeavours of the House.

February 1. A bill for the recognition of His Highness's right and title to be Protector and chief magistrate of the commonwealth of England, Scotland, and Ireland, and the dominions and territories thereto belonging, was this day read the first time. And a second time on Monday the 7th, and the debate adjourned to the following morning, when again debated and adjourned.

Whitelock says, some were very cross in this business, which caused doubts of the good issue of the Parliament.

Journals, April 6th (1659). The House resolved

that in all messages unto and conferences with the other House, the like respect, and no other, be observed by the members of this House, that is observed by the persons sitting in the other House. And Whitelock relates, that, about the same time, a representation was signed by almost all the officers of the army, and afterwards presented to His Highness, setting forth their want of pay, the insolencies of their enemies, and their designs, together with some in power, to ruin the army and the good old cause, and to bring in the enemies thereof. To prevent which, and to provide against free quarter, they desire him to advise with the Parliament and to provide effectual remedy. Now, says Whitelock, there being nothing done thereupon, the soldiers began to speak high and threatening. This, adds he, was the beginning of Richard's fall, and set on foot by his relations; Desborough, who married his aunt, and Fleetwood, who married his sister, and others of the party: and the Parliament disputed about the other House, but took no course to provide money, but exasperated the army, and all those named of the other House. He adds, that on the 17th April, the Protector sent for the officers of the army, and had conference with them.

Thursday, April 7. A report from the committee appointed to inspect the accounts of the public revenue, with the ordinary expense of the commonwealth of England, Scotland, and Ireland, for one year; with a state of the public debts: —

	£	s.	d.
The income of England, is stated to be	1,517,274	17	1
Scotland,	143,652	11	11
Ireland,	207,790	0	0
The whole issues of England, for a year,	£1,547,788	4	4½
Ditto of Scotland,	307,271	12	8½
Ditto of Ireland,	346,480	18	3
The annual income of England, Scotland, and Ireland, is	£1,868,717	9	0
The annual issues of ditto	2,201,540	15	4
The balance is	£332,823	6	4

The whole of the public debt, £2,474,290.

The proceedings upon the forementioned bill, and the vote of the House to take into consideration the constitution of the Parliament in two Houses, appear by the Journals to have occasioned great and warm debates; and Whitelock observes, much discourse and doubts of many, lest a disagreement should follow; and that some of the court and relations of Richard were not backward to promote a difference, and that Heselrigge, and Sir Henry Nevil, and their flock, were a great cause of disturbance in this Parliament: that the Parliament grew into heats, these two persons and their party labouring to overthrow the government by a Protector and two Houses of parliament, in order

to a free commonwealth.; with whom divers of the
officers joined : and that Desborough, Fleetwood,
Sir Henry Vane, Berry, and others, endeavoured to
lessen Richard's power : that he (Richard Cromwell) advised with Lord Broghill, Fiennes, Thurloe,
Wolseley, Whitelock, and some others, upon the
necessity and fitness of dissolving the Parliament;
that he (Whitelock) doubted the success of it, and
wished a little longer permission of their sitting,
especially now they had began to consider of raising money, whereby they would engage the soldiers:
but most were for the dissolution from the fear of
the army and of the cavaliers who now flocked to
London, and secretely fomented the divisions ; and
accordingly it was dissolved by commission.——
That Richard Cromwell and his council sat close
to consult what was fit to be done, among whom
were many enemies to him and his government :
that he was abused and betrayed by his near relations, and those of his council : that he (Whitelock)
was wary in his advice, but declared his judgment
honestly and for his good, when it was required :
but that Lambert and other officers of the army
consulted how they might again bring in the old
members of the Parliament, whom they had before
thrust out : that all matters were at a stand, and
the army had thoughts of raising money without a
parliament, but found they durst not venture upon
it, and thought it a safer way to restore the members of the Long Parliament : that the great officers

were advised against this measure, most of these members being supposed to be discontented for their having been broken up by the late Protector, and to distaste the proceedings of the army; and that it would probably increase the divisions, and finally bring in the King: but that the officers were determined upon restoring the Long Parliament; and that, accordingly, Fleetwood and the general council of officers published a declaration, inviting the members of that parliament who had continued sitting since the year 1648, (the year of the King's death,) until April 1653, the time of its dissolution, to return to the exercise and discharge of their trust: and Lambert and others went to the old Speaker (Lenthal) at the Rolls and presented him this declaration, and divers of the members of the Long Parliament came to him and declared their willingness to meet again, and accordingly met in the Painted Chamber on the following morning, Saturday, May 7th (1659), and proceeded in a body to the House, Lambert guarding them with soldiers. They immediately passed a declaration of their purpose to secure the property and liberty of the people, both as men and as Christians, and that, without a single person, kingship, or House of Peers, and to uphold magistracy and ministry.

The following is from the journals, Saturday the 7th May (1659). Henry Middleton, Esq. is appointed sergeant-at-arms, and John Phelpes, Esq.

clerk of the Parliament, for such time as the Parliament should think fit, not exceeding one week.

The Speaker then acquaints the Parliament, that the Lord Lambert, with divers of the officers of the army, in the name of the Lord Fleetwood, and council of officers of the army, had upon the preceding day come to him, many of the members of Parliament being then present, and delivered to him a declaration, (the preceding declaration,) which was then read; and it was referred to a committee to prepare a declaration, according to the substance of the then present debate, upon this declaration, then read. Then follows the forementioned declaration of the Commons. And letters were sent, signed by the Speaker to the several members of Parliament that were absent, desiring their attendance.

The Lord Fleetwood, Sir Arthur Heselrigge, Sir Henry Vane, Lieutenant-general Ludlow, Colonel Sydenham, Major Salwey, and Colonel John Jones, or any four or more of them, were made a committee of safety, and to continue for eight days and no longer. And a meeting was appointed of the Parliament on the following morning in the Parliament House, to seek the Lord for his guidance and blessing on the Parliament.

Lord's day, May 8. The House met this morning and spent it in praying and hearing the Word: Dr. Owen praying and preaching before them.

Monday, May 9. Major Salwey reported from

the committee of safety, that they had received good intelligence that Charles Stuart designed speedy invasion, and that many of his party were lately come into England, and that it had been endeavoured to seduce the army; and that several had been apprehended. The Lord Lambert, Colonel Disbrow, Colonel Bury, and Mr. Scot, by the desire of the committee, added thereto.

The Lord Fleetwood presented a letter from General Monck, giving an account of the quiet state of the army in Scotland, and their concurrence with the army of England. And desire that this Parliament might again sit. Also, letters from the army of Ireland.

These passages, says Whitelock, gave the more hopes to many, that this Parliament thus restored might be blessed of God, for settling the peace and liberty of the nation; and the more, because they were upon the first right and foundation of that Long Parliament, which had done so great things: and therefore divers were the better satisfied to go on with them.

A new Great Seal ordered to be prepared according to the form of the last Great Seal, made by authority of this Parliament: and the last Great Seal to be brought to the House to be broken before the Parliament. And Whitelock, referring to this new seal, says his and the other commissioners' office thereupon ceased.

Wednesday, May 11. Resolved, as the opinion

of this committee (of safety), That for the better
constituting and establishing of the land-forces of
this commonwealth, five persons, whereof the
Commander-in-chief to be one, be authorised as
commissioners, and they or any three or more of
them to nominate the commission-officers of the
said forces, and present the same to the Parliament
or council of state for the time being for their
approbation; and when approved by the Parliament
or council, that the Commander-in-chief do issue
out commissions accordingly, and to sign the same
by direction of the council of state by authority
of Parliament. Lord Charles Fleetwood to be
Lieutenant-general, and Commander-in-chief of the
land-forces in England and Scotland.

Friday, May 13. Upon the debate of the above
report, Lord Charles Fleetwood and others were
nominated commissioners: but that the commission to the Lieutenant-general and Commander-in-
chief of the land-forces in England and Scotland
shall be from the Parliament.

Friday, May 13. (post-meridiem.) A bill for
constituting a council of state, with instructions,
was read the first time.

Resolved, That the time for the continuance of
the council of state be till the 1st day of December next ensuing: that the number consist of 31;
and that ten of the number be of persons not members of Parliament.

The new Great Seal, prepared by Mr. Simonds,

was brought into the House, and the former seal destroyed.

Referred to the members of Parliament that are of the committee of safety, to take into consideration the present condition of the eldest son of the late Lord-General Cromwell, and to inform themselves what his estate is, and what his debts are; and how they have been contracted, and how far he doth acquiesce in the government of this commonwealth, as it is declared by this Parliament; and to offer upon the whole what they conceive expedient in his behalf, to the Parliament.

Whitehall and Somerset House to be sold, and the produce to be applied towards satisfaction of the arrears due to the army.

Saturday, May 21. Resolved, That to the end the legislative authority of this commonwealth may not, by their long sitting, become burdensome or inconvenient, there shall be effectual provision made for a due succession thereof.

Tuesday, May 24. Sir Henry Vane reports from the council of state, a letter subscribed H. Cromwell, dated from Dublin, the 18th May, instant; which was read, and referred back to the council of state, to take into their consideration what is fit to be done as to Ireland; and to represent their opinion to this House.

Wednesday, May 25. Sir Gilbert Pickering acquainted the House, that he and the Lord-Chief-Justice St. John had, according to the command

of the House, repaired to the eldest son of the late
Lord-General Cromwell, and acquainted him with
the sense of this House touching his subscribing a
paper sent by him to the committee formerly appointed to communicate to him a declaration and
order of this House; and that he did thereupon,
in their presence, sign the said paper with his
name, and they presented the said paper to this
House, subscribed Richard Cromwell.

The paper was this day read, and also a schedule containing a state of his debts, and an account
of his estates.

The Parliament declared their acceptance in
good part, of the expressions of the paper, and did
take upon them his debts, not exceeding the sums
contained in this schedule, and referred to a committee to consider of the payment thereof; and
that 2000*l.* be forthwith advanced to him for his
present occasions; and referred to a committee to
consider of a settlement of a comfortable and honourable subsistence on him.

Whitelock, referring to this resignation of Richard's Protectorship, observes, that an address to the
Parliament was sent from the army in Scotland,
congratulating them on their happy restoration to
the government of the nations; and seeing, say
they, that His late Highness (Richard Cromwell)
had been pleased to manifest so much self-denial
and love to his country, in appearing for the interest thereof against his own, they humbly en-

treated that some speedy care might be taken for him and his family, together with Her Highness Dowager, that there may be such an honourable provision settled upon them, and such other dignities as were suitable to the former great services of that family to these nations. They conclude with promising to the Parliament their support. This address, adds Whitelock, was signed by General Monck, and several others.

Tuesday, June 7. Resolved and declared, That the administration of the government of Ireland should be by commissioners nominated and authorised by the Parliament, and not by any one person; and that Colonel Henry Cromwell be made acquainted with the resolutions of this House, concerning the government of Ireland; and that he do forthwith repair to the Parliament, to acquaint them with the state of affairs there.

Referred to a committee to examine what was due for mourning for the late Lord-General Cromwell, and how the same might be paid for, without prejudice or charge to the commonwealth. Lieutenant-general Fleetwood acquainted the House, that Colonel Henry Cromwell was come to town, and attended to give this House an account of the management of affairs in Ireland. Referred to the council of state, and the council to do therein as they should think fit; and that Colonel Cromwell have liberty to retire himself into the country, whither he should think fit, upon his own occasions.

Saturday, July 16. Colonel John Jones reported from the committee for considering of a comfortable and honourable subsistence on Richard Cromwell — That his present clear yearly revenue, amounting (according to the forementioned schedule) to 1299*l.* over and above the jointure therein mentioned, be made up to him 10,000*l. per annum,* during his life. Lands of inheritance of 5000*l. per annum* value, to be settled upon him and his heirs, and thereupon 5000*l.*, part of the sum making up the 10,000*l.*, to be abated; and as the jointures should fall in, the sum making up the 10,000*l.* to abate in proportion.—The debt undertaken to be paid by Parliament to be satisfied by sale of the plate, hangings, &c. of Whitehall and Hampton-court.

Lord Clarendon, introductory of his account of Richard Cromwell's succession to the Protectorate, says,—Contrary to all expectation, both at home and abroad, the earthquake (Oliver Cromwell's death) was attended with no signal alteration: that it was believed that Lambert would be in the head of the army, and that Monck, in Scotland, would never submit to be under him: that besides the expectation the King had, from the general affection of the kingdom, he had fair promises from men of interest in it, and of command in the army, who professed to prepare for such a conjuncture as this; and that the disorder arising from Cromwell's death might dispose Lockhart to depend upon the best title seemed a reasonable expectation, but that nothing of this fell out: that never monarch, after he had inherited a crown many descents, died in more silence, nor with less alteration; and there was the same, or a greater calm in the kingdom, than had been before: that foreign princes addressed their condolences to him (Richard Cromwell), and desired to renew their alliances; and nothing was heard in England but the voice of joy, and large encomiums of their new Protector; so that the King's condition never appeared so hopeless, so desperate; for a more favourable conjuncture his friends could never expect than this, which now seemed to blast all their hopes, and confirm their utmost despair.

It is probable, continues His Lordship, that this melancholic prospect might have continued long, if this child of fortune could have sat still and been contented to have enjoyed his own felicity; but his council thought it necessary that he should call a Parliament, to confirm what they had already given him, and to dispel all clouds which might arise.

But His Lordship adds, there might be the more reason for it (the calling the Parliament), because the last alliance that Oliver had made with the crown of Sweden, and of which he was fonder than all the rest, obliged him, in the spring, to send a strong fleet into the Sound, to assist that king against Denmark, or at least to induce Denmark,

by way of mediation, to accept of such conditions
as the other would be willing to give him: that
this could hardly be done without some assistance
of Parliament, and that therefore the new Protector sent out his writs to call a Parliament, to meet
on the 27th January; till which day, for near five
months, he remained as great a prince as ever his
father had been.

His Lordship, referring to the disputes in the
Commons, in settling the act of recognition for
confirming Richard Cromwell's authority, and
upon their objection to the allowance of the House
of Peers to be part of the government, says, —
" The stirring these several humours, and the
drowsy temper of Richard, raised another spirit in
the army: that a new council of officers met by
their own authority, and admitted Lambert, though
no member of the army, to consult with them:
that they neither liked Protector nor Parliament,
but consulted what government to settle, that
might be better than either; yet they would not
incense them both together, nor appear to have
any disinclination to Richard, who had many of
his nearest friends amongst them." His Lordship
then mentions the army's address to him, complaining of the great arrears of pay due to the army,
and of various other supposed grievances, requesting him to represent those their complaints to the
Parliament, and to require proper and speedy remedies. He then relates the votes of the Parlia-

ment in consequence, and the army's employment of Fleetwood and Disbrow to advise him (Richard) forthwith to dissolve the Parliament; also his determination to dissolve it the next morning, notwithstanding the advice of many of his friends to the contrary, and his signing the commission for that purpose; and the Commons' adjournment for three days to prevent it, imagining, His Lordship says, that they should by that time convert Richard from destroying himself. But, adds His Lordship, the poor creature was so hared by the council of officers, that he presently caused a proclamation to be issued out, by which he did declare the Parliament to be dissolved: and that, from that minute, nobody resorted to him, nor was the name of the Protector afterwards heard of, but in derision; the council appointed guards to attend at Westminster, which kept out those members, who, in pursuance of their adjournment, would have entered into the House upon the day appointed: that thus, by extreme pusillanimity, the son suffered himself to be stripped in one moment, of all the greatness and power which the father had acquired in so many years, with wonderful courage, industry, and resolution.

His Lordship observes, that this Parliament was, in derision, called the Rump Parliament, as being the fag-end of a carcase long since expired.

. He describes their application to Richard Cromwell for his acquiescence in their new-formed government, who, His Lordship says, already humbled to that poverty of spirit they could wish, gave the committee a paper containing the state of his debts, and how contracted; also his forementioned acquiescence.

This, says His Lordship, satisfied them as to Richard; but they were not without apprehension that they should find a more refractory spirit in his brother Harry, who was lieutenant of Ireland, and looked upon as a man of another air and temper: that he had, in his exercise of that government, by the frankness of his humour, and a general civility towards all, and very particularly obliging some, rendered himself gracious and popular to all sorts of people, and might have been able to have made some contests with the Parliament: but that, as soon as he received an order from them to attend them in person, he thought not fit to be wiser than his elder brother, and came over to them even sooner than they expected, and laid his commission at their feet, which they accepted, and put the government of that kingdom into the hands of Ludlow and four other commissioners.

By way of last blow at the Cromwell family, His Lordship indulges himself in relating the following story of Richard Cromwell: he says, — It may not prove ingrateful to the reader in this place, to entertain him with a very pleasant story that related to this miserable Richard, though it hap-

pened long afterwards.   His Lordship then relates,
that shortly after the King's return, and the manifest joy that possessed the whole kingdom thereupon, this poor creature found it necessary to
transport himself into France, more for fear of his
debts than of the King, who thought it not necessary to enquire after a man so long forgotten.   He
then relates his living some years in Paris under
an assumed name, and in an obscure condition,
not having above one servant to attend him, and,
upon the expectation of a war between England
and France, his quitting that kingdom and removing to Geneva, and in his way passing through
Pezenas, a town belonging to the Prince of Conti,
who resided there, being then governor of Lan-
guedoc, to whom he was introduced as an English
gentleman, and who, after enquiring the state of
England, expressed himself thus : — " Well, Oliver, though he was a traitor and a villain, was a
brave fellow, had great parts, great courage, and
was worthy to command ; but that Richard,—that
coxcomb, coquin, poltron, was surely the basest
fellow alive : what is become of that fool ?   How
was it possible he could be such a sot ?"   He answered, he was betrayed by those whom he most
trusted, and who had been most obliged by his
father.   He quickly took his leave, and quitted
the town, and soon afterwards the Prince heard
who he was.

In the relation of this story, which is more likely
to be false than true, it not appearing to be related

by any other writer, and His Lordship giving it as
a mere story, without any authority for its truth,
he appears to take an unfeeling and unmanly
pleasure. He would probably have expressed himself differently, could he have foreseen that he
would soon be also an unpitied exile. Had His
Lordship only mentioned this departure of Richard
for the continent, much credit would not perhaps
have been due to it, as it is not recollected to have
been mentioned by any of the family; but it is
confirmed incidentally by Ludlow, who says, that
he quitted England in the vessel that had carried
over Mr. Richard Cromwell some weeks before.
As Ludlow gives no dates, the precise time of his
(Richard's) quitting England cannot now be ascertained; it was probably soon after the Restoration.

Ludlow gives a minute account of the proceedings and machinations of the principal officers of
the army (of whom himself, Fleetwood, Lambert,
and Disbrow, were some of the most active,) to
deprive Richard Cromwell of his protectorate, and
which produced the partial restoration of the Long
(Rump) Parliament. He says that Sir Charles
Coot went post to Ireland to carry the news of this
great alteration to Colonel Henry Cromwell; and
that Colonel Ingoldsby hastened after him, to consult what might be done to continue their reign;
and that all possible care was taken to maintain
themselves; and that Colonel Cromwell called a
council of officers, and proposed to them to declare

themselves ready to stand by and defend Richard
Cromwell, which they declined till they should see
what course would be taken by the army in England : also Henry Cromwell's consequent return to
England upon the requisition of the Parliament,
and his (Ludlow's) departure for Ireland as commander-in-chief of the forces there.

It is wonderful to observe the effect of party-
prejudice upon the temper and understanding of
the wisest and best of its adherents; the same
conduct in different individuals, will be praised or
censured according to the medium through which
it is viewed, of like or dislike, or as it may best
suit the purpose of the moment. Oliver Cromwell
is vilified and abused for his assumption of the
supreme power: Richard Cromwell, his son, is
contemned and despised for his relinquishment
of it.

Lord Clarendon censures Richard (this child of
fortune as he describes him) for calling a Parliament, as conducing to his fall; and a few lines
afterwards acknowledges the necessity of it. Whitelock says he did it by the advice of his council;
that every member of the Parliament took the oath
of fidelity to him as Protector; notwithstanding
which, the bill of recognition met with much opposition, and was attempted to be clogged with
many obnoxious clauses.

His Lordship also condemns Richard's dissolution of the Parliament, which he attributes to the

advice of his relations Fleetwood and Disbrow, notwithstanding the advice of many of his friends to the contrary. Whitelock says, he was betrayed by his near relations, and that Lord Broghill, Thurloe, and himself, and most others of his council, were for it; only Whitelock doubted, and wished their sitting to be a little longer permitted. His Lordship attributes this dissolution to Richard's pusillanimity. Ludlow describes the three contending parties: the commonwealth party; the Wallingford-house, or army party, so called from Wallingford-house being Fleetwood's residence; and Richard Cromwell's own party: he says they were of nearly equal strength. He has been, as hath been shown, very severe in his censures of Cromwell's dissolution of the Long Parliament; but he and his republican party are found to have no scruple in purging the House of its (to them) obnoxious members, when it suits their object of lessening the numbers, for the purpose of diminishing the strength of their opponents, by, as in this present instance, impeaching and expelling, and frightening them from the House, as Ludlow himself acknowledges with evident self-gratulation.

It appears from the preceding extracts from Ludlow, that Richard Cromwell was deceived by the republican and army party into the convening a council of officers, under the pretext of preparing and presenting to the House a plan for the regulation of the army, which, after a few meetings, was suppressed, and he appointed by the House Captain-general of the army.

Lord Broghill seems to account for Fleetwood's hostile conduct towards Richard Cromwell by the following circumstance : — That Oliver Cromwell had made him his heir; but that one of his daughters knowing where his will was, took it and burnt it before Fleetwood could come at it : that when Cromwell was asked who should succeed him, he made no reply, but said, in such a drawer of a cabinet in his closet they should find his will; but that his daughter had disposed of it elsewhere, and so they never came to the sight of it.   Neither Whitelock, or Ludlow, or Thurloe, notice this circumstance, nor does Lord Broghill give his authority for it : if Fleetwood believed it, his animosity towards Richard Cromwell would be intelligible.

His Lordship gives the following account of the above convention of the council of officers : — That while the Parliament was sitting he (Richard) likewise gave a commission to Fleetwood and Disbrow to hold a council of war at Wallingford-house, to which His Lordship received a summons, as being a general officer in the Irish army : that he went immediately to Richard to know whether he had consented to call this council, when Cromwell acknowledged he had : that His Lordship told him he feared he would repent it : Cromwell asked why ?   Because, answered His Lordship, they will certainly work some mischief against him (Richard)

and his friends; but that as yet he knew not what
it was: that Cromwell then desired His Lordship
to do what he could to prevent it;—His Lordship
replied he would go amongst them and see what
might be done: that at this meeting Colonel Disbrow proposed to purge the army of the disaffected,
by a test, that every one should swear their belief
that the putting to death the late King was lawful
and just: that His Lordship opposed all tests; but
that if they must have a test, he would offer one
more reasonable and lawful;—that every one
should be turned out of the army who would not
swear to defend the government as it was then
established under the Protector and Parliament:
that this was reasonable and lawful, because it was
to maintain the present government: that rather
than have this test and not their own, they determined to have neither: His Lordship thereupon
advised Richard forthwith to dissolve this council
of war, which would certainly do mischief if it sat
any longer; and His Lordship, by Richard's desire, drew up a short speech for him, which he
should deliver to them the next morning, to this
effect,—That he accepted their service with all
thankfulness; that he had considered what did
most aggrieve them; and that he thought the best
and properest way to redress what was amiss
amongst them, was to do it in the Parliament then
sitting, of which most of them were members;
and therefore declared his commission of holding

that council null and void, and desired them all to go to their several commands: that accordingly Cromwell, by ten of the clock the next day, went to Wallingford-house, and sat in a chair of state amongst them, which pleased some, and troubled others ; and delivered his speech, which, though it was very mild, yet gave great distaste to Fleetwood and his party : that they guessed who was the author of their dissolution, and therefore in a few days came in a body into the Parliament and complained, that they had been abused and affronted by a certain lord in that assembly (looking stead-fastly upon His Lordship), and desiring satisfaction, by an address to be made to His Highness the Lord Protector, that he would declare who advised him to dissolve the council of war during the sitting of Parliament, without the Parliament's knowledge or consent : that His Lordship then rose and moved, that at the same time, another address might also be presented, to know who advised the calling a council of war without the knowledge or consent of Parliament : for that if he was guilty, who advised the dissolution of the council without the Parliament's consent, he must be much more guilty, who advised the calling that council without it: that at this motion they all cried "Well moved!" and Fleetwood and others went their way.

That His Lordship, finding the army resolved on Richard Cromwell's ruin, advised him to cast himself upon the city, and declare for the King and a free Parliament, assuring him he would find the city favour him that way, and by it he would make his family for ever : but that Cromwell would not comply with this advice; so went on his own way till the army deposed him, and set up for themselves : and that then His Lordship went to Ireland to his command; and that had he not made good haste, he had been cut off by Fleet-wood and Disbrow, who sent speedily after him to apprehend him, but he escaped, and being upon his command in Ireland, was out of their reach.

Mr. Noble relates a dialogue between Richard Cromwell and Colonel Howard, afterwards Earl of Carlisle, in which the Colonel is described as advising Richard to vigorous measures, even the depriving Fleetwood, Lambert, Disbrow, and Vane of their lives, which he with horror rejects.

Neal, in his History of the Puritans, seems to refer to the same story, and adds that the poor-spirited Protector was afraid of blood : and that thereupon Colonel Howard made his peace with the King.

Neither of these writers referring to any authorities for this story, and the Colonel not being likely to offer such sanguinary advice, he certainly had not been taught by Cromwell to think lightly of assassination; it is not likely to be true.   It is no discredit to Richard Cromwell, nor any proof of his want of spirit, that he should be afraid of, or view with horror, the shedding of blood for his own advancement.

His firmness and resolution is very conspicuous
in his personally breaking up the council of officers,
and in his long persevering resistance of their views
of getting rid of the Parliament, who upon the
desertion of the army, through the intrigues of
Fleetwood, Ludlow, and their party, was his only,
or chief support.   In the Life of Thurloe, prefixed
to his State Papers, is the following passage, which
appears to be taken from Dr. Calamy's Life of
Mr. Howe :—" I (Calamy) was told by a friend,
that when he signified in a way of discourse to
Mr. Howe, that he had heard Richard reflected on
as a weak man, he, with some warmth, made this
return,—how could he be a weak man, when upon
the remonstrance that was brought from the army
by his brother Fleetwood, he stood it out all night
against his whole council, and continued the
debate till four o'clock in the morning, having
none but Thurloe to abet him, maintaining that
the dissolving that Parliament would be both his
ruin and theirs ?"

His memory has been treated with the greatest
ridicule and contempt, and even scurrility, for his
supposed abjectedness of spirit in this his quiet
resignation of the exalted situation in which his
father's great talents had placed him : but had he
possessed the spirit and abilities of his father, it
does not seem possible that he could have kept it.
Lord Broghill, it has been seen, allows, that he
could not resist the army's determination to ruin

him, and can give him no other advice than to
endeavour the restoration of the King. This, at
that time, was impossible; the nation was not prepared for this great change, nor would the army
have supported him. Even Monck, with an army
at his command, durst not openly declare himself,
and not till he must have had reason to apprehend
that the Restoration would be accomplished without
him. If he really had, long before the avowal of
his intention, determined upon this measure, he
must have been guilty, according to Ludlow, of
the grossest dissimulation and falsehood, in his
solemn declarations to the last moment to the
contrary, — of his determination to live and die
with Ludlow for a commonwealth; that he would
join with him and his party against Charles Stuart
and his party; that he would oppose to the utmost
the setting up of Charles Stuart, a single person,
or a House of Peers; that those that brought the
King to the block acted justly.

Bishop Burnet, speaking of Monck's supposed
merit and service in the Restoration, says, that it
was chiefly owing to the post he was in, and to the
credit he had gained; for that, as to the Restoration itself, the tide ran so strong, that he only
went into it dexterously enough to get much fame
and great rewards for that which will still have a
great appearance in history.

Oliver Cromwell's death let loose Fleetwood,
Ludlow, Disbrow, and many others, to follow their

several ambitious views, who durst not, during his
life, look him in the face; he knew them well;
they appear to have been men of inferior talents
incapable of great enterprise.   Ludlow lived to
have the opportunity of writing his own memoirs;
he sickens his readers by the account of himself
and his own little exploits, upon which he dwells
with much self-complacent minuteness.   He appears to have been a mortal foe to regal government, and never forgives, nor ceases to abuse
Cromwell, for extinguishing his favourite republic.

Rapin, upon Richard's succession to the protectorate, observes, that, though the late Protector
was both careful and capable to preserve himself
amidst the parties then in England, and to keep
them in awe, it was not in his power to extinguish
them : that when he was taken out of the world,
each party hoped to gain the advantage under the
protectorate of Richard, who had not his father's
qualities; and that to these hopes, perhaps, must be
ascribed their ready concurrence in declaring him
Protector : that the royalists justly flattered themselves that the different parties into which their
enemies were divided, having no longer a common
head capable to govern them all together, would
disunite, and that disunion be serviceable to the
King, and perhaps procure his restoration : that
those who had approved of the government by a
single person, in the deceased Protector, and had
been trusted by him, hoped to preserve the same

credit under the son which they had enjoyed under
the father, and to direct the new Protector according to their pleasure: that if the republicans
had consented to acknowledge Richard, it was
because they were unprepared to make any opposition: that the army, chiefly composed of this
party, being dispersed in several counties, the
officers had neither time nor opportunity to consult together: but that they despaired not of
finding an occasion to displace the new Protector,
and restore the Commonwealth to the state it was
in, till the year 1653, when Oliver dissolved the
Parliament which had formed it: that the Anabaptists were all of the republican party, because they
perceived the impossibility of establishing their
fifth monarchy under a Protector: that these were
the most zealous republicans, and the hardest to
be managed, on account of their singular notions,
which caused them to refer every thing to their
extravagant religion, and rendered them deaf to
any reasons not drawn from their principles.

Thurloe gives this account of them: — He says
that a new insurrection and rebellion had been
lately discovered: that it was a design of a very
strange nature, and built upon very extraordinary
pretences: that the party engaged to begin this
insurrection were those who falsely and prophanely
styled themselves the Fifth Monarchy, and pretend to have no king but Jesus; calling that which
is earthly, sensual, and devilish, the working of the

Holy Spirit and the power of Christ's love in them :
that the number and quality of the persons beginning this attempt was very inconsiderable, and,
indeed, despicable : that Thomas Vinner, a wine-
cooper, was their leader.

Rapin, in continuation, says, that there was
another set of republicans, who, regardless of religion, were governed by political views : they were
accused of having no religion, or of being properly
deists.

That the Presbyterians, who were very numerous
in England and Ireland, besides the Scots, who
were almost all of this sect, had not changed their
principles since their expulsion from the Parliament in 1648 : that they would have gladly admitted the King with a limited power, and the
firm establishment of Presbyterian government in
the church : that this principle had always caused
them to remain by themselves, without being able
to unite either with the royalists, who would
hearken to no limitation upon the King's power,
and were averse to this church-government ; or
with the republicans, who would have neither King
nor Protector : besides, that these last granted an
entire liberty to all sects that had joined the independent party ; a liberty which was inconsistent
with the principles of the Presbyterians : for that,
though the Presbyterians had, under the reigns of
Elizabeth, James I., and Charles I., taken it very
ill to be denied the free exercise of their religion

they were by no means inclined to grant others
the same liberty they had demanded for themselves.
Nevertheless, as their number was considerable,
and they might at last find a leader capable of conducting their affairs, the deceased Protector thought
it proper to manage them, and preserve their government in the church, but without obliging any
person to conform to it: that this moderation kept
the Presbyterians quiet under Oliver's government; and the more, as they could expect no
assistance from the army as it was then modelled.
But that, in remaining thus separate from all the
other parties, they disabled themselves from making any great progress against the independent
party, who took care to keep them low: that this
gave the royalists room to hope that the Presbyterians would at last be obliged to unite with them,
to free themselves from the servitude in which they
were held by the independents and republicans.

This short recapitulation of the interests of the
several parties plainly, continues Rapin, demon-
strates Cromwell's capacity, who could keep them
all in awe without a positive declaration in favour
of any one party ; that Richard proposed to begin
his protectorate with his father's maxims : that he
formed the design of making himself master of
the deliberations of his council, and of reducing
the army to receive his orders with submission:
that by these two things Oliver maintained his
authority, and if he had lived he would not have

left an officer in the army of suspected fidelity: but that, to pursue these maxims and execute this project, Richard should have had his father's capacity for civil and military affairs, his bravery and resolution, and, in a word, by a series of victories, should have been able to strike terror into all who could oppose his designs: but, that Richard had none of those great talents to command fear and respect, or to inspire his friends with hopes of a powerful protection; so that, heading no party, and being incapable to govern all, he stood exposed to their ambition and violence, without being sure of an effectual assistance when he should want it. That, meanwhile, knowing that the bare election of his person by the council, and the addresses presented to him, were insufficient to establish his authority, he believed it expedient to have his dignity confirmed by Parliament, and accordingly summoned one to meet, as before mentioned.

The expediency of Richard Cromwell's abdication, to prevent another bloody contention, is shown by the result. Those men who had been the immediate means of accomplishing this abdication, with the advantage of the army, and of all the power in their hands, could not afterwards accomplish the objects of their ambition; and finally involved the nation in the confusion that produced and terminated in the Restoration, without the necessary conditions on the King's part, and in their own utter dispersion and ruin. These conditions, the great and upright Chief Justice Hale proposed and strenuously pressed, unfortunately for the country, as it afterwards proved, unsuccessfully.

Had Richard mounted his horse, and placed himself at the head of those soldiers who might have been disposed to follow him, as he is said to have been advised, he could have done nothing effectual against the rest of the army, commanded, as it would have been, by veteran experienced officers; the attempt would have involved the nation in another civil war, more sanguinary and more destructive than the former, as being carried on by a greater variety of contending parties; and must have made way for the final victory of the royal party over all of them, and have produced the restoration of the King as a conqueror, upon his own terms. His quiet abdication, however contemptuously spoken of, merited his country's thanks.

He appears to have been of a mild and merciful disposition; and his disapprobation of violent measures for the maintenance of his situation, which must, under all the forestated circumstances, have been finally unsuccessful, has been construed a want of spirit and personal courage. Not having been bred a soldier, he had no opportunity of showing a military spirit or courage; he appears to have spent much of his time as a

country gentleman, which he might do without
imputation of his understanding, and certainly
not of his courage, which is required in a certain
degree in country sports. It may be a trifling
circumstance to mention, only as it may be used
to show that he had a degree of hardihood, that
in the keen pursuit of his favourite amusement of
hawking, Mr. Noble says, from Heath's Chronicle,
through excess of eagerness in the sport, he out-
rode his retinue; and his horse, by leaping, threw
him into a ditch, from which he was extricated by
a countryman before his attendants could come
up. This was not the act of a timid character;
and his firmness and resolution are sufficiently
evidenced in his conduct towards the council of
officers, and other forementioned instances previously to his resignation,

Some difference appears between Lord Clarendon's and Mr. Noble's accounts of Richard's
place of residence, upon his arrival upon the
Continent; — His Lordship describes him as first
residing at Paris some years, and thence going to
and residing at Geneva, and the supposed forementioned interview with the Prince of Conti, as
happening in his way thither. — Mr. Noble describes him as first going to, and residing at
Geneva; but as not long remaining there, for
reasons, he supposes, and then residing at Paris,
as Lord Clarendon relates; where he remained
(except, says Mr. Noble, another short interval

spent at Geneva, for the same reasons as occasioned his going there before,) until his return to England about the year 1680. Both these accounts cannot be accurate; but the variations are immaterial, nor is it important to ascertain his disposal of himself in the interval of the time of his quitting the kingdom and his return. His (Richard's) letters remaining amongst the family papers are numerous; they are principally written to his daughters; they are expressed in terms of the most parental affection, nevertheless at times seemingly disapproving their management of the family estates; but no appearance of their unfeeling behaviour towards him described by some writers. A family suit appears to have been depending in 1706; but the story of his personal appearance in court seems quite improbable, it being unlikely to be necessary, and unless absolutely so, not likely, from his determined retirement, to happen.

The first of his letters to his daughters, remaining with the family papers, is dated in 1687. The following is a letter addressed by him to his daughter, Ann Cromwell, at Hursley, who afterwards married Dr. Thomas Gibson, Physician-general of the army; it is dated 18th December, 1690:—" Deare; Thinck not I forgot you, though I confess I have been silent too long in returning & owning of that of yours to me; that wch was one barr, I knew not upon Mrs. Abbott's removing, how to send soe as my letter might come safe to you; and though we write nothing of state affaires, they being above our providentiall spheer, yet I am not willing to be exposed, nor can there be that freedome when we are thoughtfull of such restraint as a peeping ey. The hand by whom this comes gave me a hint, as if there were some foule play to letters directed to him. Deare heart, I thanck thee for thy kind and tender expressions to me, and I assure (if there had been cause) they would have melted me; there is a great deale of pittie, piety, and love, (what I had before was soe full, that I had not the least roome to turne a thought or surmise,) but what shall I say, my heart was full, but now it overflowes; you have put joy and gladness in it. How unworthy am I to have such a child, and I know I may venture to say, that the like parralell is not to be found: what I said was experienced matter for information; what you replyed was in behalfe of those whoe profest themselves to be the Lord's people, and they that are truly such, are as tender as the apple of his ey. I rejoyce in that we both of us love them, yet we are not to deny our reasons as to the mischiefe some of them hath been instrumentall not only in particular to a family, but in generall to the churche of Christ, besides what woes are hanging over these nations, may we not goe further, and bring in all Christendom.

I have been alone 30" years, bannished, and under silence, and my strength and saf'ty is to be retyred, quiet, and silent, we are foolish in taking our cause out of the hand of God. Our Saviour will plead, and God will doe right he hath promised; let us joyne our prayers for faith and patience; if we have heaven, let whose will get the world: my hearty, hearty, hearty affections and love to your sister and self. Salute all friends. I rest commending yee to the blessings of the Almighty; againe fairwell,

"Your truly loving father,

"R. C."

"Present me to all friends; landlord and landlady present respects and service."

None of his letters are dated from any place. In the above postscript he speaks of landlord and landlady, which must mean the (afterwards) Chief Baron Pengelly and his wife; and in a letter dated 1st December, 1691, he refers to a box not arrived, suggesting the mistake to be in the messenger demanding it in the name of Clark, when it should have been Pengelly, which seems sufficiently to prove his residence with the Pengellys, and his adoption of the name of Clark. And the following letter, dated the 25th August, 1705, written by Mrs. Pengelly to Mr. George Gibson, appearing to be Dr. Gibson's son, confirms the fact of this name and residence. The place whence it is dated is torn off. — " Mr. Gibson; Mr. Clarke received y" with the inclosed from Hursley, w^{ch}, upon his reading of it, and consideration on his pillow, he called for me, and desired me to write two or three lines to you, he not being stirring, that he could not so well answere yours by pen, as by discoursing wth you about the affair, so desires you would meet him on Monday afternoone, about three o'clock, at the Blew Bell at Edmonton, that Blew Bell that is next us heare, wheare you maye have opportunity to discourse things fully: he desirs you wold get a hors, he will pay for it: the gentleman is pretty well, and I hope will be better; we endeavour to devert him. I should have wrote to Mad^{m} at Hursley, but hope y^{rs} by Tuesday's post, will answere: wth our servis to the Doctor, is all at present from,

" Yo^{r} loveing friend,

" RACHELL PENGELLY."

" Please to call of my son and ask him how he doth, and if he have any thing to me."

It may be thought unnecessary to dwell so long upon these circumstances, but the historians of those times having deemed them worthy of attention, it becomes desirable to rectify, from authentic documents, any doubts or mistakes into which they may have fallen. Richard's signatures to these letters are generally " C. R.," reversing the initials of his name; sometimes " Richardson," sometimes " Crandbourne," — " Cranbury," — Cranmoore."

Mr. Noble speaks of Richard's known gallantry, and supposes Sergeant Pengelly, afterwards Sir Thomas, Chief Baron of the Court of Exchequer, from his alleged uncommon zeal for him as his client in the probably forementioned suit, and for some other reasons, now he says unknown, to have been his natural son. He does not give his authorities for this supposed gallantry of Richard, nor is it known to have been believed in the family. His letters are of a devotional turn. Mr. Neal, in his History of the Puritans, says of him, that in his younger years he had not all that zeal for religion as was the fashion of the times, but that those who knew him well in the latter part of his life had assured him (Mr. Neal) that he was a perfect gentleman in his behaviour; well acquainted with public affairs; of great gravity, and real piety: but so very modest that he would not be distinguished or known by any name but the feigned one, of Mr. Clarke. He was born in 1626, and married in 1649; he was therefore only twenty-three years of age at the time of his marriage, and the treaty for the marriage appears to have commenced in 1647, not leaving him much time for gallantry: nor does his father in his letters complain of his conduct in any respect, but those of disinclination to public business, and a too expensive mode of living. The presumption, therefore, seems to be, that he never was a dissolute character.

He died in the year 1712, in the 86th year of his age, in, as is said and as is probable, Sergeant Pengelly's house at Cheshunt, understood to be the house next the church, called the Rectory-house, and was buried in the chancel of the church of Hursley, in Hampshire.

Of the private character of the rest of Oliver Cromwell's children, Mr. Noble says, that the author of the History of England during the reigns of the Stuarts assures us, that all the Protector's daughters were admired, beloved, and esteemed for their beauty, virtue, and good sense; and he (Mr. Noble) adds, that they were all of them attached to the royal family except the eldest, (Mrs. Ireton, afterwards Fleetwood,) who was a severe republican.

Bishop Burnet says, — That his sons were weak, but honest men; that Richard was not at all bred for business, nor indeed capable of it: that his brother Henry had been made by his father Lieutenant of Ireland, and had the most spirit of the two; but that he could not stand his ground when his brother quitted: that the Countess of Falconbridge was a wise and worthy woman, more likely to have maintained the post than either of her brothers: that the other daughter was married, first to the Earl of Warwick's heir, and afterwards to one (meaning Sir John) Russell, both very worthy persons.

Whitelock, in his Swedish embassy, gives a conversation upon this subject of Cromwell's family, with the Queen of Sweden. The Queen asks whether his General (Cromwell) had a wife and children ; he tells her " he hath a wife and five (should have been six) children." — Queen. " What family were he and his wife of?" — Whitelock. " He was of the family of a baron, and his wife the like from Bourchiers." — Queen. " Of what parts are his children ?" — Whitelock. " His two sons and three (four) daughters, are all of good parts and liberal education." — Queen. " Some unworthy mention and mistakes have been made to me of them." — Whitelock. " Your Majesty knows that to be too frequent ; but from me you have nothing but the truth."

Bishop Burnet is certainly incorrect in describing the one or the other of Cromwell's sons as weak men. Richard, so far as he is known, does not appear so. Henry certainly was not. Cromwell's early employment of him is sufficient proof of his abilities and personal courage : partiality for his son would not have placed him in those important situations in which he is found at very early ages; it was not his practice to employ incapable men, however connected or attached. Mr. Noble says, from Wood's Fasti, and Heath's Flagellum, that his father took him into the Parliament army, raised to oppose King Charles in 1647, (when he was only twenty years of age, being born 20th January, 1627,) when he became captain of the

General, Sir Thomas Fairfax's life-guard : that in August, 1649, he went with his father into Ireland as a colonel, to quell the Roman Catholic rebellion, and Whitelock relates that he (Henry), with Lord Broghill, fell into Lord Inchiquin's quarters, and killed 160 of the enemy, and took 120 foot prisoners with their officers, and 150 gallant horse : and Mr. Noble adds, from Heath's Chronicle, that in the year following he assisted at the siege of Limerick.

Mr. Noble adds, from various histories of England, that he was in the Little or Bare-bones Parliament assembled in 1653, being one of the members for Ireland, and that in the same year he was sent again into that island to take a review of the state it was in, to discover the temper of the people, and to reconcile the minds of the disaffected to the government of his father : this, says Mr. Noble, was an arduous task; but that he performed it to admiration : that he found that the ruling powers (the republicans) had taken the most ample care of themselves, and the least of the people, and that they were so in love with their power and places, that it would be improper to permit them any longer to remain in any post of consequence in the kingdom.

Ludlow, referring apparently to this going to Ireland, (using no dates,) says that Cromwell, hav-ing changed his interest and taken off his masque, sent his second son, Colonel Henry Cromwell, into.

Ireland, to feel the pulse of the officers there, touching his coming over to command in that nation, where he arrived attended only by one servant, and landing near his (Ludlow's) country-house, he sent his coach to receive him and to bring him thither, where he staid till Lieutenant-general Fleetwood, with several officers, came with coaches to conduct him to Dublin : that having made what observations he could of persons and things in Ireland, he resolved upon his return, of which having given him (Ludlow) advice, he desired him to take his house in his way ; and to that end dined with him on the day of his departure at the Lieutenant-general's in the Castle, and after dinner went to his house at Moncktown. Then follows the particulars of a conversation between Henry and Ludlow, upon the grounds of his (Ludlow's) dissatisfaction with the then state of affairs in England, not material to relate ; after which Henry embarked for England, and, says Ludlow, upon his arrival at Chester was attended by many of the late King's party, and, amongst others, by Colonel Molson (Mosson), who enquiring of him how he left affairs in Ireland, he answered very well, only that some who were in love with their power must be removed. Mr. Noble observes, upon this respectful attention to Cromwell, that it showed the value the people in general had for him, royalists as well as others. He could at this time be only twenty-six years of age.

Mr. Noble observes, that Henry, by the wisdom and equity of his adminstration soon procured the love of the Irish, who regarded him as a blessing; that this was the sentiment of the moderate and wise of all parties; that this it was that procured him a counter-address to that presented to the Protector for the restoration of their old chief governor Fleetwood, beseeching that he (Henry) might be continued their governor; and that the nation was ruled with such skill by him, that it was become, from the most deplorable kingdom in Europe, far the happiest of any part of the British dominions, and the most satisfied with the Cromwellian reign. And a paper from the church of Dublin, dated 3d June, 1656, to be found in Milton's State Papers, and given in substance from them by Mr. Noble, but here more at large, states, " That some persons (under a pretence of love) had endeavoured to persuade the Lord Henry Cromwell that this church was much grieved and offended with his demeanour and carriage in his place of publike government; for the taking away of that false aspersion tending to the breach of love and peace, and for preventing further evills which might arise from thence, this church did then (by a competent number of their members sent unto His Lordship) assure and satisfi him, that the said information was nothing but a meere fiction (of purpose invented) to make division betwixt His Lordship and this church: and that the

father of lyes finding himself disappointed here,
in the foresaid mischievous device, hath of late,
by the like instruments in England, laboured to
asperse His Lordship and this church by insinuating unto some in authority there, that this church
in particular, and all other godly Christians in
general in Ireland, were much grieved, discountenanced, and discouraged, by reason of the countenance that is said to bee given to vice and vitious
persons in Ireland by His Lordship, or since his
command of the forces there. They, therefore,
after serious examination and consideration had
thereon, conceived it their duty to disowne and
protest against the said lying report, with detestation of soe vile a slander, and for further vindication of themselves, and manifestation of the
truth, they did in the sight of God (the searcher
of all hearts) thereby declare, that they were soe
farre from being any way discountenanced, or
haveing any cause to bee offended, grieved, discouraged, or dissatisfied, with His Lordship's demeanour and carriage in his place, that contrary-
wise they had great cause to rejoice and blesse the
Lord for him ; — for his equall justice to all, and
mercy to the poore ; for his prudent and loveing
carriage to all that feare God (though of different
judgements), endeavouring to preserve unity and
love amongst them ; for the countenance that
himself and family gave to all God's publicke
ordinances, by their constant and reverent attend-

ance on them; for the respect, countenance, and encouragement that (in a speciall manner) he gave to all the godly ministers of the Gospel. And we doe also declare (and that upon good ground) that generally all the sober-minded Christians throughout this whole land are of the same mind with us herein. Dated at Dublin, this 3d of June, 1656." Signed by many ministers.

Henry's personal worth and ability, and fitness for the high and arduous situations that he filled in Ireland, will further appear from the following extracts from the many letters to be found in Thurloe's State Papers, written by, and to and concerning him; most of which were supplied by the Cromwell family.

In a letter to Thurloe, dated 8 Martii, 53, (only twenty-six years of age,) he says, — "After a long journey by lande, I arrived heere (Dublin) upon Satterday last, in the eveninge, since which time I have not bin wantinge in my endeavours to informe myselfe of the severall tempers of men heer; and doe find, uppon the strictest inquiry that possibly I could make, that the army generally, both heer about the head-quarters, as also thosse in the other partes of the nation, are abundantly satisfied and well pleased with the present government in Englaade; unless it be some few inconsiderable persons of the anabaptiste judgement, whoe are allsoe quiett, though not very well contented; but I beleive they will receive much satisfaction from a

letter very lately come to their handes from Mr.
Kiffin and Spilsbury, in which they have dealt
very homely and plainly with those of that judgement heer: but I must say this, that if they had
been inclineable to have made disturbance, they
had sufficient encouragement frome those in cheife
place heer, whoe have managed business of late
with much peevishness and frowardness, endea-
vouringe to render the government as unacceptable as possibely they could, especially Ludlowe
and Jones, who are very highly dissatisfied, though
Jones more cuninge and close in it; but Ludlowe
hath not spared any company, or opportunitie, to
vent his venomous discontents, and that in re-
proachful and reflectinge language, very much to
the amazement of all sober men, amongst whome
he hathe rather loste than gained acceptance by
it : he hath refused to act in his civill capacitie
since the change, but will not leave his military,
because proffittable, unless it be taken from him.
You will, I suppose, consider what is fitt to be
done with such persons ; and I hope it may stirre
you up speedily to settle a government that may
signifie somethinge ; for this does verry little, unless it be to make orders to give away the publique
lands, of which they have given large proportions
to each of themselves. The uttmost that is desired
is, that all may be uppon ane equall account as to
encouragement and countenance, which I doubt
will scarce be, unless there be care taken for the

future.   I hope you received the character which
I sent at my comeing out of town to you.   Make
use only of the upper clavis to uncypher the inclosed.   I am your freinde and servante,

                              " H. CROMWELL."
    " You will shew this to my father."

    Then follows the part written in cypher, de-
cyphered by Thurloe. — " I have taken the freedome to be very plain with my brother, (Fleetwood,
Commander-in-chief,) and have, as neare as I
could, acquainted hym with what I had in trust,
and doe finde his desire rather to returne, than to
continue here ; but is willing to be at my father's
dispose : but, to deale faithfully, I doe thinke he is
a little too deeply ingaged in a partial affection to
the persons of the Anabaptists, to answer your end ;
though I do believe it rather to proceed from
tendernes than love to their principles.   He is
very well satisfyed that the government heere
should be suteable to yours, and well approves of
the two persons pitcht upon for counsellors.   To
offer my poore thought, I would take advantage by
Ludlowe's forwardness, to putt hym out of the
army, and putt Gen. Desborow in his place ; who,
with the assistance of the persons above mentioned,
will doe your business effectually, especially if you
thinke fitt for some short tyme to command my
brother over, and in his absence to constitute G.
Desbrowe his deputie.   I shall staye till the general

Henry Cromwell,
Second son of Oliver Cromwell,
and Engraved by W. Bond, from a half length Portrait,
F. Christian Pinx. Sart, in the Possession of Oliver Cromwell Esq.
Published by Longman Hurst Rees. Orme & Brown London June 1st 1820.

councill be over, which will be within those 14 daies, and then I shall hast over with speed."

In a letter from a Mr. Lloyd to Thurloe, dated the 13th of the same month of March (1653), is given an account of Henry's honourable reception upon his arrival in Ireland.

By the original commission with the Cromwell family papers, signed by the Protector, dated 24th August (1654), it appears that Henry was appointed Major-general of the army and forces of horse and foot of Ireland, directing him to observe and follow the orders and directions of the Protector, or General Fleetwood, the Commander-in-chief of said army.

In a letter of Henry's to Thurloe, dated 2d January (1655), referring to the ill usage of Colonel Hewson and others of the Anabaptists, he says, —
" I bless the Lord I doe gett strength enough to bare their reproaches beyond what I ever expected, both in respect of my youthe and naturall temper : whatever their carriage is towarde me, I trust, through grace, I shall not be withdrawne from doeing my duty, both to God and the publique ; in which, I hope, I shall soe behave myselfe, that, when it shall please the Lord otherwaies to dispose of me, they that watch for my haltinge shall have noething justly to reproach me with, or charge uppon me."

In a letter dated 10th same January, he says, —
" I hope it will appeare that I have carried myself

like an honest mane to all, notwithstanding the
harde measure I have received from some : a faire
complyance shall be from me towardes all, soe
farre as it may consist with publique safety:
Colonell Sankey himselfe hath confessed to me,
that nothinge will satisfye some of his brethren
but the saddle ; but I shall keep them frome that,
least they should make me their asse."

In a letter dated 18th same January, observing
upon the ill treatment of some officers of the army,
Anabaptists, and others, he says, — " After I had
answered those perticuler things they objected, I
told them plainly, that they might all of them of
that judgement expect equally liberty both in their
spirituall and civil concernments with any others,
and though I could not close with their principles
in my judgement, that I held myself obliged in
duty (judgeing them to be persons fearinge God)
to protect them from being imposed uppon by any;
as allsoe to keep them from doeing the like to
others: liberty and countenance they might expect
frome me, but to rule me, or to rule with me, I
should not approve of; and soe wee parted verry
farely, with a great deale of seemeing friendshipp;
and truely I ame not without hopes, but that their
may be some good come by this meeting. I am
verry sensible of the necessitie their is of union ;
and if my principles did not enforce it as a duty
uppon me, yet consideringe howe thinges are, and
are like to be in relation to the common enimy,

common prudence would make me bewarre of
increasing the number of our enemyes. Looke-
ing uppon the godliness of these men, I should
be loathe to loose them, if they be to bee kept;
but, indeed, consideringe their late practises, as
well as former, I doe not thinke that God has
given them a spirritt of government; neither
is it safe they should have much power in their
handes."

In a letter dated 6th February following, he
(Henry) says, — " I cannot be without my feares
in relation to His Highness, till I heare of his
perfect recovery. It will not become me to say
howe much the interest of these nations, and
especially of the people of God therein, depends
uppon and is wrapt up in His Highness. I have
as much reason, as well upon that account as allsoe upon a more perticular, to be earnest with the
Lord on his behalf as any. Those that may secretly
desire and contrive harme against him would
hardly escape the general calamitie that woulde fall
uppon these nations, and which they too much
endeavour to pull uppon their owne heades and
others, by their murmuringes, muttringes, and
wicked designes."

In a letter dated 2d July following (1656), he
writes, — " Sir; I have, by this post, seconded
the request, which, in my laste letter, I desired
you to make to His Highness for my retirement,
by letter to His Highness himselfe, whoe I hope

will have a due consideration thereof. I desire
the Lord to direct His Hignesse to such a course
herein as may most conduce to the glory of God,
and the peace and settlement of this poore country. Truely, Sir, accordinge to the apprehension
I have of the present state of thinges, I cannot
judge it good either for the publique or myselfe to
be longer here. I knowe not howe things are
managed; but sure I am, my enemyes (who have
been hitherto designinge to supplante me, and to
caste their reproaches upon me) insult, my friendes
droope, myself thereby rendered contemptible,
and altogether incapable of doeing further service.
I will not venture to give my opinion of your
keepinge Reynolds and Harrison, your sendeing
for Morgan. Could there be any thinge more
done to gratifie these, that have bin all this while
contriveing against me? The Lord help me to
bare these thinges with patience, and enable me
to submitt to his good pleasure."

In a letter dated 17th December following, he
says, that things in Ireland were brought to an
indifferent good pass; that the Anabaptists and
others, whose ways and principles were inconsistent with settlement and our interest, found
themselves disabled from doing much harm: that
his (Henry's) inclination was, having brought them
to good terms, not to crush them quite, lest through
despair they should attempt things dangerous, and
lest others should take occasion to become insolent

and violent, and so put us to a new trouble. Besides, that it was against his conscience to bear hard upon any, merely upon account of a different judgment, or to do any thing that might make them think so. This being done, I desire, according to your seasonable hint, to receive your further advice; and more particularly what thoughts His Highness and others have of my proceedings, and withal how affairs are like to go in England, so that I may the better know how to do my part here in the main work; to which purpose I have sent you a safe character, and, I hope, easy both to write and open, to the end that you may be more free and large thereupon.

In a book in the Cromwell family, entitled "Entries of Letters since the 24th November, 1657," is a memorandum, that "On Tuesday, the 24th day of November, 1657, the Right Hono'ble the Lord Henry Cromwell was sworne Lord Deputy of Ireland." This book contains a series of his letters to the time of his resignation of his office. He could be only thirty years of age at the time of this appointment. These letters are to be found in Thurloe's State Papers, transcribed from this book.

Preparatory to the giving these letters, it will not be improper to introduce a passage from a letter from Lord Broghill to General Montague, very complimentary of Henry's talents for the employ: it is dated Youghall, 20th same November. "They (the Irish nation) are all highly obliged to you for setling my Lord Harry amongst us; he has long (in all our opinions) deserved this office before he possessed it, and I know is a great friend to you, and a great desirer of your friendship for him. That touche you give of the condition things are still in at London, makes Ireland seem a very happy place; though where my Lord Harry doth govern, that country needs no foil to set it off."

In a letter of Henry, dated the 25th same November, he acknowledges the receipt of the commission and instructions: he proceeds, — " I must indeed acknowledge how unfitt I am for this burden; and it is my mercy that the Lord doth in these times effect his greatest designs by weak instruments, to the reproach and laying low of all carnal policy and worldly wisdome. It is my hope that the Lord, who alone has brought me hither, will not leave me in the wilderness, but will guide me through this labyrinth of my employment. The God of my father helpe and hold up my head in the evill day, when the powers of the world shall shrinke and shrivell. Indeed I account it the seal of your kindness to caution me, as you did, in this the day of my temptation." Referring to the necessary ceremonies upon taking upon himself this office, he says, that the Lord Chancellor (Steele) had advised, that to confer knighthood was a necessary part; nevertheless, considering the posture of affairs, he was unwilling to put forth that power ; but that, upon further advice, the thing being pressed as necessary, he had studied to find out a fit and proper person, and one against whom was least exception in reference of all parties : that at length he pitched upon Colonel Thomlison as being a member of the council, and one no ways famous for his formal affection to him. "I must confess, I had a farther reason, which was to declare to the world how really willing I was to obliterate the memory of that division conceived to have been among the members of the former council ; and to give this as a public act of reconciliation, even with those that were most concerned in that breach. Some other petty considerations I had, which I leave your own fancy to guess at. Having thus pitched upon the person, I used means to feel his inclinations as to the acceptance ; and I found no more reluctancy than what might be expected, but rather the contrary, handsomely dissembled ; whereupon he was knighted ; and to shew you that it was no vain itch which put me upon the action, I shall be sparinge hereafter in conferring those marks of honour. Those who we thought would have quarrelled with these ceremonys, seem at least to approve them though possibly but for the person's sake."

In a letter from Henry (then Lord Deputy of Ireland), to Thurloe, dated 2d December following, he says, — " I have, enclosed, sent you a large

letter to His Highness about the arrears of the
army. I desire you to deliver it at such a time,
when it may be read and considered, and withal
as soon as you can, for it is of near concernment
to us. You have put me upon the stage, and
therefore I desire you to continue your endeavours,
that I may in some measure act answerable to expectation; for if money be wanting, all I can do
will signify little."

In the letter above referred to, of the same date,
addressed to the Protector, he says, — " Having
by Your Highness's favour been admitted to the
government here, Your Highness might expect,
by the returne of the messenger who brought me
your commission, to receive from me nothing but
thanks, or, as some may thinke, nothing but expressions of joy for so great an honor and preferment. Nevertheless, (though without the least
derogation from what I owe Your Highness,) I
am forced to mingle with those duties some addresses of another nature alsoe. That which I am
to trouble Your Highness with at this time, is
want of monies to discharge soe great an arreare
to your army as of late hath scarce been heard of
within the three nations. I have received lately
a letter from my brother Fleetwood, so full of dis-
couragements as to this matter, that, did I not
know our condition to be lamentable and dangerous, I should have little hope to speed in this attempt. I have several times hinted our wants to

Your Highness, Mr. Secretary, and others, but being then subordinate, I thought it fitt to be urgent chiefly with my immediate superior, trusting that he, being upon the place of releife, and having himselfe left me in this entangled condition, would use all fitt remedies; but finding hitherto no effectuall answer to all former intimations, and having some reason to thinke that some make it too much their worke to frustrate my endeavours therein, the care of this business being now wholly mine, and that all miscarriages must be charged upon my single account, I must now humbly tell Your Highness, that had not this country been in an ill condition, by reason of the three months' vacancy of government, I should have even deferred opening my commission, untill, by supply of monies, I might have seen it possible for me to discharge the trust thereby committed to me, and not have given ground for all men to thinke that my greediness of honour and power is such as to make me admitt of any absurditie, to venture upon any impossibility, and to take upon me such things as must hereafter end in Your Highness's disservice and my own reproch." He then states these great arrears of the army, and the probable ill consequences of their remaining undischarged. " I humbly beg (continues he) Your Highness to weigh these truths, and not to keep me for ever engaged in conflicts and difficulties more and greater than any other man in my way doth or hath suffered. Your Highness knows how hard it is to keepe things right without money; the ill consequences of these wants may be hereafter represented as my errors and miscarriages, and it will be better for me never to have been advanced to this place of trust, than to be left without meanes to manage it, without which it must prove but an empty and dangerous title only. I hope Your Highness will thinke well of some, perhaps not so fitt expressions, which I used in giving you my apprehensions of the army. I am not willing to suggest causeless feares, nor would I speake at this rate to any other; I judge it my duty to deale faithfully upon these occasions. The Lord bless Your Highness, and direct you in that great affaire of the other House, and in what else may make for the glory of his name and good of his people committed to your care, and enable me, in the faithful discharge of my trust, and that I may in all things approve myselfe your most obedient son."

In a letter to Lord Broghill, dated 28th January following, thanking him for his kind and friendly offices with the Protector and Secretary Thurloe, he adds, — " What you have acted with His Highness and Mr. Secretary, in my behalfe, assuring them of my affections and endeavours to do things acceptable unto them respectively, I like well, but feare you have too much expressed your own affection towards mee in what you said to His Highness; but I know Your Lordship's merit in other

things will give you credit for more unlikely matters : wherefore, if Your Lordship hath lent me any
thing that was not mine, it follows that I must
labour to pay it, and discharge Your Lordship's
engagements for my good behavior."

In a letter to Lord Falconberg, dated 10th February following, he writes, — " As Ireland (like all
other reviving plantations) receives many im-
ported goods, but exports little ; so I cannot re-
pay Your Lordship's newes with newes, but must
only give Your Lordship my humble thanks, for
those your free and usefull communications, as the
interest of Your Lordship's debt upon mee ; besides, as Ireland sends forth nothing but hides, tal-
low, pipe-staves, and other coarse commodities, in
exchange of the delicacies of art and nature, so
My Lord, Your Lordship must not expect any
thing from mee, bearing any proportion to what
I receive from Your Lordship ; wherefore 'tis
something that I see in your letters not my own,
which makes me confident to draw you on to this
trouble of a correspondence with mee.

" Although the want of Mr. Secretary's intelligence leaves a great dimness upon my sight of
affaires, yett I may tell Your Lordship, without
flattery to yourselfe, or disparagement to him, that
the addition of Your Lordship's observations will
so brighten the objects I looke uppon, as to make
his prospective the more usefull unto mee ; besides, my Lord, as severall plants attract their seve-

rall and contrary substances from the same common earth, so certainly out of the same generall
masse of humane affaires men of severall minds
and inclinations will remark and be affected with
severall and very different particulars, from whence,
concluding that Your Lordship may shine upon
mee as cleare from your own orbe, as Mr. Secretary from his; I againe beg the continuance of
Your Lordship's last favours; I say, I beg, or at
least would borrow them; for I told Your Lordship you must not expect payment from me at
present.

" I was quite mistaken in my last, when I feared
as if the new-begotten House would ly crosse in
the wombe that conceived it; whereas now I see
the unnatural mother uses meanes to procure the
abortion of her owne issue; but it may be, 'tis only
the wormes or vipers (you named) lying in the guts
of the commonwealth, which have caused the frit-
tings and gnawings you mentioned; and this I
rather believe, because of the 500 maggottes
which you say are now againe busily crawling out
of the excrements of Mr. Feak's corrupted church.
But, to be serious, my Lord, 'tis a sad thing when
men of so many different waies (for such are or have
been many of those you mention), should all con-
spire for unsettlement, seeking vaine occasions to
quarrell, but it is His Highness's happinesse that
they find but words and names to snap and snarle
at," &c.

In a letter dated 14th April following, to Commissary-general Whalley, he says, — " My Lord Lockhart's confirmation of my opinion concerning your son doth likewise beget in me a good opinion of myself; for, till I heard myself seconded, I was afraid my affections towards you and him had misguided my reason in the character I formerly conceived of him.   Truly, if I had not perceived so good fundamentals in him, I should neither have advised him to the superstructure of a foreign education, nor exposed the weakness of so near a relation to the derision of strangers; but I saw there was matter, and that it was fitt to be wrought and formed.   I am of opinion that we want such men, for our foreign negotiations, as my coussin, your son, is like to be.   I give him my leave to stay for his further improvement, or other benefit, being the last return I can make for that affection I have always observed in you towards me, and our whole family."

In a letter dated 12th May following, to Thurloe, he says, — " Here is a messenger on purpose, from Col. Roger Mosson, of Mosson, in Denbighshire, by whome I am informed that Col. Mosson is secured, together with such other persons in those parts as have been officers in the late war against the Parliament. — This gentleman is a person from whome I have received many civilities in my voyages for and from Ireland; and one who hath often declared to mee that he thought it was his duty to submit chearfully to the present government, and that he was resolved never to act against it, but to follow his private affaires and mind the improvement of his estate, and discharge himselfe as became a good subject to His Highnesse. I will not undertake to say he hath kept his word, or that any other obligation lyes on him to keepe it, more than that of a gentleman and honour. Yet, neverthelesse, if you have no particular matter against his person, but that he is taken only within the compasse of a general rule, I would mediat so farre in his behalfe, as to desire you to take the best opportunity you can to gett him inlarged, he being willing to give what security shall be desired for his good deportment."

In the forementioned book, from which these extracts are taken, is a memorandum, copied also in Thurloe, — That His Excellency (Henry), intending at this time chiefly to make observations of the state of things under his immediate charge, went a progress to Cork, and from thence visited all the harbours upon the western coast as far as Bantre; and going from thence by Limerick, came to Portumna, where he met with the news of the death of his sister, the Lady Elizabeth (Claypoole); and having nothing of great emergency before him, gave the more way to melancholy thoughts and recess. This is the reason of the intermission of entry of letters, till the news that His Highness was dangerously sick gave fresh occasion.

In a letter dated 18th September following (1658), addressed to his brother, Richard Cromwell, then Protector, he declines the acceptance of the offer of his continuance in his office of Lord Deputy of Ireland ; having, he says, ever since his appointment by the late Protector, met with nothing but toil and disquiet of body and mind, thereby so exceedingly impairing his health, that it was not possible for him to undergo the like any longer : that his life was made a burden, and that had he not owed a natural and filial obedience, as well as a full subjection to His late Highness, he could not willingly have undergone it.   He adds, that he might not, unless His Highness should command him against his will, and condemn him to his grave, any longer undergo the charge : that he was not able always to live in the fire : that he did not this out of any froward humour, neither was he so vain as to design being courted : that he was willing, nay, desirous, to spend his small talents in His Highness's service, so that his task might be no more than he was able to perform ; but that he could hardly submit to a combination of pragmatical men, who, as they would endeavour to impose on His Highness, as they did upon His late Highness, so he might justly fear they would think it the nearest way to their ends, to misrepresent him to His Highness : that it was hard to express his mind by writing, unless he should swell a letter to a volume ; besides which, he had much to say

which was not fit to be written. — He requests his
permission to attend him in person for a short
time, where he doubts not, but by conference he
should give His Highness abundant testimony of
his dutiful obedience, and of his readiness and
hearty desire to serve him, and of the ways and
means which might capacitate him thereunto. For,
to say truth, says he, it were a treasonable folly,
for me to undertake a service which I beforehand
know I have not strength either of body or understanding to manage to Your Highness's advantage.
Besides, that he desired to be instructed from His
Highness's own mouth, by what principles he
should steer, lest he should ignorantly do any
thing that might justly displease. " And, indeed,
I do not dissemble if I say change of air, and
some recess is necessary for my health, which is
the more dear to me because I seldom enjoy it
twenty-four hours together. Thus I do faithfully
spread my cause at Your Highness's feet: if Your
Highness think not fitt to hearken unto my petition, I shall keep the army in due obedience, and
deliver it to whomsoever Your Highness shall
commit the charge thereof, and be truly thankful
for that protection which you allow to the meanest
of Your Highess's subjects; and publicly profess
entire love and tender affection to you as my
brother, allegiance and perfect subjection and obedience to Your Highness, as my rightful and un-
doubted supreme magistrate, and continually pray

to God for your long life and prosperous and happy reign."

In a letter dated 20th October following, Henry thus writes to Richard: — " May it please Your Highness; if the account be true which I have received of the state of affairs in England, I cannot tell what to advise Your Highness upon this sad occasion, though I confess it is no more then I looked for, only I had some hopes it might have been prevented by keeping all officers at their respective charges. But, as things now stand, I doubt the flood is now so strong, you can neither stem it nor come to an anchor, but must be content to goe adrift and expect the ebb. I thought those whom my father had raised from nothing would not so soon have forgot him, and endeavour to destroy his family before he is in his grave. Why do I say I thought, when I know ambition and affectation of empire never had any bounds? I cannot think these men will ever rest till they are in the saddle; and we of late years have been so used to changes, that it will be but a nine-days' wonder. And yet I fear there is no remedy but what must be used gradually and pedetentim. Sometimes I thinke of a Parliament, but am doubtful whether sober men will adventure to embark themselves, when things are in so high a distraction, or if they would, whether the army can be restrained from forcing elections. I know not what to advise at this distance, unless I could heare all the arguments pro and con. upon a true state of the case : yet I am almost afraid to come to Your Highness, lest I should be kept there, and so Your Highness lose this army, which, for ought I know, is the only stay you have, though I cannot but earnestly desire it. I doe alsoe think it dangerous to write freely to Your Highness, or for you to doe it to me, unless by a messenger that will not be outwitted or corrupted; for I make no question but all the letters will be opened which come either to or from Your Highness, which can be suspected to contain business. I pray God help you, and bless your counsells. The inclosed is a copy of my letter this post to my brother Fleetwood, which I send that Your Highness may see whether I am mistaken in my apprehension of things."

" To My Lord Fleetwood, 20th October, 1658, a copy whereof was sent inclosed to His Highness, in the above letter. — Dear Brother; I received the account you give of the petition of the officers, for which I give you thanks, and especially for your caution, that I should not believe any thing concerning you, till I had heard you ; truly it was seasonable advice, for I am told strange things, and pray give me leave to expostulate with you. How came those 2 or 300 officers together ? If they came of their own heads, the being absent from their charge without licence would have flown in their face, when they petitioned for a due observance of martiall discipline. If they

were called together, were they not .alsoe taught
what to say and doe?   If .they were called,
was it with His Highness's privity?   If they
-mett without leave in so great a number, were
they told their error?   I shall not meddle with
the matter of their petition, though some things in
it doe unhandsomely reflect, not only upon His
present but His late Highness.   I wish, with all
my heart, you were commander-in-chiefe of all the
forces in the three nations; but I had rather have
it done by His Highness's especiall grace and
meer motion, than put upon you in a tumultuary
unsoldierly way.   But, dear brother, I must tell
.you, (and I cannot do it without tears,) I hear that
dirt was thrown upon His late Highness at that
great meeting.   They were exhorted to stand up
for that good old cause, which had long layn
asleep; I thought my dear father had persued it to
the last; he died like a servant of God, and prayed
for those that desired to trample upon his dust, for
they were alsoe God's people.   O, dear brother,
let us not render evill for good; let us not make
his memory stink before he is under ground; let
us remember his last legacy, and, even for his sake,
render his successor considerable, and not make
him vile, a thing of nought, and a by-word.
Whither do these things tend! Surely God hath a
controversy with us.   What a hurly-burly is there
made! 100 independant ministers called together!
a councell, as you call it, of 2 or 300 officers of

a judgment! Remember what hath alwaies befallen
imposing spirits. Will not the loynes of an imposing
independent or anabaptist be as heavy as the loynes
of an imposing prelate or presbyter? and is it a dangerous error, that dominion is founded in grace, when
it is held by the church of Rome; and a sound
principle, when it is held by the Fifth Monarchy?
Dear Brother, let us not fall into the sinns of other
men, lest we partake of their plagues; let it be so
carryed, that all the people of God, though under
different formes, yea, even those whom you count
without, may enjoy their birthright and civill
liberty, and that not one party may tread upon the
neck of another. It doth not become the magistrate to descend into parties; but can the things
you doe tend to this end? Can those things be
done, and the world not think His Highness a
knave or a fool, or oppressed with mutinous spirits?
O, dear brother, my spirit is sorely oppressed with
the consideration of the miserable estate of the
innocent people of these three poor nations! What
have these sheep done, that their blood should be
the price of our lust and ambition? Let me begg
of you to remember how His late Highuess loved
you; how he honoured you with the highest trust
in the world, by leaving the sword in your hand,
which must defend or destroy us; and his declaring
His Highness his successor, shews that he left it
there to preserve him and his reputation. O,
brother, use it to curb extravagant spirits and busy

bodys, but let not the nations be governed by it; let us take heed of arbitrary power; let us be governed by the known laws of the land, and let all things be kept in their proper channells; and let the army be so governed, that the world may never heare of them, unless there be occasion to fight. And truly, brother, you must pardon me if I say God and man may require this duty at your hand, and lay all miscarriages in the army, in point of discipline, at your door. You see I deal freely and plainly with you, as becomes your friend and a good subject; and the great God, in whose presence I speak this, he knows that I do it not to reproach you, but out of my tender affection and faithfulness to you; and you may rest assured that you shall always find me your true friend and loving brother, "H. C."

"Postscript. Why were wee comprehended in the title of your address, and concluded by 2 officers? If it be not printed, pray do not cozen the world."

In a letter from Henry to the Lord Broghill, dated 2d November following, he says, — "My commission came on Saturday, and was this day opened. No instructions are yet come. May be the commission was sent before, as a bait to engage me to swallow them when they come. I must expect to be lustily thrashed, when Th. hath the making of the clog. In brief, I cannot expect

much favour from the other side; for I am told on
all hands, as well by letters as persons coming
from thence, that I am a great eye-sore; and am
told from a very good hand that they give out,
that the apprehension they had of the consequences
of my coming over was the cause of their late tumultuary meetings; and 'tis said that I am not the
only subject of their envy, but that it reacheth to
Fa. Th. and Mo., who they say are particularly
aimed at.   Indeed, for ought I hear, His Highness
hath carryed himself with prudence and resolution
enough.   I wish, with all my heart, Your Lordship
were there; and I can assure you by the last express I had from His Highness, he earnestly desires
it," &c.

In a letter from Henry to Richard, dated 3d
November following, he says, — " On Saturday last
I received Your Highness's commission for my
being lieutenant and governor-general of Ireland,
&c.; for which great honour, the reflection upon
my own unworthiness will make me always hold
myself bound in gratitude to serve Your Highness
whilst I live, although I were not (as in duty and
good conscience I am) obliged thereunto as Your
Highness's subject.   Nevertheless, I presume
humbly to acquaint Your Highness, that I had
great strivings within my breast before I could
prevail with myself to accept and open the commission, (which I did yesterday,) but doe not
thereby account myselfe any thing more at all

obliged to continue it, than I was at first to accept
it. I considered, that if I should refuse it, that
could not be done without noise and reflection
upon the state of Your Highness's affairs; and besides, I had no reason to think Your Highness sent
it upon any other terms then what I was bold
positively to insist upon in mine to Your Highness,
which was presented by Dr. Petty; and that, although no instructions came with it, I had as much
reason to think that, either you intended to send
none at all, or at least such as would not unreasonably limit me, (being assured of Your Highness's
care and favour,) as to fear Your Highness might
suffer the industry of T. and my enemies to procure such instructions as might make my commission signifie nothing; though I must needs acquaint Your Highness that all observing men, who
heard it publiquely read, took notice that the
clause, which is of the very essence of a lieutenant's
commission, and was always inserted in commissions to other lieutenants, was wholly left out of
this, namely, the power of making a deputy, and
going for England; so that I have reason to say, I
hope Your Highness will not by this acceptance
esteem me bound to continue this charge without
your licence to attend Your Highness in person
for some short time, which I humbly conceive I
have now much more cause to express than ever.
I shall not at all look back into the causes and
reasons which first induced me to make this humble

request to Your Highness, any further than to say
they remain still in their full force.   But I do now
only argue from such things as have since happened.   I find that my enemys, upon this single
issue, whether I should goe or not, have hitherto
prevailed, and so in effect have sentenced me with
an honourable banishment.   I am not conscious of
any crime which might deserve it; but if they can
denounce such judgment upon my innocence, they
will easily be able to make me criminous, by stopping all supplys from this necessitous army, who
have no more now then keeps them alive, and from
destroying our young plantations by free quarter.
This is the compendious and infallible way to doe
it; but because they will be sure of a faire blow at
me, before they give the fatal stroke, they first
cut my sinues.   They render me a persecutor of
good men, and handle my reputation so rudely
with their cobblers' thumbs, that they have already
begot a doubt amongst some good men (even my
friends) whether all be right.   And if I suffer this
continuall dropping without effectuall contradiction,
it may, for ought I know, prevail even upon Your
Highness, though the most just and wise person in
the world, or at least upon such honest men whose
good opinions I so far value, that I will rather
submitt to any sufferings with a good name, then
be the greatest man on earth without it.   And,
alas, Sir, how can I check this gangreen without
appearing there? My friends have not power to

help me : besides, 'tis doubtfull who are my friends,
and whether they do not sute their advice to Your
Highness concerning me, more to their own ends
then my safety ; and if they were never soe power-
full and just to me, 'tis not possible they should
maintain an argument touching matters or persons,
wherewith they are not fully acquainted : and my
condition is now such, that my very person is not
known (I a little doubt) to my neerest relations,
much less my disposition and manner of life. So
that, upon the whole matter, I beg Your Highness's
leave to conclude that (according to the tenor
of the two last letters I received from Your
Highness) I shall receive your licence to present
myselfe before Your Highness this humble request
to that end ; and in order thereunto, my wife being
great with child, and so like to be less able every
day to endure such a journey, I intend forthwith
to send her over. I have also, enclosed, sent a
copy of a letter (*mutatis mutandis*) from the late K.
under his hand and privy signet, to the Earle of
Strafford, which, so signed and sealed by Your
Highness, will both authorise me to come, and also
to appoint justices in my absence, which I the
rather advise should be made then a deputy, as
Your Highness's affairs here now stand. I should
be too voluminous if I should discourse all the
considerations which lead me to this opinion ; and
I forbear it the rather, because I am apt to think
that Your Highness having thought fitt to entrust

me with the charge of this place, will the more easily excuse me for presuming to offer how it may be secured till my returne. And for the army, I intend to divide it into 4 brigades, according as they now lye in the 4 provinces, and leave the charge thereof to 4 colonells, with instructions what to do in case a conjunction should be necessary, and to bring over Sir H. W. with me, and such others as cannot so safely be left here," &c.

In a letter without date (but immediately preceding Henry's resignation of his government), addressed to Fleetwood, he says, — " I received yours of the seventh of June, and your advices therein, which being but generall, I have sent Dr. Pettie to know more particularly what you would have me to doe. Upon the first rumour I sett out a proclamation to keepe the peace, when I heard the Parliament was sitting; and withall that their call was from some of the army, and that not many appeared; and that the committee of officers of severall interests kept up their meeting.

" We dispatcht from hence some, that might acquaint you with the desires of those here. I have, since His Highness's acquiescence, called together the officers, to make such addresses as they should think fitt. For my own part, I know no harm in a commonwealth way of government; and believe those now at helme to be very able and fitt for their work; yett you may think I cannot but be troubled at what has so lately befallen my relations; and do acknowledge that others may very honestly do what I cannot so handsomely. I have resisted great temptations in respect to their authority. The late newes of my being sent for, has strange interpretations putt on it by some; and I am distracted with the variety of men's opinion upon it. I desire you to lett me know how you would have me carry it, when the order itselfe comes to my hands. The officers are at worke about their address; I lett them take their own course, that the Parliament may have the true knowledge of them; they are all well disposed to settlement. Lett me hear speedily from you."

In another letter, also without date, from Henry to Fleetwood, he says, — " I received yours of the seventh instant, whereby, and by divers others letters, I take notice of the votes in Parliament concerning my coming into England : that news has so many odd circumstances, and such animadversions are made upon it, as I think it much concerns mee to know the meaning with all the speed I can : to which purpose I have sent this bearer (Dr. Pettie, as appears by another letter,) unto you, as one whom I can best trust, now my nearest concernments are at stake : wherefore, I desire you to shew your kindness to me in being free and plain with him, as to such advice as you think concerns my preservation, (for I am well contented to aim at nothing else,) and especially how I shall behave myself in reference to the summons for my

coming over when I receive them. I have made
so good use of my time, as I have not money to
bring mee. Pray give the bearer accesse to you
on my account; he does not use to be tedious or
impertinent. It concerns me to have one that I can
trust, to have such an accesse to you. I hope you
will not look upon him as to me, under the character and representation that Sir H. S. and some
others may give of him; but rather as one that
hath been faithfull and affectionate unto me, and,
I may say, to yourself alsoe, and one whome I
think, notwithstanding all that is said, is a very
honest man. I shall not trouble you with much
more: he can best acquaint you with what concerns myselfe, upon which single account I have
gotten him to come for England. As for the
public differences, I never perceived him forward
or busy in any. Dear brother, these are times of
tryall, both as to our own hearts and our friends.
I hope you will well consider of what you advise
mee as to myself, and let me have a speedy return
of your opinion. I desire the Lord to teach us
His waies, and to fitt our hearts for that condition
wherewith we have not been enough acquainted.
I have sent the letter which I intended to have
sent the House along with the army's address,
before I received the news of my being sent for:
you will see the reality of my heart therein: let
it be read, or the substance thereof more privately
communicated, as you shall think fitt upon the
place."

, The following is Henry's resignation of the government of Ireland to the Parliament: it is dated 15th June following (1659): — " Mr. Speaker; I am so unwilling to interrupt the peace of these nations, that I think it my duty to prevent even those feares and jealousies which may give any occasion thereof; and, in order thereunto, to give you an accoumpt of your affaires in Ireland, and more especially of myselfe in relation to them, and other the late transactions.

· " It hath been my unhappiness of late to receive intelligence only from common fame, and very private hands, and to be forced rather to guesse what I had to doe upon all emergencies, then to be entrusted with the cleere commands of my superiors: by reason whereof, when I heard the first general rumour of the last Parliament's dissolution, and of a likelihood of discontinuing the government under which it was called, I having no light into the intrinsick causes of that action, and knowing in generall how busy the common enemy was in all the three nations, and in what variety of shapes they appeared to act their designes; and withall, having the care of securing a more dangerous, numerous, and exasperated people, the Irish natives and Papists, I did forthwith, to answer all the severall ends of my trust, publish a declaration, requiring all officers, civill and military, to attend their respective comands, and not to hearken to any design of inovation, how speciously soever the same might bee presented to them. Soone after I received a letter from the committee of safety, recommending the peace and security of Ireland in a more speciall manner to my care, which I answered with a reall promise of complying with their advice. I did withall communicate that letter to very many officers of the army, promising likewise to transmitt the result of their consideration upon itt: and accordingly I did send over, by three worthy persons of this nation, a particular of such things, the granting thereof (as is conceived) would much settle the minds of people and the army heere, whose case and concernment are very different from those of England or Scotland. All this while I expected directions from His Highness, (by whose authority I was placed heere,) still having an eye to the common peace, by preventing all making of partyes and divisions, either among the people or army; but hearing nothing expressly from him, and yett having credible notice of his acquiescing in what Providence had brought forth as to the future government of these nations, I now thinke itt tyme (least a longer suspence should begett prejudiciall apprehensions in the minds of any) to give you this accompt, viz. that I acquiesse in the present way of government, although I cannot promise soe much affection to the late changes as others very honestly may. For my owne part, I can say, that I believe God was present in many of your administrations, before you were interrupted, and' may be soe againe; to which end, I hope, that those worthy persons who have lately acknowledged such their interrupting you in the year 1653, to have beene their fault, will by that sence of their impatience bee henceforth engaged to doe soe no more, but bee the instruments of your defence, whilst you quietly search out the ways of our peace; which stability and freedome, which, when the Lord shall restore unto you, will mueh subdue the hearts of all peaceably minded persons to your authority.

" The fower years' experience I have had of your army heere, (even under those tryalls which have provoked others,) gives me just ground to assure you of their concurrence with their brethren in England, in the way of obeying and defending, rather then of directing or awing you.

" I say, for my own part, I had an honourable opinion of the government you are now returned unto before its discontinuance, and yett I must not deny, but that the free submission which many worthy, wise, and conscientious persons yielded to the late government under a single person, (by severall wayes, as well real as verball,) satisfied me alsoe in that forme. And whereas my father, (whom I hope you yett looke upon as noe inconsiderable instrument of these nations' freedom and happinesse,) and since him, my brother, were constituted chiefe in those administrations, and that the returning to another forme hath beene looked upon as an indignity to those my neerest relations, I cannot but acknowledge my owne weaknesse as to the suddain disgesting thereof, and my owne unfitness to serve you in the carrying on your further superstructures upon that basis.   And as I cannot promote any thing which inferres the diminution of my late father's honour and meritt, soe I thanke the Lord for that hee hath kept me safe in the great temptations, wherewith I have beene assaulted to withdraw my affection from that cause, wherein he lived and dyed.

" I have a tenderness to peace, which (as I conceive, depending rather upon the worthiness of governors then formes of government,) renders me contented to wait upon Providence, in the expectation of that mercy, being ready to yield up my charge to any whom you shall send to receive itt ; and beseeching the Lord to be your mighty councellor and prince of peace.   I remaine, &c.

" H. CROMWELL."

Here concludes the entries of the letters of Henry Cromwell in the forementioned book, during his continuance in his office of Lord-deputy of Ireland.

In a letter in Thurloe's same State Papers, is a letter dated 21st June, 1659, from Mr. John Barwick to Sir Edward Hyde, afterwards Lord Clarendon ; he says, — " What the letters told you of

H. Cromwell's defyance and submission was not true in either particular. He hath hitherto stood *in æquilibrio,* taking no notice at all of the Parliament as the supreme authority (as they call it), but proceeding on in his former course as if his brother were still Protector. He is neither so active as he might be to play his own game, nor so plyable as they would have him here to comply with theires. And his dullness is the more inexcuseable, because he has all the encouragement he can desire to shake it off. The common soldiers and inferior officers of his army are very great zealots against the Anabaptists. The people of Ireland, generally, are against his submitting to the Parliament: the nobility and gentrie are willing to make up his army to 20,000; and the city of Dublin alone proffer to pay 2000 of them. All this I am told by a very sober and discreet person, who heard it from 470, 103, 2, 187, (Lord Meath,) who was there the 9th instant; and yet, notwithstanding all this, he was then very pendulous which way to take. It is true, indeed, he had not then heard of the rejecting of his message, nor of his being voted out of the government, nor of his being sent for hither. And how those may work upon him, this relater knowes not; but otherwise he suspected the worst as to his own inclination. But for all that, he is of opinion a good game may thereby be played, if things be well managed, though he should doe as his brother did, &c. If I

should swallow the flying reports, I could tell you
better newes thence, and it is certain, that Henry
Cromwell's last letter does not please them at
Westminster; and the same may be sayd for the
last letter from Monk: and that which adds to the
discontent is (as I am told), that both of them harp
upon one string, (which makes them suspected of
some understanding each of other,) they are both
for having all the members received into the House
that sat in it in 48."

Mr. Noble says, The Protector being displaced,
Henry was desirous of keeping Ireland for His
Majesty, knowing that he was less obnoxious to
the King than to many of the commonwealth's
men.

This may be true, but it does not appear to be
given from any authority. Of Henry's spirit and
abilities, there can remain no doubt; and, supported by the affections of the Irish nation, he
might have made a considerable stand against the
then ruling powers; but the contest must have
been, if finally successful on the part of Henry,
most sanguinary. Could he have foreseen the
King's restoration so soon afterwards, he might,
with this assistance, have kept his ground, and
have greatly forwarded it, by retaining Ireland for
him: but the then state of things did not seem to
afford the least probability of that event; it was, at
the last, the act of almost the moment. Perhaps it
is, even now, uncertain whether Monck meant the

restoration or his own elevation. Henry could,
therefore, have no object in his resistance but the
continuance of his own power, which he was not
likely long to retain against the force he must have
encountered. Accordingly, as he expresses himself in his forementioned letter to the Speaker,
being unwilling to interrupt the peace of these
nations, and to prevent those fears and jealousies
that might give occasion for it, and for other the
reasons given in this his letter, he acquiesces in
the then newly adopted government, and surren-
ders his charge. This was agreeable to the rectitude and uprightness of his mind, appearing in all
his letters and actions, during his public life. He
was not eager of power, nor would he retain it at
the expense of the nation's peace.

Rapin says, he peaceably submitted ; though in
all probability, if he had been inclined to resist,
the new governors would have found it difficult to
remove him : that he was extremely beloved in
Ireland, both by the army and the English inhabitants, having never injured any person, but on
the contrary obliged every one, as far as lay in his
power : but that, doubtless, not thinking himself
secure of success, and receiving no orders from his
brother, he was unwilling to undertake so important
an affair : that all the historians are unanimous in
their praises of him, and generally believe, that
if he had been Protector instead of his elder brother, the officers would have met with their match,

or not attempted what they undertook against
Richard.

Mr. Noble says, it is almost needless, after what
has been already given, to speak of the rectitude
of his character, and the goodness of his understanding; but that as nothing that can be produced in so good a cause should be omitted, he
gives some short sketches of both, from various
persons, whose judgments might be relied on.   He
then quotes Doctor Leland, whose History of Ireland, he says, is strictly impartial, as saying that
Henry was penetrating, just, and generous.   Also
the passage from Neal's History of the Puritans,
where he says, that Henry was a wise and discreet
governor, and by his prudent behaviour kept the
Irish in awe, and brought the nation into a flourish-
ing condition : and that while he was in Ireland
he behaved with such a generous impartiality as
gained him the esteem even of the royalists themselves: also another passage from Leland's History,
wherein the Protector Oliver is described as bearing this honourable testimony of his merit, — that
" he was a governor from whom he himself might
learn."   In a letter from Lord Fauconberg to
Henry Cromwell, dated 8th June, 1658, giving
him an account of his (Lord Fauconberg's) honourable reception at the court of France, by the Cardinal, (here given also by Mr. Noble,) he says,
" the Cardinal admires Your Lordship very much,
as all the world must needs doe, but none ever to

that degree, as Your Lordship's," &c.   And in a
letter dated 10th September, 1657, from Sir An-
thony Ashley Cooper, (afterwards Earl of Shaftes-
bury,) to Henry (in Thurloe, and here also given
by Mr. Noble,) apologising for not answering a
letter of Henry's, he says, — " for there is noe
person in the world more desires to retain Your
Lordship's affection and good opinion.   You have
many love His Highness's sonne; but I love
Henry Cromwell, were he naked, without all those
glorious additions and titles, which, however, I
pray may continue and be encreased on you.   My
request for myselfe is, that you love me," &c.

Dr. Bates, become, as before observed, a bitter
enemy of the Cromwell name and family after the
Restoration, relating the appointment of Henry to
the command of the army in Ireland, says, that
Cromwell having for two years made a trial of his
juvenile prudence, raised him to a higher degree:
that he made it his chief business, in the first place,
to restore the worship of God, though not to its
ancient beauty, yet to some better order, by degrees giving back the churches and pulpits, which
were wholly possessed by the Anabaptists, to the
ministers: and that he caused his own child to be
publicly baptized in the cathedral church; a rare
thing at that time: that he protected the preachers
from all affronts and the troublesome interruptions
of the sectaries in time of divine service.   Now,
continues Bates, does the college of Dublin, which

had been long neglected, raise its head out of obscurity, Henry himself being chosen the chancellor or patron thereof: and that he bought at his own charges the library of Archbishop Usher, and made a present of it to the college. This probably is a mistake, Cromwell being said to have purchased it. Nor, says he, was he less careful of the civil than of ecclesiastical affairs; for justice in the courts began now to show itself as much as it could under a tyrannical and violent government; stately houses were built in the cities, and the country abounded in pasture and corn, and trade began also to flourish : that he (Henry), moreover, allowed a free access to all, and liberty of petitioning; nay, and illustrated his bounty with some kind beams towards the royalists, by easing those who had been forfeited and sequestrated, remitting one-half of the money that had been imposed upon them; giving gracious words, liberty of playing with him, and many times admitting them to his table. In another place, referring to the forfeiture of the Irish Papists' estates and the imposition for the discovery of them, of a strict oath of abjuration upon suspected persons, he says, in the execution thereof Henry showed himself merciful, and very seldom put any to that trial.

The Restoration must have placed the Cromwell family in a state of the most painful suspense, particularly Richard and Henry. The King's declaration from Breda promises a free and general

pardon to all who should, within forty days after
its publication, lay hold thereon, and should, by
any public act, declare their so doing and their
return to the loyalty and obedience of good subjects, excepting such persons as should thereafter
be excepted by Parliament. This exception left
them, Richard and Henry, at the mercy of the
Parliament, the majority of which appear to have
been Presbyterians, consequently inveterate enemies of Cromwell and his family. The King and
his advisers must have been well aware of their
advantage in this exception, which might be extended to every person obnoxious to the King or
to his ministers, leaving the odium of its exercise
upon the Parliament; who appear to have used it
freely. Neither Richard nor Henry were among
those that were excepted in the act of pardon and
oblivion, afterwards passed;—they had no concern in the King's death. Richard probably owed
his safety to his not having been concerned in any
of the public transactions of the preceding times,
except his assumption of the Protectorate. Henry
may be considered as obtaining the benefit of the
act, through the intercession of his numerous and
powerful friends of the royal party, many of whom
were under various obligations to him in the exercise of his public capacity. This will, in some
degree, be seen by the following papers remaining
with his family.

In Henry Cromwell's petition to the King, a

draught whereof is amongst these papers, he declares his hearty acquiescence in the providence of God in restoring His Majesty to his government: that all his actions had been without malice to His Majesty's person or interest: that he did, all the time of his power in Ireland, study to preserve the peace, plenty, and splendour of that kingdom; encouraging a learned and orthodox ministry; giving not only protection but maintenance to several bishops there; placed worthy persons in the seats of judicature, and magistracy; and was (to his own great prejudice) upon all occasions favourable to His Majesty's professed friends. He therefore prays His Majesty's clemency; offering to his consideration his loss of 2000*l. per annum*, which he held in England, and in consideration whereof his wife's portion was paid to his late father, and therefore praying His Majesty's grant for such lands in Ireland (then already in his possession upon a common account with many others) as should by law be adjudged forfeited, and in His Majesty's disposal; and that, forasmuch as he had laid out near 6000*l.* upon the premises, His Majesty would recommend him to the Parliament in Ireland to deal favourably with him concerning the same, and answerable to his deportment in that nation. Upon the back of this draught is one of a declaration of His Majesty's loyal and faithful subjects residing in Ireland, who had been eye-witnesses of Colonel Henry

Cromwell's behaviour in Ireland during the time of his power there : that he never, to their knowledge, expressed any malice against His Majesty's person or interest·: that he suffered much from the fanatic and sectarian party : that he did countenance the known laws of the land, and discipline of the church ; place men of sobriety and good repute in the several offices of the nation ; did not only protect but also allow maintenance to the several bishops remaining in Ireland, and was the only refuge and support of His Majesty's professed friends. In consideration of all which, and to express their gratitude to him for the kindness they had received from him, they recommend him to His Majesty's grace and favour.

The following are two original letters to Henry Cromwell from General Monck. The first is addressed " To the Right Ho^ble the Lord Henry Cromwell, these, — At Sr Francis Russell's house, in Chipnam, in Cambridgeshire, near Newmarkett." It is dated Cockpitt, 3d June, 1660.

" My Lord ; — I received Your Lp's leter of the 30th of May. — And for those lands wch Yo^r Lp's father settled on yo^u uppon your marriage, being lands given in satisfaction of arreares, there will bee little doubt but yo^u will possess and enjoye them. But what was conferr'd by guift may be in some hazard. I shall be ready to doe Yo^r Lp what service I can, and remaine Y^r Lp's most humble servant,   " GEORGE MONCK.'

The other of these letters is dated Cockpitt, 9° June, 1660, and addressed " For the Ho^{ble} Col. Henry Cromwell, these,—att Sir Francis Russell's, att Chippenham, Cambridgeshire. — S^r I rec^d yo^rs, and as to yor coming uppe, I thinke itt will not bee yett convenient, butt when itt is seasonable I shall acquaint you with itt, wch is all att p'sent from yor very loving friend and serv^t.

" G. Monck."

These letters appear to be signed, but not to be written, by General Monck.

The following is a copy of a letter, appearing by the indorsement to have been written by Henry to the Duke of Ormond. It is without date. — " May it please Your Grace ; — Although I have beene long in towne without any wayes expressing my sense of Your Grace's favours towards mee, and acknowledging that I owe my whole unto that generous protection and patronage you have vouch-safed mee ; yett, now my time of stay here drawing to an end, I doe humbly presume to assure Your Grace, that there are few howers in the day wherein I doe not remember those your kindnesses, and thanke God that it ever fell in my way to doe that which was acceptable to Your Grace. It is in vayne for mee to make many promises of what I will doe for Your Grace in acknowledgement hereof, God having disposed my heart to retirement and acquiescence in that state of life which both best

becomes mee and incapacitates mee for other performances.   Wherefore I most humbly beg Your
Grace to accept of such thanks as a few words can
expresse, and of my hearty wishes that Your Grace
may receive from other hands those more reall services that are due from mine, since by the Providence of God I myselfe am become insolvent.   It
troubles mee that I should give Your Grace any
new trouble, but pardon mee this once, if I beg
Your Grace at some fitt time to assure His Majesty
of my loyalty to his service, and that I lament my
unworthiness and incapacity to expresse it.   Although by His Majesty's great mercy and indulgence set forth, as well by his speciall letters as
his publick declaration, I might keep Portumna
until my —— yet, I am so conscious of My Lord
Clanrickard's better service to His Majesty than
of my own, that I am contented to part with it before; but what prejudice such a president might
doe to the English interest in Ireland I know not,
wherefore I leave the present disposall of the house
and parke of Portumna, so farre as I have to doe
with itt, wholly to Your Grace, having given order
to my agents that it may be disposed of forthwith,
according to your pleasure; for it is but just that
I, who have received all from His Majesty's mercy
and Your Grace's favour, should dedicate a part
to your justice, which I heartily do."

The following is a letter from Sir Thomas
Chichely, addressed to Colonel Mark Trevor, on

behalf of Henry. It is dated 15th October, no
year, but probably 1660, the year of the Restoration: — " Sir; I understand by My Lord Harry
that he intends to desire you to doe him the favor
as to recomend his affaires to My Lord Chan^{llr}
(must be Lord Clarendon): I would also beg a
favour of you, which is to present my humble
service to him, and let him know (if you will
honor me so much as to ioyne me in the suite)
that I am an humble sutor to him on his behaulfe,
and that I know not any one who hath obliged
the King's party more when it was in his power,
and I am confident will give as good a testimony
of his loyalty when he shall have an opertunity
to shew it ; and this I really believe, who am, &c.
                          " Tho. Chicheley."

A Mr. Edward Worth, in a letter to Henry,
dated 6° Junii, 1660, (place not mentioned from
whence written,) says, — " May it please Yo^r Lo^p,
God hath even wonderfully mooved the tongues
of all men to speake off Yo^r Lo^p with that affection
that the highest of the opposites stand amazed, and
profess they cannot heare on their strictest enquiries, any thing suggested by any person against
you. I doe not, therefore, in the least kind doubt
but Yo^r Lo^p will see a very cleare settlement of
yor interesse in Ireland (unless what concernes
the Lady Dowager), nor doe I despaire of yor
estate from My L^d of Worcester. Certainly the

already experience of God's goodnes in moving y᷎
hearts of all sorts to affect you, is a good earnest
of yet further mercies designed for you and (I am
sure) a great ingagement quietly to depend on
such a God.

" The Lord Broghill, S᷎ Paul Davis, S᷎ Maurice
Eustace, Col. Hill, &c. are safely landed at West-
chester, and expected here to-morrow or next day.
If there should be any further scruple moved
concerning Yo᷎ Lo᷎, they will be good additional
succo᷎ to your serv᷎ here.   But noething is likely
to attaine a settlement that relates to Ireland till
a parliam᷎ be called there to settle it.

The L᷎ of Ormond expresseth a great aptnes to
serve you; but it is thought better that his Lady
should breake the ice to the King, than that he
or any other man should doe it.

I humbly p'sent my service and duty to my Lady,
begging the Lord to be nigh her in the needfull
time of trouble.   When I receive Yo᷎ Lo᷎
summons, I shall performe y᷎ duty and ingagem᷎
of, &c.

" EDW. WORTH."

" I forbeare to instance particular persons,
because they are many with whom I speake, and
all agree to serve you."

A letter to Henry, dated 3° Novemb. 60, without signature, saying that the writer had seen his
(Henry's) pardon fully completed : — " That that

day, Sir George Lane   and himself
(the writer) had wayted upon Mr. Secretary
Nicholas, with directions from the King and L^d
Ormond, about his (Henry's) letter, and that he
was appointed to wayte late agayne that evening."
He adds, that Lord Broghill, Sir Charles Coote,
and Sir Maurice Eustace, were to be justices of
Ireland; that all the old council were to be continued, and a supply made as in ancient times.

A paper, signed by the King (Charles II.),
"CHARLES R.," and dated 13th April (1661), addressed to Sir Maurice Eustace, Lord Chancellor of
Ireland, Roger Earle Orrery (late Lord Broghill),
and Charles Earle of Mountrath (late Sir Charles
Coote), Justices of Ireland, commissioners appointed to execute the King's declaration for the
settlement of that kingdom. It states, that
whereas the King, by his letters patent of the
6th of November then last, had declared, that no
distinction should be made between Henry Cromwell and any other adventurer, for what hee held
in Ireland as such. And that by other letters
patent of the last of February following, the lands,
&c. lying in the baronyes of Dunboyne and
Ratoth, in or neere the towne of Portuna, sett out
in satisfaction of 7039*l.* 16*s.* 8*d.* of soldiers'
arreares, and in the county of Tipperary, possessed
by him on the 7th of May (1659), should be confirmed unto him, his heirs, and assigns, under the
Great Seale of Ireland, " Although wee then

knew that a considerable part of the said lands, and of his interest as an adventurer, were derived from persons attainted by the late act of parliament, entituled, An Act of Attainder," &c., and stating that the King had given and granted to several the estates of the persons attainted by that act. Therefore declares, that out of these grants, and out of any future grants of these estates, be excepted the lands possessed by the said Henry Cromwell on said 7th of May, in satisfaction of soldiers' arreares, and such other lands as should or might be sett out in satisfaction of 850*l.* of adventure come to him by assignment or other conveyance or assurance: — " In all which it is our pleasure that hee be settled and confirmed as any other adventurers or souldiers are or may bee; and in case any of the lands hee holdeth bee not confirmed by our declaration of the 30th of November, wee doe hereby graunt him liberty to purchase the same for and with any of the considerations by our said declaration allowed.

" Signed by His Ma^tie^s command,

" WILLIAM MORICE."

" Entred at the Signett Office, 20th April, 1661.

" JOHN NICHOLAS."

A certificate, signed E. Manchester, by G. Carterett, Anglesea, Denzill Holles, dated Whitehall, 25th of March (1662), addressed to His Royall Highnesse, (presume the Duke of York): — That they had examined the pretensions of Henry Cromwell to certain lands by him possest in Ireland, and were satisfied that part thereof was in satisfaction of his owne personall arreares, and part in satisfaction of his late father's arreares: and that, in case his said father's were a chattell and personall estate, that then the said debentures were not forfeited as not possest by Oliver Cromwell at the tyme of his death : on the other side, that if the said debentures were reall estate, and of the nature of lands, then wee think itt necessary that the said Henry Cromwell, to maintaine his right, should prove that the said debentures were made over unto him for a valuable consideration : it having onely bin alledged that 4000*l.* was paid for Oliver's pretences to the said lands amongst other things, by Sir Francis Russell, upon the marriage of his daughter to the said Henry Cromwell.

On another side of the same paper is a declaration, dated Munday, the 7th day of April (1662), by His Royall Highnesse and the commissioners for managing of his revenue.

That upon consideration of the petition of Sir William Russell and others, purchasers of certain lands in Ireland theretofore, by the pretended powers sett out to Henry Cromwell, in satisfaction of his and Oliver Cromwell's arrears: and upon perusall of His Majesty's gracious declaration for the settling of the kingdom of Ireland, His Royal Highness was satisfied that the said lands were comprehended within the intention of the said declaration to be enjoyed by the present possessors thereof, notwithstanding the act of attainder; and therefore was content that a provisoe should be brought in (to the bill for settling the affaires of Ireland) for the saving and reserving of the said lands unto the present possessors. (Signed by CHARLES PORTER, Clerke of His Royall Highness's Councill.)

And on another side is a copy of a clause in an act of Parliament, (presume the Irish Parliament, the title or year of the reign not given,) enacting that all the lands, &c. in the baronyes of Dunboyne and Ratooth, and county of Meath, whereof Henry Cromwell was, by himselfe, his tenants, or assignes possessed, the 7th of May (1659), bee settled and confirmed unto Sir William Russell of Langhorne, Baronett, and Doctor Jonathan Goddard, their heirs and assignes for ever; and that the lands, &c. lying in the province of Connaught, whereof the said Henry Cromwell was in like manner possest on the said 7th of May, be settled upon and confirmed unto John Russell, of Chippenham, Esq. his heirs and assigns for ever, to be held upon terms of His Majesty's declaration of the 30th of November (1660); and that 850*l.* be satisfied unto the said John Russell as an adventure, in such manner as by the same act was appointed in the case of any other adventurers.

The above Sir William Russell and John Russell

were trustees for Henry Cromwell ; but the family appear, by a statement amongst the family papers, to have been afterwards illegally dispossessed of these estates by some of the then Clanrickard family, whose ancestor, Ulick Burke, is stated to have been proprietor thereof in the year 1641, and as being General of the rebels in the Irish rebellion, and by act of Parliament attainted, and his estates forfeited. This statement describes the heir of the above Ulick Burke as having been illegally restored to these estates, and that the then Earl of Clanrickard was in actual rebellion against the then King William and Queen Mary : and the object of the statement is an application to Their Majesties on behalf of Henry Cromwell's son for the restoration to him of these estates. No further proceedings therein appear; but the Cromwell family, according to this statement, seem to have been unfairly deprived of this property.

A licence was granted in February (1664–5), signed by the Earls of Manchester and Anglesea, and Lord Ashley, to Henry Cromwell, to visit London for 21 days : and another by the Earl of Suffolk, as Lord-lieutenant for the counties of Suffolk and Cambridge, dated 12th October (1665), permitting him to visit his relations at Newmarket and Chippenham.

Henry appears, in a statement amongst the family papers, to have purchased, in 1661, in the names of two trustees, Sir Thomas Chicheley and Sir John Trevor, an estate called Spinney-abbey, in

the parish of Wicken, near Soham, in Cambridgeshire, of between five and six hundred pounds per
annum, where he resided the remainder of his life,
and died 23d March (1673), in the 47th year of
his age. Mr. Noble, from the Nonconformist
Memorial, says that he conformed to the church
of England, and in that communion died.

The Restoration produced a striking revolution
in the national manners; departing from the strictest religious and moral habits, the people became
generally immoral and vicious; religious profession
became quite unfashionable, and exposed the professor to scorn and ridicule, and even to the suspicion of disloyalty. The most active in the late
transactions were generally the foremost in their
endeavours to obtain the forgiveness of the then
ruling powers; and to satisfy them of the sincerity
of their contrition for the parts they had taken
under the late several governments, they were the
forwardest to vilify and ridicule those with whom
they had acted. Bishop Burnet says, — " Those
who had been concerned in the former transactions
thought they could not redeem themselves from
the censures and jealousies that those brought on
them, by any method that was more sure and more
easy, than by going into the stream and laughing
at all religion; telling and making stories to expose
both themselves and their party as impious and
ridiculous." Hence all those bitter sarcasms and
ordinary and improbable stories, and all the rib-

aldry in poems and political ballads and other
publications that have been handed down, and
found currency in all subsequent times. Many of
the most distinguished writers of those times basely
sacrificed their talents, and their veracity and consistency, to the idol of the day; to please whom,
they hardily and most barefacedly unsaid all they
had before said; eulogizing Cromwell to the skies,
during his life, and upon the occasion of his death;
and, not more than two years afterwards, boldly
and unblushingly coming forward, and in effect
declaring themselves to have uttered deliberate
falsehoods, by then setting him forth as the worst
of characters. Nothing can excuse this baseness
and meanness of mind. The King himself, the
object of their adulation, must inwardly despise
and detest these men, and must feel their fulsome
panegyrics, instead of serving his cause, to be, on
the contrary, prejudicial to it in the highest degree,
in reviving and perpetuating the civil and religious
distinctions of past times, and those party feuds
and animosities, which he appears in his forementioned Breda declaration so anxious to bury in
oblivion; therein expressly declaring, that no crime
committed against him or his late father, the late
King, before the publication thereof, (excepting
as to such persons as should be excepted by Parliament,) should ever rise in judgment, or be
brought into question against any of them to the
least endangerment of them, either in their lives,

liberties, or estates, or (as far as should lie in his power) so much as to the prejudice of their reputations, by any reproach or terms of distinction from the rest of his best subjects; he (the King) desiring and ordaining, that thenceforward, all notes of discord, separation, and difference of parties, should be utterly abolished amongst all his subjects, whom he invites and conjures to a perfect union among themselves, under his protection. And that because the passion and uncharitableness of the times had produced several opinions in religion, by which men were engaged in parties and animosities against each other, which, when they should thereafter unite in a freedom of conversation, would be composed or better understood, he declares a liberty to tender consciences, and that no man should be disquieted or called in question for differences of opinion in matters of religion, which should not disturb the peace of the kingdom.

These numberless, abusive, and scandalous publications show how ill the wishes, or rather, perhaps, the promises, of the King, were complied with. The heats and animosities, and prejudices thereby excited, have hardly yet subsided.

Cromwell's most inveterate and most powerful enemies were the Presbyterians and Commonwealth's men; both these parties aimed at his destruction, as the great obstacle to their own schemes of aggrandisement and dominion: and, in preservation of himself, he overpowered them, and assumed the supreme authority; the necessity whereof, Rapin observes, was clearly shown by the confusion which prevailed in England soon after his death.

Cromwell, in his answer to the arguments of the committee of the House of Commons upon their humble petition and advice, desiring him to assume the title of King, says, That he assumed the authority with which he stood invested, at a time when immediate ruin was falling down upon the nation, which no other man durst attempt to prevent, when opposite factions were rushing into war, because no man durst interpose and command peace. What were the dangers that threatened, and upon what principles the factious and disobedient attempted to interrupt the public tranquillity, it might not, he says, be at that time improper to explain.

Accordingly he proceeds: That the Parliament which had so vigorously withstood the encroachments of the regal power, became themselves too desirous of absolute authority, and not only engrossed the legislative, but usurped the executive power: that all causes, civil and criminal, all questions of property and right, were determined by committees, who being themselves the legislature, were accountable to no law; and for that reason their decrees were arbitrary, and their proceedings violent: oppression was without redress, and unjust

sentence without appeal : that all the business of
all the courts of Westminster was transacted in
this manner, and the hardships were still more
lamented, because there was no prospect of either
end or intermission : for that the Parliament was
so far from intending to resign this unlimited authority, that they had formed a resolution of perpetuating their tyranny; and apprehending no
possibility of a dissolution by any other power,
determined never to dissolve themselves : that
such and so oppressive was the government planned
to us and for our posterity; and under these calamities must we still have languished, had not
the same army which repressed the insolence of
monarchy, relieved us with the same spirit, from
the tyranny of a perpetual Parliament, a tyranny
which was equally illegal and oppressive : that
when, after their dangers and labours, their battles
and their wounds, they had leisure to observe the
government which they had established at so much
expense, they soon perceived that unless they made
one regulation more, and crushed this many-headed
tyranny, they had thitherto ventured their lives to
little purpose, and had, instead of asserting their
own and the people's liberty, only changed one
kind of slavery for another : that they therefore dissolved the Parliament, which would never have
dissolved itself : and that the nation might not
fall into its former state of confusion, they entreated
him (Cromwell) to assume the supreme authority

under the title of Protector; a title not implying
any legal power of governing in his own right, but
a trust consigned to him for the advantage of another: that this trust he had faithfully discharged;
and that whenever the means of settling the public should be found, he was ready to give an account of it, and resign it : that the necessity which
compelled him to accept it, was, indeed, not
wholly produced by the illegal resolutions of the
Parliament, but was much heightened by the un-
governable fury of wild fanatics and tumultuous
factions, who, to establish their new schemes,
would have spread slaughter and desolation through
the kingdom, and spared nothing, however cruel
or unjust, that might have propagated their own
opinions.   He then shortly describes the views of
the different parties; and adds, that it was unnecessary to say what must have been the state of a
nation, in which either of these parties had exalted
themselves to power, and how usefully that man
was employed, who, stepping on a sudden into the
state of dominion, had spirit to control, and power
to suppress them : that the reproaches thrown upon
his conduct by the ignorant or ill-affected he
sometimes heard, but with the neglect and scorn
which they deserved : that he was acquitted by
his own conscience, and, he hoped, by the best
and wisest men : that he was convinced he was
called by Providence to the power which he possessed, and knew that he desired it no longer than

was necessary for the preservation of peace, and the security of liberty; that liberty which he had never violated, and that peace, which, amidst murmurs and discontents, threats and complaints, he had never suffered to be broken. — That he aspired to unlimited authority, and therefore assumed ·a title unknown to the nation (Protector), was a reproach easily cast and as easily contemned: that his power had been the offspring of necessity, and that its extent had been bounded only by the occasions of exerting it: that if a settlement should be then proposed, and, previously to it, a legal establishment of his authority, it might be limited by them, the Parliament: that, under whatever title it should be conferred upon him, that title would then be valid, and those limitations could not be transgressed. In another place, he says, that he had never interrupted the course of justice, and that all the judges could attest, and, he believed, affirm with equal confidence, that it had not been more obstructed by any other impediment than in former times.

The same account of the ambition and tyranny of the Long Parliament is given by Cromwell in his foregiven interview with Whitelock, who admitted the truth of it, and, in more than one place in his Memorials, observes upon and censures them for it.

This (Cromwell's) assumption of the supreme power, in the absence of monarchy, certainly kept

things together, and left the country not only
unimpaired, but raised it to the highest elevation
of prosperity and reputation; and in this state it
came into the hands of the King, Charles the
Second. But all these advantages were thrown
away and lost in his and his brother James the
Second's inauspicious reigns, who might have been
expected to have profited by the examples of those
arbitrary measures that led to the troubles of the
two preceding ones of their father and grand-
father, Charles, and James the First.

The Restoration certainly did not produce the
good effects to be hoped and expected from it; but
it brought back the ancient mixed monarchical
form of government by King, Lords, and Commons, to which the nation had been accustomed,
and to which they might be supposed to be attached, and to which all our laws apply. Cromwell's comprehensive mind appears, at the first
meeting after the King's death, for the purpose of
considering of the form of government to be
adopted in consequence of that event, to have seen
the necessity of the preference of this form to the
others then proposed; it may be said, this preference might owe itself to his view to the possession
of the supreme power; this, however, must be
uncertain; the short continuance, nevertheless,
of the republican form, and the improper and violent exercise of its power, proved the correctness
of his preference. Indeed, it does not seem cal-

culated for duration or national happiness, in this,
or perhaps any other country; it must be revo-
lutionary, subject to commotion and change, as
having no fixed head or power to prevent a perpetual
struggle for the ascendancy of mere physical
strength, and conceived mental ability. On the
contrary, the quiet and uninterrupted descent of
the crown, as in this country, under the various
restrictions and regulations of known and fixed
laws, effectually checks and prevents those convul-
sions to which popular governments, whether of a
republican or of an elective monarchical form, must
necessarily be subject. The crown, certainly, in
this case of hereditary succession, may descend,
as has been objected, upon a weak or unworthy
head : infirmity and imperfection are inseparable
from all human institutions and contrivances; but
our excellent laws will be always found a sufficient
protection against these possible inconveniences;
our constitution, as it now stands, is the gradual
result of long experience, and is and has been
found to be the best calculated for duration, and
for the true and permanent happiness of its people.

Mr. Gibbon, in his Decline and Fall of the
Roman Empire, observes, — " Of the various forms
of government which have prevailed in the world,
that of an hereditary monarchy seems to present
the fairest scope for ridicule. Is it, says he, possible to relate, without an indignant smile, that on
the father's decease, the property of a nation, like

that of a drove of oxen, descends to his infant son,
as yet unknown to mankind and to himself; and
that the bravest warriors and the wisest statesmen,
relinquishing their natural right to empire, approach the royal cradle with bended knees and
protestations of inviolable fidelity? Satire and
declamation may paint these obvious topics in the
most dazzling colours; but our more serious
thoughts will respect a useful prejudice, that establishes a rule of succession independent of the
passions of mankind; and we shall cheerfully acquiesce in any expedient which deprives the multitude of the dangerous, and indeed the ideal,
power of giving themselves a master. In the cool
shades of retirement, we may easily devise imaginary forms of government, in which the sceptre
shall be constantly bestowed on the most worthy,
by the free and incorrupt suffrage of the whole
community. Experience overturns these airy
fabrics, and teaches us, that in a large society, the
election of a monarch can never devolve to the
wisest, or to the most numerous part of the people;
that the superior prerogative of birth, when it has
obtained the sanction of time and popular opinion,
is the plainest and least invidious of all distinctions
among mankind; that the acknowledged right
extinguishes the hopes of faction, and the conscious security disarms the cruelty of the monarch;
that to the firm establishment of this idea, we owe
the peaceful succession, and mild administration of

European monarchies; to the defect of it, we must attribute the frequent civil wars through which an Asiatic despot is obliged to cut his way to the throne of his fathers."

Judge Blackstone, in his Commentaries on the Laws of England, at the conclusion of his chapter "Of the King and his Title," observes, — " That the extremes, between which the true constitutional notion of the right of succession (which he had immediately before stated) steers, are each of them equally destructive of those ends for which societies were formed, and are kept on foot. That where the magistrate, upon every succession, is elected by the people, and may, by the express provision of the laws, be deposed (if not punished) by his subjects, — this may sound like the perfection of liberty, and look well enough when delineated on paper, but, in practice, will be ever productive of tumult, contention, and anarchy. And that, on the other hand, divine, indefeasible, hereditary right, when coupled with the doctrine of unlimited passive obedience, is surely, of all constitutions, the most thoroughly slavish and dreadful. But that, when such an hereditary right, as our laws have created and vested in the royal stock, is closely interwoven with those liberties which we have seen in a former chapter are equally the inheritance of the subject, this union will form a constitution, in theory the most beautiful of any, in practice the most approved; and, I trust, in duration the most permanent. It was," adds the Judge, "the duty of an expounder of our laws to lay this constitution before the student in its true and genuine light: it is the duty of every good Englishman to understand, to revere, to defend it."

THE END.

LONDON:
Printed by A. & R. Spottiswoode,
New-Street-Square.